Frank Guttman has provided an exhaustive account of the political career of a significant, yet neglected figure in twentieth century Quebec. In this biography, he has underlined the components, which shed light on the transition of radical liberalism into the twentieth century. This book is a beautiful case study to stimulate thought about the inter-connections of twentieth century liberalism and nationalism. The debate remains enriched by the experience of a man who Frank Guttman has illuminated as a bright star.

—Yvon Lamonde, Professor, McGill University.

Frank Guttman's meticulous research on T.D. Bouchard adds greatly to our understanding of the complex relationship of liberalism and nationalism in 20th century Quebec.

—Brian Young, Professor, McGill University.

Frank Guttman has provided an exhaustive account of the political career of a significant, yet overlooked figure in twentieth century Quebec.

—Ronald Rudin, Professor, Concordia University.

This study analyzes the historical context of the struggle that Bouchard led to defend democracy in Quebec in the tradition of the *rouges* of the 19th century and against xenophobia, anti-Semitism, clericalism, the Quebec nationalists, free speech, and his great accomplishments in local and provincial governments. The style is neither academic nor boring. The book fills a void and is a major contribution to the history of Quebec and Canada particularly about the history of ideas and politics of the time.

—Yves Lavertu, **Author**

THE DEVIL
FROM
SAINT-HYACINTHE

THE DEVIL FROM SAINT-HYACINTHE

A Tragic Hero

Senator Télesphore-Damien Bouchard

Frank Myron Guttman

iUniverse, Inc.
New York Lincoln Shanghai

The Devil from Saint-Hyacinthe
Senator Télesphore-Damien Bouchard

iUniverse books may be ordered through booksellers or by contacting:

iUniverse
2021 Pine Lake Road, Suite 100
Lincoln, NE 68512
www.iuniverse.com
1-800-Authors (1-800-288-4677)

ISBN-13: 978-0-595-40302-8 (pbk)
ISBN-13: 978-0-595-84678-8 (ebk)
ISBN-10: 0-595-40302-6 (pbk)
ISBN-10: 0-595-84678-5 (ebk)

Printed in the United States of America

This book is dedicated to the memory of my father,
Joseph Guttman, who taught tolerence for all peoples.

Contents

ACKNOWLEDGEMENTS

I am grateful for the collaboration and help given by Jean-Noel Dion, archivist of the Historical Society of Saint-Hyacinthe. I wish to express my gratitude to the numerous Bouchard family members whom I interviewed; and to Mme. Claire Simard Odermatt, who provided me with Cécile-Ena's cache of private letters and memorabilia. I am grateful to the late Elspeth Chisholm, who named me legatee of the unpublished manuscript she wrote on Bouchard's life, a document that contained many original interviews with the actors of the period. Professors Ronald Rudin, Yvan Lamonde and René Durocher have kindly provided me with comments on the text. Ronald Rudin suggested the title, "The Devil from Saint-Hyacinthe." I am also thankful for the kind guidance of Professor Brian Young in my readings of Quebec and general history over the past fifteen years, and for his patient reading of this manuscript. I am also indebted to my sister-in-law Greta Nemiroff-Hofmann, to Pierre Anctil, and to Françoise Beauregard (Bouchard's grandniece) for their careful reading of the manuscript and their helpful suggestions. In addition, I would like to thank Moishe Dolman for his careful editing of the text. Finally, I am indebted to my wife, Herta, who has supported me throughout this endeavour, and has critically commented on the text.

PREFACE

I have written about Télesphore-Damien Bouchard's life and times because Quebec historians have ignored him. There is no published biography of Bouchard. And yet he was a major influence and an outstanding personality in Quebec politics from 1912 to 1944, a precursor of the "Quiet Revolution," during an era generally dismissed as "the Great Darkness." Perhaps it is because I feel that to tell the story of Bouchard's life is to help to lay to rest a widespread myth, namely, that before the "Quiet Revolution" of the 1960s French Canada was nothing more than a xenophobic monolith dominated at every level by an all-powerful, reactionary Roman Catholic Church. It is my view that this narrow-minded preconception may indeed have been the reality for many members of the elite—the graduates of the *colleges classiques*. However, I maintain that the people of Quebec have always been more open-minded generally than most peoples.

My own interest in the life of Télesphore-Damien Bouchard is neither impersonal nor random. As a Jewish Quebecer, I was attracted to his sympathy for the underdog, and his battle against the xenophobia of the right-wing nationalists of his time. His story serves to illustrate that enlightened people lived in Quebec, individuals who were receptive to the ideas and some of the customs of the First Nations, and later others, who welcomed immigrants escaping persecution in Europe.[1] My grandparents arrived in Canada over 107 years ago. In every Quebec town, and even villages, Jewish storekeepers got along well with their fellow citizens. Jewish peddlers were welcomed into farm homes around the province with hospitality. Although T.-D. Bouchard was in many respects ahead of his time, he was perhaps in the same respect, part of this long and honourable tradition. Thus, the story of his life and times are important for the people of Quebec, and indeed for everyone interested in Quebec history to recall. T.-D. Bouchard was a man of the people, not a representative of the elites; and so, despite his outspoken anti-

---

1   I use this old-fashioned, well-established term, French Canadians, in order to avoid the ambiguity of "Québécois" which covers, or should cover, all citizens of Quebec. One could use the term, French-speaking Québécois.

clericalism and despite his unwavering opposition to any form of prejudice and to the separatists of his day, the people of his native Saint-Hyacinthe elected him to public office repeatedly for over thirty-nine years.

From 1935 until 1944, Bouchard was one of the outstanding actors on the Quebec political stage. Before this period, however, he had been a prominent figure. In many respects, he was far ahead of his time. First elected to the Legislative Assembly in 1912 as Member for Saint-Hyacinthe, Premier Louis-Alexandre Taschereau appointed him Deputy Speaker of the House in 1928 and as Speaker in 1930. Finally, he entered the provincial cabinet in 1935. An advocate of compulsory education and of the creation of a Provincial Department of Education, he also called for the municipalization and eventual nationalization of electric power, for enlightened labour laws, and for women's suffrage. In 1944, after the nationalization of the Montreal Light, Heat, and Power and Beauharnois Power companies, Premier Adélard Godbout appointed him the first president of Quebec-Hydro and senator in Ottawa. He fought against the "undue influence" of the Church in temporal affairs and against graft and corruption in awarding contracts for public works. Yet, at the end of his career, he had become a tragic hero in Quebec history, vilified for his attacks on the narrow-minded, ultramontane nationalists. (See page 2 for an explanation of the terms "ultramontane" and "Gallican.")[2]

I was educated in the English Protestant school system of Quebec. In my day, French schools did not admit non-Catholics, and not even English-speaking Catholics. The Protestant schools, which we attended, barely tolerated Jews. I completed my undergraduate studies at McGill University, where I obtained my BSc (Hon. Physiology) in 1952, and then went to the University of Geneva for medical school. (In 1952, there was still a *numerus clausus*, a quota limiting Jewish entry into McGill medical school.) Later I completed my training at Montreal's Jewish General Hospital and at the Sainte-Justine Hospital for Children—also in Montreal—where I spent seventeen years of my professional life. It was at the Sainte-Justine Hospital that I began to feel myself part of

---

2   In these footnotes there are two memoirs cited. I will refer to *Mémoires,* the published French version of Bouchard's selected autobiography—*Mémoires.* I, *Ma vie privée,* II, *Gravissant la colline,* III, *Quarante ans de tourmente politico-religieuse,* (Montréal: Éditions Beauchemin, 1960)—and also to *Memoirs* (English—unpublished), found in the Quebec City ANQ, *Fonds* T.-D. Bouchard, P 10/18 & 19. The unpublished version in English contains many more details of family life than the published French version.

Quebec life and learned to appreciate that which I had missed growing up in the ethnically mixed Montreal neighbourhood of Outremont. The Outremont of my youth was partly Anglo-Saxon, partly Jewish, and partly *Canadien*. Although my family lived next door to French-Canadian families, we had absolutely no contact with them, even though my parents spoke both national languages, and though my mother grew up in French-speaking Quebec City. My uncle, who was a commercial traveller in Saint-Hyacinthe, actually knew T.-D. Bouchard. My father was also acquainted with him. At home we subscribed to his newspaper, *Le Haut Parleur* (the Loud-Speaker), published in the 1950s that I read regularly. Thus, neither Bouchard nor his ideas were foreign to me.[3]

Although I have spent the greater part of my life as a pediatric surgeon, history has always interested me. The books of Barbara Tuchman stimulated my interest in general history, and it was through the work of Francis Parkman that I became attracted to the study of French-Canadian history. Both Tuchman and Parkman were non-professional historians who nevertheless possessed a knack for bringing history to life. (Many of Parkman's biased conclusions are now disputed.) Extensive reading has also fostered my interest in Quebec history. In spite of its right-wing and anti-Semitic bias, Robert Rumilly's *Histoire de la Province du Québec* is a valuable source of information regarding the ultramontane-Gallican disputes, as is his biography of Maurice Duplessis (*Maurice Duplessis et son temps*).[4]

---

3   Professor E.H. Carr has noted that all historians have a unique background that influences their views. Therefore I have presented my upbringing for all to note. As Carr observed: "Study the historian before you study the facts…When you read a work of history, always listen for the buzzing. If you can detect none, either you are tone deaf or your historian is a dull dog." Prof. Carr gives this advice to the student of history in *What is History?* (London: Penguin Books, 2nd edition, 1987), p. 23.

4   Rumilly, *Histoire de la province du Québec*, Vols I–XXXIV (Montréal: Fides). Roberto Perrin derides Rumilly's history as cheerful gossip, as do many modern historians. Roberto Perrin, in *Rome in Canada; The Vatican and Canadian Affairs in the Late Victorian Age*, (Toronto: University of Toronto Press, 1990) p.8. He remarks: "Rumilly for his part was a chronicler, interested above all to get his reader to follow him from the beginning of the story until the end. His characters are vividly portrayed, perhaps too vividly, with all their peculiarities and eccentricities. In the end they appear as personalities out of an *opera bouffe*. If they fight, it is only for form's sake, since they are all members of one happy family which no issue can seriously divide." Pierre Elliot Trudeau is supposed to have joked that Rumilly is a good professor "des histoires"—"of stories." Nevertheless, Rumilly remains a valuable source of material not found elsewhere; and is often cited by many serious historians of the period.

Both Rumilly and another Duplessis biographer, Conrad Black, thought very highly of T.-D. Bouchard. There have been, however, no biographies of Bouchard. All we have is a single Master's thesis on the period 1935–1944, which corresponded to the pinnacle of his career.[5] There is also an unpublished biography written by the late Elspeth Chisholm. In writing this book I wish to continue the current trend, which emphasizes progressive forces in Quebec. This trend was established by Professor Jean-Paul Bernard in his seminal study on the "Reds" of the mid-nineteenth century: *Les rouges, libéralisme, nationalisme et anti-Cléricalisme au milieu du XIX siècle.*[6] The "reds" described by Bernard were the followers of the *Parti Patriote* who took part in the Rebellions of 1837–38. They were anti-clerical supporters of responsible government who at times advocated annexation to the United States. Although Bernard concludes his study on a negative note concerning the survival of the radical *rouges*, I maintain, along with Fernande Roy, that although the flame of their views may have been dimmed, it was never extinguished. Roy asks: "Was liberalism triumphant or dominant at the turn of the century? That remains to be seen, but in any case, liberalism was definitely an active force, not confined to the fringe of ideological debate."[7] The work of illuminating the lives of these radical *rouges* has contin-

---

5   Robert Saint-Germain and Jacques Bibeau, M.A. Thesis (History) *Télesphore-Damien Bouchard; Un Chef du Parti Libéral; (1935–1944)* Université de Sherbrooke, *novembre* 1973.

6   Jean-Paul Bernard, *Les rouges, libéralisme, nationalisme et anti-Cléricalisme au milieu du XIX siècle,* (Montréal: Les presses de l'Université du Québec, 1971). See also M. Ayearst, "The *Parti Rouge* and the Clergy," *CHR,* 15, 1934, 390–405.

7   Fernande Roy, *Progrès, Harmonie, Liberté. Le libéralisme des milieux d'affaires francophones au tournant du siècle.* (Montréal: Boréal, 1988), p. 283. See also Fernande Roy, *Histoire des idéologies au Québec aux XIXe et XXe siècles,* (Montréal: Boréal Express, 1993) p. 45. "Did the defeat of the reds really mean the end of liberalism in Quebec? Of course not." and p. 115, "Liberal ideas were present in Quebec society since the end of the eighteenth century. They became entrenched, with time into the next century, and became dominant in the twentieth century." See also Séraphin Marion who in 1962 wrote that the history of French-Canadian radicalism had not been written. He cites the life of Honoré Beaugrand as an example of an important figure whose biography has yet to be written. "The history of French-Canadian radicalism has not yet been written. If ever a historian decides to fill this hole, he must devote one of the important chapters of the work to the study of a highly colourful person, politician, author, crotchety, asthmatic, and yet an extensive traveller, soldier, journalist, lecturer, pamphleteer, who attempted with force, in vain, to graft the ideas of Republican France to the soil of Canada…Honoré Beaugrand." *Cahiers des Dix,* 27, 1962, p. 13.

ued with Patrice Dutil's discussion of the life of Godfroy Langlois,[8] Professor Yvan Lamonde's work on Louis-Antoine Dessaulles of Saint-Hyacinthe,[9] Yves Lavertu's biography of Jean-Charles Harvey;[10] and more generally by the contributions of Paul-Andre Linteau, Rene Durocher, Jean-Claude Robert (Vol. 1), Linteau, Durocher, Robert and François Ricard. (Vol. 2), and Dickinson and Young's *Short History of Quebec.*[11] Michael Oliver's *The Passionate Debate*, Ramsay Cook's *French-Canadian Nationalism*, Serge Gagnon's *Quebec and its Historians: The Twentieth Century,* Jacques Monet's *The Last Cannon Shot,* Denis Monière's *Le Développement des idéologies au Québec, des origines à nos jours,* and Ronald Rudin's *Making History in Twentieth Century Quebec* have all greatly added to my understanding of Quebec history.[12]

In his book *Quebec before Duplessis*, Bernard Vigod demolishes the myth of the "great darkness," which is supposed to have existed before 1960.[13] Admittedly, during the Duplessis years, Quebec was set back in many ways. There was, however, "light" before the Duplessis premiership of 1944–1959, and before the "Quiet Revolution" of '60s. The Felix-Gabriel Marchand, Simon-Napoléon Parent, Lomer Gouin, and Louis-Alexandre Taschereau Liberal provincial gov-

---

8   Patrice Dutil, *Devil's Advocate: Godfroy Langlois and the politics of Liberal Progressivism in Laurier's Quebec,* (Outremont: Robert Davies, 1994).

9   Yvan Lamonde, *Louis-Antoine Dessaulles, Un seigneur libéral et anticlérical,* (Montréal: Fides, 1994).

10 Yves Lavertu, *Jean-Charles Harvey, le Combattant,* (Montréal: Boréal, 2000).

11 Paul-André Linteau, René Durocher, and Jean-Claude Robert, *Histoire du Québec contemporain,* Vol I, *De la confédération à la crise,* Vol II, with François Ricard, *Le Québec depuis 1930 (*Montréal: Boréal, 1979–1989), John A. Dickinson and Brian Young, *A Short History of Quebec,* (Mississauga, Ontario: Copp Clark Pitman, 1993).

12 Michael Oliver, *The Passionate Debate,* (Montreal: Véhicule Press, 1991). Ramsay Cook, *French-Canadian Nationalism,* (Toronto: Macmillan, 1969). Serge Gagnon, *Quebec and its Historians; The Twentieth Century,* (Montreal: Harvest House, 1985). Jacques Monet, *The Last Cannon Shot,* (Toronto: University of Toronto Press, 1969.) Denis Monière, *Le Développement des idéologies au Québec, des origines à nos jours,* (Montréal: Québec/Amérique, 1977) and Ronald Rudin, *Making History in Twentieth Century Quebec,* (Toronto: Univ. Toronto Press, 1997). See also Yvan Lamonde and Claude Corbo, *Le rouge et le bleu, une anthologie de la pensée politique au Québec de la conquête à la révolution tranquille,* (Montréal: Les presses de l'Université de Montréal, 1999), Yvan Lamonde, *Histoire sociales des idées au* Québec, *1760–1896,* (Montréal: Éditions Fides, 2000).

13 Bernard L. Vigod, *The Political Career of Louis-Alexandre Taschereau.* (Kingston and Montreal: McGill-Queens Press, 1986).

ernments (1897–1936) witnessed moderate social and economic progress[14] and enacted progressive labour legislation. Quebec accepted the federal old age security benefits plan in 1935.[15] As emphasized by the Quebec historians Linteau, Durocher, and Robert, over a long period there was a gradual evolution, during which French Canadians took control of their society, particularly in the areas of business and the arts.[16] The career of T.-D. Bouchard clearly reflects this development.

During his political life Bouchard was called a "renegade of God," a Freemason, and an atheist. In spite of these accusations, the Catholic French-Canadian people of Saint-Hyacinthe elected Bouchard alderman in 1905, at the age of 23; Member of the Legislative Assembly in 1912, at age 30; and mayor in 1917, at 35. Excluding a brief period of defeat, he was repeatedly re-elected MLA and mayor over a 25-year period, until his resignation in 1944. This demonstrates that contrary to popular mythology, the people clearly refused to follow the dictates of some of their priests, who usually supported Bouchard's opponents.

The French-Canadian people have never been monolithic in their outlook. Broad-minded and bigoted attitudes have coexisted since the establishment of the colony of New France. Even Quebec's bishops were divided in their views on the relationship between state and Church. In chapter 1, I shall develop the theme of this conflict in a short historical review of the Quebec into which Bouchard was born and raised; and in which he matured politically. The politico-religious struggle was to become the most important battle of Bouchard's life.

---

14   Félix-Gabriel Marchand, Liberal Party leader, was premier of Quebec from 1897 to 1900, followed by Simon-Napoléon Parent from 1900 to 1905, Lomer Gouin from 1905 to 1919, and Louis-Alexandre Taschereau from 1919 to 1936. Thus the reign of the Liberals lasted 39 years.

15   Antonin Dupont, "*Louis-Alexandre Taschereau et la législation sociale au Québec, 1920–1936,*" *Revue d'histoire de l'Amérique française,* 26,3, 1972, 397–426.

16   L.-D.-R., I & II.

Chapter I

"Clericalism is the corruption of religion, as nationalism is
the corruption of patriotism."[1]

THE POLITICO-RELIGIOUS STRUGGLE: PROBLEMS IN CHURCH-STATE RELATIONS

Born in the nineteenth century, Télesphore-Damien Bouchard began his political life early in the twentieth. His was the struggle to diminish the role of the Roman Catholic Church in the social, educational, and political spheres of Quebec life. The political wars of his day were intense. He consistently fought his opponents' fire with his own. In order to understand his passionate participation in the political life of his time, it is important to be aware of some of the intense battles of the day. These debates were influenced by the large influx of French clergy fleeing Republican France in the late nineteenth century, an immigration encouraged by Monsignor Ignace Bourget, the Bishop of Montreal. This clergy was imbued with ultramontane, anti-Freemason, monarchist, and xenophobic views.[2] Yet just as Quebec opinion as a whole was never limited to one perspective, neither was that of the Church itself. This chapter provides an overview of some of the events that may explain the "fire" driving the political beliefs of Télesphore-Damien Bouchard.

---

1   T.-D. Bouchard cited in *Le Devoir*, June 25, 1944.

2   2 Léon Pouliot, *Msgr. Bourget*, (Montréal: Beauchemin, 1955). See also Nadia F. Eid, *Le Clergé et le Pouvoir Politique Au Québec*. (Montréal: Éditions Hurtubise, 1978), Fernand Dumont, "Idéologies Au Canada Français (1850–1900): Quelques Réflexions d'Ensemble." *Recherches sociographiques* 10 (1969): 145–69, Laurier Lapierre, "Les Relations Entre l'Église et l'État Au Canada Français." In *L'Église et le Québec*, edited by Marcel Rioux, 31–45. (Montréal: Éditions du jour, 1961), Séraphin Marion, "*Libéralisme Canadien-Français d'Autrefois et d'Aujoud'hui*." *Cahiers des Dix* 27 (1962): 9–45, Marcel Trudel, *L'Influence de Voltaire Au Canada, Volume II, de 1850–1900*. (Montréal: Les Publications de l'université Laval, Fides, 1945).

The central, bitter controversy of the nineteenth century in Quebec was that regarding the role of the Roman Catholic Church in a modern, essentially secular state; and particularly its responsibilities in politics, social services, and especially education. The terminology we shall be using to discuss this debate about the fundamental function of the Church and how it played out in Quebec can actually be traced back to seventeenth-century France, where the Church was subject to the monarch. The king appointed his own bishops. In recognition of the power exercised over them by the temporal ruler, the clergy quite understandably adopted what came to be referred to as the "Gallican" approach to Church-State relations; that is, they decided to abide by the principle of "render unto Caesar what is due to Caesar, and render unto God, what is God's." In Quebec, this was generally the position of the *rouges* (members of the Liberal Party, as opposed to the *bleus*, members of the Conservative Party). Nevertheless, there were Liberals who were close to the Church. Some even maintained a perspective that approached the ultramontane viewpoint, and there were Conservatives who were out-and-out Gallican.[3] Literally, "ultramontane" means "over the mountain"; that is, over the mountain from France, towards Rome—the only true political capital for a believing Christian, or so ultramontane doctrine held. Ultramontanism's adherents believed that the Church had no obligation to submit before a national secular state, but rather that it was supranational—that it was to obey the Vatican, and was superior to any individual state, especially in the domains of social service and education. During the latter half of the nineteenth century and into the twentieth, the political stage in Quebec was actually shared by four groups: the conservative-ultramontanes—known as *castors* (beavers)—who advocated a theocratic state;[4]

---

3   George-Étienne Cartier was a Gallican Conservative leader, as was the first provincial premier, Joseph-Adolphe Chapleau. The Gallican-ultramontane battle divided the Conservative Party for a number of years. See Frank H. Underhill, "The Development of National Political Parties in Canada," *Canadian Historical Review*, 1935, XVI, 367–387. See also H. Blair Neatby and John T. Saywell, "Chapleau and the Conservative Party in Quebec," *CHR*, 1956, XXXVII, 1–23.

4   The "*castors*" was the name given to a group of dissident ultramontane Conservatives founded in 1882, when one of their leaders, François-Xavier Trudel signed a pamphlet, *Le pays, le parti et le grand homme*, with the pseudonym, "*Castor*." They opposed the Conservative anti-clerical premiers Joseph-Adolphe Chapleau and Joseph-Alfred Mousseau, because they were judged to be too close to the Gallican Liberals. Yvan Lamonde believes that the *castors*, without a solid structure, faded away by 1908. (Personal communication). However, the

anti-clerical Conservatives who were strongly Gallican; Liberals, known as the lukewarm *rouges,* who were usually passively and sometimes actively pro-clerical; and the radical *rouges,* who were anti-clerical and staunchly Gallican.[5] This great European ideological debate had been transported over the ocean to Quebec in such a manner that, by the end of the nineteenth century, it came to dominate political discourse and cut across party lines.

It is noteworthy that the first bishop of the colony of New France, François Xavier de Laval-Montmorency—known as Laval—only received his appointment in 1764, after an eleven-year delay caused by strife both within France and between France and Rome.[6] Bishop Laval was an ultramontane, but, as we shall see, many of his successors had a more nuanced view of the Church-state relationship. In the early part of the nineteenth century, the power of the Church was in decline.[7] However, by mid-century, the Church's power had

---

views of the bigoted, ultra-religious, xenophobic population certainly persisted until the 1960s. See appendix on the Order of Jacques Cartier, p. 367. See also Herbert F. Quinn, *The Union Nationale, a Study in Quebec Nationalism,* (Toronto: University of Toronto, 1963).

5   J.A.A. Lovink, "The Politics of Quebec: Provincial political Parties 1897–1936", Doctoral thesis, Department of Political Science, Duke University, 1967. Lovink makes the point that the parties were divided internally, as noted here.

6   Francis Parkman, *France and England in North America,* (New York: The Library of America, 1983). vol. 1. pp. 1164–1222. The battle was between the Sulpicians who supported L'abbé de Queylus as Bishop and the Jesuits who supported Laval. See also Terrence J. Fay, *A History of Canadian Catholics; Gallicanism, Romanism, and Canadianism,* (Montreal and Kingston: McGill-Queen's University Press, 2002). Fay terms the early Church in Quebec Gallican, and it is true that Laval was appointed by the King, after pressure and manoeuvring by the French Jesuits: but he was ratified by Rome, which took over the missionary endeavour in 1622. Laval's attitude towards the Governor of New France was certainly ultramontane. He felt that the Church was above the state and fought the governor frequently. See also Eid, who analyzes the ultramontanes but does not speak about the Gallican church in Quebec at all. Perhaps she felt that there was none. See also Roberto Perrin, *Rome in Canada, The Vatican and Canadian Affairs in the Late Victorian Age* (Toronto: University of Toronto Press, 1990), and Paul Crunican, *Priests and Politicians: Manitoba Schools and the Election of 1896,* (Toronto: University of Toronto Press, 1974).

7   Linteau, Durocher and Robert, p. 232. The authors attribute this decline to the fact that the Church's position was still not clearly defined in law during this period, thus rendering its properties insecure; as well as to the upsurge in liberal ideas. "From 1840 on, these obstacles were removed. The Church was fully recognized juridically and the anti-clericalism of a part of the French-Canadian leadership did not survive the defeat of 1837–38."

increased. Yet in spite of this increase in ultramontane influence in Quebec, Rome, as Roberto Perrin and Paul Crunican have demonstrated, never sided with Bourget, or with his successor as leader of the ultramontanes, Monsignor Louis-François Laflèche. This flies in the face of the popular view of the Ontario Orangemen (fanatic Protestant anti-papists), according to whom Rome ruled Quebec. Instead of promoting a sectarian Quebec Church, Rome, although headed by ultramontane popes, always ultimately favoured some separation of Church and state in Canada. The Vatican's aim was to avoid provoking a religious war; and to protect the increasing English-speaking Catholic population of Canada, as well as the Catholics of the United States.[8]

The *Institut canadien* made an important contribution to the Church-state debate in Quebec. A group composed mostly of liberal Montrealers, especially from the radical wing of the party founded the *Institut* in 1844. Non-radicals such as Wilfrid Laurier and George-Etienne Cartier were also early members. The *Institut* had Protestant members. It sponsored debates and discussions on problems of the day, as well as on scientific and literary topics. Its premises contained halls for public debates, halls for reading, and an extensive library that became the focus of their dispute with the bishop. The library was suspected of including many books banned by the Church. Bourget bitterly opposed the *Institut*,[9] and it eventually disbanded due to his continuous pressure on it, which included the excommunication of members who did not resign.[10] Nevertheless, before its collapse, the *Institut canadien* succeeded in making its influence widespread.

The ultramontanes did not view the end of the *Institut* as a pretext to lay down their arms. Canadian liberals were, in their eyes, no different from the republicans of revolutionary France. Thundering edicts came forth from the ultramontane press. *Le Nouveau Monde* wrote in 1876: "We must crush the liberal snake, liberalism in any form, no matter who professes the doctrine,

---

8   See Perin, and see Crunican.

9   Théophile Hudon, *L'institut canadien de Montréal et l'affaire Guibord: une page d'histoire*, (Montréal: Librairie Beauchemin, 1938). See also L.-D.-R., I, p. 238.

10   Susan Mann (Trofimenkoff) Robertson, "The Intstitut Canadien, an essay in Cultural History," Master's thesis, University of Western Ontario, 1965. See also Susan Mann Trofimenkoff, *Visions nationales une histoire du Québec*, (Saint Laurent; Éditions du Trécarré, 1986), p. 178–180, as well as L.-D.-R., p. 238.

whether M. Laflamme, M. Doutre, M. Langelier and M. Dessaulles."[11] From the presses of *Le Franc-Parleur* came a brochure entitled "A Glance at European Liberalism and Canadian Liberalism. The Demonstration of their exact identity."[12] Bourget, celebrating his seventy-seventh birthday in 1876, circulated a pastoral letter stating that in order to avoid putting his soul in danger, a Catholic had to learn to recognize a "Catholic liberal" by these beliefs: that the Church should be subordinate to the state or should be separate from the state; and that the Church and its priests should only be concerned with spiritual matters.

This partisan clerical intervention led to conflict in the courts over the issue of "undue influence" during elections.[13] In 1881, just before T.-D. Bouchard's birth, a bitter battle broke out in a contested federal election in Charlevoix, in which Alexis Tremblay, a Liberal, lost to Hector Langevin, a Conservative and brother of the bishop of Rimouski. The parish priests of the region had taken an active part in the election, the results of which Tremblay contested. Tremblay's lawyer, François Langelier, a prominent Liberal and a respected academic, created a sensation when he claimed "undue influence and spiritual intimidation" by local priests in favour of Langevin. The trial was presided over by Judge Adolphe-Basile Routhier, a Conservative and the author of the famous "Catholic program" of 1871, according to which the state was to be subordinate to the Church.[14] The people of Quebec followed the trial passionately. Newspapers of every political stripe published inflamed editorials. Several ultramontane newspapers and Monsignor Langevin demanded the dismissal of Langelier from Laval University, where he was a professor of law and political science.

The trial took place during the months of July, August, and September in Malbaie and attracted the excited attention of the province. Langevin testified, admitting that before he agreed to be a candidate, his organizer had met with local priests. He admitted that he and Israël Tarte, the Conservative organizer, urged voters to listen to the advice of their priests. Witnesses testified that Father

11   *Le Nouveau Monde*; le 12 *février* 1876; cited in R. Rumilly. HPQ II p.43. Rodolfe Laflamme and François Langelier were prominent Liberals, as were Joseph Doutre and Loius-Antione Dessaulles. All were members of the Liberal radical wing and members of the *Institut*. See also Lamonde, on *Dessaulles*.

12   Rumilly, *HPQ*, II, p. 43.

13   Perrin, p. 35, 62–63, 95–99, 105–107.

14   Judge Routhier was also the author of words of the national anthem, "O Canada." He had been the unsuccessful Conservative candidate twice in the county of Kamouraska.

Sirois had warned parishioners at Sunday mass that they should not trust the anti-clerical (Liberal) party, which wanted to abolish the tithe and thereby starve the clergy. Sirois declared that if the Liberals gained power, they would persecute the clergy. It was even possible that blood could flow. The only way to avoid this tragedy, said Sirois, was to fight against Liberals. A farmer, Fleurent Paquet, and five others testified that the sermon caused many people to change their votes. Elzèar Danais stated that the loss of the election by Tremblay was due to the sermon of his priest. Zephirin Bergeron reported that Father Langlais noted that the Pope's flag was blue—the Conservatives' colour—while the Liberals' colour was red—the same colour as the flag of Garibaldi, leader of the anti-papal Italian nationalist revival.[15] One of the most impressive witnesses was Rieule Asselin, father of Olivar, a loyal *rouge*.[16] He was mayor of Saint Hilarion and deacon in Father Langlais's church. Jules Tremblay testified that he changed his vote because he feared being condemned to hell. Many other witnesses testified in the same manner. There was evidence of clerical influence in Saint-Urbain, Saint-Fidèle, and Saint-Jérémie. Father Roy informed his parishioners that children of Liberals insulted his party, the Conservatives. Rumilly states: "Most of the witnesses, illiterate farmers, understood that a Liberal vote implied a serious sin."[17] It was evident that the clergy contributed to the defeat of Tremblay. It remained to be seen however, whether this contribution constituted illegal "undue influence."

Newspapers on both sides of the debate relished reporting the trial. Writing in *Le Canadien*, the Conservative organizer Israël Tarte was so outrageous that Judge Routhier, an ultramontane, held him in contempt of court. Abbé Alexis Pelletier, who wrote diatribes against the Liberals under the pseudonym "Luigi" in *Le Franc-Parleur,* was reprimanded by Archbishop Elzèar-Alexandre Taschereau, who said: "Polemicists of Luigi's kind do more harm than good to the cause which they defend."[18] When the trial was over, 175 witnesses had

---

15   Garibaldi was the leader of the new Italian state, which fought against the temporal hold of Pope Pius IX on Italian territory. Quebec was involved in the war to protect the Pope through its volunteers, the "Zouaves." Louis Frechette, the poet, fought for Garibaldi.

16   H. Pelletier-Baillargeon; *Olivar Asselin et son temps.* (Montréal:Fides, 1996). p. 24. (Olivar Asselin, a journalist, was active with the Henri Bourassa nationalists of the early twentieth century. See Chapter 4).

17   Rumilly, *HPQ,* II, p. 49.

18   Ibid., p. 49.

been called to the stand. According to Rumilly, "The intervention of the clergy appeared to have been established, the legitimacy of the intervention was the subject of discussion."[19] The Liberal newspaper of Senator Fabre asked where it all would end. "Intelligent people, Liberals and Conservatives, wonder where the system would lead us if left in place … in each Parish there would be one great voter, the priest, and in Parliament only representatives of the priests."[20]

Rome fretted about this trial. Cardinal Alessandro Franchi, Prefect of Propaganda in Rome, wrote to Taschereau seeking accurate information about the problems caused by this intrusion into clerical affairs, asking; "what prudent ways he would suggest to eliminate these difficulties."[21] Along with the other bishops of Quebec, in the autumn of 1875 Taschereau had signed a pastoral letter, initiated by Bourget, condemning Liberal Catholics. However, on May 25, 1876, Taschereau published on his own initiative another pastoral letter, which placed the two political parties of Canada, the Liberals and the Conservatives, on an equal footing.[22] This second letter was an attempt to differentiate his view from the ultramontane stand of Bourget, Langevin, and Laflèche, all of whom refused to sign. This demonstrates that the Quebec clergy was by no means monolithic.

In 1876 Bourget resigned as Bishop of Montreal. The ultramontanes initiated a campaign to ask the Pope, Pius IX, to refuse the resignation. They dispatched Laflèche of Trois-Rivières to Rome to support Bourget, and to ask the Holy Office to condemn the "great contemporary error." Meanwhile, Taschereau had also sought advice from Rome. Bourget was thought to be on his deathbed and received the Last Rites. Before the final judgment in the "undue influence" trial, Rome sent news that Bourget's resignation had been accepted, just as he made what was, in the eyes of his followers, a most miraculous recovery. The Pope appointed Edouard-Charles Fabre, brother of a Liberal senator, as Bourget's replacement.[23] In the same mail came the announcement that the Pope had

---

19   Ibid., p.50.

20   Ibid., p.52.

21   Ibid., p. 45.

22   Fay portrays Taschereau as a weak leader. However, according to Paul Crunican: "(Fay) probably goes too far in downgrading the talents of Canada's first Cardinal Taschereau." Book review of *Rome in Canada,* in the *Catholic Historical Review,* 177, 1991, 344.

23   Brian Young, "Edouard-Charles Fabre," *Dictionary of Canadian Biography,* XII, (Toronto: University of Toronto Press, 1990.)

granted the University of Laval a pontifical charter. This was another defeat for Bourget—for twenty-five years he had been attempting to establish an institution of higher ecclesiastical learning in Montreal. These two acts of the Vatican were widely interpreted as strengthening Taschereau's position. Taschereau wrote; "The Holy Father has approved our neutral attitude towards the various political parties of our country ... why then, concerning questions where religion has nothing to say, come people who inflame the mind by making one believe that faith and morals are in danger?"[24] The people understood these words as a condemnation of ultramontane priests.

Judge Routhier delivered the predicted judgment. He granted that the clergy had influenced the vote—but only a little. The law defined undue influence as the use of force, intimidation, or threats, which the court found were not present in this case. In British jurisprudence, Routhier had found no precedent in which a sermon constituted undue influence. Routhier dismissed the cause, and upheld the election of Langevin. Tremblay then appealed to the Supreme Court. While the Supreme Court deliberated, Langevin published a special pastoral letter protesting against "erroneous and harmful principles." He refused to grant the courts the right to rule on the abuse of power, or to decide on the right of the Church to withold holy rites to someone on the grounds of their political activity. Langevin inveighed against "Catholic liberals" and condemned the following propositions: that Parliament is omnipotent and can make laws that oppose religious practice; that the liberty of voters is absolute; that civil courts can determine whether a particular sermon is abusive or whether the clergy has the right to refuse holy rites; that this refusal of rites constitutes undue influence; and that one must obey a law which one considers unjust. Anyone who agreed with these proposals, Langevin wrote, was unworthy to receive the sacraments of the Church. This pastoral letter caused a sensation throughout the country. Liberals and the Protestant press called it an effort to influence the Supreme Court. Even *The Gazette*, a conservative newspaper, criticized the bishop of Rimouski and denounced the idea that the Church could determine the limits of civil power and the law.

On February 23, 1877, the Supreme Court announced its verdict. On behalf of his colleagues, Judge Jean-Thomas Taschereau (cousin of the Archbishop) announced that the court had unanimously decided to reverse Judge Routhier's decision and annul the election of Hector Langevin. They did not disqualify

---

24   Rumilly, *HPQ,* II, p. 53.

Langevin but fined him six thousand dollars in costs. The decision, written in French, attentively sketched the history of the election and the opinions of Langevin and his priests:

> All these sermons accompanied by threats and declarations that it was matter of conscience to obey the clergy, were of a nature to induce a great number of voters, who were required to hear Sunday sermons after Sunday, to believe that they would commit a serious sin or that they would be deprived holy rites if they did not act in accordance with these instructions. Such acts have to be qualified as acts of the worst kind of undue influence, because these declarations and these threats were made from the pulpit, in the name of religion, and addressed to men well disposed to listen to the voice of their priest, to men with little or no education.... A system of general intimidation has been created, and one can conclude that the voters have not been able to exercise of their rights freely.[25]

The Liberals were triumphant, yet the Conservatives and the ultramontanes did not hesitate to attack the Supreme Court's decision. Israël Tarte, Langevin's organizer, insinuated in his newspaper *Le Canadien* that the Archbishop had influenced his cousin, the judge. Taschereau severely reprimanded Tarte. Tarte accepted blame and repented. Taschereau must have been somewhat ambivalent, because after having met with all the bishops of Quebec, he signed a joint declaration on March 26, taking note of the judgment with "deep pain," and requesting that the legislators find a suitable remedy. A telegram from Rome instructing the bishops not to comment on the judgment of the Supreme Court arrived too late. Their joint announcement had already been published.

In the repeat election, the same candidates, Tremblay and Langevin, represented their parties. Taschereau forbade the priests to comment on the election, although Father Sirois asserted that the decision of the Supreme Court did not impress him. Langevin's organizer circulated a pamphlet in which the judgment was discussed and in which Tremblay was accused of using the Supreme Court to attack the Pope and the bishops. The Supreme Court itself was described in the pamphlet as "consisting of four Protestants and two priest eaters (*mangeurs de prêtres*)." Moreover, the authors accused the Liberals of advocating that priests be imprisoned or fined. They went on to say that all the priests of the province were against Tremblay. "Those with doubts should seek the advice of

---

25   Ibid., pp. 70–71. Rumilly quoting from the judgement

their priest, who will tell them that a vote for Tremblay this year is even worse than last year." In the end, Langevin was re-elected, but his majority fell from 211 to 60.

In the interim, another legal battle intensified this debate. In December 1876, Judges Louis-Napoléon Casault, John McGuire and Thomas McCord annulled an election in Bonaventure, disqualifying the Conservative, P. C. Beauchesne, as a candidate for seven years. Judge Casault, who wrote the decision, was also a law professor at Laval University. Since Bonaventure was in the diocese of Rimouski, the bishop, Jean Langevin, supported by Laflèche, demanded that Cardinal Taschereau dismiss or disavow Casault. Taschereau replied that it was important to distinguish between the judge who could be criticized, and the professor of law, who was above reproach. In any case, in consideration of the views of some bishops, as well as of the delicacy of the affair, Taschereau decided to submit the problem to Rome. In a letter to Laflèche, Taschereau wrote:

> When one compares the propositions condemned by Msgr.Langevin with the judgment of Judge Casault, one wonders if they are from the same person? Using scissors, by editing right and left in the text, in the manner of Protestants in reference to the Bible, have they respected the context, which would have explained all in a reasonable manner? Do the propositions of the judgment represent such an absolute certainty, making them reprehensible in the eyes of Msgr. Langevin?[26]

Langevin then sent Canon Godefroy Lamarche to Rome to demand the dismissal of Casault. Luc Letellier de Saint-Just, a minister in the federal Liberal government, drafted a memorandum to the Pope. Although a *rouge*, Letellier de Saint-Just was responsible for a federal charter establishing the Catholic University of Ottawa, and so the Oblate Fathers of Ottawa held him in high esteem. Lamarche added his own memorandum condemning "liberal Catholics." He explained that the Canadian constitution guaranteed the Catholic Church full rights and liberty from persecution; that there are in Canada Catholic liberals who form the Liberal Party, which is harmful and radical; that the Archbishop of Quebec "has been deficient in this struggle, and seems to crush its most valiant

---

26   Msgr. Taschereau to Msgr. Laflèche; letter of December. 26; Archives de L'Archévechie de Trois-Rivières.

warriors by his authority."[27] In Rome, Abbé Benjamin Paquet, friend and advisor to Taschereau, presented his views: that there were no "Catholic liberals" in Canada; that the professors and the spirit of Laval University were beyond reproach and Roman Catholic; that "the complaining Bishops leave much to be desired; that Msgr. Taschereau is very superior to them"; and finally, "that these blindly partisan priests compromise their character and their position by their political sermons and their electoral interventions."[28] A friend of Paquet in Rome was none other than the influential Cardinal Franchi, who promptly had Paquet appointed Apostolic Protonotary. Abbé Paquet questioned the "serenity" of the bishop of Rimouski, Langevin, and his complicity with his brother, the elected member.

Rome had had its fill of Canadian problems. Deluged by all these depositions, including one by Letellier de Saint-Just, the Holy Father decided to send an Apostolic Delegate to Canada: the Bishop of Ardagh, Ireland, Monsignor George Conroy. Pope Pius IX mandated Conroy to study and report to the Sacred Congregation, but Pius also gave him secret instructions: to eradicate the division between the Quebec bishops and to accept Taschereau's views. These secret instructions, eventually published by Taschereau, suggested that the cause of the troubles was clerical interference in politics without "sufficient pastoral prudence."[29] The bishops were to be reminded that the Holy Congregation had already expressed the view of Rome in 1868 and again in 1874 (July 29), that

> Another cause of the same disadvantage is found in the too great interference of the clergy in political businesses, without worrying enough about pastoral discretion. The suitable remedy to this excess of zeal … [is] that at election times, they confine their advice to voters to what is found decreed in the Provincial Council of 1868. It will be necessary to add that the Church by condemning liberalism *does not intend to condemn all and or any political parties which are perchance called liberal, since decisions of the Church relate to some errors opposed to Catholic doctrine and not to a determined political party …* the latter damage without any other basis, by declaring one political party of Canada condemned by the Church, namely the reformist

---

27   Rumilly, *HPQ*, II, p. 74. see also Crunican, Fay, Rioux, Lapierre and Perrin.

28   Rumilly, *HPQ*, II p. 75.

29   *Mandements du Québec*, NS II, 271.

party, a party formerly warmly supported even by some Bishops.[30] [Emphasis added.]

The Pope's secret instructions began with an admonition that one of the main problems was the public disagreement among bishops, not only in their attitudes in political debates but also in other well-known conflicts—that is, the desire of Montreal to establish a university, which was considered by Quebec to be ruinous for the future of Laval University. The pope proposed a solution: that with the assistance of Conroy the bishops of Quebec decide together what public policy should be adopted. Regarding the political question, the extracted quotes are clear enough to assert that Rome did not agree with the ultramontane view of the relationship between the Church and the state, at least in a state such as Canada with its two major religions. "The bishops should take care to avoid a stain on the honour of the Church by having priests accused of undue influence in civil court. That the bishops must be prudent, especially in political affairs, to avoid a religious war with the Protestants of Canada." The Protestants were already worried and irritated by the clergy. The document continued: "In addition, it is necessary that the clergy always avoid naming people from the pulpit, especially to discredit them at election time, and that it never use the influence of the ecclesiastical ministry for particular purposes, if these candidates do not threaten the true interests of the Church."[31] This last phrase allowed the ultramontanes some latitude of interpretation.

Thus, Conroy had clear and well-outlined instructions. He met with all the bishops of Quebec, Ontario, the rest of Canada and Newfoundland. He listened to everyone. To maintain an aura of independence, he rented a residence in the countryside of St. Foy instead of staying in the Archbishop's Palace. He accepted invitations from everyone, visited Trois-Rivières and Sorel, and attended a banquet given in his honour by the Lieutenant-Governor, Letellier de Saint-Juste. The Pope, who had developed ultramontane views in the wake of the 1848 revolutions and who had promulgated the doctrine of the infallibility of the Pope in 1870, nevertheless demonstrated sensitivity to the specifically complex nature of the Canadian federation. The Vatican listened to the English and some French-Canadian bishops of Canada who cautioned against taking political sides. Roberto Perrin has written that the third most important city

---

30   Rumilly, *HPQ*, II, p. 76.

31   Ibid.,

in Canadian history was Rome, and that contrary to the belief of the Ontario Orangemen, the popes of the late nineteenth century had not been in favour of the ultramontane view in Canada. Pius IX, although ultramontane and opposed to modernity, had to accommodate increasingly secular European regimes and the complexity of Canadian religious divisions. In a bull published in 1854, he proclaimed the dogma of the Immaculate Conception, and in 1864, he issued a syllabus condemning 80 errors, among them the belief that the Pope should reconcile himself to "progress, liberalism, and modern civilization." Nevertheless, by this stage he felt the necessity of accommodating the Church to the realty of increasingly secular European regimes and the intricacy of Canadian and American religious divisions.

Thus, we see that a historical review of the conflicts within the Catholic Chuch during the nineteenth century challenges the myth of the monolithic Quebec church.

LAURIER'S SPEECH OF 1877

While Conroy deliberated during the summer of 1877, the Liberals organized a large meeting at the Music Hall in Quebec City, at which they would hear a speech by the new leader of the French-Canadian wing of the party. On June 26, 1877, Wilfrid Laurier, a rising star in the Liberal Party and soon to be appointed to the federal cabinet, delivered perhaps one of the most influential speeches of his career—and, indeed, in Canadian history.[32] The T.-D. Bouchard collection of documents housed at the *Archives Nationale du Québec* in Quebec City contains a well-thumbed copy of this speech. Many of the themes of this address were later to form the basis of Bouchard's own speeches; and therefore it merits analysis.

At the time of the address, Laurier was about to replace Joseph Cauchon as leader of the Quebec wing of the Liberal Party of Canada. Laurier detested Cauchon, believing him to be a man of neither principle nor conviction. In fact, Laurier refused to join the Liberal cabinet of Alexander MacKenzie until after Cauchon was named Lieutenant-Governor of Manitoba—were he in the cabinet, Laurier would have felt compelled to vote against Cauchon's appoint-

---

32   Real Belanger, "Sir Henry-Charles-Wilfrid Laurier," *DCB, 1911–1920, XIV*, (Toronto: University of Toronto Press, 1998). 610–628.

ment.[33] As a French-Canadian leader in an English-majority state, Laurier's aim was to define the objectives of the Liberal Party from a national viewpoint. In early May, he wrote his speech, a frank declaration of his liberal faith and submitted a summary to Prime Minister MacKenzie. The Prime Minister replied on June 22 that after having discussed the speech with Rodolphe Laflamme and several others, he recommended its postponement until after Conroy had concluded his mission. "It would be the safer course," he wrote. Joseph Schull, Laurier's biographer, comments that this was almost a command for Laurier to remain silent.[34] After much agonizing meditation, Laurier wrote to Mackenzie that he would be as prudent as possible, but that "undue influence" was a subject that demanded a declaration. He absolutely would have to speak about it.[35] The Conservatives were planning to amend the relevant law at the next session of the provincial Parliament, and the Liberal Party would be be thought foolish if it were to acquiesce to this amendment. According to Laurier, "Unless we do something to form the opinion of our friends here, they will leave (the fold)…. It seems to me that if we can not speak clearly in a common language, which we have to speak some day, the destiny of our party is in a desperate condition."[36] He added that if Mackenzie insisted, he would refrain from speaking. He would await MacKenzie's advice, but due to time constraints this advice would have to be sent by telegram to Laurier's hotel in Quebec City. "I am at your disposition, and I will respect your judgment," he wrote. When no telegram arrived, Laurier proceeded to the Music Hall, where he found an enormous crowd of 2,000 members of the province's intellectual, political, and social elite. The thirty-six-year-old rose to declare his beliefs:

> I know that, for a great number of our compatriots the Liberal Party
> is a party composed of men of perverse doctrines and of dangerous

---

33 Joseph Schull, Laurier, (Toronto: MacMillan, 1965), p, 114. Alexander MacKenzie formed the first Liberal government of Canada in 1873. His election was due mostly to the Canadian Pacific Railway scandal. The scandal involved Sir Hugh Allan, head of the CPR, contributing $900,000 to the Conservative Party election campaigns of Sir George-Étienne Cartier and Sir John A. MacDonald. See Brian Young, George-Étienne Cartier, (Montreal & Kingston: McGill-Queens University Press, 1981). pp.122–124.

34 Schull, p. 116.

35 Belanger also notes Mackenzie's attempt to postpone the speech. He also judges the speech to have had a major impact on Canadian politics. DCB, XIV, 1998, p. 615.

36 Schull, p.118.

trends, walking knowingly and deliberately towards revolution … victims and dupes of principles by which they are unconsciously but fatally guided to revolution … for others … Liberalism is a new form of evil, a heresy … some have systematically belittled us, others have in good faith maligned us.… All accusations against us … can be resumed … 1. Liberalism is a new form of error, a heresy already virtually condemned by the head of the Church; 2. A Catholic cannot be Liberal.… I know that the Head of the Church has condemned Catholic liberalism. But I know and I say that Catholic liberalism is not political Liberalism.[37]

Calmly, Laurier defined the creeds of Conservatives who favoured the continuation of the status quo and of liberals who were more prone to favour changes towards progress. He quoted Macaulay's definition of the two opposing ideas:

Everywhere there exists a class of men who attach with love to all that is ancient … even when they are convinced … that a change would be advantageous, they consent however only with regret and repugnance. There is also another class of exuberant hopeful men, bold in their ideas, always going forward, prompt to discern imperfections in what exists, little gauging the risk and disadvantages which always accompany improvements, disposed to look at all change as an improvement.[38]

Laurier explained that progress—the reforms to which all of humanity aspires—could be realized without agitation, without perturbation, without violence. Canadian Liberals, he said, followed the pattern established by the Liberal Party of England, who without any instrument other than the law had carried out a series of reforms that had made the English people the freest, most prosperous, and happiest in Europe. In French Canada, however, the bloodier histories of continental Europe and France tended to be studied and used as examples. "It is true that there exists in Europe, in France, in Italy, and in Germany, a class of men with the title of liberal," Laurier explained, "but they are only liberal in name, and they are the most dangerous of men. They are not liberals. They are revolutionaries.… With these men we have nothing

---

37   W. Laurier, *Le Libéralisme Politique,* Speech given at the Canadian Club in Quebec City, June 26, 1877, pp. 2, 4–5 in ANQ; *Fonds* Bouchard P 10/16.

38   Laurier, p. 10.

in common, but it is the tactics of our adversaries always to associate us with them."[39] Laurier asserted his belief that abuse is to be found in all aspects of human affairs; and that this should be remedied. He then presented a passionate confession of his faith in liberalism:

> Liberalism appears to me from all points of view superior to the other principle. The principle of liberalism resides in the essence of our nature, in this thirst for happiness that we bring with us in this life.... Our soul is immortal, but our means are limited. We gravitate, without ceasing, towards an ideal, which we never reach. We dream of the good, we never reach the better ... we discover there horizons which we had not even suspected. We push headlong, and in these horizons, explored in their turn, we discover some others which push us on again and always further.... This condition of our nature is precisely what makes the grandeur of man, because it condemns him fatally to movement, to progress: our means are limited, but our nature is perfectible, and we have infinity as a playing field. Thus there is always place for improvement of our condition, for the improvement of our nature, and for the accession of a greatest number to an easier life. Here is again what, to my eyes, constitutes the superiority of liberalism.[40]

According to Laurier, the identification of the Liberal Party with Catholic liberalism would result in a single-party state; and that party would be the Conservative Party, controlled by the ultramontanes. Laurier then reviewed the history of the Canadian Liberal Party, which was born following the demise of its precursor, the Patriot Party, after the 1837–38 Rebellions. Until 1840, almost all French Canadians belonged to the Patriot Party. In the 1840s Louis-Hippolyte Lafontaine led the party towards a more moderate view opposed by the *rouges* and Louis-Joseph Papineau upon his return from exile. Later, in the 1850s, a youthful, greatly talented, and more impetuous generation leaned more towards the radicalism of Papineau, and proclaimed a program of twenty articles, including the annexation of Quebec to the United States.[41] Laurier affirmed that this program was no longer the policy of the current Liberal Party. Those with calmer and more reflective views replaced the rash youth of this wing. As is well

39 Ibid., p. 20.

40 Ibid., p. 13.

41 Ibid., p. 22.

described in a book by Jean-Paul Bernard on liberalism of the mid-nineteenth century, the Liberal Party became "pale red."[42] This is confirmed by Laurier's view that, "As for the old programs, all the social parts no longer remain; nothing at all, and as for the political party, what remains are only the principles of the Liberal Party of England."[43]

In Laurier's view the very pale red wing of Lafontaine joined with the Conservatives of Upper Canada to become the Liberal-Conservative Party. Frank Underhill has described the formation of national political parties in Canada. Early on—in the 1850s and 1860s—parties were extremely unstable due to independents elected in too many constituencies. "Front-benchers and back-benchers" frequently passed "with remarkable ease from one political camp to the other."[44] In fact, Macdonald complained that after independents had been bought, "they often refused to stay bought." The party then abandoned the title of "Liberal" and enacted changes to its program. Laurier inveighed indirectly against the Quebec Conservative Party, which in 1871 had adopted the "*programme catholique*," according to which Catholic politicians should be subject to the policies of the Holy See.

> I no longer know what name to call this party. Today, those who seem to hold the upper hand call themselves the ultramontane, the Catholic party. If Mr. Cartier returned today on earth, he would no longer recognize his party. Mr. Cartier was faithful to principles of the English constitution. Those today … who hold the upper hand, openly reject the principles of the English constitution.… They understand neither their country nor their period. All their ideas can be traced to those of the reactionaries of France.… They adore Don Carlos and the Count of Chambord.… They shout "Long live the King!" I accuse them of judging the political situation of the country, not according to what goes on here, but according to what happens in France. I accuse them of wishing to introduce here ideas whose

---

42   Jean-Paul Bernard. See also H. Blair Neatby, *Laurier and a Liberal Quebec: a Study in Political Management*, (Toronto: McClelland & Stewart, 1973) Neatby discusses the question of Catholic liberals and Montreal schools.

43   Laurier's speech, p. 23.

44   Frank H. Underhill, "The Development of National Political Parties in Canada" *CHR*, 1935, XVI, 367–387. The author remarks that Macdonald is reputed to have said that he was for protecting the rights of the minority, and that the rich are always a minority!

application would be impossible in our state of society. I accuse them of working laboriously and unfortunately too efficiently, to lower religion to the simple dimension of party politics.... You want to organize a Catholic party. *But have you not thought that if you had the misfortune to succeed, you would gather to your country calamities whose consequences it is impossible to anticipate? You want to organize all Catholics as a single party, without other bonds, without any other basis than the community of religion, but have you not thought that, by this action, you will organize the Protestant population as a single party, and that then, instead of the peace and harmony which exists today between the various elements of the Canadian population, you bring war, religious war, the most terrible of all wars?*[45] [Emphasis added]

Laurier then went on to state that the clergy had an absolute right to express their views; but no right to coerce their congregations:

I tell you that there is not a single liberal Canadian who wants to prevent the clergy from taking part in politics.... In the name of what principle of liberty would they wish to refuse to the priest the right to participate in political affairs? In the name of what principle of liberty would they want to refuse to the priest the right to have political opinions, and to express them; the right to approve or disapprove public men and their acts; and to teach the people what they believe to be its duty?... No! The priest should preach as he wishes, it is his right. Never will this right be contested by a Liberal Canadian. The constitution we have invites all citizens to take part in the affairs of state.... However, this right is not unlimited. We do not have absolute rights. The rights of each man in our society finish at the precise place where they encroach on the rights of another. In political life, the right of intervention ends where it would encroach on the independence of the voter. The constitution of our country rests on the freely expressed will of each voter. The constitution expects that each voter register his vote freely and voluntarily ... The law keeps a jealous eye to see that the opinion of the voter is expressed such as it is, that if in a county, the opinion expressed by a single voter is not his own real opinion, but an opinion aroused the fear, by fraud or by corruption, the election has to be cancelled.[46]

---

45   Laurier, pp. 25–26.

46   Ibid., p. 31.

Laurier explained that it is legitimate to change opinion by persuasion, but never by intimidation. Persuasion changes the conviction of the voter. Intimidation, however, does not change a person's mind; rather, it prevents the expression of his true free will and obstructs the aim of the Canadian constitution. Intimidation renders "responsible government" an empty phrase; and eventually, here as elsewhere, repression would bring explosive violence and ruin. Laurier outlined the possible consequences of such an approach, and he concluded his speech by mentioning the secret instructions of the Pope to Monsignor Conroy to avoid the sparking of violent religious conflict in Canada. Laurier finished his address with a tribute to the free British institutions that had allowed French Canadians to remain French and Catholic—though under the British flag—without a single British soldier in the country.

This speech established Laurier as the imposing national leader of the French Canadians within the Canadian Liberal Party. Laurier entered Alexander MacKenzie's cabinet in 1877. A by-election was called in October of 1877 for the Arthabaska riding, where Laurier lived because of a suspicion of tuberculosis. The Conservatives, led by Hector Langevin, did not follow the British custom of not contesting an election involving a standing minister. Laurier was subsequently beaten by 24 votes in a bitter, dirty campaign in which much money and major Conservative power was invested. Laurier observed that "I was beaten in a district of 3,200 voters, where 3,800 expressed their opinion."[47] Months later, he was elected in the riding of Quebec-East, where he kept his seat for many years. Nineteen years later, Laurier became the first French Canadian to be elected Prime Minister of Canada.

At this moment, a conjoint pastoral letter signed by the Quebec bishops under the direction—and coercion—of Conroy, proclaimed that the condemnation by the Pope of "liberal Catholicism" did not apply to any political party in Canada. The priests were reminded that "the decree of the Fourth Council of Quebec forbids you explicitly to teach from the pulpit or elsewhere that it is a sin to vote for any particular political party; even more, it is forbidden to announce that you would refuse holy rites for this cause. *You must never give your personal opinion from the pulpit.*"[48][emphasis added]

The priests were obliged to read this letter to worshippers on Sunday, October 11, 1877; but the population nevertheless understood where clerical

---

47   Wade, p. 369.

48   *Mandements de Québec*, N.S. II, 52; *le 11 octobre*, 1877.

sentiments remained.[49] The ultramontane newspapers did not restrain their criticism of Taschereau and Conroy. When Conroy died on his return passage to Rome, ultramontanists saw it as a sign of divine providence. Perhaps because of the proscription against clerical influence in the next provincial election—in May 1878—the Swiss Protestant Henri-Gustave Joly de Lotbinère won a slim majority for the Liberals. This did not prevent some clerics from coining the now-famous expression *"le ciel est bleu et l'enfer est rouge"*—heaven is blue and hell is red.

FREEMASONRY

Bouchard was frequently accused of being a Freemason. The Quebec clergy had adopted the hatred that the French Church (of France) felt towards Freemasonry. While French Freemasonry was anti-clerical, English Freemasonry was a non-political movement of brotherhood and good works, and was not related to atheism.[50] In fact, the King of England himself, as well as much of English and Upper Canadian high society, were quite open about their Masonic membership and connections. In 1904, Abbé A. Dumesnil—Superior of the Seminary of Saint-Hyacinthe during the school years of Télesphore-Damien Bouchard—wrote a secret memo to Msgr. Donato Sbarretti, the Apostolic Delegate to Canada. Dumesnil circulated it only to the clergy. Its title was "The Hidden Aspect of a Great Intrigue—Liberalism and Freemasonry: The Reason for the Resignation of Monsignor Bourget."[51] A mysterious "PMG" distributed this document publicly some years later. In his *Mémoires* Bouchard asserted that

49   O. D. Skelton; *Life and Letters of Sir Wilfrid Laurier*, vol. 1; Toronto, p. 212
     "A farmer is said to have told his curé: I cannot vote for Mr. Laurier for you tell me that if I do I shall be damned. I cannot vote for Mr. Bourbeau for you tell me that if I do not follow my conscience I shall be damned. I cannot abstain from voting for you tell me that if I do not vote I shall be damned. Since I must be damned anyway I'll be damned for doing what I like. I shall vote for Mr. Laurier." Rumilly, *HPQ*, III, p. 76.

50   According to Philippe Bernard and Henri Dubrief, the more the Church in France shed its anti-republicanism between the Great Wars, the more the Republic's own "religion"— Freemasonry—declined. Bernard and Dubreif, *The Decline of the Third Republic, 1914–1938*, (Cambridge: Cambridge University Press, 1985) p. 260.

51   This pamphlet can be found in the collection of published speeches in ANQ *Fonds* T.-D. B. P-10/42. Abbé A. Dusmenil, *"Les dessous d'une grande intrigue. Libéralisme et Franc-maçonnerie. La raison de la démission de Msgr. Bourget."*

the belief that he was the source of the public revelation of this document contributed to the bitter hatred of the clergy towards him. In the memo, Dumesnil divulged his close rapport with Bourget—he had accompanied Bourget to Rome without his own Bishop's permission—and repeated all of the ultramontane views regarding liberalism and Freemasonry. In his introduction, the anonymous "PMG" could not resist making the observation that Abbé Dusmenil wrote very bad French for a retired college superior.[52]

In the memo, Dumesnil describes valid reasons for Montreal to have its own university—namely, the great distance and high cost, which students from Montreal needed to overcome in order to be educated in Quebec City. Since the establishment of Laval in 1854, it had attracted few students from Montreal; and those it did attract were mostly those with rich relatives. However, since Laval was now to have a branch in Montreal—one that would include a new medical school—the real question became who would control it. Would it be the Archbishop of Quebec or the Bishop of Montreal? The agreement imposed by Conroy broke down again in 1879, when Laval tried to establish its own medical school in Montreal. Hôtel Dieu Hospital remained loyal to the Victoria School and refused entry to students of the new school. (Hotel Dieu Hospital medical diplomas were issued by Victoria College in Coburg, Ontario, by a special arrangement.) The doctors of Hôtel Dieu subsequently appealed to Rome. Despite the injunction by Bishop Fabre against public discussion, the press seethed with accusations of liberalism, Gallicanism, ultramontanism, and rebelliousness.

Neither the ultramontane press, Bishop Laflèche, nor the retired Bishop Bourget ended their crusade in favour of the view that in Canada the Church must be superior to the state. They continued their campaign despite the repeated edicts of Rome; and despite the fact that papal infallibility was already accepted dogma. The ultramontane press accused the Pope and Archbishop Taschereau of "*inadequate comprehension of the facts, and of being tainted by the influence of Freemasonry.*"[53] Despite the Council of 1868 and the 1877 announcement by the bishops of Quebec under the influence of Conroy, the ultramontanes, led by their bishops, continued their "holy war" to the delight of the liberal press and the anti-clerical movement. In a series of articles in *Le Journal de Trois-Rivières,* Laflèche once more outlined the ultra-

---

52   Ibid.

53   *Journal de Trois-Rivières;* L.-O.David, Histoire p.161–2; cited in Wade. p. 375.

montane view regarding the relationship between the Church and the state. In these articles he called for the repeal of the "undue influence" law. These articles were then circulated in the form of a brochure. From his retirement, Bourget endorsed Laflèche's opinion, expressing his disagreement with the compromises made by the bishops—compromises made by Fabre, Conroy, Taschereau and the other bishops of Quebec regarding the university question. Taschereau accused Bourget of undermining the authority of his successor by counselling his (Bourget's) former diocesans to resist the will of their bishop and, by extension, that of the Pope. Again the ultramontane press (*la bonne presse*)—to whom Bourget was now a saint—contested the view from Quebec. Their newspapers accused Laval and Taschereau of allowing harmful principles, encouraging modern progress, and tolerating Protestant professors. Nevertheless, the Legislative Assembly, supported by both the Conservatives and the Liberals, passed the bill establishing Laval's Montreal branch.

Rome now heard from Canada once again. The ultramontane Senator Trudel— soon to be joined by Bourget himself—represented the cause of Montreal, while Bishop Racine of Chicoutimi and Grand Vicar Hamel travelled to Rome to support Taschereau. The Pope decided once again in favour of Laval; and reiterated his admonition that liberal Catholicism was not to be confused with political liberalism. On September 13, 1881, the Pope instructed the bishops to consult the Holy Congregation before seeking the repeal of the "undue influence" law.[54] In a pastoral letter of February 1882, Taschereau reported on this victory and condemned the kind of discussion that "excites the minds of men to the detriment of religion and public business."[55]

The conflict, however, did not end there. Laflèche refused to be silenced. Taschereau had demanded that the Church hierarchy issue a joint declaration condemning journalists who disobeyed the Holy Father by attacking Laval University and Taschereau himself. Laflèche signed; but soon he withdrew his signature and departed for Rome to explain this action. According to Wade, "He was coldly received by Pope Leo XIII who told him that there was no advantage to review the question and that his presence was not necessary in Rome, where the band of so-called defenders of Montreal have become tire-

---

54   Rumilly, *HPQ.*, III, p. 75–80.

55   *Mandements de Québec.* II N.S. 265.

some to the Holy Father."[56] Taschereau, learning about this snub promptly published the results of Laflèche's trip. Once again, despite the concept of central authority, the ultramontane press did not hesitate to attack the Archbishop. They also challenged Cardinal Giovanni Simeoni, Director of Propaganda, for having "insulted a Bishop and priests whom good Catholics of Canada have learned to venerate for their piety and their devotion to the Holy Office."

This "heresy hunting"—the term is employed by Wade—became "intoxicating" for some.[57] For example, Jules-Paul Tardivel, who established the ultramontane newspaper *La Vérité* in 1881, wrote: "The problem of Laval is a question of fact, and without being heretical or even a bad Catholic, one can say that the Pope is in error on this question."[58] Laflèche's newspaper, Le *Journal de Trois–Rivière* declared: "For one reason or another, it is certain that the Holy Father may be influenced, for a certain time into error on questions of fact and doctrine."[59] Laflèche remained in Rome to compose a memorandum on "the religious problems of Canada," printed in Rome and in Canada in 1882. He continued to maintain that liberalism, Gallicanism, and nationalism were the fundamental errors of the period. Liberalism, for Laflèche, was little better than a plague. "The snake of Freemasonry," he suggested, had been tempting Taschereau. Approved by Rome, Taschereau issued a counter-memorandum. Laflèche refused to obey Taschereau's demand that all complaints be submitted to the Superior Council of the University; and again Laflèche directed his attack at Rome. Simeoni wrote to the Archbishop that Laflèche's accusations were "vague and without proof." Despite Rome's insistence on a settlement, the atmosphere of ideological warfare in the province of Quebec refused to dissipate.

The Holy See felt compelled to intervene once again. On March 25, 1883, a pastoral letter containing a new decree of the Propaganda was read in every Catholic church in Quebec. In it, the Pope ordered that all attacks against the University of Laval and its branch in Montreal were to cease. He stressed that any violation of this edict would constitute disobedience to the Holy Father. The letter pointed out that the previous seven years had witnessed many regrettable examples

56   Wade p.373

57   Ibid., p.375

58   *La Vérité*; David; Histoire. P.162; cited in Wade, p.375.

59   *Journal de Trois-Rivière;* David, *Histoire* p.161–2; cited in Wade, p. .375.

of such disobedience. The diocese of Quebec City, the Vatican observed, had remained above reproach in this matter.[60]

Nevertheless, the battle continued. It was rumoured that the Vatican would soon punish Laflèche by dividing his diocese. Its rich southern section, along the south bank of the St. Lawrence River, would become a new diocese called Nicolet. Bishop Taché of St. Boniface wrote to protest this measure to Taschereau, who replied that Taché seemed to consider Laflèche a martyr persecuted by the majority of Quebec bishops, the Sacred Congregation of the Propaganda, and the Sovereign Pontiff himself! He refused to circulate Taché's letter. Laflèche's supporters accused Grand Vicar Hamel of sympathy for Masonry because when Hamel was rector of Laval, he had defended some Protestant doctors who might have been Freemasons.[61]

Laflèche, as stubborn as ever, yet again departed for Rome; while the Congregation received a flood of letters from his partisans. The ultramontanes of the Catholic Circle of Quebec, led by Dr. Landry, accused the ecclesiastical authorities of a scandalous tolerance. When Landry refused to retract this charge, the university annulled his honorary professorship. Jules-Paul Tardivel defended Landry in *La Vérité*. The newspaper was then banned from the seminary, the university, and the Archbishop's Palace. The Archbishop published a canny pastoral letter on June 1st, noting that since adherence to a secret society must be penalized by excommunication, all accusations of Freemasonry would be forbidden, and could be only be made by the Ordinary of the diocese. Doctor Landry's son denounced this pastoral letter to Cardinal Monaco of the Inquisition. Amidst this flurry of back-and-forth denunciations, Rome yet again dispatched its own envoy to the battlefield.

The new apostolic delegate, Dom Henri Smeulders of Belgium, arrived in October of 1883. Petitioners, including those recently returned from Rome, besieged Smeulders. He visited Bourget. Taché came from St. Boniface to defend his friend Laflèche. The ultramontanes circulated a petition demanding a general canonical inquiry into Canadian religious difficulties. Smeulders

---

60 *Mandements de Québec*, N.S. II, 349–56; Taschereau's pastoral, March 19, 1883; Propaganda decree of Feb. 27, 1883.

61 This theme was repeated in a private letter from Abbé Maheux to Télesphore-Damien Bouchard some seventy years later. Maheux noted that the Freemasons published membership and leadership lists, including home addresses, in newspapers at the beginning of January of each year, in contrast to the secret Order of Jacques Cartier, which did not. *Fonds* Bouchard, ANQ P 10/11.

persuaded Laflèche to abandon this idea, and was assured that the papal envoy considered the division of his diocese neither necessary nor useful. This time, Archbishop Taschereau himself went to Rome, where news soon came from the Cardinal Prefect of the Propaganda informing Dom Smeulders that Rome would make any decision regarding the division of the diocese of Trois-Rivières. This repudiation served to weaken Smeulders's authority. On August 23, Rome reconfirmed Quebec City's victory. Laval University, including its branch in Montreal, was recognised as the sole Catholic university in Quebec.

In his memoir, Dumesnil reports that Bourget, returning from a session with the Pope on the question of the university, did not say anything. A few years later, however, Bourget encouraged Dusmenil not to despair, assuring him that the university would come to Montreal. "We will have it, our university," he said.[62] During this trip with Bourget to Rome, Dusmenil learned in a conversation with a very highly placed ecclesiastic of the curia that the Pope would never support a bishop against an Archbishop. As a measure of the Pope's approval of Taschereau, he was named the first cardinal in Canadian history in 1886. At the same time, Edouard-Charles Fabre, Bourget's successor in Montreal, became Archbishop—an appointment that Laflèche, pointedly, did *not* receive. Meanwhile, Dom Smeulders, won over to the cause of the ultramontanes and repudiated by Rome, left Quebec the very day Taschereau returned from Rome. The public was certain where Rome's sentiments lay when Taschereau's representative Abbé Gravel of Saint-Hyacinthe became the first bishop of the new diocese of Nicolet, formed by the subdivision of Trois-Rivières. Even then, those members of the clergy still under Laflèche's influence kept the opinions of the ultramontanes alive; and their press remained vociferous. As described by Wade, "The authoritative and apocalyptic approach to modern problems that Laflèche shared with Bourget, were [sic] deeply rooted."[63]

The campaign waged by the ultramontanes truly seemed to betray elements of paranoia. In his secret memoir, Dumesnil revealed what in his opinion was the true reason for the resignation of Bourget as Bishop of Montreal.[64] Dumesnil claimed that this was the result of the session with the Pope, in which Bourget informed His Holiness that several of his newly appointed cardinals

---

62   From brochure Dumesnil, ANQ *Fonds* Bouchard. P-10/42.

63   Wade, p. 381.

64   L'Abbé Dumesnil; *Mémoire adressé à Msgr. Sbaretti*, 1904, *Fonds* T.D.B.: ANQ P-10/42, p. 14.

were Freemasons. The bishop's own trusted informants had revealed this to him. In response, the Pope apparently "shrugged his shoulders." Perhaps the Pope was merely indifferent to these accusations. More likely, he was reacting with impatience to such aberrant nonsense. However, based on the consistently wild nature of some of the ultramontane attacks, one wonders whether Dumesnil was actually suggesting that the Pope himself was part of the conspiracy.

BATTLES INTO THE TWENTIETH CENTURY; *LA BONNE PRESSE*

In 1960, Abbé Maheux P. D. wrote in the introduction to T.-D. Bouchard's autobiography that young people of the current generation—in this atomic age—upon learning of the infantile disputes of the nineteenth century would think that they were dreaming.[65] However, as noted by Bouchard, the debate between the Gallican and ultramontane views of the relationship between state and religion continued well on into the twentieth century.

> About 1900, the clericals renewed their interference in politics … they gave orders to take over the press, youth movements, patriotic associations, benefit societies. They encouraged the creation of secret societies and invaded mutual help fraternities and trades … It was necessary to destroy democracy and liberalism…. The government of the people by the people had to yield place to a theocracy.[66]

Maheux was certainly wrong in thinking that "infantile disputes" are relics of the past; that "in the atomic age" modern science would somehow be able to quell bitter political battles.

French monarchists exerted a powerful influence on Quebec politics. Their newspapers, *La Vérité* and later, in the 1890s, Marie-Amédée Denault's *La Croix de Montréal*, followed the doctrines of *La Croix de Paris*.[67] Founded in 1883

---

65   Arthur Maheux, P.D., Préface. T.-D. Bouchard: *Mémoires*. I.

66   T.-D.B *Mémoires*. Vol. III p. 33.

67   Louis Veulliot followed the preachings of Edouard Drumont, whose *Le testament d'un antisémite*, (Paris: E. Dentu, 1891) and *La France Juive*, (Paris: Librairie Marpon et Flammarion, 1886) were extremely popular in France and Quebec. The alleged liaison between the perfidious Jews and Freemasonry was detailed by Copin-Albancelli in *Le drame maçonnique; la conjuration juive contre le monde Chrétien*, (Paris/Lyons: La renaissance française, Librairie Emmanuel Vitte, 1909).

for "Catholics who need to know," *La Croix de Paris* became one of the most important dailies in France.[68] Its adherents followed the ultramontane teachings of Pope Pius IX, who preached against the "enemy within." In 1889, *La Croix de Montréal* added new elements to its program of Catholic militancy. This was a trend, according to Phyllis Senese, "that went beyond its preoccupation with its devotion to nationalism to embrace anti-Semitism."[69] *La Croix* declared: "No more thieves, no more atheists, no more persecutors, no more Freemasons, no more Jews, no more Prussians, no more foreigners to govern France. Nothing but honest men. Nothing but Catholics. Nothing but French."[70] Its xenophobia was clearly not restricted to Jews. Tardivel, editor of *La Verité de Quebec*, was the son of a French-Canadian father and an American mother. When he entered the Seminary of Saint-Hyacinthe at sixteen years of age, he spoke only English. With the zeal of a convert to a heady doctrine, Tardivel espoused the ultramontane cause, serving as a sounding board in Quebec City for the views of Bishop Laflèche.[71] Tardivel tended to be more French than the *Séminaire de Quebec,* and more Catholic than Laflèche. He attacked Laval University with charges of Freemasonry and, borrowing from his idol Louis Veuillot, found the dark hand of the Grand Orient—the Freemasons—not only in the schools of law and medicine, but also in the very household of the Archbishop.[72]

These powerful forces continued to influence Quebec politics and the political career of Télesphore-Damien Bouchard. Indeed, the power of the Catholic Church in Quebec's political and social life lasted until the Quiet Revolution in the 1960s. To see how these potent forces influenced Bouchard, we will now begin an examination of his life.

---

68 Jean-Denis Bredin. *The Affair; The Case of Alfred Dreyfus.* (Paris: George Brazillier Inc. 1986), p. 281. Bredin estimates the circulation of "la bonne presse" in France to have been about 1,000,000, including 170,000 copies of *La Croix de Paris* and its rural editions, as well as *La Libre Parole*. By contrast the circulation of the Dreyfusard press was about 40,000. This has its parallel in Quebec, where according to Rumilly near the end of the nineteenth century there were 31 conservative newspapers as opposed to 7 liberal ones. Rumilly. *HPQ* III, p. 139

69 Phyllis A. Senese, "*La Croix de Montréal*; 1893–95," *CCHA. Historical Studies,* 53, 1986, pp. 81–95.

70 Ibid., p. 90.

71 Pierre Savard, "Jules-Paul Tardivel", *DCB,* (Toronto: University of Toronto Press, 1994) XIII, 1009–1112.

72 Wade; p. 375.

Chapter II

THE FAMILY BACKGROUND; FAMILY TALES

"He would go far, that baby, for good or for evil." So spoke Dr. Eugene St. Jacques to Julie Rivard and Damien Bouchard after the birth of their son Télesphore-Damien on December 20, 1881.[1] Many years later, Doctor St. Jacques, now mayor of St. Hyacinthe, would tease his city clerk and secretary T.-D. Bouchard about his early prophesy. In this chapter, we will examine some of the early influences that helped T.-D. Bouchard to choose his path in life.

Neither in the unpublished English version nor in the published French version of his autobiography does Télesphore-Damien Bouchard write much about his mother, Julie Rivard. This is perhaps not surprising, since she died when he was only five years old. Julie had married Bouchard's father, Damien, on October 20, 1872.[2] After one of the frequent big fires in Saint-Hyacinthe destroyed his parents' first house in 1876, they lived in a shack on Concord Street, which was located in the back yard of one of Damien's friends, Joseph Bazinet. Julie became pregnant seven times; but as was the case with many women of this era, only three of her children lived to adulthood. Two children died, one in infancy and the other of smallpox. The eldest, Joseph-Émile, was born on August 24, 1877. Damien then built his second little house at 98 St. Antoine Street—later known as Fourth Street. In this house, his second son, Télesphore-Damien, was born on December 20, 1881. Marie-Eve Angelina, the third surviving child, was born on December 10, 1883. Bouchard's mother died at the age of thirty-three, while giving birth to a stillborn child. His father remarried shortly afterwards.

In his memoirs, Bouchard errs about the dates of the death of his biological mother and the remarriage of his father. This is not altogether surprising, as such

---

1   During his youth Bouchard was known as "Young Damien" or D.-T. Later in life he was widely known as Tée-Dée. In English this was contracted to Teddy. He signed his early articles at the Seminary and in *L'Union* as "D-T".

2   Church records.

mistakes can often be attributed to old age or to the selective memory loss inherent in all memoirs.[3] He wrote the published memoir during his retirement, after suffering several strokes.[4] In the French version, he writes that when his mother died he was barely two years old.[5] In the English version, he first wrote "barely" five years; "barely" is then crossed out and replaced by "hardly."[6] According to church archives, however, Julie died on May 5, 1887;[7] and therefore Bouchard's age at the time of the event was five years, four and a half months. In the English version, Bouchard describes the death of his mother in a vivid and poignant manner, remembering very precise details.

Damien and Julie Rivard, T.-D. Bouchard's Parents, circa 1869

---

3   Peter Gossage, *Families in Transition, Industry and Population in Nineteenth Century Saint-Hyacinthe*, (Montreal & Kingston: McGill-Queen's University Press, 1999). Gossage notes that there was high infant mortality and high adult mortality in the late nineteenth century, especially in parturient women; and that second marriages were common. p.180

4   T.-D.B: Published French version *Mémoires*. (Montréal: Les Presses Beauchemin, 1960), Volumes I, II, III.

5   Ibid., I, *Ma vie privée*, p. 31.

6   TDB, *Memoirs*, Chapter V, p. 13.

7   Extract of Acts; Cathedral of Saint-Hyacinthe.

My mother was very industrious and active. She made soap from meat scraps ... and offal of animal flesh we picked up from the butcher or from the homes of neighbours. While pregnant with her last child, she contracted, in handling the material from which she made soap, a malignant anthrax, from which victims seldom recovered. The infection, which showed itself first in a threatening black spot, almost of the size of a ten-cent piece on the left arm, provoked a premature delivery, and she was not able to fight through the infectious fever which followed. The last time that I saw her alive was the eve of the tragic night she died. I can still see her, her left arm wrapped in bandages, frightfully swollen, resting on one side of her sickbed. At the moment she passed on, I remember that my father, terrified by the drama that had just come to an end, went out of her room, his eyes haggard; he took me in his two hands and, lifting me above his head as if to preserve me from some danger rampant in the house, cried: "Your mother is dead; your mother is dead; what's to become of us?" Gathering me to his bosom he burst into scalding tears, hugging me nervously.[8]

Julie thus died an acute death, her illness lasting no more than a week. Until that unfortunate event, her son seems to have had a happy childhood. Bouchard claims that his father remarried in the autumn of that year. The truth, however, is that with the dispensation of his priest Damien married the widow Elisabeth Landry Fauteux on June 15, 1887—less than six weeks after the death of his first wife.[9] Why did Damien feel the need to remarry so quickly? Had Damien known Mrs. Fauteux for a long time? We do not know the answer to this question; but we do know that the childless Mrs. Fauteux had recently returned from New England after her first husband's death to live with her mother and sister in St. Dominique, a village adjoining Saint-Hyacinthe.

To understand Damien's haste, it is necessary to examine his personal history. At only seven weeks of age, he had been "borrowed" (adopted) by his Aunt Marceline, and separated from his parents and siblings. This surely was not a pleasant experience. Now, after Julie's death, he was responsible

8   T.D.B.*Memoirs* Chapter III p. 17.

9   Church records. ANQ, P-10/40.

for the welfare of three small children aged nine, five, and three. We could presume that after the shock of his wife's sudden death—and recalling what had happened to him in his infancy—he may have feared dividing his family, having to place his children with various relatives or in orphanages, as was customary in those days.[10] Damien had a full-time job as a leather-cutter in a shoe factory, which had a very strict rule requiring employees to work six days a week. Therefore, Damien Bouchard may have chosen a precipitous marriage for his children's sake; but the widow he married proved a fine woman who became, in time, a real mother to his children. She came to earn their love. Bouchard in his memoirs may have been confused about the dates relevant to his father's second marriage, but he was clear about the strong emotions surrounding it:

> It was in this house on Saint-Antoine Street that my mother died in March, 1886. [sic] I was then only four years old [sic] and we were left orphans, at an early age, on my father's hands. He refused to separate from his children. Instead he entrusted one of our aunts, Parmélie, the wife of Phineas Rivard with our care, and she came to live with us for about six months, the period that my father remained a widower [sic].... At the end of the fall [sic] my father married again. His second wife was a widow who had returned of late from the United States with her mother, to live with one of her sisters in the village of Saint-Dominique, some six miles from Saint-Hyacinthe. She was a tall woman of very good appearance, humble, but of distinguished air, reflecting her fine character and good heart. She entered our home like the guardian angel to those whom a good mother, called by destiny to the Great Beyond, had been forced to leave behind.[11]

---

10   Gossage, p. 122.

11   T.D.B.*Memoirs*, Chapter V p. 13.

Damien Bouchard, Circa 1887

Télesphore-Damien wrote a great deal about his stepmother, whom he truly loved. In both the English and French versions of his autobiographies, he refers to her as "mother". The former Elisabeth Landry had her work cut out for her. "She accepted as a sacred duty the heavy responsibility of bringing up three adopted children as if we had been her own, and she carried that responsibility to the letter.... We soon could not help seeing that she loved us as if we had been her own flesh and blood."[12] Her life, however, was complicated by the hostility of some members of the Bouchard family. "A group of our relatives got together to make her life as unpleasant as possible for her. The most ardent in this role was my great-aunt Marceline, whom we considered almost a grandmother, since it was she who brought our father up."[13] T.-D. writes that he never understood

12   Ibid., p. 14.

13   Ibid., p. 14.

this enmity; and he still did not understand it even seventy years later. Perhaps he did not consider that to Marceline and other relatives, Damien was "their boy." Elisabeth dealt with this animosity like a true Christian, writes Bouchard. "Neither [sic] have I heard my stepmother say a word against anyone. When she realized that she was under the attack, she made no reply. She suffered in silence, and since she was a fervent believer and a perfect Christian, I am convinced that, among many prayers ... many were addressed to God to ask pardon for those who ill-treated her.... She was the personification of goodness."[14] No doubt, the injustice of Marceline's persecution of his beloved stepmother had a deep psychological effect on young Bouchard. His memoirs are a testimony to his sympathy for her plight.

Damien and Elisabeth Landry Fauteux, 1887

---

14 Ibid., p. 14.

Saint-Hyacinthe, where Télesphore-Damien Bouchard was born, is a thriving town. The Yamaska River plays an especially important part in the leisure activities of its citizens.[15] The river flows past the southern and eastern edges of the town. Above Saint-Hyacinthe the river is deep, and navigation is possible. Below the town, however, there are dangerous rapids. Known in the past as "Maska" or "Little Maska," the village of Saint-Hyacinthe established by the first *colons* around 1748, began to grow after the establishment of the Saint Lawrence and Atlantic Railroad in 1848.[16] Saint-Hyacinthe is surrounded by a fertile plain and is situated on the route from Montreal to the northeastern United States The well-drained land and a warmer climate than most regions of Quebec combined to encourage the growth of agriculture. By the 1870s Saint-Hyacinthe had become industrialized. Aided by municipal tax benefits light industry expanded. Notable local factories manufactured items such as shoes, leather products, and knitted goods. In the century between 1870 and 1970, over twenty-six factories in the textile industry alone made Saint-Hyacinthe their home.[17] The Casavant organ factory manufactured organs bought by churches from all over the world. Eventually, five former employees of the Casavant Company formed their own organ manufacturing company. All of Saint-Hyacinthe's factories employed low-paid women and children in addition to their male workforces.

Saint-Hyacinthe eventually became a popular destination for many sports: hunting; horseback riding in the woods alongside the Yamaska River; fishing; paddling; bicycling; snowshoeing, and ice skating. The town was also home to many religious institutions. The list of these is long: *Les Soeurss de la Congrégation Notre Dame; Les Soeurs de la Charité de Saint-Hyacinthe; Les Soeurs de la Présentation de Marie; Les Soeurs Adoratrices du Précieux Sang; Les Soeurs de Saint Joseph de Saint-Hyacinthe; Les Soeurs de Sainte Marthe de Saint-Hyacinthe; Les Frères Maristes*; a *Noviciat Dominicain; Les Frères du Sacré-Cœur;* and *Les Frères de Saint-Vincent de Paul.*[18] Thus, the town was able to nourish both body and soul.

---

15   Société d'histoire régionale de Saint-Hyacinthe, *Saint-Hyacinthe; 1748–1998,* (Sillery: des Éditions Septentrion, 1998).

16   Gossage, p 46–48.

17   *La société d'histoire Régionale de Saint-Hyacinthe,* p. 255.

18   Ibid., p. 151.

Télesphore-Damien Bouchard in front of the family home on Fourth Street, also known as St Antoine Street. [circa 1941]

The private papers of T.-D. Bouchard's daughter Cécile-Ena contain an imaginative account of the supposed relationship between the Bouchards of the Saguenay region and the Bouchards of Saint-Hyacinthe. This account was hand-written in English, presumably by T.-D. Bouchard himself.[19] The tale begins with the crossing of the

---

19   T.-D. B: A hand-written story, in English, presumably by T.-D.B. Found in the private papers of Cécile-Ena Bouchard, kindly provided to the author by Mme. Claire Simard Odermatt:

A FRENCH-CANADIAN SAGA; THE ETERNAL STRUGGLE

"Two Bouchards Claude and Nicholas standing on the deck of the "Vagicud" were admiring the panorama of New France. Wide space, forests no ends [sic], immense river in which the little ship rocked. They would be in Quebec four days hence. What a joy after months bad crossing in a crowded ship. Nicholas had met on board the beautiful Zostra girl, a singer from Madrid, accompanied by her father [the word "family" is crossed out]. The girl was escaping the inquisition. They had the misfortune of being Jews. The father was a moneylender, an honest man. Reina Zostra was a most beautiful young girl, that type of exotic beauty which ancestors' Moorish blood had perfected.

As for Nicholas, eldest son of a Normandy brickyard owner, why he had crossed over with his brother was that the sea and the fabulous tales of New France had attracted him. He was a six-footer, blond hair and very blue eyes that look you straight. He was of sturdy stock and the

Atlantic by two putative Bouchard brothers: Claude, the ancestor of the Bouchards of the Saguenay/Lake Saint Jean region; and Nicholas, the ancestor of the Bouchards of Saint-Hyacinthe. In fact, it does not seem that the two historical Bouchards were closely related. Claude was the son of Jacques and Nouelle of St.-Côme-le-Verd in the region of Perche in France. He arrived in Quebec in 1650, first settled near Quebec City, and later moved to the region of the Petite Rivière de St. François. From there, the family migrated to the region of Lac St. Jean. In 1950, this family celebrated the 300th anniversary of its arrival in Canada.[20]

Nicholas, however, was the ancestor of the Saint-Hyacinthe Bouchards. He was the son of Clement and Louise (née Brassard) of Antilly-les-Marais, in the French

---

new venture pleased him. As soon as he would get to Quebec Reine would study his religion and he would marry her.…As for Claude, he had not met his destiny on board, he would wait and see, he was two years younger than Nicholas, but as sturdy as he. They looked so much alike that if it hadn't been for his soft black velvety eyes, you could have easily mixed them up. He looked at his brother with respect and joy to see him so happy, it was indeed a good augure [sic]. "Well, brother, this New France, what say you? I think it is marvelous, Nicholas, look at those beautiful trees, those green waves and that crisp air which smells so fresh." "I hear Claude that winters are very hardy, but you and I won't let that bother us." At that moment father Zostra rejoined them, "Let us hope my boys that these skies will be more clement to us than were the European ones." He was an elderly man, not tall, with grizzly hair, the characteristic nose of his race, with dark and intelligent eyes, he was short and skinny. His life had been a hard one, at the early age of four his family had roamed from country to country peddling and finally they had chosen Madrid for their home, once their gain had amounted to a good sum allowing them to establish a commerce there. Thank God his mother and father had not lived to see the horror of the inquisition, his brother has fallen pray to these fanatics and he in order to save his family had to escape like a criminal. Not only Jews were victims of the Great Inquisitor, that cause the greatest sadness but Christians also had to pay the price if they were too broadminded or did not pore into the coffers of the church. He wondered as he looked at that beautiful scene if their God they worshiped was aware of these horrors. Surely it could not be, Yes Reina wanted to become a Christian but what was he to do, maybe he should follow suit as he knew quite well that the new world was also in the hands of the Inquisitor. It was hard to put away a lifetime of religious custom to enter another one, but for his daughter which was more than his life he felt he should try and learn more about the Christian doctrine. It would not do to let Reina marry and him not be near her when she needed him most. Forgive me Stella, this was his wife's [sic]. When he had left in the cemetery at Madrid, a heart attack had taken her a year ago when it was decided that they would flee to New France. She had brooded for weeks and finally in the morning he found her dead at his bedside."

20   ANQ, TDB, P 10/42. *Arrivé de Claude Bouchard au Canada, Tricentenaire des familles Bouchard. Fête du 11–3 septembre 1951. Album souvenir.*

diocese of La Rochelle, Aunis.[21] The two origin sites of the relevant Bouchard clans—La Rochelle and Perche—are in widely separated regions of France. The date of Nicholas's arrival is supposed to have been around 1658.[22] On September 30, 1670, Nicholas married Anne Leroy, daughter of Pierre Leroy and Anne Fleury. They had six children. (See family tree.) The Leroys hailed from St. Hilaire-sous-Romilly in the diocese of Sens Champagne-Bourgogne in France. For the first three generations these Saint-Hyacinthe Bouchards lived near Quebec City. Jean-Ignace was the first of the Bouchards (of the Saint-Hyacinthe Bouchards) to have married in Saint-Hyacinthe itself, when in 1797 he wed Marie-Angélique Zostre.

Saint-Hyacinthe in the late eighteenth century was a village of a few hundred souls. The first *colons* had arrived between 1756 and 1779. In 1805, the village's 89 houses held 72 families including 56 bachelors, 60 unmarried women, and 111 children. In 1831 the first census of the town revealed a population of 1,107.[23] Jean-Ignace Bouchard and Marie-Angélique Zostre had at least six children. The two that concern us are Basile—Télesphore-Damien's grandfather—and his sister Marceline, a fearsome character whom we have already encountered in this chronicle. Basile married Lucie Lavallée in Saint-Hyacinthe on May 29, 1843. Their son Damien was the father of Télesphore-Damien. It seems that Damien was one of the youngest of their children. When he was seven weeks old, his aunt Marceline approached her brother Basile and his wife. She offered to take Damien off their hands and raise him in her house in Saint-Hyacinthe. Basile was a poor farmer in the vicinity of Acton Vale, near Saint-Hyacinthe. He had "wrested from the virgin forest and the refractory soil a meagre existence for his wife and children."[24] Later, Basile bought a farm some thirty miles from Saint-Hyacinthe, in the parish of St. Théodore d'Acton. He worked this farm with his family; and he rarely left it. T.-D. remembered seeing Basile only once in Saint-Hyacinthe, when he came to visit Damien. "He was a very old man," T.-D. Bouchard remembered, "with shoulders stooped from the weight of years, its head covered by crisp still black hair, answering laconically when spoken to, but otherwise silent."[25]

---

21 See family tree.

22 T.-D.B., *Memoirs.* Chapter III, p. 10.

23 *Société d'histoire régionale de Saint-Hyacinthe; Saint-Hyacinthe; 1748–1998;* (Sillery: des Éditions Septentrion, 1998), p. 25.

24 TDB, *Memoirs*, Chapter III, p. 4.

25 Ibid., p. 19.

Descendants of Clement Bouchard

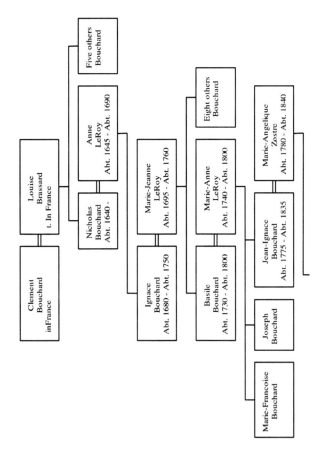

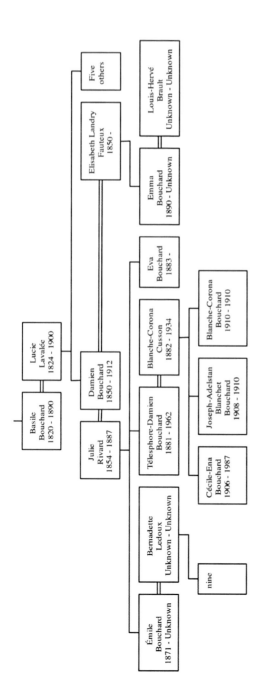

The family tree of the Saint-Hyacinthe Bouchards.
Nicholas Bouchard is the first to reach Canada's shores, circa 1658

It is impossible for the hand-written genealogical story found in Cécile-Ena's papers to be true. Most likely it was concocted by the exuberant imagination of T.-D. Bouchard; and was nothing more than an expression of his poetic, romantic nature. In this tale, he alleges that the two "brothers," Claude and Nicholas, were travelling on the same boat as a Spaniard from Madrid—Zostre, or Joste, or Jauste—who is accompanied by his daughter. This supposedly Jewish family, according to Bouchard, had escaped the Inquisition. Such an encounter would have been highly improbable in 1658, since the Jews had been banished from Spain by Queen Isabella in 1492. Certainly, a woman named Marie-Angélique Zostre (or "Jauste") did join the family when Jean-Ignace Bouchard, Télesphore-Damien's great-grandfather, married her in Saint-Hyacinthe on October 14, 1797 (or, as mentioned in the family genealogy, possibly in 1799)[26]—one hundred and forty years after Nicholas Bouchard's arrival in Canada. Marie-Angelique's father's name was Christian; an implausible one for a Jew. Her mother, on the other hand, was born Marguerite Rinkin, a name that is Germanic and could be Jewish. The fact that the Zostres named their daughter Marie-Angélique might indicate that the mother, Marguerite, had converted to Catholicism. Regardless, Télesphore-Damien believed that his great-grandmother was Jewish. He shared this belief with Dr. Harold Segall,[27] an eminent Jewish cardiologist in Montreal who was often consulted by Bouchard's family.[28] The manner in which he alludes to his great-grandmother makes clear his suspicions of her origins:

> Independence of character was always a salient trait in my family. The cult of individual liberty, pushed to extreme limits, was the cause of most of our ancestors leaving Europe at a time when religious fanaticism was still sovereign and master. Then the individual was called upon to believe whatever the fanatics who had control of the brute force provided by the civil authority, chose to dictate, with the only alternative of going to the stake or taking the long, hazardous road of exile, leaving behind them all their worldly goods and chattels to the glory of God but to the personal profit of their executioners.... It was Marie-Angélique Joste who brought into our family the blood of

---

26 Archives of the Seminary of Saint-Hyacinthe.

27 H.N. Segall. Personal communication.

28 Frank M. Guttman; "The Bouchards of Sainte-Hyacinthe and Dr. H. N. Segall." *Essays in Honour of the 90th Birthday of Dr. H.N. Segall.* (Montreal: The Osler Library. McGill University Press, 1989), p. 320.

the victims of European pogroms, driven from home for the crime of worshipping God otherwise than as prescribed by their persecutors.[29]

Note the references to victims of European pogroms and to people being driven from their homes for the crime of worshipping God in a different manner than that mandated by the authorities. These statements are certainly applicable to Jews. T.-D.'s convictions regarding this question were reinforced by his Great-Aunt Marceline's stories about her mother Marie-Angélique. Bouchard writes:

> She told me, like a tragic fairy tale, of the life of the Jostes in the old country. They were numerous and powerfully rich, they lived in a superb chateau in a great city. They had many horses in vast stables and a multitude of servants; their carriages were reputed to be the most luxurious that could be built. They were merchants who acquired millions honestly, in business; they were honourable people, who gave much to the poor. There were many rogues who wished them ill because they had succeeded in making money … the "swine" she would say "who worked to ruin them." The happiness of the Jostes was an object of envy.… Envy and jealousy gave birth to every type of calumny, and especially of racial hatred, to arouse the imbecility and the wickedness of the vulgar crowds against them … to move public authority itself to have some of them murdered by fanatics and others driven from the country while their persecutors, like highway robbers, laid hands on their immense fortune. "They stole everything, everything" my old aunt said, her eyes blazing with anger; to complete the tragedy my grandmother [sic—she was his great-grandmother] was robbed here, of a dress covered with brilliants, of a value of thousands and more thousands of Ecus. The Joste family, trying to save a little of their fortune, had brought many high priced diamonds, which they hid in the folds of this dress, over which had been sewn, with gold and silver thread a multitude of other precious stones … my grandmother [sic] not caring to keep the dress at home for fear of having it taken from her by robbers had entrusted it to the care of a churchwarden who asserted he had handed it over to the parish priest. My grandmother died and the heirs claimed the dress. The priest to whom it had been entrusted was also dead and his successors replied to the heirs that the churchwarden had never deposited the dress for safekeeping, but had evidently stolen it if it had ever existed. And thus the jewels of the family disappeared. And this is why we are poor. That is why we have to dig the ground with our finger-nails and drag

---

29 T.D.B. *Memoirs*, Chapter III, p. 6.

the river with nets for fish in good weather or bad, or else starve to death and then they want us to love the priests and the rich people who lead us around by the nose.… This family of foreign extraction was Catholic in our country. Was it so in Europe? Mystery.[30]

Bouchard seems to have been convinced that Marceline's recounting of family history suggested a Jewish origin for Marguerite Rinkin.

Around 1865, Bouchard's father Damien began work as an office-boy in the chambers of Honoré Mercier, a young lawyer who had just hung out his shingle in Saint-Hyacinthe.[31] Despite the bitter opposition of some segments of the public, Mercier—a future premier of Quebec—was a fervent believer in improved and obligatory popular education.[32] In some parishes angry taxpayers burned down schools—often at the instigation of the parish priest or "righteous" lay parishioners. This atmosphere of uneasy discussion and sometimes violent political dispute influenced Mercier's office-boy. Damien wished to acquire an education. Against Marceline's strong opposition, he enrolled in night school. She asked him why, if *she* had succeeded in earning a living without having an education, he thought *he* needed one? She claimed that a lot could be learned simply by living and by observing nature. Despite Marceline's objections, he continued his course of study. Evening classes had become a tremendously popular phenomenon in the province. To the astonishment of the authorities, there was such an overwhelming amount of interest that the number of late-night classes had to be increased.[33] At school, Damien learned reading, writing, and mathematics. During the day, he began his apprenticeship as a leather-cutter at the Côté factory. According to T.-D.:

> His education was summary enough, but it enabled him … to become a popular labour leader, and later, to lay aside his leather knife and set up in business as a merchant and an innkeeper. If his book knowledge was scanty, it was nevertheless sufficient for him to realize to the full the value of an advanced education, and to convince him that his children must have the best schooling that his means would enable him to give them. It

---

30   Ibid., p. 7.

31   See Pierre Dufour and Jean Hamelin, "Honoré Mercier", DCB, XII, (Toronto: University of Toronto Press, 1990) pp. 719–728.

32   L.-D.-R., p. 243.

33   Ruby Heap, " Un chapitre dans l'histoire de l'éducation des adultes au Québec: Les écoles du soir, 1889–1892." *RHAF*, 34,1981, pp. 597–625.

is due to this fervour on my father's part that I was able to go through all the grades of primary and classical education available in my town.[34]

Bouchard describes his father as a model worker—one who eventually became a friend of the Côtés and who was later promoted to the position of foreman. His employers, Louis and Victor Côté, had founded their shoe factory in 1865.[35] Louis Côté had invented two improvements in the manufacture of shoes: a procedure for finishing off soles; and a machine for stiffening them. This second invention had revolutionized the shoe industry throughout the world and merited an honourable mention at the International Paris Exhibition of 1886.[36] The Côtés' large factory had acquired the first steam engine in the city. Except for a brief interval, Damien worked for the Côtés for about thirty-three years. For the short interval aforementioned, he was employed as a foreman at a larger enterprise—the Séguin and Lalime Shoe Factory—which had offered him a one-third increase in salary. However, Séguin and Lalime lacked the fraternal spirit of the Côté factory, where Damien had appreciated the companionship and the close communication between employers and workers. He therefore resigned and returned to the Côtés' where he became a leader of the workers. This leadership did not damage his relationship with his employers. Damien felt that workers would have to be united to better protect their rights, since most employers did not treat their workers as well as did the Côtés. Damien became the president of the local branch of the union known as *Les Chevaliers du travail* (the Knights of Labour), a precursor of the union movement of twentieth century. Unions, then as now, were unpopular with the establishment. The Knights were American in origin and English in language, and therefore particularly suspect. The bishops of Quebec strongly condemned the organization.[37]

---

34 TDB, *Memoirs*, Chapter III, p.6.

35 Contrary to public opinion the Côtés were not brothers. Gossage, p. 48.

36 Ibid., pp.70–71. Gossage notes that Louis Côté was a prolific inventor. His first patent was submitted in 1870 for a sole sewing-and-finishing machine. Over the next 35 years Côté filed 31 more patents. In a close demographic and sociological analysis of late 19th century changes in the industrialization, population, and fertility of Saint-Hyacinthe, Gossage underscores the linkages between industrialization, capitalist industrialism, population, economic change, changes in the structure of families, the advent of female breadwinners, and the role of family in mediating relationships.

37 TDB, Chapter III, p. 6 See also; L.-D.-R., I, and II, p. 211. Cardinal Taschereau obtained a papal condemnation of the Knights of Labor in 1884. Monsignor Fabre in Montreal, who

The Bouchard family circa 1894. From left to right: Eva, Damien, possibly one of the Guay children, Émile, Emma, Elisabeth Landry Fauteux Bouchard, Télesphore-Damien.

Marceline, the adoptive mother of Damien Sr., was effectively T.-D.'s grandmother and a very important influence in his life. She took a special interest in him, calling him by the nickname of "Mistigri," an appellation he claims to have never understood.[38] Her motive for adopting Damien had been to lighten the burden of her brother Basile, who had a large family to take care of. She also wished to make her house livelier by the presence of a child. Marceline shared

---

was more sympathetic to the workers, opposed this. In 1887 Cardinal Gibbons of Baltimore obtained a cancellation of the papal interdiction.

38   *Bélisle Dictionnaire Nord-Américain de la langue Française* states that *mistigri* is a *"chat familial"* or family cat—therefore it is strange that T.-D. did not understand this term, although Bélisle was not available in his time. (Montréal: Librairie Beauchemin, 1979) The term is not found in *Robert* and *Collins Senior Dictionary* (4th edition, New York: HarperCollins, 1995).

the family tradition of being somewhat solitary.[39] According to T.-D., she felt that since she was able to tame crows, robins, and squirrels—her family prior to the adoption—a child would not be difficult. Therefore, Damien grew up with nature as brother and sister.

Marceline was illiterate, like many people of her generation.[40] A professed misanthrope, she never left her house unless it was necessary. She had no idea of the value of education and therefore; "deprived her young nephew of the greatest blessing anyone could have bestowed on him. Had she known its worth, she surely would have seen that he got it in abundance. But Damien grew up, like most of his buddies, with no other learning than the main lines of the shorter catechism and, when he passed from childhood to adolescence, he still could not read fluently."[41] Marceline was both brave and independent. She lived alone in "Petit Maska" and although single, she managed a house and earned her livelihood from a farm, which she worked herself. She added to her income by fishing—by line and by net—in the Yamaska River. She had a reputation for fearlessness among the youth of the city. Marceline took great pleasure in demonstrating her skill in guiding her boat through the rapids, "matching the strength of her mighty muscles against that of the turbulent waters as she held the bark to its course with a single oar."[42] Some said that she had no equal in boat-handling in the swift current of the dangerous river.

Aunt Marceline categorically avoided attendance at church. It seems that as a young girl she found a gold pen on the steps of her church after Sunday services. She gave it to the priest with the request that he announce its recovery but return it to her if no one stepped forward to claim it. She heard nothing about it for months. One day, she met the priest on the street with the pen hanging

---

39   T.-D. Bouchard, Memoirs, X, p. 10.

40   At the beginning of the 19th century, Father Girouard, whose name is prominent in the streets and the academy of Saint-Hyacinthe, denounced the huge illiteracy rate when he noted the extraordinarily high number of X's as signatures on official documents. He launched a campaign to promote education. Msgr. C.P. Choquette, *Histoire de Saint-Hyacinthe: Société d'Histoire Régionale de Saint-Hyacinthe: Saint-Hyacinthe 1748–1998:* (Sillery: Septentrion, 1998); p. 164, In the 1891 census, 31.96 percent of Quebeckers were illiterate, versus 8.18 % in Ontario—cited in Jean-Paul de la Grave, *Histoire de l'information au Québec,*(Montréal: Éditions de la Presse, 1980.)

41   TDB, *Memoirs,* Chapter, V, p. 5.

42   Ibid., p. 4.

around his neck. She immediately and publicly berated him, calling him a thief. From that day forward, she never set her foot across the threshold of the church, although she did accept sacred rites before her death at a ripe old age.

The saga is, in a way, a repetition of the family mythology concerning Marie-Angelique's experience with the trustworthiness of church officials concerning her jewel-laden dress. T.-D. was thus subject to vigorous anti-clerical diatribes from babyhood on. The liberal influence came not only from Marceline. His father was a *rouge* and Liberal Party organizer for the lower town (the working-class district). His maternal grandfather, Séraphin Rivard, was also dedicated to the *rouges*. Both family tales and tradition combined to inspire anti-clerical and liberal doctrines in the lad. As noted in studies of French-Canadian society, the *rouges* did not mix socially with the *bleus*, especially in smaller towns and villages.[43] Marriages between them were not common. The Bouchards and the Rivards had long *rouge* roots.

As a child, T.-D. had a deep attachment to Séraphin Rivard, his maternal grandfather. Like his aunt, his maternal grandfather had a strange, unexplained nickname for him: "Charles."[44] Séraphin earned his living as a water-carrier, charging ten cents a barrel. He was tall and strong. This served him well in his occupation. He would back his cart at a well-selected spot fifteen feet into the river, fill his barrels, and proceed with his heavy load to customers along potholed roads. Pulled along by his mare Flora, and with his grandson beside him, he wended his way along roads that were sometimes very rough, especially in the spring or after heavy rains. T.-D.'s father Damien would leave for work at seven in the morning and finish work at six in the afternoon, with one hour off for lunch. Since Séraphin's work was irregular, he spent many hours with T.-D. "As soon as I was able to stand without help, I began to slip out of the house to go looking for him in his house, his stable, or his yard. I see him still ... his smiling face and imposing stature, with outstretched arms inviting me to sit on his ample lap.... I can truly say that I grew up in his arms."[45] As an older lad, T.-D. would accompany Séraphin on his deliveries. When the road was rough and the

---

43   Horace Miner; *Study of St. Denis;* thesis Univ. Chicago, and (Chicago: Phoenix-Univ. Chicago Press. 1939), p. 58.

44   Sister Isabelle de la Presentation, PhD, Émile's daughter and T.-D.'s niece, reports that people on the street would call him Charlie, and he told her he did not know why. (Personal communication.)

45   T.D.B.: *Memoirs*: Chapter IV. p.2.

covers not tight enough—causing the water to splash on him—his grandfather would laugh. However, when the water splashed on Séraphin, "… he would give vent to formidable curses on the people, the municipal authorities, who made such a mess of road maintenance."[46]

There were also nonpolitical divisions in French-Canadian towns and villages—though these did not necessarily follow the same red/blue split. In addition to the debates about clericalism and nationalism, there were economic rivalries. Séraphin hated competitors in general—and one in particular, called Boisseau. "There was one competitor whom he most particularly detested," T.-D. remembers, "and strangely enough the nephew of this man … was destined along with his son to become one of my worst enemies in the political field."[47] Bouchard wondered if the "bitter rivalry between two water-carriers created an atavistic heredity of hatred between the two families …" Armand Boisseau ran successfully as an independent Liberal in 1919 against T.-D. in the provincial election, but was then convicted of fraud and sent to jail.

Séraphin owned his own home on St. Antoine Street, heating it with tree stumps and roots that he gathered on the property of the priests at the seminary. For the poor of the city, this was considered to be a fair exchange: free wood for those with horses and rigs traded for the hard work of clearing the land that the priests intended to farm. Séraphin did not consider this charity, since it was of mutual benefit. Bouchard often would accompany his grandfather on these outings, admiring the strength of this giant of a man hewing away with pick and axe. His grandfather also taught him much about natural history, botany, and zoology:

> It was while spending long hours with my grandfather on the college grounds that I learned to love the open air … the solitude of field and forest…. The morning air still fresh and cool…. While the chips flew under the heavy blows of his axe … I wandered barefoot through the fields exploring for new types and species of berries. My grandfather seemed glad to act as my natural history teacher … never tired of my interminable questions. He would willingly interrupt his work to tell the names of many of the living creatures that I saw for the first time in my life and to acquaint me with their habits, their way of living … with the characteristics of plants …[48]

---

46   Ibid., p. 2.

47   Ibid., Chapter IV, p.3.

48   Ibid., p 5.

According to his grandson, the folk of the lower town considered Séraphin Rivard a "model citizen." He neither smoked nor drank. He was very strong and enjoyed the respect of everyone in the neighbourhood. Often, he was called on to restore the public peace when arguments had degenerated into riots. He was the only man who could master T.-D.'s uncle and godfather, Télesse Guay. In his earlier, quarrelsome days Télesse tried to match his strength with that of Séraphin, but he lost every time. He was also a big man who, when under the influence of liquor, would "clean up" a bar by throwing everyone out—owner and customers alike—and smashing bottles, furniture, and mirrors in the process. In the 1890s, the Saint-Hyacinthe police force was small, and none of the constables were willing to take on the job of arresting Télesse—they all knew that he would rather let them shoot him than submit to handcuffs. When Télesse was busy emptying a pub, the police stayed prudently out of the way and sent for Séraphin. Télesse quieted down when he saw his father-in-law—as big as himself, and sober. The next day, Télesse would pay for everything he had broken, and would then stay sober and be a "model citizen" for many months.

According to T.-D., Uncle Télesse was "the finest fellow in the world"—when sober. Télesphore (Télesse) Guay was his birth mother's (Julie Rivard's) brother-in-law (he was married to Julie's sister) and another powerful childhood influence on him. Télesse and his family lived in three small rooms upstairs in Damien's house. Séraphin lived next door. This was an extended family compound.[49] Télesse Guay was one of the best-paid workers in the Duclos and Payan tannery,

49   The street directories of Saint-Hyacinthe located at the Séminaire de Saint-Hyacinthe give the earliest available family addresses:

1883: Damien–98 rue St. Antoine and Séraphin Rivard–100 rue St. Antoine.

1887: Damien moved to 84 St Antoine, listed as "cordonnier-shoemaker."

1885: Marceline is listed as living at 23 Piété.

1894: Damien has moved to 54, 56, and 58 rue Cascades and listed as "marchand-merchant." In 1898 Damien is listed as "commis." 65 Cascade and Emile as "Hôtelier innkeeper" at 65 Cascades. Marceline at 67 Cascades.

1900: Émile, hôtelier 72 rue St. Simon and Marceline back at 34 rue Piété. Damien fils now listed as "étudiant-student."

1904: Damien, bourgeois-gentleman, 173 rue Girouard and D.T. éditeur de *L'Union*, 173 rue Girouard.

1907: Damien listed as gardien au ménage 79 rue Lafromboise and in

1915: Now T.-D. is listed as "député-MLA," 320 rue Girouard.

1927: T.-D. at 351 Girouard and 1934 355 Girouard.

1942: 21ième Street—corner of Morison and Ste. Anne.

but then developed tuberculosis. Dragging his huge frame around the streets with difficulty, he could hardly hold himself up on the curb. Télesphore-Damien was by then in his early teens. In his memoirs, he describes watching the pitiful scene unobserved from his window, after which he closed the door of his room and wept. Three months after Télesse finally succumbed to the disease, his widow died in childbirth with her fourth child. Damien fulfilled a promise to his brother-in-law and took two of his children. The eldest was mute and was sent to a special school in Montreal. Another generous couple took in the new baby. T.-D. states that his parents adopted the two that remained as their own children, but all traces of these Guay children seem to have vanished from family lore.[50]

His grandfather Séraphin, described by T.-D. as "a believer but indifferent to external religious practices," was constantly present for him.[51] He was also passionate about politics. In those days without modern media or communication, people discussed politics passionately and debated all aspects of political programs. After church service every Sunday, there was the *petite messe du dimanche*, where party politics were debated, gossip collected, and strategy planned. Damien was the chief organizer of the Liberals for the lower town. He was extremely loyal to the Liberal leader, Honoré Mercier. The leaders of the "upper town" (the wealthy district) would come down to consult with him. Saint-Hyacinthe was generally a Liberal town in the tradition of the Dessaulles family and its Papineau connection.[52] Louis-Antoine Dessaulles (L.-J. Papineau's nephew) was very involved in the liberal *Institut canadien*." From Confederation until the 1940's, the Liberals rarely lost elections in Saint-Hyacinthe. "Politics occupied so large a part of the life of our people that even the children were as preoccupied as their parents. Economic principles, social theory, and religious beliefs all centred on politics. The 'blues' accused the 'reds' of being anti-clerical and disguised socialists, and the 'reds' accused the 'blues' of being reactionaries and clericals."[53] For the Bouchards and the Rivards, politics was a form of religion.[54]

---

50 Interviews with several family members failed to illicit any information about the Guay children.

51 T.D.B.: *Mémoires*. I, p. 109.

52 Yvan Lamonde, *Louis-Antoine Dessaulles, Un seigneur libéral et anticlérical*, (Montréal: Fides, 1994).

53 Ibid., p. 99.

54 As an illustration of family involvement and the political mores of the day, an interview on Radio-Canada with Jacques Bouchard is of interest. Jacques, who died recently, was the

"My grandfather attributed to politics the importance of religion. His devotion to public affairs was so remarkable that my father introduced him to the Liberal chiefs of our town."[55] In 1892, when T.-D. was 11 years old, he attended a public debate with his grandfather, who detested heckling. "He wanted to listen to the orators of the two parties … a loudmouth was insulting Honoré Mercier … as he refused to shut up … Grandfather landed a heavy punch which broke his jaw … the incident lasted only a moment, the heckler faded out … My grandfather put his jacket back on, crossed his arms, and calmly listened to the speaker."[56] His grandfather's strength, as well as his politics, no doubt greatly impressed the young boy. Séraphin was extremely upset at the defeat of Honoré Mercier and of the federal Liberals in the elections of 1892. However, in 1896 he stayed up late at night to hear the news of Laurier's victory. T.-D. remarks that it was "a true triumph, while the pessimists and anti-British repeated that the Protestants would never elect a French-Canadian Catholic as Prime Minister in Ottawa."[57] Séraphin died on Dec.10, 1897, at the age of 77, after expressing his joy that the Liberals had gained power federally with the election of Laurier, and provincially with the election of Marchand: "Now I can die in peace!"

Another strong influence on young Bouchard was the head of the local Liberal Party, Jean-Baptiste Blanchet, a lawyer who loved practical jokes. Once, when he was scheduled to speak at an *assemblée contradictoire* (a public debate), he disguised himself in the clothes of "*un habitant*" (a peasant) and hid at the back of the room. The Conservative speakers began confidently, happy that they would only be debating with two young students. Then, from the back of the hall, Blanchet called out: "You lie!" A speaker finally asked this fellow dressed in peasant clothes to come up to debate with him. The amused audience realized who he was, and then enjoyed his considerable oratorical skills, to the dismay of the *bleus*.

---

grandson of Émile and thus a grandnephew of T.-D. He was the founder of the well-known publicity company, BCP. The interviewer remarked that the Bouchards were always involved in local politics, and inquired when was the first time he had voted. The answer was: *"Je crois que j'avais sept ans; deux fois!"*—"When I was seven years old, I believe. Twice!"

55   T.D.B.*Mémoires*, 1. p. 111.

56   Ibid., p.112.

57   Ibid., p. 109–110.

PRIMARY SCHOOL; LOCAL INFLUENCES

In 1887 Télesphore-Damien Bouchard registered at the Girouard Academy—the public school of the Hay-Market ward. The school was under the direction of the Brothers of the Sacred Heart. Damien would allow none of his children to skip school for minor problems; only for serious illness. Slight colds, chilblains, or a mild colic were no excuse. Of course, Marceline considered this view too extreme for her favourite nephew. She complained to Damien, who replied that it was wrong to give in to children's whims when their education was at stake. Marceline would reply that it was his new wife who had stuffed his head with this crazy idea that children must have an education. It was not necessary, she claimed, to kill them for the sake of making them learned.[58]

Class picture circa 1888. An 'X' marks Télesphore-Damien.

During one summer holiday, T.-D. cut his foot on some glass while playing barefoot in the river at the edge of St. Antoine Street. This resulted in a dispute between Marceline and Elisabeth. Marceline accused T.-D.'s stepmother of not caring for him. As he described it, "Marceline spoke bitter words to my

---

58   T.-D.B., *Memoirs*, Chapter V, p. 15

stepmother who as was her habit replied that she maybe was wrong in not notic-ing.... had she known she would have asked my father to let me stay home."[59] The soft answer seemed to increase Marceline's anger. When Damien arrived, he heard the full story and saw his wife quietly crying. He listened silently, then turned to Marceline and said that, "his wife was mistress in his home and that no one—not even she whom he loved as a mother—had the right to come in and trouble her." He took his wife gently by the arm and led her into another room, wiping away the tears still welling up in her eyes. "Aunt Marceline stood as if frozen by the icy tenor of her adopted son's words, then with a last look of pity towards me, went out of the house."[60]

For many months, Marceline was not seen on St. Antoine Street. T.-D. con-tinued to visit daily, amusing himself in her productive garden. On holidays he went fishing with her in the lower stretch of the river. Both Aunt Marceline and Damien used T.-D. to inquire as to the state of the other's health, while pretend-ing not to be interested. T.-D. understood his role as liaison officer between these two "who refused to admit to each other that they loved one another like mother and child.... I carried it out to the letter."[61]

Bouchard notes that homework was not difficult, especially since he had help from his mother, as well as from his older brother Émile. At ten years of age he underwent his first communion. It was an important milestone in the life of a child. Damien gave a large party for family and friends. It would seem that Télesphore-Damien was a bright student at primary school; bright enough to encourage his father with early high expectations that T.-D. was capable of further study, and could become a lawyer.[62] Another indication of his early promise was an offer made by Father Proulx to sponsor his education. Young Bouchard was very pious, attending daily mass at the workers' chapel of St. Genevieve. Father Proulx saw his potential and suggested to Mme. Bouchard that he would be willing to support T.-D.'s higher studies for the priesthood. While this was very much to her liking, Mme. Bouchard knew of her husband's wishes for T.-D., and declined the offer.

---

59   Ibid., p. 19.

60   Ibid., p. 19.

61   Ibid., p. 21.

62   The records from the primary school, the Girouard Academy, are no longer available for these years.

Many children ask questions about death and the hereafter, but the young Bouchard's own personal experiences most surely accentuated his interest in these issues. Not only did he witness his mother's death and that of his uncle Télesse, but also he was very much aware that of the three children born to his mother before to his own birth, two had died—one in infancy and another of smallpox.[63] In his memoirs, Bouchard notes that when he was young, children were born to French Canadians as frequently as they were at the time of his writing (about 1947), but in previous generations they were swept away by the Grim Reaper almost as fast as they came into life. In addition to deaths in the family, he lost several school-friends early on—one at the age of nine. Despite his own tender years, Télesphore-Damien was one of this friend's pallbearers:

> I can still see the lily-like whiteness of his angelic face.... The mother had perfumed the death chamber with violet essence; I do not know what feeling of horror and loss pervaded my being when the inert, marble-like features reappeared [on reopening the casket] ... whenever I recognize the odour of violets, I see my young schoolmate, the smile fixed in death, entering eternity in a rose-hued sky.[64]

When T.-D. was fourteen, his friend Léon Archambeault died of tuberculosis. Once again, T.-D. served as a pallbearer. He mused on the mystery of death and on his early mistrust of the narrow-minded views taught at the seminary. "I ... did not see in the phenomenon of Death and future torment the terrors found therein by my masters ... I had formed a much more human conception of Christ and God than those around me."[65] In April of 1900 a distant cousin whom T.-D. admired, Guillaume Cartier, returned from the United States, where he had been a successful acrobat in a major traveling circus. Guillaume was dying—in the final stages of pulmonary tuberculosis—at the tender age of 30. Over the one week he agonized at Bouchard's home, T.-D. spent all of his spare time with Guillaume. The doctor warned that Guillaume had little time. Despite having been, to all intents and purposes, just introduced, it was

---

63 In the 1870s and 1880s there were several epidemics of smallpox in Quebec. Due to their distrust of vaccination compared to the English, the French Canadians suffered many more deaths and illness. See Michael Bliss; *Plague: A Story of Smallpox in Montreal*, (Toronto: Harper-Collins Publishers, 1991).

64 T.-D.B., *Memoirs*, Chapter XII, p. 8.

65 Ibid., p. 8.

Télesphore-Damien whom Guillaume called for when he started feeling worse; and it was T.-D. who held Guillaume as he died. In his memoirs, Bouchard reflects on this episode:

> Death had become to my mind a simple natural phenomenon, bringing ... neither horror nor fear. Man has his term of life ... which, having had a beginning, must have an end.... The death of man remains for me a reality, which must be contemplated as the simple termination of physical life, no more to be surrounded by mystical phantoms and bogeys.... These ideas did not prevent me from being a faithful church member ... my teachers acquired the impression that I was travelling along the rugged edge of the dangerous precipice of religious doubt.... In my first year in philosophy I was required to compose, in cookhouse-Latin, a fairly long thesis against skepticism; I found it recently amongst my old papers.... I had difficulty reading it, and still more in understanding it.[66]

Thus, from a young age Bouchard was concerned with philosophical and scientific questions. In his memoirs, he refers to an episode which greatly impressed his young mind, and which demonstrates his scientific curiosity:

> I was splashing about in the mud puddles ... my attention was attracted by what at first appeared to be a black thread, some four or five inches long, which was moving in the yellow, stagnating water.... I stopped to re-examine this unusual sight: How could the wind stir up the liquid substance lying in the bottom of a hole the sides of which are level with the ground? ... But there was no wind.... The black thread was moving ... its spiral movements resembled those of a grass snake ... I persuaded myself that it was a horse-hair. Yet, how could a horse-hair move thus by itself when in the water? ... I thought that some of those tiny animalcula ... present in stagnant waters, clinging to the hair gave it ... the spiral motion ... scrutiny soon made me give up this idea: the horsehair was perfectly smooth, and seemed to move by its own internal action.... What mysterious force set in motion this piece of horsehair?[67]

---

66   Ibid., p. 11.

67   Ibid., p. 13.

Years later, in his final year at the seminary, he discussed this problem with his science teacher, Monsignor C.-P. Choquette. T.-D. was convinced that this moving horsehair was proof of the existence of "spontaneous generation." In answer, Choquette smiled and replied that Bouchard was wrong—that his story was preposterous and that he must have been dreaming or imagining movement. Since Bouchard had such high esteem for his professor (an esteem which was reciprocated), he almost believed that he had dreamt the whole thing; but inwardly he knew that he had observed a biological phenomenon. He mulled over this problem for a long time. One day, while preparing a paper for his biology class, he inadvertently came upon the answer. "While looking over the nomenclature ... I came upon the name and description of my metamorphosed horsehair.... scientifically known as a Nematoda found in ponds and brooks ... vulgarly called Horsehair worm because of its likeness to a horsehair. The description corresponded in every detail to the black animated thread ... I had seen as a child."[68]

This story demonstrates many of the fundamental aspects of T.-D. Bouchard's character: his curiosity, his intelligence, his stubbornness, and his drive to always be right. "It is easy to understand that I could not as a mere child have recognized the threadworm when its existence was not known even by my professor of science who had attributed the tale ... to a dream. What seems strange is that each of us tried to explain the thing as being mysterious: I by my problematic conjectures and he by the haziness of a dream."[69]

This same Choquette was remarkably rooted in science,[70] and was also the author of a history of Saint-Hyacinthe in which he makes many laudatory comments about one of his eminent pupils, T.-D. Bouchard. "We learned to appreciate the activity, the tenacity of Bouchard's objectives. We attribute to him Napoleon's words: 'If possible, it is done, if impossible, it will be done.'"[71] Bouchard states that he never forgot the advice given by his old master. "I have

---

68   Ibid., p. 16.

69   Ibid., p. 16.

70   Télesphore-Damien Bouchard, *Memoirs*, XII, p. 19.

71   Msgr. C.P. Choquette. Chan. P.D. *Histoire de la Ville de Saint-Hyacinthe*. Richer et Fils. 1930. Monsignor Choquette was a remarkable and unusual priest, scientist, and teacher. He proposed the adoption of a triphasic, 60-cycle format for the first municipal power plant of its type in North America, in 1894. The province of Ontario, which nationalized its hydro power early on in the twentieth century (1903), adopted a diphasic, 25-cycle format, which was transformed into the triphasic one in 1949 at the cost of $200 million. p. 437.

always believed in the simple and in the simple I have found beauty, truth, and justice. I have been an unswerving enemy of the involved and the mysterious, because I have found in their nebulous tenets the sources of evil, ugliness, false-hood, and injustice."[72]

THE ENTREPRENEURIAL SPIRIT

Saturday was market day in Saint-Hyacinthe. Saturday was also the day Mme. Bouchard prepared *"les bines"* for Sunday, carefully selecting each small, shiny bean. Young Bouchard brought a numbered pot, the prepared "bines," to the baker, who would cook them slowly overnight for Sunday's feast. It was here that Télesphore-Damien first fell in love with "Poucette," the baker's daughter. Poucette was a few years older than T.-D.; and so the love affair was one-sided. T.-D. tried to show his love for Poucette by many means, but she returned his affection in a "sisterly" fashion. This feeling lasted from the age of eight to his early teens, when, reinforced by the news of her involvement with an older boy from the upper town, he finally understood that his emotional investment was futile.

Two of Saint-Hyacinthe's characters also greatly influenced young Bouchard. One was "Titoine Jesus, *notre Barnum local*" (our local Barnum), whose real name was Antoine Flibotte-Schmidt.[73] Because of his beauty as a baby, he had been called *l'enfant Jésus*. Smallpox, however, had marred his good looks at a young age. He was an acrobat and clown. Little T.-D. loved him. At an early age, he helped Titoine put on theatrical works. Thus began a lasting interest in theatre. T.-D. admired Titoine's wonderful, balanced nature. Another person young Bouchard admired was "L'ours Bigaré," commonly called a *"quétenne ambitieux,"* in this case a contradiction in terms.[74] *"Quétenne"*, thought to be a local term, originating in Saint-Hyacinthe, char-acterises someone of the lower rungs of society—poor, unreliable beggars. Therefore, one could not really be "an ambitious *quétenne*." The origin of the word had always been mysterious.[75] Bigaré was an innkeeper who loved to exhibit his prowess—in wheelbarrow races, or by taking winter swims in the river after making sure the whole

---

72   Ibid., p.19.

73   T.D.B.*Mémoires*. I, p. 38.

74   Ibid., p. 42.

75   Jean-Noël Dion; "Aux Origines du Quétaine"; *Le Courrier de Saint-Hyacinthe*. March 9, 16, 23, 1988. Bouchard discovered the origin of the word when as mayor he asked one Joe Martin, a shiftless beggar, if he knew the origin of the term. Martin announced that it was a

town knew when this was to occur. Once, to demonstrate mind over matter and win a bet, he jumped barefoot onto a hot stove. There was no sound save for the sizzle of burning flesh. These antics served to publicize his business. Damien Bouchard would always moralize to his children, underscoring that Bigaré had many admirable qualities: candour; fairness; frugality; bravery; and a strong work ethic.

Damien himself held this same attitude towards work. He wanted to become wealthy in order to provide his children with the best possible education. He was constantly reminding them that their goal was to improve themselves, just as he had. One was, however, not to advance on the backs of others. "We should seek happiness by deserving the esteem of our fellow citizens."[76]

T.-D.'s development as a young capitalist began very early. From the ages of five to ten, he rummaged in garbage to collect scrap-iron, rags, and bones to sell for pocket money. After his confirmation at the age of ten, he felt—considering his newly acquired "manhood"—that this was not dignified enough. The influence of his father's disapproval no doubt had something to do with this change in attitude. "My father," he reports, "like all the Bouchards, who dreamed of becoming a successful merchant, trader, or industrialist, his own master instead of being a hired man of others, looked with definite disfavour at the spectacle of his son rummaging in rubbish heaps."[77]

Next, Télesphore-Damien went into partnership with Pivelé, a classmate, who had "flashing restless eyes betraying an unusually active mind."[78] Pivelé was one of the brightest children in the class, having carried off the first prize in catechism. He was also the best at games and a champion marble player. Pivelé came from an even poorer family than Bouchard. T.-D. financed Pivelé's gaming skills at marbles by betting with other classmates on Pivelé's prowess. After some time, the partnership had accumulated enough capital to start up another business. The two friends bought a small cigarette-rolling machine and began to manufacture contraband smokes. They each contributed an equal share of capital to this enterprise. "Hidden in the upper story of Pivelé's father's shed, I rolled cigarettes … and

---

family name. His real family name was Quétenne-Martin. Several generations in his family demonstrated the typical traits, Bouchard claimed, "genetically" passed down.

76 T.-D.B, *Mémoires,* I, p. 51.

77 T.-D.B, *Memoirs,* Chapter VI, p. 1.

78 Ibid., p. 2.

Pivelé, much less afraid of the police than I was, sold the smokes on the street."[79] Some time later, Télesphore-Damien suspected that Pivelé was not fairly sharing the profits from street sales, and as a result they liquidated the company. T.-D. decided to abandon the illicit business. He gave Pivelé the machine, and they divided their stock. Since T.-D. was afraid to sell his several hundred cigarettes, he kept them for personal use. His addiction grew until one day he became intoxicated. From that time on, he could not smoke cigarettes, although in later life he became a cigar smoker. Several years after the collapse of their joint venture, Pivelé decided to set up an illegal still in his father's basement. Since he knew that T.-D. was more knowledgeable in science than most in the class, Pivelé approached him for some advice. T.-D., however, no longer trusted Pivelé and answered "vaguely that I did not think it would be easy to find a glass that would resist the changes of temperature required for the condensation of the vapour."[80]. In adult life, Pivelé became assistant cashier at a large factory in town, eventually absconding with thirty-five thousand dollars obtained by padding the payroll.

Damien then arranged for T.-D. to become a delivery-boy at the Market Square grocery, owned by his friend Victor Merserault. For use in the new job, Damien bought his son a little four-wheeled wagon. According to T.-D., "the pay was not fabulous for my age and the times: four dollars a week."[81] Before this regular job—carried out after school and during holidays—the young entrepreneur would station himself at the market on Saturdays to help women carry their heavy loads home. Afterwards, when he had become strong enough, T.-D. would spend time at the Côté factory during summer holidays to learn the leather-cutting trade. Sitting beside his father, he would shape the pieces of lower-grade leather used as lining or accessory parts of the shoe. "I helped his work along," he recalls, "by doing, under his kindly eye, such parts of his work as could be safely entrusted to the inexperienced hands of an apprentice. I did this work with much pleasure during two school vacations but an accident … cut my second term short and made me drop my earlier idea of learning my father's trade."[82] While sharpening a knife, T.-D. slipped "either by clumsiness

---

79 Ibid., p. 4.

80 Ibid., p. 6.

81 Ibid., p. 7. One could question whether he really earned $4.00. Perhaps with tips this makes sense. But $4.00 is half of his father's pay as foreman!

82 Ibid., p. 8.

or inattention" and managed to stab himself right through the left hand, ending his apprenticeship for that holiday. That incident aside, many of the relationships formed at the factory were helpful to T.-D. in his later political career.

When Elisabeth Landry-Fauteux married Damien in 1887, she had given him her fortune of six hundred dollars—saved from her own and her late husband's earnings in the spinning mills of New England, and perhaps from some insurance money. That sum seemed adequate to enable Elisabeth to return home to St.-Dominique. This was the ambition of so many of the French Canadians driven to emigrate by the huge population increase of the nineteenth century and the poor soil of Quebec.[83] Damien used this money to reduce his mortgage on the house on Hay-Market Square. With constant, prudent saving, Damien was able to buy another piece of land at 84 Saint Antoine Street, where he engaged his cousin, Joseph Chenette, a leading builder of the day, to build a new house that faced the market. His drive to change his social status and improve his economic situation brought Damien to the decision in 1890 to buy a grocery, wine, beer, and liquor store from his friend François Renaud, a building contractor. In order to help him run the store, Damien took Émile, aged 13, out of school. Émile never seemed to have resented this. The store was at the corner of Cascades Street (the main thoroughfare), and Saint Pascal Street. Thus, Damien relocated his home to the new spacious residence that had additional storerooms. He sold the house on Saint Antoine Street to Euclide Normandin. Bouchard describes Normandin as typical of the many French Canadians who were talented and successful in business:

> This Mr. Normandin was one of those enterprising French Canadians of whom our town had quite a number at the period of its rapid industrial development toward the end of the last century.... in 1918, I met him again in ... Los Angeles where ... he was head of a big shirt-manufacturing business ... at home he had been the owner of a flourishing saddlery shop and also a prosperous luggage and leather-goods store.... He succeeded there [in Los Angeles] and his Saint-Hyacinthe house, under the able direction of its new owner, grew to be one of the biggest of that town

83   S. Mann Trofimenkoff; *Visions Nationale,* (St. Laurent: Éditions Trécarré, 1986), Chapter IX. More than 500,000 left before 1870. See also p. 42. *Histoire du Québec Contemporaine.* L.-D.-R. From 1840 to 1940 the estimated emigration to the U.S is 925,000: From 1860 to 1900 it is estimated at 500,000—source cited: Yolande Lavoie, *Les mouvements migratoires des Canadiens entre leur pays et les États-Unis au XIX et XXe siècles.*

... which disprove[s] the silly legend that French Canadians are neither good for trade nor for industry.[84]

Acting in defiance of the law forbidding the sale of liquor by the glass in an establishment that had a permit to sell by the bottle, Damien served beer, gin, and whiskey by the glass. The beer was served "sour" or, in winter, served *ferrée*. Émile or T.-D. had the job of heating an iron-tipped rod until red-hot in the fire and plunging it into a glass of beer, thereby setting off a caramelized vapour—hence beer *ferrée*. On some nights Émile or another musical person would play the violin. There would be music and dancing. In contrast to Damien, neither Émile nor Télesphore-Damien drank. The hapless Damien, however, enjoyed his *"stimulant de whiskey blanc."*[85] T.-D. states that although his father was not an alcoholic, "quite frequently he would be high."[86] In this state he began to neglect the business. His troubles increased when he was denounced to the authorities, brought to court, and condemned to pay a fine for serving alcohol by the glass. His gregarious nature further compounded his troubles. When tipsy he would be very generous to the local hangers-on. Some of the locals would deliberately get Damien drinking, repeatedly filling his glass while playing cards for high stakes. Thus, one day in 1894, Damien lost everything—his savings, his wife's savings, even his children's piggy bank savings—a scene painfully etched in T.-D.'s memory. Damien could not pay his

---

84   T.D.B.*Memoirs*; Chapter VI. p.11. Bouchard comments on the mythic concept that French Canadians were not as ambitious, and enterprising as their English compatriots.

When I reviewed the Saint-Hyacinthe newspapers of 1880–1890, I noted that a preponderance of the advertisements were for stores and industries seeming to belong to French Canadians.

Bouchard's views are echoed by those of Antonio Barette, who followed Duplessis and Suavé as premier of Quebec. Antonio Barette, *Mémoires*, (Montréal: La Librairie Beauchemin, 1966) Barette complains that most of the industries and stores of his town of Joliette, which were founded by French Canadians in the late nineteenth and early twentieth centuries were then sold to 'others' because of the wishes of French Canadians to 'take it easy'. Barrette then supplies a long list of Joliette industries that had been sold while they were flourishing enterprises. He notes that in all these cases the proprietors exchanged their industry for security; and that the major part of Montreal commerce was in large part established and directed by French Canadians. Barette concludes this chapter with a psychological explanation—that perhaps French Canadians are too fearful of the future.

85   T.D.B.*Mémoires*, I, p. 77.

86   Ibid., p.77.

creditors, and had to declare bankruptcy. To extricate himself from this quag-mire, Damien was fortunate to have the help of his friend François Renaud, who enabled him to buy back the business in Émile's name at a public auction in August of 1894. This kept the family name on the storefront, with Damien actively in charge. From that time on T.-D. hated alcohol and gambling. He never bought lottery tickets nor speculated in any way—even in the stock market. "Since that time I have detested games of chance … even though I was often presented with the opportunity to succumb to temptation. I never felt the urge to increase my capital by playing cards, buying lottery tickets, playing roulette, or speculating in the market."[87]

Damien was optimistic about his son's future. While Émile had to leave school to work in the family store, T.-D. was encouraged in all his studies—especially in English and arithmetic. "My father," he writes, "imagined that one day I would become the most educated person in Saint-Hyacinthe."[88] Damien expressed the wish to see T.-D. become a member of a liberal pro-fession—preferably a lawyer. In the store Télesphore was already helping Damien with English customers and salesmen from English firms. In T.-D.'s grade school, English was taught daily. An Irish priest who only spoke English taught arithmetic. As he retells it: "The members of the [primary] school board of that time were of the same opinion as my father and all other intelli-gent citizens [to encourage the learning of English]. The Brothers had not yet been poisoned by that evil propaganda which later caused them to only make a pretence of teaching English, making quite sure that the children would never learn it."[89] In the words attributed to Bishop Laflèche of Trois-Rivières, "Apprenez l'anglais, mais apprenez-le mal"—learn English, but learn it poorly. Bouchard complained that the seminary taught English according to Laflèche's dictum—there was only one hour of instruction per week. All the English he learned in school was in grade school. On his own, he studied English by con-sulting catalogues of American companies selling mechanical and electrical devices for teaching the practical sciences, physics and chemistry. He bought some of these small experimental machines, with which he made considerable progress in his personal knowledge:

---

87   Ibid., p.80.

88   Ibid., p.84.

89   T.D.B.*Memoirs,* Chapter VII, p. 23.

I learned at an early age something of the strange phenomena of electro-chemistry, electro-static and electro-magnetism. I also knew enough English to carry on conversations with the machinists who came to install the first direct current dynamos to operate in our town … [who] explained to me the general principles of the operation of these generators, of which the hard carbon brushes rubbing against the outer surface of a cylinder made of insulated copper, threw off greenish sparks, which gave the room a peculiar odor. Mr. Wilkinson, the chief electrician, explained to me that this odour was due to a gas liberated by the action of the sparks. He also gave detailed information as to how the wires and the lamps must be laid out in order to use the current for lighting.[90]

At the time Télesphore-Damien was all of 13 years old. Throughout his life he was a true self-taught man. Later on Msgr. C. P. Choquette, his physics teacher and later *superieur* of the seminary, was to comment: "Voltage, amperage, the economic coefficient of these dynamos, absorbed calories, cycles, the power of these motors, he understood it all, learned it all, and he spoke about it all with the competence of an expert."[91] Subsequently T.-D.'s nephew Jean Bouchard, an electrical engineer, testified that his uncle knew as much as he did.[92]

During this period T.-D. continued his vain efforts to charm Poucette by attempting to become proficient as an acrobat. He only succeeded in enduring several severe accidents. He also continued to try to impress her with his thespian skills—establishing the foundation of his future oratorical competence. Damien and Émile often would take part in riding competitions and hunting. Télesphore-Damien did not participate in these activities. On Sundays Damien and the family would go on family picnics up the river to a favourite spot: la Pointe aux Fourches, where the Yamaska is joined by the Black River, which is coloured by the peat swamps on its banks. The peninsula of Pointe aux Fourches became a park—Union Park—surrounded by a fine forest. On Sundays, excursion steamers would bring the citizenry from Saint-Hyacinthe. There were two boats plying the river: the *Eagle* and the *Yamaska*. These boats towed a barge, which on calm days could haul up to 300 people to the park.

---

90   Ibid., p. 24.

91   Msgr. C.P. Choquette, *Histoire de la Ville de Saint-Hyacinthe*, Richer et Fils. 1930, p. 440.

92   Jean Bouchard, personal communication, cited by Chisholm, Arch. Nat. Ottawa.

One of the favourite attractions was the pigeon- and trap-shooting contest, of which Damien and Émile were ardent devotees. Once, while demonstrating how to take aim with what he thought was an unloaded gun, Émile came close to wounding his stepmother in the next room. Émile knew that his father never left his gun loaded, and had taken aim at the stovepipe to show T.-D. how to hold the gun. What he did not know was that François Renaud's gun—which was loaded—had been placed next to Damien's gun. Émile squeezed the trigger. Both boys were shocked to hear a loud detonation, and more alarmed to hear a scream from the next room. There they found Elisabeth in a faint—but unwounded. The bullet had passed just in front of her, knocking off her glasses. Damien reprimanded Émile, who defended himself by saying that he had taken aim at the stovepipe and had made sure that no one was in the line of fire. Damien was able to give the boys a ballistics lesson on the path of a bullet through a hollow space, the physics of which impressed T.-D. very much, since the path is not usually in a straight line. At the age of 11, this lesson was imprinted on his mind.

At the age of 12, Télesphore-Damien was helping regularly in the store, weighing out rice, sugar, biscuits and other groceries, beer, whiskey, and lamp-oil (kerosene). Damien cautioned his sons not to eat the profits—if they took something, they had to pay for it. Otherwise, it was possible to become poor. Occasionally T.-D. would sneak a hard candy from the front counter. One day his father entered the room just as T.-D. placed a particularly large one in his mouth, forcing him to attempt to swallow the candy. It became stuck in his windpipe, and he turned blue. Damien placed T.-D. on his lap, turned him over and slapped his back. This resulted in the dislodgement of the candy, which flew across the room. Kept in bed for a few days to recover, T.-D. suffered moral pangs regarding his deed, especially since neither his father nor mother had mentioned it. "Never again," he writes, "did I risk stealing the tiniest piece of candy; my gluttony was cured forever."[93]

Télesphore-Damien Bouchard thus grew up in a caring, tight-knit French-Canadian family in Saint-Hyacinthe. He had a strong, ambitious father; a loving stepmother; and grandparents and siblings with whom he shared close relationships. His character, formed early on, seems to have been non-conformist, inquisitive, and devoted more to study of the arts and sciences rather than to sports. The non-conformists throughout his paternal and maternal families

93   T.D.B.*Memoirs,* Chapter, VIII, p. 7.

served as models for the admiring young T.-D. As we will see in the next chapter, he could be strong-minded and determined to follow his own path. That path was illuminated by the strong influence of his family—his Great-Aunt Marceline, his maternal grandfather, Séraphin Rivard, and his father Damien—all anti-clerical and staunchly Liberal.

Chapter III

AT THE SEMINARY

The story of Bouchard's enrolment at the Seminary of Saint-Hyacinthe is an indication of his concern for his family and his inner conflict about causing a financial drain on them. About the time of the failure of the store and the relaunching of the business under Émile's name, Damien had a heart-to-heart talk with Télesphore-Damien. He told his son that he would do whatever he could to send him on to a higher education. If T.-D. wanted to pursue his mother's hope that he study for the priesthood Damien would support him, but he really hoped that T.-D. would become a lawyer. Since Émile was now older, he and Elisabeth could take care of the store, while Damien would return to leather cutting to make ends meet. Damien had approached several friends to help out with the tuition fees and the money required to pay for books and uniforms. At that time the vast majority of children from T.-D.'s neighbourhood did not attend school for long; and very few attended secondary school. Most entered the workforce at a young age. But T.-D. was ambivalent. He did not want to saddle the family with an extra burden. He shook his head in refusal. Damien was so disappointed that he told T.-D. that if his poverty continued he would go to see several wealthy friends to guarantee support for the completion of studies. In the event of poor times or Damien's death, Damien's former employer Magloire Côté, the owner of the tannery Sylas Duclos, and the merchant Victor Mesereault were all willing to guarantee support. Still T.-D. refused to reconsider. "I was unwilling to impose further sacrifices on my parents who had already done so much for me, even if they wanted to make them."[1]

Bouchard's stubbornness discouraged his father. Time was pressing. There were only three weeks left until school began. It took two weeks to make the compulsory uniform. Thus, only one week remained for Télesphore to

---

1   T.-D.B. *Memoir,* (English) Chapter VIII. p.25

change his mind. While his father and his mother moped about, obviously distressed at his decision, he kept his resolve. A week went by and then another; there was no change of heart. Damien then told T.-D. that he had registered him in the Académie Girouard's one-year commercial course. "I thanked him and told him that I would be ready at the opening date."[2] The night before school started T.-D. had a terrible nightmare. He awoke thinking that he was on the edge of a precipice. He was drenched in a cold sweat. He arose without telling his parents about it, and went off to the commercial course. On the way he walked more and more slowly.

> [I was] ... fighting an irresistible force that urged me to move in another direction. My head was on fire. I no longer knew what to do. I wanted to turn back, but I also felt a strong attraction drawing me toward my former school ... as I laid my hand on the gate an irresistible impulse turned me around willy-nilly and I made all possible speed back home where I informed my mother and father that I would go to the big college the following day and that from then on, no power on earth would stop me from finishing my higher education as they desired. When they recovered from their astonishment, my parents gave voice to their happiness.[3]

Damien hurried to enroll his son, explaining the circumstances to Monsignor Dumesnil, the superior, who agreed that it was better to break a rule than to thwart a most evident vocation for the altar. He gave special permission for T.-D. to attend class without the required uniform for two weeks. Elisabeth accompanied T.-D. to the tailor's to be fitted for his school uniform—called a "Swiss" because of a striped braid along the main seams of the frock-coat. Thus began his higher education.

---

2   Ibid., I, p. 26.

3   Ibid., I p 26.

Saint-Hyacinthe Seminary, circa 1895.
Télesphore-Damien is in the second row, fourth from the right.

When T.-D. entered the Saint-Hyacinthe Seminary in 1894, the majority of the class of 20 were the children of bourgeois families from the upper town. Only two or three were of working-class origin. Even though Damien was now a merchant, he was known to be a former manual worker, so T.-D. was labeled as coming from the "lower classes." Two-thirds of the students—primarily those from farms in the countryside—were boarding at the school. When T.-D. began, the city students only attended school in the morning. At first, during holidays the students were permitted to stay home. Later, this policy changed: even during the holidays the students had to stay in residence. The aim was to produce obedient and submissive sons. As we have noted, this was a period of intense political battles not only between the "blues" and the "reds," but within these loyalties as well—most notably between the Conservative ultramontanes and the Conservative anti-clericals (who were nevertheless Catholics). As T.-D. reflects:

> Later, a new regulation was imposed requiring the external students
> to do their homework at the college. The priests in charge of the

institution decided that since during their free time the students were no longer under their direct surveillance ... our souls could be exposed and lost. So they reduced our leisure hours in order to prevent the development of habits which could snuff out the spirit of submission, which they required of students of the seminary.[4]

Social class divided the students as well as their residential status (i.e., whether or not they were live-in *pensionnaires* or town-dwelling day students) and by family party affiliation. T.-D. had two good friends at the seminary. One, Hector, came from a poor family and lived on T.-D.'s block. He later became a priest in a small parish in the United States, but returned home at a young age to die of tuberculosis. The other friend was Frédéric (also called Dudley in the published *Mémoires*), who would become a doctor in a poor district of Montreal. T.-D. and Frédéric remained friends throughout their school years. Frédéric was the son of a woollen-factory foreman of Scotch origin who was both an agnostic and a socialist. Because of the deep divisions in the seminary, Télesphore often was the target of ribbing. He was small for his age (and was to remain so) and not particularly good at sports. Nevertheless, "I often traded punches with them.[5] ... More often than not the boy from the Hay-Market got the worst of these scraps, but *his honour was vindicated.* That was the most important point: the bleeding stopped ... skin grew back, but *had I crawled before an insult or a challenge, neither side would ever have forgiven it.*"[6] (Emphasis added.) What we can assume is that T.-D. would not have forgiven himself. He believed in defending his honour by attacking even if the chances of winning were slight, and without regard as to the consequences. He was quick to perceive insults and always reacted vigorously, never letting one go unchallenged.

> I often got into trouble with my schoolmates who thought themselves of too high a rank to deign to share their play with me. Their insolent pride intensely displeased me ... in spite of my physique, not one of an athlete; I was obliged to settle our differences with my fists. Often, I did not win, the child of the Hay-Market had damage to his nose or scraped ear, by the child of a family from the upper town; but *always honour was saved. After all, that is what is most important ... it could*

---

4   T.D.B.*Mémoires* I p. 89.

5   T.D.B.*Memoirs.* Chapter IX, p. 4

6   Ibid., p. 5

not be a question of retreating before an adversary who insulted you or provoked you ... because to shirk one's duty would constitute in the eyes of all an unpardonable fault, or even cowardice.[7] [Emphasis added]

This unyielding pride turned out to be his lifelong yoke, a defect in his character that eventually proved to be the cause of his precipitous political downfall in 1944, after his maiden speech in the Senate.

Although T.-D. was always labeled a Freemason, an atheist, or a renegade, he was not a "freethinker"—a non-believer—even as a young student. Nevertheless, he was friendly with some prominent graduates of the seminary who were active, publicly avowed freethinkers. One of these was Francis Robert, a young worker who would spend his entire Friday pay on alcohol in Damien's tavern. He later became a teetotaler. "He was Liberal in politics, and a non-believer in religion."[8] T.-D. had a warm relationship with him. Another influence was Raphaël Fontaine, "a free-thinker and one of the most brilliant and erudite lawyers in the province."[9] Fontaine was the author of a political satire, *"Un duel à poudre"*—quite popular in Saint-Hyacinthe. He later became a judge of the Superior Court.[10] Neither of these two men tried to shake T.-D.'s faith, which at the time was very strong. Bouchard continued to attend mass, but his belief had limits: "Even though I was religious, I never shared the superstitions of so many people, and I never believed in divine intervention into the ordinary realities of life."[11] This statement reflects the early influence on T.-D.'s life of Grandfather Séraphin, Marceline, and his father. An example of this is the reaction of Damien to a fire at the farm of the Grey Nuns, which left thirteen people dead on May 13, 1898. Townsfolk immediately assumed that there was some religious significance associated with the fact that the number of victims corresponded to the date on the calendar. When they went on to predict that: "The Saviour will create a miracle. St. Joseph's statue will not burn," Damien became enraged at what he felt was sacrilege, declaring: "It is an insult to God to say that he would save a stone statue while thirteen people perished!" Shortly

---

7   T.D.B.*Mémoires*, 1. p. 94.

8   Ibid., p.119

9   Ibid., p. 120

10   When Fontaine died, true to his beliefs, he requested cremation, which was not permitted by the laws of Quebec. His son had to arrange this in Boston.

11   T.-D. B. *Mémoires* I, p.120.

after, the statue fell.[12] Damien thus represented a rational counterbalance to certain prevailing superstitious attitudes.

When someone disappeared in the river, some credulous souls threw "blessed bread" into the river in order to discover the site of the body. When T.-D. mocked these people, his mother scolded him severely.[13] He obviously thought a lot about religion and recognized that belief is an act of faith not explicable by rational argument. Nonetheless, it was not surprising that the seminary decided that there were too many freethinking graduates; and that the externs had too much unsupervised free time.

The students reflected the political battles of the times. Télesphore-Damien was an outsider both politically and socially. Although attentive to religious duties, he was identified by his family's well-known anti-clericalism, and especially by the sale of alcohol at Damien's/Émile's tavern. In his class there was an unknown practical joker who constantly perpetrated hostile, juvenile acts on the staff, such as filling inkwells with sand and leaving excreta on a professor's desk. Years later, the most innocent-looking, quiet student in the class confessed to having been the vandal. However, at the time of these acts it was Télesphore-Damien Bouchard who, because of his background, wound up more often than not being scapegoated for crimes he did not commit; and was punished by being given the strap.

During holidays and in his free time Télesphore-Damien helped in the tavern, working as a bartender. There was a billiard room attached to the tavern in which Émile became a champion. T.-D. often took bets when he was sure of Émile's capacity to beat a customer. In this way, he earned enough extra money to take piano lessons with Léon Ringuet, leader of the municipal band. After three years, he was confidant enough to give private piano lessons to further augment his income, although he states that he really did not have a good ear: "My parents sang well, but I did not inherit their talent ... through work and perseverance I learned to play several popular tunes ... I became professor of piano ... None of my students received prizes." Later on in life he composed the lyrics for several

---

12   Ibid., p. 121.

13   Ibid., p. 120–121.

songs arranged by Ringuet. *"Maska ma belle"* was composed to honour his wife. Other songs included "The Apple—Forbidden Fruit."[14]

In his first year at the seminary he did very well. He never placed first in his class, but usually ranked fifth, sixth, or seventh at the end of the year. Elspeth Chisholm's unpublished biography of T.-D. Bouchard claims that Bouchard was a mediocre student, but examination of the records shows that this is not true.[15] Most years he obtained either first, second, or third prizes for individual subjects.[16] During his years at the seminary he was active in the debating society, in a

---

14 All the songs with words written by T.-D. Bouchard are found in ANQ 10/41 and T.-D.B. *Mémoires;* Volume 1. p.106.

15 From Cécile-Ena's critical comments on Elspeth Chisholm's biography on T.-D.B., Simard-Odermatt collection.

16 Archives Séminaire. Saint-Hyacinthe. Livres des notes. 1894–1901
Class Records: 1894–1902. ASHS.
1894 ELEMENTS LATINS; 13 yrs. old; general standing 8–9 in class of 20. June 20, 1895. Prizes: Second in Latin; third in English grammar; and third in English reading.
1895 SYNTAX
10–15 percent of the students were day students. TDB was 4th to 7th in various class grades out of a class of 20. Final general grade: 5th out of 20. Prizes: Third *Thème Latin,* Third, *Version Latin,* First in arithmetic.
1896 METHODE
General list: 5th to 6th during the year. Final grade: 6th of 20.
1897–98 VERSIFICATION
First trimester; 8/33; second trim. 7/33; third, 5/30. Year-end general list: 6/32. Prizes: Second—*Version Latin;* Second—*Version grecque;* First—*Narration française,* Second—Canadian History, First Greek translation.
1898–99 BELLES-LETTRES
First trimester: 4/30 (19/30, There are two different notations). Second trimester: again two notations: 5/28 and 24/28. Final, again: 5/28 and 20/28. Prizes: Third—*thème Latin;* Third *Version grecque;* First—French composition; Third—Literature; Second—Greek translation. First—Modern History; General list—first trimester: 5/28, second trimester: 4/25. Third trimester: 5/26. Prizes: Second—*version latine;* Second—*Discours français;* Third—Modern history, Second—Greek translation; First—algebra; Second—*Oraison funèbre de Corde (Bossuet) Apprise et Commentée,* Second—*version anglaise.*
1900–01 PHILO 1
First trimester: 2/28. Second trimester: 8/28. Third trimester: 5/28. Prizes: Third—"logique et métaphysique"; Third—Mathematics; First—Botany.
1901–02 PHILO 2
First trimester: ('Messieurs Beauregard, Bouchard, Forbes, Lavigne, Phaneuf, et Tanguay were absent for most of the trimester because of the smallpox epidemic, which was the reason

theatrical group he had organized, and in a literary-discussion society he had also helped organize. He was also the editor of the school newspaper *La Lyre,* which led him to contribute articles to the local press. Eventually, before the end of his studies and with the permission of the superior, he became the Saint-Hyacinthe correspondent for several Montreal newspapers, notably *La Patrie.* He was allowed to do so with the understanding that he would simply be recording *les faits divers* (local news) without expressing his personal opinions.

When he was seventeen, Bouchard wrote a play about the 1837–38 Rebellion.[17] L. O. David's book *Les patriotes de 1837–38* inspired him. The play, entitled *Le fils du Meunier* (The Miller's Son), was very well received. The *Cercle Montcalm,* an amateur group of actors directed by Aimé Blanchard, first presented it on April 4, 1899, in the city hall of Saint-Hyacinthe. The metropolitan papers reviewed it favourably. Wilfrid Chicoine of *L'Union* (reprinted in *La Patrie)* wrote a nice review.[18] Mayor Euclide Richer said; "I came because of duty, and I stayed with pleasure."[19] In view of its success the actors insisted on giving another benefit performance for the author, "Jean-Baptiste Le Canadien" (Télesphore-Damien Bouchard). Blanchard advised postponing further performances of the play until summer, when the new hall of the *Cercle Montcalm* would be ready. However, Bouchard was worried that people would forget about it, and so arranged for the second performance one month later. It was an artistic success but a financial failure, leaving T.-D. in debt to the tailor's where he had had a fine suit made in anticipation of the play being a financial success. In an attempt to recoup his loss, Bouchard organized his own troupe of amateurs and presented the play in several neighbouring towns. The resulting artistic and financial success enabled Bouchard to pay off his debt to the tailor.

The play demonstrates the influence of his anti-English schooling. At the end of his studies, Bouchard reread the play and had a dramatic change of mind. "Like all French Canadians I saw myself a martyr to English fanaticism. It was in this

---

why the seminary was quarantined and the day students kept out.) 6/28. Second trimester: 12/24. Third trimester: Was he absent again? He was 6/28 in physics taught by Msgr. C.P. Choquette. A classmate was Ph. Desranleau—future priest, and Bishop. Samuel Casavant was one year ahead of T.-D.B. The superior in 1894 was Msgr. A. Dumesnil.

17   T.-D.B., *Mémoires,* I, 124. The rebellion both in Upper Canada (Ontario) and Lower Canada (Quebec) was centred on the issue of representative and responsible government against the British oligarchy. See Allan Greer.

18   *La Patrie,* 6 *avril* 1899.

19   T.D.B., *Mémoires,* 1. p. 124.

spirit that I wrote my play, and my success was less due to its literary value than to its Anglophobia."[20] Bouchard subsequently refused permission to other amateur groups to stage the play, and only with much hesitation did he allow the student society literature class to transcribe it into its register at the seminary.[21] At the risk of his eternal damnation—at least as threatened by some of his professors—T.-D. began to doubt the seminary's teachings of hatred and bigotry towards the English. "They stuffed our heads with hatred for the English."[22] He began to read texts not approved by his teachers.

In October of 1900, Damien moved his tavern to a new location on the central marketplace. It continued to be a favourite watering hole for students, many of them apprenticed to leading lawyers and notaries. To celebrate the victory of the British at Ladysmith in South Africa, the town arranged a fireworks display. Anti-British, pro-Boer sentiment was very strong among the students, and they held a counter-demonstration. The storefront of Damien's tavern served as a platform for student's speeches. Elementary-school and college students learned and sang popular lyrics that were xenophobic and anti-English. The song "Mon chapeau de paille" became the battle hymn of the ultra-nationalists. Bouchard reports that the author was thought by some to have been Canon Lionel Groulx.[23] This was never confirmed, since it was the common custom in those days to write under pseudonyms.[24] Bouchard remarks that if the Brothers had really taught Christian charity and forgiveness, they

---

20   Ibid., p. 125

21   *Fonds* T.-D.B; ANQ; A handwritten copy exists which is not legible, P 10/41

22   T.-D.B., *Mémoires,* 1. p. 126

23   Ibid., p. 126

24   Ibid., p. 127, "In St. Denis, near the forest,
     A day of storms and battle, For the first time I wore my straw hat,
     Without consideration for my beautiful hat, Against the English, the bastards.
     We battled without rest, with our straw hats."
     L'Abbé Charles-Emile Gadbois priest at the St. Hyacinthe Seminary edited a book of songs, "La bonne chanson"; where he altered the phrase, "Against the English," to read "Against the enemy." Another example of this type of song, again attributed to l'Abbé Groulx is the adoption of a Flemish song: "They will never have/They will never have/They will never never have/The soul of New France/Let us say again with courage/They will never, never/They said with foolish pride/We will take you, proud race/And your language and your haughty soul/In peace we will nail your coffin/Much as our kneeling mothers/Our ancestors in white caul/Near our cradles of revenge/Let us repeat again the words of home…"

would not have taught such songs in school. Thus, he observes, it was not surprising that the theme of his first thespian effort was anglophobia.

Another enterprise, which attracted Bouchard initially, was the Ouija board, which was supposed to tell the future to a believer who would ask it questions. T.-D. quickly learned how to manipulate the board. He found people too credulous after many clamoured to pay him for answers to their questions. Even though he told them it was a hoax, they did not believe him and requested more time on the board. Finally, convinced that he would not persuade them, he threw the board into the garbage. This is an early sign of his integrity and probity—characteristics that would remain with him throughout his political and personal life, often creating difficult relationships with political colleagues not accustomed to such behaviour.

At the end of the nineteenth century there were three local newspapers in Saint-Hyacinthe: *Le Courrier de Saint-Hyacinthe,* a conservative paper owned by J. de la Broquerie Taché; *La Tribune,* a pale "red," liberal-clerical paper owned by Colonel Denis; and *L'Union,* a "red" paper owned by Lewis Morison. In the fall of 1899, at the beginning of Bouchard's career as a journalist, there was an open war in the Liberal Party between Morison and Denis, the latter of whom defended the federal Member of Parliament for the riding, Michel-Esdras Bernier. Morison and Bernier had been close friends until a financial falling-out after which they remained bitter, irreconcilable enemies. Morison headed one group and Louis Côté, who was seeking the mayoralty, led the other. The dispute was accentuated when Bernier—then Minister of Revenue—named his son-in-law Dr. Émile Ostiguy—a former Conservative organizer—as the head of Liberal patronage. Morison attacked Doctor Ostiguy in his paper, calling him a *cornac*—an elephant-keeper. Moreover, he challenged the *Tribune's* liberal commitment by noting that its editor, Camille Lussier, was really a Conservative. Lussier was also the local correspondent for *La Presse* of Montreal, in which he mocked and contradicted T.-D.'s local reports in *La Patrie* because of Bouchard's close relationship with Morison. Worrying about his job at *La Patrie,* T.-D. replied vigorously in *L'Union.* The fight deteriorated into name-calling: Lussier called Bouchard *un blanc-bec* (a greenhorn) and Bouchard called Lussier *un barbon* (an old fogy). Surprisingly, in October of 1899, Denis fired Lussier and asked T.-D.—*le blanc-bec*—to be editor of his paper. The weekly salary was one dollar. Bouchard remarks, "Even though I did not have the required experience, he was convinced that no one would doubt my liberal orientation."[25]

---

25   T.D.B., *Mémoires*, 1, p.137

During this period Télesphore fell in love once again—this time with Blanche-Corona, the daughter of an innkeeper of St. Hilaire, Napoléon Cusson, who had been a gold miner in the United States. The story of their first meeting is touchingly related in T.-D. B.'s *Mémoires*. Bouchard had not been aware that his friend Nöé Dussault had planned to introduce him to Blanche-Corona. Nöe embarrassed him further by suggesting that he should demonstrate his skills at the piano. He was mortified since he had not been party to the scheme and appeared in an old pair of patched pants. He had worn the pants to go to Montreal in order to buy electrical supplies to install in Émile's inn, which equipment would permit clients to buzz waiters for more drinks. Both he and Blanche-Corona were extremely uncomfortable. Nevertheless, he had already fallen in love with "the beautiful child with chestnut brown hair and blue eyes."[26]

Young Télesphore-Damien circa 1900

---

26   Ibid., p.146.

Blanche-Corona Cusson

Bouchard visited Saint-Hilaire regularly by train. The trip took 20 minutes, and the return train left at midnight. He liked the Cussons and enjoyed their company. Because the Cusson family was open-minded, he was not concerned that his growing reputation as a *rouge* would damage his relationship with Blanche-Corona. Four times a week he went by train for the evening to St. Hilaire to see her. He wrote her many letters and telephoned regularly. He was very much in love. Blanche-Corona came to Saint-Hyacinthe to meet his parents, family and friends. While he was madly in love, she was more hesitant. She told him the truth—that she hoped one day to be able to say that she loved him, but for the moment she regarded him as a dear friend. Three weeks before her eighteenth birthday, while sitting on a bench overlooking the river, she asked him tenderly, "If a woman felt a frank and simple friendship towards a man who in return loved her, could she be happy with him if she linked her destiny with his?"[27] With both of them in tears he replied that he did not know; but "I had confidence that with time and while sharing the intimacy of a home, friendship could easily change into feelings of love."[28]

Blanche's birthday was three weeks later, on November 15, 1900. Télesphore used the occasion to present her with an engagement ring. She hesitated, but then accepted amid tears. They decided to have a two-year engagement. They would marry when she was twenty, and he twenty-one (and out of the seminary). One year later Blanche-Corona returned the engagement ring. She explained that as much as she admired and respected him, the feeling was not the same as that she had felt towards another young man several years earlier, which had not been reciprocated. She was not sure she should marry without being madly in love. This was a repetition of Télesphore's earlier long preoccupation with the baker's daughter, *la Poucette*. He was devastated. He stopped seeing Blanche-Corona and buried himself in his many activities. In the meantime, the local priest denounced Cusson's inn as a den of iniquity because of the sale of alcohol. Unfortunately, Cusson decided to take the curé to court. He lost his case and was financially ruined. He moved to Montreal, where he became a tramway driver. Through frugality, and in spite of a large family, Cusson eventually saved enough to open an inn at the corner of Atwater and Notre-Dame Street in Montreal.

Bouchard lists his activities in his last year at the seminary: doing home-work; acting as local and regional affairs correspondent for *La Patrie*; editing *La Tribune*, a weekly; helping out at Damien/Émile's inn; spending several hours per week in St. Hilaire; editing the student newspaper, *La Lyre*; and acting as literary secretary of the Saint-Jean-Baptiste society, which was at that time an *académie de débats*.[29] He was a very busy young man. In spite of his reputation and obvious relish at being outspokenly *rouge*, he was elected class president. With his characteristic sense of persecution, he writes that contrary to custom, notation of his presidency is omitted from his class picture. However, Jean-Noel Dion—archivist of the *Société régionale d'histoire de Sainte-Hyacinthe*—remarks

---

27   Ibid., p.156

28   Ibid., p. 158

29   T.-D.B., *Mémoires*, II, 29. *La Lyre*, Class literary review founded in 1899. ASSH, Series L., section A, file 15.

that not all class pictures did, in fact, indicate who was the class president.[30] A group of "blue" students did try to depose Bouchard as president of his class, offering the position to David Lavigne, who was always first in class. Lavigne refused.[31] Again, with his well-developed feelings of persecution, Bouchard notes that in the debating society he was always given the more difficult side to defend. He proudly boasts of his ability to argue the more difficult position of the debate: "Would French Canadians be sorry if Canada had become unilingual-English?" He won by arguing that "one does not desire what one does not know—*ignotti nullo cupido.*"[32]

Télesphore had no fear of public speaking because of his theatrical experience. At the age of eighteen he was asked by the (now) Liberal organizer Dr. Émile Ostiguy to speak in several rural parishes in favour of his father-in-law, Bernier. When asked to submit his expenses for his speaking engagement, he requested fifteen cents for his telephone call to St. Hilaire, since he had been forced to cancel a visit to Blanche-Corona at the last minute.[33] Télesphore-Damien had many supporters within the Liberal Party organization because of his father's connections and because of his own growing fame. The local Liberal leader, M. Frégeau, remained a loyal supporter through thick and thin for many years, as did Joseph Bissonette—Bouchard's tailor, who was an alderman in the municipal council.

Two examples of exchanges with his professors reveal the narrow-minded atmosphere at the seminary.[34] T.-D. had a warm relationship with his professor of literature, who wrote lovely poetry about spiritual and worldly love. Bouchard published these poems in his *rouge* newspaper, signed anonymously as "Albin." Somehow, it was suspected that there was a connection between T.-D. of the seminary and the unknown author, who was thought to be one of the priests. One day this priest stopped talking to Télesphore, and stopped submitting material.[35] Some time later, Bouchard met "Albin" alone in the garden and

---

30   Jean-Noël Dion: personal communication

31   ASSH, Class records.

32   T.-D. B., *Mémoires.* II, p.142

33   He was given 25 cents.

34   The motto of the Seminary was *"Foi et Instruction"*, Société d'histoire regional de Saint-Hyacinthe, p. 170

35   T.-D. B, Mémoires, II, p. 152. The last poem from Albin; *"Joie d'aimer"* appeared in *L'Union,* 19 *juillet* 1901.

learned that the Grand Vicar had tricked the priest into admitting authorship by claiming falsely that Bouchard was the source of the revelation. The Grand Vicar had claimed that Bouchard had told him who Albin was. Since the priest was convinced that the Grand Vicar would never lie, nothing T.-D. could say would change his mind—so he said nothing. The second example is the story that Télesphore reports of being asked by one of the newly ordained priests if he had ever read Voltaire. When he replied that he had read several extracts, the priest told him that he had started to read Voltaire, but stopped because he was afraid that he would lose his faith. Bouchard remarks, with some irony, "If he thought that there were mistaken ideas ... why stop reading ... could he not criticize the text?"[36] Bouchard muses that perhaps it was just a trap to check his reading list.

In his last year in school the province was hit by a smallpox epidemic. As he had lost a child in a previous epidemic, Damien had vaccinated his children. Just before this new epidemic, they were vaccinated again. T.-D. reports that he and his siblings had an attenuated attack. The seminary was quarantined, the *pensionnaires* were kept inside, and the day students were allowed to stay at home.[37] A good part of the semester was lost. Vaccination was much more common in the English community, who therefore suffered a much lower death rate than the French community, among whom there was a stiff resistance to vaccination.[38] In his book on the 1885 smallpox outbreak in Montreal, Michael Bliss points out that it was certain doctors—some prominent ones were English—who were influential in this anti-vaccination campaign, especially among the French population.[39] They responded negatively in spite of a vast campaign by the clergy in favour of vaccination. Bishop Fabre himself set an example by ordering priests to urge their parishioners to be vaccinated.

Near the end of Bouchard's studies, Morison offered him the job of administrator of *L'Union*, at a salary of $9 per week. This was the same salary as his father's as foreman in the shoe factory. He replied that the offer was very tempting, but he wanted to finish his studies and go on to study law. Morison

---

36   Ibid., p. 151

37   ASSH, Class records.

38   Michael Bliss, *Plague; A Story of Smallpox in Montreal,* (Toronto: Harper-Collins Publishers, 1991)

39   Ibid., p. 127–128

persisted. Canon Ouelette, superior of the seminary, agreed to allow him to work, on condition that he pay his debts to the seminary. So T.-D. threw himself into this exhausting job, working into the wee hours of the morning and taking long, solitary walks to console himself for his lost love. As a consequence of the heavy burden—a job and studies—his schoolwork suffered. In his final year he did not rank well, and for the first time received no final prizes. Lost time due to the smallpox epidemic may also have contributed to his relatively poor results.

Although everyone thought that Francis Morison was a rich man because he dressed with sartorial elegance, he died a pauper. His father, who had participated in the 1837 Rebellion, had left him a considerable fortune. His father was arrested after the failed rebellions, but then released without trial. Morison himself studied law but disliked its adversarial nature. He became publisher and editor of the *rouge* newspaper *l'Union*. He owned property, stocks, and two toll bridges. However, at the time Télesphore knew him he was impoverished and going blind. Thus T.-D. did not receive his promised salary. This type of business practice led the previous administrator to jump ship to join Lieutenant-Colonel Denis at *La Tribune*. Télesphore paid up his obligation to the seminary with borrowed money.[40]

AT THE END OF SEMINARY STUDIES

On January 13, 1903, Bouchard registered in the law faculty of the University of Montreal; but he does not mention continuation of law studies in his memoirs. He most likely dropped the plan to study law because of his natural affinity to journalism, which fit with his intense interest in political life and his pugnacious nature. In addition, journalism was a satisfying profession that quickly accorded him major responsibility. He continued to work for Morison, whom he regarded as "a real father." Morison had no children, and at this time had no friends. He was isolated and had been rejected by former sycophants. Morison attributed his financial troubles to his long-time, now-soured partnership with Michel-Esdras Bernier. Bouchard was in a quandary because he liked and respected both men.

---

40   T.-D.B., *Mémoires*, II, p.164. He states that he borrowed money to pay. In another version he recounts how he kept a purse found outside the school with $15.00 in it. This was just the amount owed. On the advice of his father he advertised the find, intending to pay back the money to whoever claimed it—but no one did.

Télesphore lived free of charge at his father's inn. His only regular income was his salary from *La Presse* of $22 per month [sic] for his articles on local activities and politics.[41] His theoretical salary of $9 per week as manager of *L'Union* went to pay the editor, the accountant, the compositors, and the printers. His main expense was clothing. Télesphore-Damien was never a great sportsman like his father and his brother Émile. He never learned to dance. He was not what might be called a *gai luron*—a happy-go-lucky person. He was always a bit more solemn and mature than his age would suggest. He never had much fun at soirées because of his inability to dance, and so he avoided them as much as possible.[42] Elspeth Chisholm suggests that as a short man, he was embarrassed to dance with girls his own height or taller.[43] Bouchard's great interests lay on the artistic side of life. He loved music, theatre, debating and reading. At a young age he became interested in the attempt to introduce a universal language, Esperanto.[44] With a socialist friend, Albert St.-Martin, he founded a discussion club, *"Club de la Prévoyance"* (The Foresight Club).[45] They discussed the nationalization of the railroads. The right-wing forces founded the *Club des Ouvriers* that he joined. In 1902 Bouchard and his friends founded *le Cercle littéraire,* where actors, singers and musicians attended and presented their skills. The club encouraged the

---

41   From the salary level of the time this would seem to be high.

42   C.-E. Bouchard, personal communication.

43   T.-D.B., a biography, Elspeth Chisholm, National Archives, Ottawa.

44   This simplified language, invented by Dr Ludovic Lazarus Zamenhof, had a limited number of rules. Zamenhof believed Esperanto would serve to increase international communication and understanding, thereby leading to increased brotherhood of nations and peace on earth. Zamenhof, an ophthalmologist, was born on December 15, 1859, in the town of Bialostock, in the part of Poland which was then a part of the Russian Empire. The town's population had been made up of several major ethnic groups: Poles, Belorusians and a large group of Yiddish-speaking Jews. Zamenhof was saddened and frustrated by the many quarrels between these groups. He supposed that the main reason for the hate and prejudice lay in mutual misunderstanding caused by the lack of a common language that would play the role of a neutral communication tool between people of different ethnic and linguistic backgrounds. In 1887 the book titled as *"Doktoro Esperanto. Lingvo internacia. Anta parolo kaj plena lernolibro"* ("Dr. Hopeful. International Language. Foreword And Complete Textbook") was published. For Zamenhof this language was not merely a communication tool, but also a means of spreading his ideas on the peaceful coexistence of different peoples and cultures.

45   *L'Union,* 6 *juin* 1902.

use of Esperanto, giving regular classes. In 1902 Télesphore played the role of Harpagon in Moliere's *l'Avare*.

T.-D.'s inquisitive personality also led him to an interest in hypnotism. One day Doctor St.-Jacques asked Télesphore to accompany him to the theatre to witness the performance of a "Dr. Onofroff." When volunteers were requested from the audience, T.-D. presented himself. Under hypnosis he held himself rigid as a board and was lifted to stretch between two chairs four feet apart. Then he did not react when a large hatpin sterilized in an alcohol lamp was thrust through his upper arm. Bouchard denied being hypnotized, stating that he was aware of everything but was just co-operating to see how far the "doctor" could hoodwink the public.[46] With his curious distorted logic, he attempted to comprehend the phenomenon of hypnotism—explained in those days as the physical flow of magnetic fluid. He states: "It did not take me long to figure out the psychological explanation of his strategy; he obliged me to lie each time he commanded me to obey him."[47] In fact, Doctor St. Jacques and his daughter were convinced that Télesphore had been mesmerized, but he continued to claim otherwise. His was the type of personality that found it difficult to accept loss of self-control.

People were so taken by T.-D.'s capacity to receive the magnetic fluid that friends, and even people from the countryside, wanted to induce him to hypnotize them. Finally he succumbed to their repeated importuning—as he notes, from an intellectual desire to see if he could repeat the exercise while continuing to regard the process as "charlatanism." He began by transmission of thought—by demonstrating that he could find a hidden object while holding on to a rod, which the subject also held. By sensing the inadvertent movement of the subject towards the hidden object, he was more often than not capable of finding the object. When he could not do so, he would simply announce that there was not enough transfer of fluid. His friends could not understand why an impoverished student should not use this talent to increase his income. Télesphore refused to make money from something he regarded as dishonest. Even though he succeeded in hypnotizing several people, he continued to think that they were faking it, as he felt he had faked it. One day Arthur Fontaine, one of his best subjects, did not wake up on command after spending over fifteen minutes rigid between two chairs and having his arm pierced by a hatpin. The audience became alarmed, asking if his rigidity was not cataleptic, but cadaveric! Although frightened, T.-D.

46   T.-D. B., *Mémoires*, II, p. 17.

47   Ibid., p. 17.

did not convey his fear to the audience. He told them that this was a well-known phenomenon. When the transfer of magnetic fluid was strong it sometimes took longer for someone to awaken. With patience, the subject would wake. Everyone would have to remain in the room until he awoke, even if it took until the next day. Then T.-D., noting a deep sigh from Fontaine, again made several passes with his hands, commanding him to awake; and so he did. With this episode, Bouchard ended his career as a hypnotist, once again displaying his personal integrity—he would not exploit a technique that he considered fraudulent.

After mass on Sundays, Liberal Party stalwarts met at what was termed *la petite messe du dimanche* (Sunday's little mass). Lawyers, businessmen, doctors, workers and party organizers met in the offices of Jean-Baptiste Blanchet to gossip, discuss strategy and prepare for action during periods of municipal, provincial and federal elections. People of many views came together, including radicals, freethinkers, moderates and even Catholic militants. All, however, were opponents of Church intervention in political life. Bouchard attended as a reporter for *La Presse* and *La Patrie*. He continued this tradition later on, when he was leader of the Liberals, conducting the meetings in his office at *L'Union*. Bouchard was not a fanatic Liberal Party adherent. He understood the complexity of political orientation in Quebec. For example, in his *Mémoires* he plays tribute to the political life of the Conservative leader Sir George-Etienne Cartier.[48] In his first editorial as owner of *L'Union* he wrote that it was a liberal

---

48   Ibid., p. 24–29. Cartier participated in the 1837 Rebellion. Then he did not agree with the radicalism of the Liberals of the 1850s and so became active in the Conservative Party. In general, the Church supported the Conservative Party. However, in the 1872 federal elections, the Church supported the Liberals in a battle between Louis-Aimé Jetté, a clerical *rouge*, against George-Étienne Cartier, an anti-clerical *bleu*. In fact, Cartier lost that election most probably due to Church intervention. Monsignor Bourget, the bishop of Montreal, held Cartier to task for his anti-clericalism, and especially because of Cartier's defence of the Sulpicien cause in Montreal, against Bourget. As well, Cartier was active in negotiations to eliminate the seigneurial system of land holding. Bourget's friend, Canon Lamarche, published diatribes against Cartier because of his revision of the Civil Code. He was tainted with a label of *"Gallicanisme prononcé."* Cartier was a sincere Catholic. The accusation of Cartier's Gallicanism was referred to Rome and declared unjustifiable. It was at this period that the *castors* attempted to introduce the *Parti catholique*—the Catholic program—formulated by the future judge Routhier. See Brian Young, *Cartier*.

newspaper, which nevertheless would be independent from the Liberal Party, criticizing it when necessary.[49]

In spite of Bouchard's efforts to improve the finances of *L'Union* by mending fences with Bernier, Morison continued to feud with him. T.-D. was quite depressed. Instead of succeeding in getting the two together, their hostility grew. Bernier obtained $11,000 from Ottawa to buy land between Saint-Antoine and Saint-François Streets for an esplanade. Morison wanted to mount a campaign against this project, but Bouchard resisted, persuading him not to do so. One Friday there was only $68 in cash available to pay all the workers of the press and staff. He needed $40 more. He managed to obtain $10 from Aimé Beauparlant, and he finally went to his brother Émile for the rest. The situation was not improving.

Bouchard became editor of *L'Union* in 1902. His fiery rhetoric soon filled its pages. On December 19, 1902, he answered an article of a "M. Léon," which had appeared in *La Tribune* and criticized the Literary Circle. This exchange continued over the next few issues of the two newspapers. In this exchange, one gets the impression that "M. Léon" is stunned by the furious attack on the part of twenty-one-year-old Télesphore-Damien Bouchard, who wrote: "Mr. Léon is certainly thoughtless or someone interested ... to do harm to the newborn Literary circle ... he is badly informed ... it is completely false that there is discord between members of the circle.... What the devil got into Mr. Léon?"[50] T.-D.'s polemical articles in *L'Union* attracted the attention of people in Saint-Hyacinthe. Some friends encouraged him to continue the struggle in this aggressive tone, but others feared that his style presented a danger to the reformists who were facing a tough upcoming municipal election. He replied that it was time to declare one's views:

> I answered that it was time to end some of the old practices ... of being elected under false pretences. If the majority of the people do not share our ideas, it is necessary to convert them to these ideas before thinking of taking power. *Power, which is not sustained by public opinion, can not be solid ... if one serves his own interests, it would be better not to think about gaining power.*[51] [Emphasis added]

---

49   *L'Union*, 11 mars 1904.

50   *L'Union*, 19, 26, 30 *décembre* 1902.

51   T.D.B., *Mémoires*. II, p. 106.

It is noteworthy that Bouchard kept to this formulation of his political beliefs throughout his life. If he could not convince the electorate of the wisdom of his program, he did not deserve to be elected. He would accept defeat of a project or a bill, but would keep up his educational campaign to convince the public that he was right. Before the *Club de la Prévoyance,* Bouchard exposed the program of "our group." The first necessity was to put the municipal house in order before attempting to reform the province. In most municipalities, common abuses had slipped into public administration. Large industrial and religious corporations had succeeded in creating a heavy public debt by legalizing tax exemptions, grants to manufacturers, gifts and subsidies. This debt weighed heavily on the shoulders of the ordinary taxpayer. Therefore:

> The major reforms recommended by our group were: the abolition of tax exemptions and grants in money to manufacturers; special taxation of religious communities for public lighting; expenses for fire protection; the construction and maintenance of the pavement, sidewalks and sewers in front of their properties; the levy for the supply of water based on the value of the property ... as well as ... the municipalization of the production of electricity.[52]

On the local scene, Bouchard tried to improve the representative nature of the municipal council and municipal elections. Big business and real estate developers easily controlled the aldermen. Many did not pay municipal taxes. There was much graft and favouritism. Saint-Hyacinthe had a huge religious establishment of convents, seminaries, monasteries, hospitals and other religious institutions, which were also exempted from paying taxes.[53] Half of the main street was fronted by these buildings, as they still are. They required water, sewage, snow cleaning, maintenance and fire and police protection. Télesphore-Damien was one of those who felt that these institutions should be taxed. At the time, to be a candidate alderman, one was required to be a property owner and to have at least $400, free of debt. In order to have a vote, income taxes had to be paid

---

52   Ibid., p. 108.

53   The list of religious institutions in Saint-Hyacinthe as noted in the Société *d'histoire régionale de Saint-Hyacinthe,* p.151*: Les Soeurs de la Congrégation Notre Dame, Les Soeurs de la Charité de Saint-Hyacinthe, Les Soeurs de la Présentation de Marie, Les Sœurs Adoratrices du Précieux Sang, Les Sœurs de Saint Joseph de Saint-Hyacinthe, Les Sœurs de Sainte Marthe de Saint-Hyacinthe, Les Frères Maristes, Un Noviciat Dominicain, Les Frères du Sacré-Cœur, Les Frères de Saint-Vincent-de-Paul.*

at least four days before to the election. Bouchard fought to change these laws to allow tenants to be eligible for election as alderman or mayor. At the *Club National Ouvrier*, Bouchard introduced a motion demanding that the financial requirements for alderman and mayor be dropped. In 1904, "our group" succeeded in electing four aldermen favourable to these progressive ideas, out of five in total. Of course, women were not allowed to vote.

As we have seen, in this period "priest-politicians" frequently interfered in public matters. The Workers Club, which had fallen into the hands of the clericals, invited the Reverend Roberge to speak on social questions. "This Abbé possessed a resonant voice and the gift to impress crowds."[54] Roberge spoke against the ideas of nationalization and the municipalization of public utilities. He condemned the administration of the Intercolonial Railroad by the state, as well as the administration of water services, streetcars and electrical lighting by municipalities. All international union chiefs were only exploiters of working Canadians (i.e., French Canadians), he declared.[55] Since, at the town hall, "our group" was recommending the municipalization of electricity, Abbé Roberge's speech provoked an immense reaction, both locally and regionally. A month later, workers of "advanced ideas" and the "internationals of Montreal" organized an excursion to Saint-Hyacinthe. In a grand hotel, two hundred persons participated in a "lively evening."[56] They proposed the formation of a new, and true, workers club.

In 1904, Bouchard participated in a delegation to Ottawa that left a lasting impression on him concerning political mores, and increased his admiration for his hero Laurier. Morison was suffering physically and financially. His vision was failing, and he could neither read nor write. His railroad was put under guardianship, and this led to the bankruptcy of the Bank of Saint-Hyacinthe, in which he held a major share. A delegation composed of MP Blanchet, Senator Dessaulles, ex-mayor Euclide Richer, Mayor Eugene St. Jacques, Aimé Beauparlant, J. R. Brillon, Joseph Morin and including Télesphore-Damien Bouchard, proceeded to Ottawa to meet with Laurier. Because Morison had helped the Laurier campaign, there was reason to hope for federal assistance, especially since Blanchet and Brodeur—the new Minister of Revenue—were old friends of Laurier. The Prime Minister listened attentively and said that he

---

54   T.-D.B., II, p. 93.

55   Ibid., p. 94.

56   Ibid., p. 94.

could not do anything. "He belonged to the old school that held that the state should not intervene in private enterprise."[57] The delegation, surprised by the firm rejection, reminded Laurier that if the government did not help the bank, the election of Liberal candidates would be severely compromised in future elections in Saint-Hyacinthe. Reacting strongly, Laurier stated: "My government may fall, but I will not use public funds to protect the interests of a particular person."[58] These words remained engraved in the brain of T.-D. as words of a great leader and as a model he tried always to follow—a difficult, hard principle, guaranteed not to make him a lot of friends in his political life.

In spite of his youth, Bouchard was recognized as one of the Liberal Party leaders. The Young Liberal Association of Saint-Hyacinthe elected him president. He became an implacable enemy of the "nationalists" who were attacking his hero Laurier while they remained nominal Liberals. Always a defender of the French-Canadian nation, he felt that progress was to be made through education, bilingualism and co-operation with the English majority of Canada. The clerical nationalists referred to this scornfully as *la bonne entente.*

In 1903, the issue of a flag for Quebec burst into public debate. The Jesuits and many other of the *castor* wing promoted the sacred-heart flag, *le Carillon du Sacre-Coeur,* which depicted the sacred heart of Jesus within a version of today's *fleur-de-lis* Quebec flag.[59] There were some, including priests, who wished to continue to use the tricolour of France, commonly flown for celebrations. The Orangemen of Ontario supported the use of the Union Jack. The bishops decided to prohibit the use of a sacred flag (the one with the sacred heart) for non-religious purposes. Bouchard gave a talk to the *Cercle Montcalm* during which he advocated putting aside this divisive issue, since it did not serve the

---

57   Ibid., p. 53.

58   Ibid., p. 53.

59   The debate about a Quebec flag began in 1901 and lasted until the 1940s. See Jules-Paul Tardivel, *"Le Nationaliste et le drapeau national," la Vérité,* 15 mai 1904, p. 4. Reply of Olivar Asselin, *"M. Tardivel et nous," le Nationaliste,* 22 mai 1904, p. 4. Elphège Filiatrault, *"Nos couleurs nationales,"* Saint-Jude, *février* 1905, pp.7–8, 12. See also Elphège Filiatrault, *"Notre drapeau national," la Patrie,* 14 *avril* 1904, p. 10. Henri Bourassa, *"Il a raison," le Devoir,* 20 *septembre* 1910; *"La Question des drapeaux," le Devoir,* 23 *septembre* 1910. Laurent-Olivier David, *La Question des drapeaux suivi de Noblesse oblige,* (Montréal: Librairie Beauchemin, 1926), p. 11–18; C.-J. Magnan, *"Le Carillon-Sacré-Coeur, drapeau national des Canadiens français, Québec," l'Action catholique,* 1939, p. 31.

national purpose. It divided the two founding "races." He remarks that the audience did not receive his message with much sympathy.[60]

Another issue that for many years was to preoccupy T.-D. and many Quebec politicians both on the right and the left was the question of public energy. Saint-Hyacinthe was the pioneer in this domain, having installed the first small hydroelectric plant in North America at Rapides Plate in 1894, under the direction of Bouchard's science teacher, Msgr. Charles-Philippe Choquette.[61] The local power company raised rates 25 percent—to $3 per square foot of gas and 15 cents per kw/hr of electricity. T.-D. likened the issue of municipalization of electric power to the supply of municipal water. He noted the success of Glasgow at that time, and of Ontario, which had nationalized Ontario Hydro in 1903.[62] Bouchard was an early advocate of the municipalization of electricity in order to lower rates by competing with the power "trusts." Later, he became a strong promoter of the nationalization of these exploitative "trusts."

T.-D. Bouchard became proprietor of *L'Union* on December 1, 1903, when the ailing Morison prevailed on T.-D. to take over the newspaper, the printing company, and the building. The sale price was $300, which Bouchard borrowed from the mother of the bookkeeper, endorsed by the bank, plus nine hundred dollars in outstanding back wages. He was not yet twenty-two years old. His lack of funds did not discourage him—to say nothing about his debts. He had "an ardent desire to succeed in order to please those dear to me.... Timid as most French Canadians, it was only in thinking about defending justice that I succeeded in overcoming this complex of fear."[63] Bouchard clearly announced that while his paper was devoted to the Liberal Party, he would not be a "slave of all Liberal politicians. *L'Union* ... will maintain its freedom of thought and action."[64] In the first issue announcing his ownership of *L'Union* in January of 1904, Bouchard quoted extensively from an 1892 papal encycli-

---

60   T.-D.B., *Mémoires*, II, p. 37

61   Monsignor Choquette was not only a pioneer in electricity, but also one of the first Canadian researchers in radiography, astronomy and radiophonic transmission. *Soc. D'histoire régionale de Saint-Hyacinthe*, p. 170.

62   T.-D.B., *Mémoires*, II, p. 75.

63   T.-D. B., *Mémoires*, II, p. 45.

64   *L'Union*, 11 *mars* 1904.

cal that denounced excessive priestly intervention in politics.[65] This encyclical was chiefly directed against the ultramontane monarchists of France, but had repercussions in Quebec on Tardivel and *La Croix de Montreal*.[66]

Morison knew that T.-D. would maintain the traditions of the *L'Union*, and probably hoped that his withdrawal would help T.-D. to obtain more government printing jobs withheld during Morison's dispute with Bernier. Bernier became a member of the railway commission, and was succeeded as Minister of Revenue by Louis-Philippe Brodeur, who was one of "our political group." Meanwhile, a large majority of Saint-Hyacinthe voters elected Jean-Baptiste Blanchet in a federal by-election, in spite of his avowed freethinking. With the founding of the *Le Nationaliste*, Bouchard took the opportunity of announcing the policy of his own Catholic newspaper by beginning with the entire text of the Pope's bull on popular Christian social action. "We publish the whole text because of its intrinsic value and because the author has directed all Catholic papers to do so."[67] Bouchard remarks that this text was copied from another newspaper and (with tongue in cheek) that he hopes to receive an authorized text from the bishop.

> Is *L'Union* suspected of not being Catholic? We have never preached against doctrine nor been excommunicated. Our paper is not a pious paper and we will not run a regular theological column.... Our distance from purely religious questions should not be confused with hostility ... It is a condition of a Catholic newspaper to have at least one page of a sermon ... especially an article in favour of the sacred-heart flag. Without such, no salvation.[68]

These were battling, provocative words. This battle cry of *L'Union* was like a red flag for the ultramontane press, and Tardivel was soon to mock Bouchard in *La Verité* by teasing him about his inelegant French. "The French language is the

---

65   *L'Union*, 10 *janvier* 1904. As pointed out by Roberto Perrin, Pope Leo XIII constantly reminded Catholics to obey state authority. In his encyclical *"Au milieu des solicitudes"* of February 16, 1892, addressed to France, the Pope commented on church-state relations. He defended the concordat between the church and the state. In Canada he was constantly concerned with the militancy of the ultramontane Catholics who equated the French language with Catholicism, forgetting that the language of the majority of Catholics was not French. With the influx of Irish Catholics, this attitude became more relevant.

66   Jules-Paul Tardivel and *La Croix* have been discussed in Chapter I.

67   T.-D. B., *Mémoires,* II, p. 47–51.

68   Ibid., p. 47.

guarantee of the faith."[69] Was T.-D. being disingenuous when he replied that this could not be true, since the language of the Church was Latin? Tardivel accused *L'Union* of being anti-French Canadian. Bouchard brought an action against *Le Courrier de Saint-Hyacinthe* for naming him a Freemason. He denied being a member of the Masons at that time, although it seems that he was an active member briefly in 1898, at the age of seventeen.[70] The court rendered a verdict of "no bill," meaning that there was no insult in being called a Freemason. As is the case frequently in Quebec politics and no doubt elsewhere, the label stuck to him throughout his life.[71]

A MARRIAGE PROPOSAL

During this period T.-D. courted several eligible young women. In order to forget his unsuccessful amorous venture, he began to go out with "a lovely Canadian of Irish origin."[72] Soon it was apparent that she preferred a young doctor from Montreal. Another disappointment! One young woman—still in convent school—fell in love with him, and they became engaged. She became ill with pneumonia and died within three days. Blanche-Corona was reported to have been upset at hearing the news of this engagement. Bouchard also paid court to the bookkeeper, who had arranged his loan to buy *L'Union* through her mother; but he realized that his heart was still with Blanche-Corona, and that what he felt for this employee was gratitude. Meanwhile, a mutual friend let him know that Blanche-Corona followed his suit against *Le Courrier* with great interest. T.-D. was also informed that she was following all his various activities in searching for a wife.

In the spring of 1904, Télesphore-Damien passed through Montreal. He visited the Cussons, who were doing well financially. Left alone with him, Blanche-Corona told him that she had considered entering a convent after their breakup, but that an aunt who was a nun told her not to enter the orders because of a romantic disappointment. He had learned from a brother-in-law that she really loved him and

---

69   Ibid., p. 50.

70   Again in 1917 he sued Joseph Bégin, director of *La Croix,* for calling him a Freemason and won $100 in damages. In court he admitted that he had been a member at a young age but had resigned in 1910.

71   A political science professor once asked me if T.-D. B. was not a Protestant.

72   T.-D. B., *Mémoires,* II, p. 15.

defended him against criticism. He was thus emboldened to tell her that his love for her was undiminished. He also suggested after this long talk that he would be attending the St. Louis World Fair as a delegate of the journalists of Quebec—and would that not be a nice place for a honeymoon? He returned to Saint-Hyacinthe in a buoyant mood. The following Sunday he returned to Montreal and, after two hours of discussion, Blanche-Corona agreed to marry him.

The ceremony was to have taken place at the church of the Cussons, in St.-Henri, but it had burned down. Since they were not his parishioners, the curé of neighbouring St. Cunégonde Church refused to allow them to marry. When Napoléon Cusson said, "Well, if we cannot have a Catholic wedding, let us go get a Protestant one," the curé then agreed. (It is amazing how many times the Bouchards ran into obstacles when dealing with the Church.) Father Doyon, a Dominican priest of Saint-Hyacinthe, celebrated the mass blessing their union on May 12, 1904, in the *Hospice de la Charité* in Montreal. The ceremony cost was $6.[73]

---

73 The night before his marriage T.-D. underwent the rites of passage—the burial of his life as a bachelor. This ancient custom had been highlighted in the past by a mock funeral. "The bridegroom was forced to lie down on bed-boards or a cot made to resemble a coffin while a solemn or bawdy eulogy was read over him." Gerard J. Brault, *The French-Canadian Heritage in New England*, (Kingston and Montreal: McGill-Queen's University press, 1986), p. 36. According to the account in *L'Union* of May 14 1904:

Happy Burial: Numerous friends of Mr. D.-T. Bouchard gathered on Wednesday night at the Hotel de Canada to bury his life as a bachelor....About 60 people were present. The subscription list contained over 100 names. A purse of $60 was given to the hero of the celebration. Mr. Belisle gave the initial speech in spiritual and jovial form due to his lengthy experience in doing so. Mr. Bouchard expressed his happiness and said that he was touched by this expression of friendship. The rest of the evening was spent happily with songs, music, and jolly speeches. It is unnecessary to add that toasts to the health of future marrieds were proposed several times. The principal speakers were Mr. Beauparlent, Marin, René Lussier, and H. Casavant. All were unanimous in congratulating their young friend for his courage shown in venturing on such an unknown and doubtful path at the age of 22, when old bachelors of 30 and 35 did not enter without fear.

On the same page:

Mariage—vendredi le 13 mai: The marriage of Mr. T.-D. Bouchard to Miss Corona Cusson took place at St.-Cunégonde, in the Sisters of Charity chapel...The young couple were accompanied respectively by their fathers. The Reverend Father Doyon, of the Dominican convent of St.-Hyacinthe, who spoke touchingly, wishing the young couple a long and healthy life, gave the nuptial blessings. A family dinner

Télesphore-Damien and Blanche-Corona Cusson in 1904

EARLY MARRIAGE; THE YOUNG JOURNALIST AND ALDERMAN

The married couple boarded a special train for St. Louis to attend the 1904 World Fair. Other journalists on board, upon discovering that the two were on their honeymoon, celebrated the event with them. In St Louis crowds from all over the world gathered to rejoice in humanity's advancements since the Louisiana Purchase hundred years earlier.[74] The exposition was extraordinary;

---

followed at the home of the bride's father. The young couple left that evening by train for the World Exposition at St. Louis, as part of the journalists' group. Our best wishes go with them.

74   The exposition celebrated an important event in American history, commemorating the conclusion of the treaty of April 30, 1803, between Napoleon Bonaparte, then First Consul of the French Republic, and Thomas Jefferson, author of the Declaration of Independence and third president of the United States. It brought to an end the anxiety of the previous administrations of Presidents Washington and John Adams about a possible resumption of the wars between France and Great Britain for ascendancy in North America. The land area acquired from France was huge. It encompassed all the land lying between the Mississippi

many exhibits focused on new technological advancements: radium, submarines, wireless telegraphs, gas power (replacing coal), airplanes, electricity and automobiles. As a practical machine, the automobile was just a few years old.

On their return, the newly married couple moved into an apartment arranged by Blanche-Corona's parents above the printing rooms of *L'Union*. Mrs. Cusson, whom Bouchard greatly admired, helped with the decoration of the apartment, the choice of furniture, and its placement. It was a brick building with pretty dormer windows upstairs facing Girouard Blvd.[75] Bouchard was very pleased. "This home was nothing like a castle, but my wife, who had moved to Saint-Henri, took possession of her new residence, happy and radiant."[76] In his memoirs, T.-D. once again boasts about having "climbed the hill." The grandson of a water-carrier, born in miserable circumstances in the lower town near the Hay-Market, continued to climb the social ladder. He repeated this theme throughout his life, in his memoirs and in his speeches. He always chose to emphasize his plebeian origin, but at the same time, he would boast about his success in climbing the social ladder. Saint-Hyacinthe physically lent itself to the idea of "climbing the hill."[77] In Saint-Hyacinthe, there is an upper town and a lower town. "I had abandoned the lower town to establish my home on the hill, on Boulevard Girouard."[78]

Blanche-Corona—often simply called Corona—was never very robust. She became pregnant five times, losing the first baby through miscarriage at three months of pregnancy, and the last through miscarriage in 1911. Their first child born at term was Bernadette Cécile-Ena, who arrived on March 15, 1906. Télesphore's brother Émile and his wife carried the small child to the baptismal font. "The baby was frail at its birth. Her mother herself

---

River and the crest of the Rocky Mountains, up to the Canadian border. The territory included Louisiana, Arkansas, the Indian Territory, Oklahoma, Missouri, Kansas, Nebraska, Iowa, North and South Dakota and Montana; as well as part of Minnesota, Wyoming and Colorado. It indirectly provided access to Washington, Oregon, Idaho, California, Nevada, Utah, Arizona, New Mexico and Texas. The treaty allowed for the extension of the United States to the Pacific Ocean.

75   T.-D.B., *Mémoires, Quarante ans de tourmente politico-religieuse*. Volume II. p. 57.

76   Ibid., p. 57.

77   *Société d'histoire régionale de Saint-Hyacinthe*, pp. 13–23.

78   T.-D.B., *Mémoires*, II, p. 58.

not endowed with a strong constitution, but thanks to the good care which she bestowed on her girl under the sagacious direction of the physician, our fears disappeared and Cécile-Ena began to thrive."[79] Here we have an interesting theme of the family life of Télesphore and Blanche-Corona: the fragile health of Mrs. Bouchard contrasting with the vigour of Cécile-Ena, a true daughter of the vigorous T.-D. "Our hopes were not disappointed [in the good health of his daughter and also in the belief in the efficacy of "good" physicians]."[80] The family often had need of doctors. Two years after the birth of Cécile, a boy was born on his sister's birthday. This time it was Mr. and Mrs. Joseph Bissonette who held the small baby on the baptismal font. Since Télesphore-Damien and Joseph Bissonnette were two great admirers of the late Jean-Baptiste Blanchet (the freethinking MP)—and with Corona'a approval—the baby's name was to be Joseph Adelstan Blanchet Bouchard. Once again, there was a confrontation between the Bouchard family and the priests:

> We were welcomed there by Father Sénecal, who appeared at first very warm. However, his brow grew furrowed when, after asking what names would the child be given, the godfather replied: "Joseph, Adelstan, Blanchet." The priest looked at me with a disapproving air: "Yes, I said, Joseph Adelstan, *Blanchet*." "Blanchet—" replied Father Sénecal, "but this is not a saint!" "How would you know?" replied his godfather. "There was no one better in the world. If there is a heaven he has to be there." The priest judged it prudent to remain silent and to proceed with the baptism.[81]

Tragically, this boy died at fourteen months of age from whooping cough.[82] On May 21, 1910, Corona gave birth to a second girl, named Blanche-Corona. She also died at a young age, from dysentery, on December 8, 1910. "This was my last child, and it is with a deep feeling of sadness that I followed her coffin to the to the cemetery, where hardly twelve months ago I followed the

---

79   Ibid., p.126.

80   Ibid., p.126.

81   Ibid., p. 174.

82   According to Cécile-Ena her brother died at twenty-two months of age. Church records give the date of death as May 21, 1909, thus really fourteen months.

mortal remains of my son, who died at fourteen months of age."[83] Blanche-Corona had another miscarriage; then, in 1911, at the age of twenty-eight, she had an operation on the cervix of the uterus. In 1914, she underwent "the big operation" *(la grande opération)*—a hysterectomy.[84] Therefore, there was enough cause for sadness and mourning in this family. Cécile-Ena observes that from childhood she played the role of nurse to her mother, who was bedridden more often than not.[85] "I never knew my mother in good health. From the age of five years, I began my apprenticeship as a nurse. She was small and delicate."[86] Blanche-Corona obviously confided in Cécile-Ena regarding the true nature of the relationship between herself and her husband. In his published *Mémoires*, T.-D. also candidly describes the one-sided love that he felt for his wife; and writes that she had hesitated to marry him because she did not feel a deep and passionate love for him. Cécile-Ena reveals that she was aware of her mother's ambivalent attitude towards her husband. "Fate did not spoil her. She was disappointed in love before meeting my father. He knew about it and took the risk of marrying her, hoping that she would forget her first love."[87]

She also evaluated her father's character:

> This man, full of vitality, not spoiled during his youth and adolescence, had to fight for his place in the sun. He could not understand the tenderness required by a young girl broken by life. As with most of our men he did not understand women. He only knew struggle because, even at a young age, he had to defend himself as the little

---

83   Ibid., p. 216.

84   Medical records, Dr. H.N. Segall and personal communication.

85   Cécile-Ena Bouchard. *Mémoires*. Sainte Marguerite Station, PQ *le 27 mai* 1975. *Dédié à "mon ange gardien, Mme. Claire Simard Odermatt. Centres d'Archives du Séminaire de Saint-Hyacinthe. AFg.126;4*
"Souvenir et Portraits":
"Born in 1906 in St-Hyacinthe, being the daughter of T.-D. Bouchard was not easy. I have only vague memories of my infancy. First there was the death of my little brother, born exactly two years after me, who took my place somewhat. He died of whooping-cough at 22 months of age [sic]. Later I lost a little sister, aged eight months, of dysentery. I was the only survivor. I don't understand it. All my life I was surrounded by disease, hospitals, doctors, and nurses, for myself or my parents."

86   Ibid., p. 1.

87   Ibid., p. 1.

guy from the Hay-Market. An honest worker, devoted to the task of succeeding, entirely good-hearted, under a thick skin, he did not know how to create the family atmosphere that my mother and I needed so badly. Perhaps that is the lot of politicians. I grew up in an atmosphere of contention and battles.[88]

Confirming Cécile-Ena's impression of her mother, Dr. Harold Segall remarks that Mrs. Bouchard was small and weighed little: 93–100 pounds.[89] He describes her as depressive.[90] In correspondence between Cécile and her parents, and even in that between Télesphore-Damien and Corona, constant repetitive themes are a continual concern for a safe and agreeable trip, and their state of good or bad health.[91] Among Cécile-Ena's papers covering the years 1920–34, there is much communication among the three concerning Mrs. Bouchard. Later, after Corona's tragic death in 1934, there was much correspondence between Cécile and her father. There was an almost morbid concern for daily, sometimes twice-daily contact—by telephone, by telegram or through the intervention of a third party. Cécile confirms this in her memoirs: "If I was absent for one day either at Granby or Montreal at friends', I had to telephone to have news from her and to report on my doings so that she would not worry about me. We were closely bound up each with the other."[92] They were a prime example of an "enmeshed family."[93]

Mrs. Bouchard ceased to be hostess and companion early in Bouchard's political life, and soon Cécile took over this role, probably from her mid-teens. Blanche-Corona refused to accompany T.-D. on his trip to Spain in 1929, when he was the guest of the Congress of World Mayors. Instead Cécile, now aged twenty-three, accompanied him. In their letters from that trip they express their mutual concerns for remaining constantly in contact, and especially their sense of guilt, writing that if

---

88   Ibid., p. 3.

89   H.N.Segall, medical records and personal communication

90   Ibid.

91   Letters from the collection of Claire Simard-Odermatt

92   C.E.B.; *Souvenirs*; Papers from Claire Simard-Odermatt, p. 20.

93   Salvador Minuchin, *Families and family therapy*, (Cambridge: Harvard University press, 1979).

Mrs. Bouchard did not feel well they would interrupt their trip and return immediately.[94] Nevertheless, they remained away from home for more than two months.

Cécile describes her childhood with some bitterness, referring to being picked on while going to school in Saint-Hyacinthe as the daughter of the high-profile T.-D. "I was therefore raised in an atmosphere of fighting, envy, jealousy, and hate ... I never felt very happy in Saint-Hyacinthe, any more than my mother, who came from Montreal."[95]

In the same spirit as her papa, Cécile-Ena was tenacious and stubborn. Several people have emphasized how much the daughter and the father had similar strong personalities.[96] At the age of ten, Cécile underwent another disappointment when the family once again collided with the clergy. The priest refused to allow her to undergo first communion because he claimed that she did not know her catechism well enough.[97] Her father consequently decided to enrol his daughter

---

94   Private correspondence; From the papers of C.E.B.—Claire Simard-Odermatt

95   C.E.B.; *Souvenirs* p. 4. Cécile studied in the Convent of Lorette, where she felt that her classmates ostracized her. Each day she ran the gauntlet of blows on the lovely Girouard Boulevard—even today shaded by magnificent century-old trees—to be attacked with pebbles in the summer or snowballs in winter, thrown by children of the bourgeois, *les soit-disant huppés de la société maskoutaine*—"the so-called posh of Maskoutain society." They laughingly shouted: *Bouchard qui vend des patates au demiard*, alluding to her origins in the lower town where her grandfather Damien sold potatoes from his basement in the early years of his store. She was a spoiled child according to her own recollection: "by a mother who feared so much to frustrate me that she left me with the bad habit of drinking my milk from the bottle until six years of age," to the great despair of her father and her maternal grandfather. One day while living at her uncle Domina's home in Notre Dame de Grace, Montreal, while her mother was hospitalized, this habit suddenly came to an end. "One lovely morning, he [Uncle Domina] looked me deeply in the eye and said: give me your bottle. He took it out onto the balcony behind his house, and Pam! My bottle and its milk spread out in the lane with the sound of thunder. I never again drank a drop of milk."

96   Jacques and Marcel Nichols; Gérald Longtin; Nurse Gauthier, who nursed Bouchard for many years after he became ill; Personal communication.

97   From Cécile-Ena's *Souvenirs*. p. 5. "The day of [sic] the Great Solemn Communion was held, I was the only one to stay on her bench while my companions went to the Holy Table...the priest claimed that I did not know my catechism well enough...my father had insisted that I would be at least confirmed...a hard knock for me...whatever one thinks, Damien Bouchard was fundamentally a believer. In the province of Quebec, one has always confused anti-clerical with anti-religious...today [1975] we have gone much further than T.-D. Bouchard would have dared to go."

in an English public school in Saint-Hyacinthe for two years. He then sent her to board at the Trafalgar School for Girls in Montreal. Probably the unfamiliar environment did nothing to relieve her anxiety. She was not the only one to suffer because of the reputation of her father. His brother Émile had eleven children, two of whom, Isabelle and Madelaine, became nuns. Sister Isabelle (of *Les Soeurs de la Présentation*) was born in 1912 and now resides in Saint-Hyacinthe.[98] She remembers having the dubious distinction of being known as the niece of T.-D. Bouchard, and thus being suspect in the eyes of her superiors at the convent.

During the first year of Bouchard's marriage, business was not great. T.-D. had returned to work with renewed vigour, but the income from the printing plant was minimal. He sought the approval of his Member of the Legislative Assembly (MLA) to reduce costs by publishing his paper only three times a week. Since Bernier and Morison were no longer on the scene, T.-D. entertained hopes of attracting more government contracts. He did receive some contracts and did manage to reduce his costs and improve his financial position. With his credit improved, he obtained mortgages to buy the building containing the printing press, enlarged the workshop and installed new offices. He built a large hall for public meetings and for meetings of the Liberal Club. This also served as the site for the "little Sunday Mass" (*la petite messe du dimanche*) and the *Club de la Prévoyance,* which limited its activities to municipal business.

On August 29, 1904, J.-B. Blanchet, the federal MP, was killed in a railroad accident near Richmond, sixty miles from Saint-Hyacinthe.[99] Bouchard was to have accompanied him on the train, but at the last minute Blanche-Corona prevailed on him not to go because she felt that he was overworked. He was very upset by the death of Blanchet. The party chose Aimé Beauparlant to replace Blanchet. Beauparlant was another *rouge* of the old school of Papineau, Dessaulles and Doutre;[100] and was a former editor of *L'Union.* In the federal

---

98   Personal communication. Soeur Isabelle obtained her PhD from Laval University. Her doctorate thesis is on Paul Claudel. Sister Madelaine was also a teacher in Fall River, Massachusetts.

99   In the *Société d'histoire régionale*'s history of Saint-Hyacinthe Blanchet's name is omitted from the list of Federal Members of Parliament. He was MP only for several months in 1904 when he was killed in the train accident.

100   Louis-Joseph Papineau, Louis-Antoine Dessaulles and Joseph Doutre led the *rouges* forces of the 1837–38 rebellions in Quebec. In the 1840s and 50s they opposed Louis-Hippolyte LaFontaine's group of French-Canadian politicians who joined with Upper Canadian

election of 1900 Laurier and his team won again. On the provincial scene, the Liberals made a sweep, with fifty-nine Liberals and six Conservatives elected. Simon-Napoléon Parent became premier and Joseph Morin was elected Member of the Legislative Assembly [MLA] for Saint-Hyacinthe.[101]

At the age of twenty-two, Télesphore-Damien Bouchard, now the president of the Young Liberals, began to be noticed. His friend the tailor Joseph Bissonnette urged him to submit his name as an alderman for the municipal council, arguing that during the past four years Bouchard had regularly attended municipal council meetings as a reporter and was very much aware of municipal problems. Bissonnette added that, with his help at the council, they could implement many progressive changes.[102] The program of their group included revising the electoral laws allowing renters to vote; fighting against high electricity rates; and taxing church property. T.-D. ran in District 3 but was defeated thanks to a Conservative campaign rife with fraud.[103] The Conservative candidate had sent a letter to voters explaining that he had withdrawn his candidacy, that there would be no replacement, and that voters should cast their votes in favour of Bouchard. However, he never *officially* withdrew, and the day before the election, his election workers (and the priest) went door-to-door, encouraging people to vote for the Conservative candidate. The Conservatives also used the old stratagems of not eliminating dead voters from the list and transporting the old and handicapped to polling stations. Meanwhile, the Liberals had been lulled into inactivity by the pseudo-withdrawal of the Conservative candidate. Thus they did not attend to the routine electoral tasks usually done at election time. Of 115 eligible voters, 109 voted. Télesphore-Damien received fifty-two votes against fifty-seven for his adversary. He wanted to call for a recount, but

---

(Ontarian) Liberals to form the less radical Liberal-Conservative Party, which then became the Conservative Party led later by John A. Mcdonald and George-Étienne Cartier.

101 After Marchand's death in September 1900, Parent was called on by the Lieutenent-Govenor to become premier and form a cabinet. He continued as premier until August 1905, when the caucus voted him out of office and appointed Lomar Gouin as premier. This is one of several examples of different ways of thinking about the power of the party leader—no longer applicable today, but prevalent in the early part of the century in federal and provincial politics. Christopher Moore, 'A Way of Thinking: Ideas and Practice of Political Leadership in Canada 1900–50' (http://orghistcanada.ca/files/conferencepapers/2002/5a-Moore).

102 T.-D.B., *Mémoires*, II, p. 61.

103 Ibid., p. 71.

Bissonnette persuaded him to be patient. Another seat became immediately vacant when it became apparent that the elected candidate had another official job. Three weeks later Bouchard was elected without opposition. Thus, at the age of twenty-three, he began a long and productive career as an elected official.

In Saint-Hyacinthe Bouchard held a privileged position as publisher of the local Liberal newspaper. More important, however, was his role as the local correspondent for the Montreal daily *La Presse*. This allowed him to attend meetings of the Conservatives. At one of these meetings, convened to choose a candidate to oppose the Liberal candidate Beauparlant, the chairman, Dr Cartier, noted Bouchard's presence and declared that that there was a spy in the hall. Bouchard rose from his seat and acknowledged that he was present as representative of *La Presse*, and if the chair wished, he would leave and report this expulsion in the Montreal press.[104] Cartier granted permission to stay, on condition that T.-D. report the truth. Bouchard notes with irony that the Conservatives probably came to regret the terms they imposed, for he gave a faithful journalistic account of the speech of the retiring MLA for the county of Wolfe, Jérome-Adolphe Chicoyne. Chicoyne was a Conservative of the school of George-Etienne Cartier who, to the astonishment and embarrassment of the audience, gave his opinion that Beauparlant was an honourable man. In his opinion, the voter had a choice between two honourable gentlemen. Moreover, he went on to express his admiration for Sir Wilfrid Laurier, the Liberal Prime Minister of Canada. The audience received this speech coldly. The Conservative press ignored it entirely. Bouchard reported it completely—and jubilantly.[105]

The train accident that killed Blanchet had severely injured Colonel Denis, the proprietor of *La Tribune* (the clerical-liberal newspaper). When some of Denis's workers began a strike, he sold them the business in order to demonstrate its lack of profitability and because of his own poor health. The printers' strike then spread to the other two newspapers. The owners of *Le Courrier de Saint-Hyacinthe* offered the workers a deal in which they would resume work and rent the premises and press for a very low price. They refused and agreed to continue at their present salaries. Bouchard offered his employees an increase of 15 to 35 percent, which they refused. Therefore, he closed his newspaper but continued to operate his presses to fulfill printing contracts—only the typesetters were on strike, and other employees could manage this work. He was in a

---

104 Ibid., p. 63.

105 Ibid., p. 63–64.

difficult situation because there was a need for a Liberal newspaper in the city just before municipal elections. *La Tribune* was failing, and closed a month later. Since he came from the working class, Bouchard sympathized with the need to earn an equitable salary. His workers also understood the disastrous state of the newspaper's finances. They knew that T.-D. did many technical tasks himself, working late into the night in order to make his business a success. Therefore, he fought the strikers by suspending the publication of *L'Union*.[106] Four days later, he was able to publish again with the help of one of the four strikers.[107] He did not rehire two others because he had ordered new, more modern, typesetting machines that required less manual work. Through this experience he became convinced of the benefits of benevolent capitalism, and came away with a lasting distrust of union leaders. Although he was of working-class origin, he felt strongly that an owner had the right to reward an efficient worker, to dismiss an ineffective worker, and not to be constrained by union rules.

Since he had already been attending meetings as a journalist for several years and, more importantly, since he was not of a reticent nature, the new alderman was very active on the municipal council. Three weeks after his election, council appointed him to a committee studying municipal by-laws. He immediately drafted a series of resolutions.[108] He proposed that sessions be held on Tuesday evenings rather than Friday evenings, because Fridays suited neither workers nor small shopkeepers. Friday was payday, and therefore that evening when much of the population made its weekly purchases. His political friends—even Joseph Chenette—did not follow the lead of the new alderman: his was the lone vote for his motion. Louis Lussier, a reactionary alderman who opposed education for the working class, objected to the proposal as well. Lussier observed that farmers not only had the advantage of warming themselves at the expense of the municipality on Friday evenings, but could also profit from this education in the school of civic affairs by attending council meetings. The audience reacted to his words with an outburst of laughter.

In July of 1905, the young alderman Télesphore-Damien Bouchard was once again alone in opposing a request that a particular firm be granted a partial tax exemption. The company had requested a fixed price for water at the ridicu-

---

106 *L'Union,* 6 *décembre* 1904.

107 Ibid., 10 *décembre* 1904.

108 AMSH, 24 *février* 1905.

lously low sum of $25 per year for a period of ten years. When the request was introduced to the council, T.-D., citing a procedural by-law, insisted that preliminary notice of eight days be given before any decision is taken. Although the shareholders of this firm were among his political friends, he forced the council to postpone discussion until the next session. The next week, with the hall packed with spectators, Bouchard delivered a prepared speech. Having learned it by heart, he delivered it with a passion that surprised his colleagues:

> Next, there will be complaints about the bankruptcy of municipalization, public administration, while instead there should be complaints about the bankruptcy of character and of energy among representatives of the people.... As for me, I vote against this regulation, which I find illegal and in opposition to the interests of the city. Threats of some of my colleagues will not prevent me to do what I believe to be my duty. I don't give a damn for my seat.... My conscience and my ideas inspire my votes and not those of others.[109]

Soaked in perspiration after his speech, he was again alone in his vote against this regulation.[110] He describes the spectators as all sharing his opinion. This episode represents another example of both his extraordinary dedication to the truth as he saw it and the ferocity with which he held firm to his opinions in spite of pressure from his political friends. It was a portent of his whole political life. His stand bore fruit the next month when the council faced a similar request. In this case the concerned principals were Doctor Ostiguy and Joseph Huette, one of the *rouges* and a close friend of T.-D., who had placed advertisements for his plumbing business on the front page of every issue of *L'Union*. Once again the sale of water at a low rate had been proposed. This time the council unanimously agreed with T.-D.'s resolution to double the previous annual rate.

T.-D. began to use his newspaper to attack the "enemy," especially the extreme ultramontane press. One of the most vociferous in this regard was *Le Travailleur* of Chicoutimi. On July 14, 1905, Bouchard published an article by Jules Hirtz commenting on the French Revolution of 1789.[111] While con-

---

109 T.-D.B., *Mémoires*, II, p.110.

110 Bouchard perspired enormously during fiery speeches throughout his political life. When an MLA, and especially when he was Leader of the Opposition, he would often go to his room at the Chateau Frontenac after an important speech to change his drenched shirt.

111 *L'Union*, 14 juillet 1905.

demning its bloody excesses, Hirtz wrote about its great result; that is, a society founded on the principle of equality and not privilege, and based on the "rights of man." The article concluded that free and compulsory primary and secondary education would result in a knowledgeable electorate who would choose their constitutional governments, thus avoiding revolution. Hirtz recommended that the privilege of voting should be compulsory. In the spirit of the time, Hirtz stated that this program would improve the moral and material well-being of the people. The editor of *Le Travailleur* sharply criticized Hirtz's observations concerning the French Revolution, and T.-D. responded in an article entitled "Misleading Pseudo-Patriots" (*Patriotards endormeurs*).

> ... [It] is enough to bring tears to the eyes of those who believe, or profess to believe, that the most advanced people on the globe are those whose homeland borders the banks of the Saint Lawrence River. If, by chance, a French Canadian is honest enough to confess that we have something to learn from other nations, the bigots and chauvinists quickly cry out irreligion and the lack of patriotism. Every new idea brings necessarily the ruin of religion and the homeland; if one dares speak about the establishment of a Minister of Public Education, which exists in all countries with the exception of the Province of Québec, of Spain and Russia ... they write ... that one is after the Bishops; if one comes out in favour of compulsory and free education, one wishes to exclude the teaching communities and make our people atheists; if one speaks of a compulsory vote, these visionaries cry out tyranny. The screams of these so-called defenders of religion are so deafening that intelligent people would think that religion is false and precarious since the least step forward in the realm of ideas will result in its ruin ... According to *Le Travailleur*, a French Catholic should not love France, no doubt because he is no longer tyrannized by despotic kings ... no longer slaves under the irons of the old aristocracy.... In Saint-Hyacinthe the people are educated enough to condemn the excess committed during the French Revolution, but also to recognize that it is that revolution which placed all Frenchmen on an equal footing, made intelligence and virtue superior to birth and class.[112]

---

112 *L'Union*, 1 *aôut* 1905.

The year 1905 was during the period of infamous pogroms in Russia, with widespread massacres of Jews. The Kishinev massacre was the occasion for world-wide condemnation, including that of Canadian religious and political leaders. Sir Wilfrid Laurier condemned this religious persecution in ringing tones from the steps of Parliament in Ottawa while participating in a demonstration of support for the victims. However, once again, *petit Poucet* of *Le Travailleur* gave his view of what should be:

> I would do everything to send away from our dear country the most outstanding of all scourges, the plague of peoples, the Jewish people. I would not persist in the inconceivable stupidity of welcoming them with open arms. A detestable race ... which seeks constantly to suffocate true civilization, to destroy Christianity, to undermine nations, *who carry on their forehead the indelible mark of their horrible crime, and who, deicide throughout the ages, endeavour everywhere to destroy Divine religion founded by Him who with their hatred they nailed to the Cross of Calvary.*[113] [Emphasis added]

At the time, there was widespread anti-Semitism, especially among the nationalist-Catholic population of Quebec, as well as among the English/Scottish population of Quebec.[114] Yet T.-D. bravely expressed the views of the common people who, in most towns in Quebec, respected the travelling Jewish peddlers, dealt with them on a personal level as human beings, and then accepted the established shopkeepers. T.-D.'s response was not long in coming. In 1905 these were strong and courageous words—defending the Jews and suggesting that French Canadians would do well to follow their example of hard work, their prudence and their pursuit of knowledge:

---

113 T.-D.B., *Mémoires*, II, p. 101.

114 See Jacques Langlais and David Rome, *Juifs et Québécois français, 200 ans d'histoire commune* (Montréal: Fides,1986), see also Victor Teboul, *Mythe et images du Juif au Québec Essai d'analyse critique,* (Montréal; Éditions de la Grave, 1977), *"Juifs et Canadiens", deuxième cahier du cercle juif de langue française,* edited by Naïm Kattan, (Montréal: Éditions du Jour, 1967), Michael Gary Brown, *Jew or Juif? Jews, French Canadians and Anglo-Canadians 1759–1914* (Philadelphia: Jewish Publication Society, 1987). Arthur Daniel Hart, *The Jew in Canada: A Complete Record of Canadian Jewry from the Days of the French Régime to the Present Time* (Toronto-Montreal: Jewish Publications, 1926). Benjamin G. Sack, *Canadian Jews: Early in This Century* (Montreal: National Archives, Canadian Jewish Congress, 1975).

Decidedly, Petit Poucet did not shudder when reading of the horror, which the savage Russians of his species have just committed amongst the Jews ... in massacring men, women, the elderly, and children because they belong to the damned race ... Petit Poucet should have fumed when learning that Sir Wilfrid Laurier ... gave a speech at a meeting held to bring aid to the unfortunate victims of these atrocities.... This hatred of Jews, which fills his heart, how can we explain it other than blind prejudice? Are the Jews of today responsible for a crime committed by a certain number of their compatriots, nineteen hundred years ago? ... Does this agree with the words of He who said ... "Forgive them for they know not what they do." Petit Poucet heal yourself before wanting to heal others. Learn that your hatred of Jews is an unjustified prejudice and learn that among Jews there are very honest men as there are scoundrels amongst French Canadians. All peoples are constituted in the same way.... There are a large number of French Canadians who would not waste their time in studying and following the good sense of economy of a certain class of Jews, their sobriety and their sense of hard work. If some become rich, it is because they save what they earn with difficulty instead of drinking it up at the local tavern; many French-Canadians would become rich by following their example.[115]

On December 15, 1905, T.-D. succeeded in having the council adopt a measure to amend the municipal charter. Among these amendments was a project to allow for the taxation of religious orders. He reasoned that the city needed money to build roads, sidewalks and sewers; as well as to adequately light streets and maintain a fire department.[116] But he subsequently lost the battle when a revision of the vote was granted and the resolution overturned. Nevertheless, the religious communities, perhaps because they were frightened, consented to pay a rising annual rate in compensation. Their water rates were increased, and they agreed to pay council a fixed amount of money in lieu of a special tax.

The compromise proposed by the religious corporations resulted from the realization of the clerical faction of Saint-Hyacinthe that there was a climate in Quebec favourable towards the initiative of the council. The Liberal cabinet would not have hesitated to grant what the city authorities had requested. Joseph Morin, a *rouge*, represented the county in the legislature. In addition, Lomer Gouin, the new

115 *L'Union*, 26 *décembre* 1905.

116 AMSH, December 15, 1905.

premier, was open to progressive ideas on education.[117] Gouin even proposed to name the Secretary of the Province an *ex officio* member of the Council of Public Education. The bishops who controlled that council crushed even this modest initiative that proposed the principle of direct participation of the government in the administration of this body, which was not responsible to the electorate.

On November 24, 1905, the municipal council adopted a request drafted by Bouchard demanding respect for the spirit of a contract signed by Seigneur Jean Dessaulles when he donated the Hay-Market to the city.[118] Dessaulles donated this large piece of land to the city to be used as a marketplace. Instead, much to the chagrin of the residents of the neighbourhood, it had become a garbage dump—a place to store used machinery and rubbish. Bouchard wanted council to set fines in order to clean up the area. "I had not forgotten the population of the poorest quarter, where I was born, and where I had lived the first years of my childhood."[119] The future mayor notes: "This date marks the beginning of the beautification of the countryside which I had undertaken … it resulted in the reputation of Saint-Hyacinthe as one of the most charming cities in the country."[120] The municipal elections of January 1906 grew near. In District 2—the workers' quarter—the Liberals had decided to replace an unreliable alderman. In District 5 the lawyer Louis Lussier once again represented the clerical Conservatives in this, their stronghold. Although defeat in this district was probable, the Liberals decided to fight Lussier. In District 3, T.-D. did not have to undergo re-election, having been elected for a period of two years in 1905. The battle was intense. *Le Courrier* succeeded in stirring up the bigots of the city. Some University of Laval students threw rotten eggs at a Protestant minister, Mr. Maje, who had come to preach in the province; and *Le Courrier* published an article approving the students' activities. The same newspaper had also approved the conduct of these same students when they welcomed Sarah Bernhardt—the greatest actress of the period and the glory of the French

---

117 Dickinson and Young, (*A Short History*) point out that the aristocratic and elitist regimes of Gouin and Taschereau are to be evaluated as "conservative nationalists. Industrial progress was the bedrock of their three decades of provincial power…progress meant rapid exploitation of natural resources, low taxes, minimal interference with business, and a paternalistic attitude to labour." p. 250.

118 AMSH, 24 *novembre* 1905.

119 T.-D. B., *Mémoires,* II, p. 112.

120 Ibid., p. 112.

theatre—by throwing rotten eggs at her because she was Jewish. In *L'Union* of December 16, 1905, Bouchard replied angrily, demonstrating his open mind and originality of thought:

> *Le Courrier* tells us that it refuses to see in this escapade of Quebec youth a serious offence. What would it have said if a Catholic lecturer in Toronto had been the object of an identical reception to that reserved for Sarah Bernhardt and for Mr. Maje? The editor of this holy paper would have poured waves of ink to blacken the character of those who would have been guilty of this medieval act of intolerance. One would have seen in his article a mad choice of epithets: backward, intolerant, fanatics, etc. *Le Courrier* ... denies to Mr. Maje the right to come to proclaim his ideas in the province of Quebec because the great majority of our fellow citizens are Catholic. If this reasoning is right for our country, it has to be for another; if it is true today, it had to be true nineteen hundred years ago ...

And with canny insight into hypocrisy, he went on to declare that:

> If the first apostles had been prevented from preaching their religion, where would the beautiful Catholic and Christian doctrine be today? If nobody has the right to spread his doctrine in a country where the great majority of individuals do not share it at all, why therefore do we send out missionaries? ... *Le Courrier*, which well deserves to be the organ of all our tremendously well-known bigots, makes it a crime for Sir Wilfrid Laurier to have condemned the Russian atrocities towards Jews ... he sees the Jews only as crooks.... How little he knows this people! Jews are exactly like the French-Canadians, the English.[121]

T.-D. did not fear to tackle the "enemy" frankly and aggressively. He felt that his role was to expose the thinking of bigots, even on the eve of a municipal election in which the electors had to decide if they were to be governed by partisans of progress and liberty of opinion, or by intolerant people.[122] In District 2 the progressives were victorious, but in District 5 Lussier won again.

---

121 Ibid., Bouchard is referring to Sir Wilfrid Laurier's condemnation of the Kiev and Kishenev pogroms in 1905.

122 Ibid., p. 124.

The day following the municipal elections of 1906, the major issue before the council was the project to construct a municipal electrical power plant for street-lights, public structures and water pumps. The contract with the local company had expired. Alderman Samuel Casavant was in favour of the construction of this plant at first, but then changed his mind, thus influencing several other members of the council. "This change of mind of a citizen whose sincere conviction could not be put in doubt deprived us of the support of some members of council ... this change of heart was one cause of his [Casavant's] defeat later on, when he was a candidate for the mayoralty."[123] Casavant rallied some aldermen to award a five-year contract to the local electric company. They attempted to adopt the regulation without receiving the voters' ratification. Bouchard raised an objection, invoking a clause in the municipal charter obliging council to submit all expenditure exceeding $8,000 to a popular referendum. Since this was a project of $20,000, a referendum was required. At that time, the right to vote was limited to property owners. Thus, those in favour of municipalization anticipated a defeat for their cause. That is, they felt that the approval of the contract with the private company was likely. Meetings held throughout the city provided T.-D. with the opportunity to explain his views on the municipalization of electricity.[124] A young engineer from Montreal, Léon Beauchamp, was hired to submit a plan to build an electrical plant powered by gas motors for the sum of $27,000. The supporters of municipalization managed to receive 141 votes, but their opponents received 176. Considering that the main force of the progressives would in the future be tenants, this vote can be regarded as a victory for Bouchard's cause. In any case, it augured well. "This result represented a success for our cause because it demonstrated clearly that we had the people with us."[125]

At a subsequent council meeting, Télesphore-Damien raised the question of the municipal debt.[126] He had calculated that the city was losing $30 every week because the debt was spread out among several creditors. He believed that it was the duty of the council to request submissions for the consolidation of the debt. "Mr Bouchard states that he does not intend to make a motion to this end immediately. He wants to give the council time to reflect, but he wishes

---

123 Ibid., p. 124.

124 *L'Union*, 6 *février* 1906.

125 T.-D.B., *Mémoires*, II, p. 125.

126 AMSH, 17 *février* 1906.

to see this consolidation, which has dragged on for two or three years, reach a solution in the next few weeks."[127] Some five months later, on June 6, T.-D. once again drew the attention of the council to the consolidation of the debt. He reminded his colleagues that they had decided to study the question in committee, and that nothing had been done. Finally, the committee established some solid figures. The city could consolidate the current debt by emitting bonds for $170,000 bearing an interest of 4 percent payable semi-annually for a period of forty years. Bouchard ended his intervention by asking the chairman of the finance committee, Dubrûle, to give notice that at the next session he, Dubrûle, would propose such a motion. Dubrûle agreed with T.-D.'s request, declaring that at the next session he would propose the consolidation of the debt. On August 3, the council adopted the measure by a vote of five against four.[128] It was a victory for Bouchard, but a narrow one.

At a town council meeting some time after T.-D. became alderman, Louis Lussier claimed that rocks grow with time; in the spring stones were larger than in the fall. The startled council then heard T.-D. say that if this were the case the council should plant stones—eventually they would have a paved road! Bouchard was very grateful for the next observation from Samuel Casavant, the well-respected alderman and Conservative, who in a serious tone backed up Lussier's observation: "Keeping a straight face he said that M. Lussier was right. Last evening … on Girouard Boulevard … he saw a rock with roots at least six inches long!"[129] Lussier was embarrassed both by the explosion of laughter and by the source of this observation—his Conservative ally, Casavant.

The next debate at council was about the purchase of an auxiliary electrical pump for the fire department. After close study of the problem, Bouchard decided against the purchase. He observed that Saint-Hyacinthe had as many pumps as any city of its size, and more than most. In case of the failure of the Holley pump during a fire (this was a steam pump with a capacity of 2,000,000 gallons of water), the city was far from being at the mercy of fire. In reserve, there was the new aqueduct with a Blake pump, which had a capacity of 800,000 gallons, two small pumps with a total capacity of 500,000 gallons, and two fire-pumps available at the fire station. He emphasized that the main pump had

127 Ibid., 17 *février* 1906.

128 AMSH, brought to the attention of the Council, June 6, 1906, notice of motion, July 20, and passed Aug. 3, 1906.

129 T.-D. B, *Mémoires* II, p. 75.

done its duty during a cataclysmic fire in the city in 1903. If before that fire the city had increased the auxiliary reserve with new pumps, it would not have saved any more houses. In addition, since 1903, houses were built of brick rather than wood, and roofs were made of metal instead of shingles, as previously. Once again, Bouchard had demonstrated his serious study of municipal issues, his independence, and his concern with the expenditure of public money.

> Some of our aldermen appear to be suffering from megalomania, this moral sickness, to do everything in a grand style, acquired easily when others pay. Today it is an electrical pump for $9,000, tomorrow it will be a circuit pipe, $8,000 ... the sewer to serve those who do not pay any taxes in Districts 1 and 2, $10,000; next week ... it will be necessary to ask the Legislature for the authority to raise property taxes.[130]

On the municipal front, "our group" led the struggle for good administration and the improvement of schools. The leading champion of scholastic reform in Quebec at the beginning of the century was unquestionably Godfroy Langlois, MLA from Saint-Louis. The *Club de la Prévoyance* invited him to deliver a lecture on public education on May 13, 1906. On the dais were the notables of the city: the mayor; the two members of Parliament, provincial and federal; some sympathetic aldermen; and several major manufacturers and labour leaders. Before a large crowd in the town hall, Langlois explained the necessity of creating a ministry of public education, of implementing schoolbook uniformity, and of establishing free and compulsory education. The federal MP, Beauparlant, emphasized the importance of educational reforms. At the end of the meeting Bouchard thanked Langlois.

Bouchard indeed was always receptive to the promotion of educational reforms. He advocated uniformity of books in schools, a measure aimed at avoiding useless expenses for parents who often moved into different school districts and were forced to buy a whole new set of books in the new district. He also called for the creation of a single school commission and for the collection of school taxes by the municipal treasurer, so that taxpayers would not have to pay their taxes at two different offices. When Casavant became president of the school commission, he ordered book standardization and an increase in the

---

130 *L'Union*, 12 *juin* 1906.

number of hours of English instruction, to the great surprise and dismay of the clerical group.[131]

Just six months before the municipal elections of January 1907, Télesphore-Damien's opponents spread the false rumour that T.-D. would change districts so as to avoid a defeat. They said that he would propose his candidacy in District 2, a district more favourable to someone coming from the Hay-Market. In *L'Union* Bouchard denied this rumour. *La Presse* reported his denial. Bouchard said it reflected the determination of the Knights of Columbus to defeat him in the next election. They sought a clerical liberal to oppose Bouchard. After several attempts without success, they found Mr. Poirier, a clothing manufacturer, a good man respected by all his fellow citizens—a fearsome adversary, at that. Instead of the ten supporters required on the list submitted to the election agent, T.-D. obtained forty-four. Among them were the most important citizens and proprietors: G.-C. Dessaulles, ex-mayor; Doctor St. Jacques, the mayor; the federal and provincial Members; and several merchants, manufacturers and labour leaders. At the end of December, *La Tribune* repeated the false story that Bouchard feared the verdict of the voters of District 3 so much that he would ask his friend Huette to not present himself as a candidate in District 2, and leave the field free for himself. Bouchard replied that Denis, the publisher-proprietor of *La Tribune*, was a poor judge of the intentions of the voters of District 3, since he had been defeated twice when he had presented himself in that ward.

T.-D. regarded this municipal election as the most difficult of his long public career.[132] The anti-clerical Conservatives joined with *rouge* Liberals against an amalgam of the clerical *bleus* and clerical liberals, under the leadership of Doctor Ostiguy. There were two *assemblées contradictoires*—public meetings. Poirier sponsored the first, which took place in the hall of the central market. As he was not a great speaker, he limited himself to thanking those who had encouraged him to run, and promised to do his duty if elected. His speech was over within three minutes. Bouchard rose, declaring that he had come to learn what one could criticize regarding his performance at city hall, since there was opposition to his continuing to represent his district. Hearing no accusation against himself, he declared that he had nothing to add, since Poirier was really only the front man of the Ostiguy clique. Fontaine, Casavant and Lussier spoke in favour

---

131 In 1929, Samuel Casavant and Télesphore-Damien were on the same ship to Europe, and shared many reminiscences.

132 T.-D.B. *Mémoires,* II, p. 141.

of Poirier. Joseph Bissonette and Émile Marin replied for T.-D. The crowd was then surprised to see Bouchard climb up again onto the stage, where he declared that, since his adversaries had not dared to accuse him of anything, he would present his own accusations against them in their own meeting. For forty-five minutes Bouchard let loose, castigating Fontaine, Casavant and mostly Ostiguy, to demonstrate that it was personal interest and religious and political fanaticism that had turned them against him. Neither was he kind to the Knights of Columbus who, he said, opposed him under the pretext of defending religion, which no one was attacking. Their ultimate goal, he continued, was to keep the people in ignorance. He replied to accusations about his vote at the council concerning the consolidation of the debt; about his opposition to the purchase of an unnecessary electrical pump; and about the construction of a sewer to serve the Sisters of Presentation. Surprised by the heat and ardour of his attack, the partisans of Poirier remained glued to their seats. Although the clerical faction had sponsored that meeting, T.-D.'s supporters seemed to be a majority of the audience. Bouchard then announced his own meeting for the following Sunday, in the same hall, and invited his opponents to participate. There, according to T.-D., his adversaries were roasted even more than at the first meeting. This success gave renewed energy to his followers.

At eleven o'clock on the morning of election day an organizer of the Conservatives offered a bet of $1,500 that Bouchard would be defeated. He expected that it would be impossible to find someone with sufficient confidence to cover this sum among Bouchard's friends, and that the lack of takers would influence those voters who traditionally waited to vote for the winner. Eusèbe Morin came to the rescue by accepting the bet. However, the agent of the clericals then withdrew his offer. He reappeared later in the day with a second proposition: while conceding victory, he offered a bet of $1,500 that T.-D.'s majority would not exceed twelve votes. Bouchard's organizers had calculated an expected majority of fifteen votes. Once again, T.-D. succeeded in covering the bet, laying down $500 himself and getting the owner of a small metal workshop to contribute the lion's share.

At five o'clock in the afternoon, the counting of the ballots began. The hall was full, and an excited crowd massed outside on Market Place. The electoral officer declared Bouchard the winner by nine votes. He had won the election, but he and his friend had lost their money, which initially threw a chill on the celebration. As soon as the news of the election of T.-D. was known, cheers and hurrahs from the immense crowd on the Market Place were heard throughout the city. His friends carried Bouchard in triumph to the Canada Hotel, where he addressed the assembled citizens. Émile Marin also gave a well-received speech.

> The demonstration that evening was the most momentous to have ever taken place in Saint-Hyacinthe to celebrate a municipal election victory. The philharmonic band provided the music. About a thousand persons formed a parade in front of the residence of Mr. Bouchard, and with torches impregnated with the glow of petrol … they paraded through the streets.… The procession ended at the residence of Mr. Bouchard, where speeches were delivered … Mr. Bouchard, Mr. Messier, Dr. Ulric Jacques, Mr. Jos. Bissonnette and Joseph Robert spoke. The crowd then moved to district five to the committee headquarters of Mr Messier. There Mr Émile Ouellette and Mr. D.T. Bouchard made charming speeches.[133]

On the day following the election, the first municipal council appointed committees. Bouchard was appointed chairman of the finance committee on January 18, 1907.[134] To be appointed to this position at the age of twenty-five attests to the recognition of his talents and knowledge of public affairs. That same evening he charged the town clerk to place the documents of the recorder's court secretary—who was also the chief of the municipal police—under lock and key. With the help of an accountant they learned that the chief of the police had deposited several sums of money for his personal use, which had been collected for the city. Summoned to the office of the clerk, the chief admitted to having diverted the sums indicated on the list that the accountant drew up. When Bouchard asked him if he wished the council to investigate before taking the required measures, he replied that he preferred avoiding useless procedures and that he would resign. He submitted his resignation to the council in an overflowing hall. The chairman of the police committee proposed that they refuse the resignation, the case being too serious for the chief to escape so easily. The council adopted the motion unanimously. T.-D. then presented a motion demanding the dismissal of the chief and a complete audit of the books. The three aldermen belonging to the Knights of Columbus voted against this proposal, stating that it was unjust and that it denied the chief the right to

---

133 L'Union, 15 janvier 1907.

134 AMSH, vol. 8. p. 689.

defend himself—even though he had already admitted his guilt and refused the proposed inquiry. The council voted for dismissal by seven votes to three. The following month this ex-chief of police accepted the job of janitor at the Knights of Columbus Hall, which confirmed in Bouchard's mind that the man was very much one of the members of this organization. The exposure of this person may also have been the real reason for the opposition to T.-D. as chairman of the finance committee the next year, 1907. The Catholic Church of New England also attacked the Knights of Columbus. *La Tribune* of Woonsocket, Rhode Island, wrote: "This Catholic Freemasonry which claims to be the right arm of the Church in America will taint the cause that it wants to defend."[135] From the pulpit, Abbé Sullivan condemned the Knights of Columbus.[136] He asserted that nobody benefited from these societies.

In reviewing the minutes of meetings of the municipal council, one notes that our young alderman spoke out very frequently. Bouchard had an opinion on all subjects: sewers; licenses; sidewalks; municipal tax exemptions of industries; the hiring of city employees; and the awarding of contracts. In other words, he took an interest in all questions of city management. In addition, he was often the most technically and legally informed city councillor. Although he claimed to be among the majority of "our group" at the council—seven against three—he was more often than not the lone voice for or against a resolution, or at least with the minority. It is not surprising that his competence, his rectitude and his persistence ruffled his colleagues.

On May 4, 1907, Bouchard organized a banquet to celebrate the nomination of Georges-Casimir Dessaulles as Senator.[137] The father of Senator Dessaulles, Jean Dessaulles, had been the *seigneur* and one of the founders of Saint-Hyacinthe, and Member of Parliament for Lower Canada. Later, he had become a Member of the Legislative Assembly in Quebec. Through his mother, Rosalie Papineau, Dessaulles was a nephew of Louis-Joseph Papineau. These connections perhaps explain Saint-Hyacinthe's long radical *rouge* Liberal tradition. During the rebellion of 1837, Rosalie Papineau Dessaulles hid her brother from British troops. St. Denis, the site of one of the main battles of the rebellion, is close to Saint-Hyacinthe. Louis-Antoine Dessaulles, a brother of Georges-

---

135 T.-D.B. *Mémoires.* II, p. 151

136 *La Presse,* 20 *février* 1907.

137 *L'Union,* 4 *mai* 1907.

Casimir and a radical *rouge*, was a prominent leader of the *Institut Canadien*.[138] All provincial and federal Liberals came to show homage to this veteran fighter for the "dark red" Liberals. "The speaker briefly reviewed the party's past and dealt with the burning question of public education in more detail."[139] After several speeches, it was "D.-T." Bouchard's turn (his name was misspelled in the report), and he proposed the health of the Liberal Party. "The speaker briefly reviewed the Liberal Party's past and dealt with the burning question of public education in more detail."[140]

Following the municipal elections of 1908, the council entertained a motion to replace Bouchard as chairman of the finance committee with Casavant.[141] Doctor Jacques, seconded by Huette, proposed an amendment to the contrary: that Bouchard be reappointed chair of the committee. To support his amendment, Jacques drew attention to the exemplary fashion with which Bouchard had accomplished his task to the satisfaction of all, and he did not see what reasons could motivate those who wanted to remove him from the position of chairman. Huette protested against the injustice of removing alderman Bouchard, who had produced such good results at the finance department. Carpenter explained his proposed change by saying that positions are not fixed, and that last year there had been an injustice when he himself had been not appointed chairman of the roads committee! Fournier declared that he was in favour of Casavant because he was a rich man and that Bouchard was poor. Casavant's wealth, he believed, would permit him to be more useful to the city.

---

138 see Yves Lamonde, *L.-A. Dessaulles*.

139 *L'Union*, May 4, 1907. Dessaulles's speech contained the following passage (quoted in its entirety in *L'Union*): "My age allows me, gentlemen, to speak you of the past. My liberal convictions go back to the heroic period of the history of the Liberal Party. For the duration of the government of the Union of Upper and Lower Canada, the Liberals were rarely in power...The electoral struggles of these times were harsh; the most difficult today seem very peaceful as compared to those of that period. All methods were accepted to combat the Liberals. Religion was a great force that was employed against them and God knows what hypocritical abuse was made by some. The Conservative Party gave itself a cover of sanctity. It had the monopoly of virtue, the good, the true principles. It had at its service thunderbolts and threats that are happily now not used...The people have understood, even though it has taken a long time, that it is not those who shout 'Lord' the loudest who will see the kingdom of heaven."

140 Ibid., May 4, 1907.

141 AMSH, *Procès verbaux du conseil*, 17 *janvier* 1908.

Bouchard rose to make a speech, which received so much applause from the large audience, that Mayor St. Jacques had to demand silence. With the bravado that characterized his whole life, T.-D. declared that he would not take the easy way out offered: to leave without protest. He refused to kowtow. As was his style, he preferred "to face the storm standing upright and to receive the blows of partisanship and envy directly, and not with his back turned."[142] (This was a recurrent theme in his speeches, reminiscent of his attitude in seminary.) He reminded his colleagues that from the beginning of his chairmanship he had stopped municipal squandering. For a change, the recorder's court had a surplus this year. At the same time, he had succeeded in decreasing expenses. Despite his poverty, he had negotiated loans at four and a half percent. He challenged his opponents to criticize his administration. In fact, the real reason for replacing him given during a meeting of the committee was that his jealous adversaries did not want to see Bouchard's name noted in the metropolitan newspapers as "Chairman of the Finance Committee," but possibly, they were really upset by his discovery of the chief of police's dishonesty. When Carpenter tried to reply, Bouchard interrupted repeatedly, causing laughter in the audience. The vote was for Casavant by six against two (with Bouchard abstaining). Bouchard then refused to accept the chair of the markets committee, declaring that he was not in a better position to fill the role of chair of the market committee than that of the finance committee. On June 20, 1908, Casavant proposed the adoption of the budget for the current year.[143] T.-D. Bouchard opposed the motion and pointed out that the budget had not been prepared conforming to the article of the charter obliging the council to allow for a 5 percent margin on receipts for unforeseen expenses. Faced with these objections, Casavant withdrew his motion.

Thus, we see that throughout his early schooling and seminary education, Bouchard demonstrated the traits that would characterize his whole life: honesty; adherence to principles; entrepreneurship; scientific curiosity; and an impetuous, defensive nature. He would defend his cause even if he would harm himself by doing so. In the next chapter, we shall describe the political realignments that took place at the beginning of the twentieth century, especially among the nationalists.

---

142 Ibid.

143 AMSH, *Procès verbaux du conseil*, 20 *juin* 1908.

Chapter IV

THE NATIONALISTS

> French-Canadian politics are the politics of nationalism. Only when
> this basic datum is accepted is it possible to reconcile the paradoxical
> extremes of French-Canadian thought.[1]

The beginning of the twentieth century marked a period of political
realignment in Quebec. A new movement was formed, an amalgamation of
the nationalists and *castors*. This movement included some anti-clerical nationalists, but its majority linked nationalism and religion. Its leader was Henri
Bourassa. His principal followers were Armand Lavergne and Olivar Asselin.
Lavergne was the son of Laurier's law partner Joseph Lavergne,[2] while Asselin
was an extremely nationalist yet anti-clerical, journalist who had doubts about
religion and was very concerned with democratic reforms.[3] On February 28,

---

1   M. Oliver, *The Passionate Debate; The Social and Political Ideas of Quebec Nationalism*,
     (Montreal: Véhicule Press, 1991), p. 15. See also Herbert F. Quinn, *The Union Nationale, A
     study in Quebec Nationalism*, (Toronto: University of Toronto Press, 1963).

2   Emilie Lavergne, Joseph's wife, had a close intellectual relationship with Laurier. Rumours,
     spread by the Conservatives, held that Armand was the son of Laurier and Mme. Lavergne.
     Schull, p. 161–163.

3   H. Pelletier-Baillargeon; *Olivar Asselin et son Temps*. (Montréal: Fides, 1996).
         At this time, the Nationalist newspaper *Le Nationaliste*, with Olivar Asselin as
     editor, produced a regular supply of caricatures, epigrams, accusations and rumours
     of graft, calling Jean Prévost, Minister of Colonization and Mines; "Jean-sans-tête"—
     witless Jean. Each week they reported some new crime attributed to the minister. They
     accused him of selling mining properties at low prices to speculators who then resold
     them at a higher price, and of granting concessions to a Belgian syndicate headed by
     a certain Baron de l'Épine in return for electoral contributions. When Jean Prévost
     sued Asselin for defamation, Asselin offered to establish proof. This offer resulted in
     transforming the cause into a criminal trial. Turgeon, Minister of Crown Lands, was

1904, the first edition of *Le Nationaliste,* their newspaper, was published with Asselin as editor, aided by Jules Fournier.

In 1896, the county of Labelle elected Henri Bourassa as Member of Parliament as a Liberal, the party of Wilfrid Laurier. Bourassa then broke with Laurier on the issue of Canada's participation in the Boer War. Laurier was against Canada's involvement, but due to jingoistic-imperialistic pressure from the English majority in the country, he had to allow volunteers to fight. Henri Bourassa had inherited the gift of remarkable oratory from his grandfather, the radical *rouge* Louis-Joseph Papineau. This connection with Papineau

---

also attacked almost as much as his colleague Prévost. The nationalists hoped that in case of success—that is, the acquittal of Asselin—they would be able to induce Lavergne and Bourassa to resign their federal posts and launch them as leaders of a provincial coalition with the Conservatives to defeat the government of Gouin. Even Rumilly comments: "*Le Nationaliste* disregarded all moderation, abandoned all prudence, in the fury and the repetition of its attack…the articles of Asselin resulted in a sensational trial, which in turn fed extremely violent polemics." Rumilly, HPQ, XIII, p, 62. In June of 1907, this famous trial of Asselin vs. Prévost ended. No verdict was rendered—the jury was not able to agree; six were in favour of acquittal and six in favour of condemnation. However, the public and the press took it to be a loss of face for Asselin. In addition, the Conservative judge, Bossé, who presided over the trial, concluded that the Minister of Colonization and Mines was innocent. He also held that Turgeon, Minister of Lands and Forests, was innocent of charges. The crown attorney formally accused the notorious Belgian Baron de l'Épine, the source of Asselin's accusations, of perjury. According to the conservative newspaper *The Gazette*: "It does not suffice to oppose one word against another in similar circumstances. If Mr. de L'Épine has perjured himself, the means to punish him should be adopted without delay. The province awaits the steps suitable in this sense." (*The Gazette*, June 4, 1907.) Because the jurors could not render a verdict, the affair was to resume. But according to Hélène Pelletier-Baillargeon "justice virtually acquitted Asselin." (H.P.-B., p. 399.) This is not the viewpoint of Rumilly. "Thoughtful people would condemn the spirit of Nationalism. By his excesses, Asselin separated well-disposed persons from his cause…. He ridiculed religious journals, especially *La Vérité* of Quebec and *La Croix de Montréal.*" And again, in contrast to what Pelletier-Baillargeon asserts, ("*Elle ne sera jamais reprise*") Prévost resumed his suit against Asselin according to Rumilly.

In the same vein, August Noël wrote to his brother-in-law Armand Lavergne: "If Asselin really wishes to see the success of the nationalistic program, why does he fire on friendly troops combating the same enemy? Asselin is a hateful person, and, unfortunately, he is a fanatic who if he had been well balanced and in a right mind, he would have perhaps been grand…between the success of his cause and the hatred of a certain class of religious people, he will always sacrifice his cause." (Rumilly, *HPQ,* XIII, p. 62).

turned out to be a source of great confusion because many Liberals who initially supported Bourassa became disillusioned by his anti-Laurier stance.[4]

On August 8, 1906, the population of Saint-Hyacinthe experienced the eloquence of the new political group's leader. The purported subject of his speech was the federal Lord's Day Act, sponsored by the Attorney General, Samuel Aysleworth. Protestant Canada supported this "blue Sunday" law, while the majority of French Canadians opposed it. Bourassa knew that *Maskoutains* (people of Saint-Hyacinthe and vicinity) supported his criticism of this legislation. Indeed, the municipal council approved a motion introduced by Bouchard condemning the Aysleworth bill and inviting the MP from Saint-Hyacinthe, Beauparlant, to vote against the bill even though the Liberal government had presented it. The *Cercle Montcalm* had sent an identical protest. Beauparlant did vote against the measure, and had supported Bourassa's amendment rejecting the bill. In the House, Beauparlant stated: "In my opinion the disposition of this question should depend on the persuasiveness of the priest, the minister of religion, rather than the authoritative voice of the legislator.... I am in favour of all legitimate liberties; I consider that the proposed legislation is an infringement of these liberties."[5] Filled with indignation, Bouchard notes that the organizers did not invite Beauparlant to the meeting held just just three weeks after the vote in the Commons where Beauparlant had supported Bourassa. The reason,

---

L'Avenir du Nord called Asselin a "souilleur de réputations"—one who soils reputations. *La Presse* wrote; "Since its inception *Le Nationaliste* has not found an agreeable word for anyone. That is without doubt due to the character and temperament of its director. For him, in life, everything is bad, everything is reprehensible." (*La Presse*, 3 juin 1907.) And again, from *La Croix de Montréal*, the newspaper of the Catholic ultramontane right: "Mr. Prévost comes out of this trial with his head high, as does Mr. Turgeon and Mr. Asselin, who had promised us scandalous revelations. Asselin emerges diminished, with the reputation as a man who seeks to satisfy a personnel grudge through his exaggerated and unjust articles." (Cited in Rumilly, HPQ, XIII, p. 63.) In the civil suit of Turgeon against *Le Nationaliste*, Asselin asserted that he was not under oath when he wrote in his newspaper: therefore he was not compelled to tell the truth. Judge Cimon, a former Conservative MP, fined him and stated that to his regret the law did not permit him to send Asselin to prison. As Rumilly remarks: "Many people condemned the background and the form of *Le Nationaliste's* campaign, as did Judge Cimon." (Rumilly, HPQ, XIII, p. 63.)

4   Laurier is quoted as saying: "Having known Mr. Papineau, I can in some measure understand Mr. Bourassa. Having known Mr. Bourassa, I can in some measure understand Mr. Papineau." Schull, p. 461. As Schull remarks: "Down through the years from grandfather to grandson…ran that linking strain of brilliant, bitter futility." p. 461.

5   From the speech of M. A. Beauparlant, M.P. cited in T.-D.B., *Mémoires*, II, p.132.

he claimed, was that Bourassa's speech was to be nothing more than a bitter attack on Laurier:

> The barbed diatribe, which poured forth from the Member of Labelle against Sir Wilfrid Laurier and his cabinet, disappointed the Liberal partisans of the grandson of Papineau. The bias ... to diminish the Prime Minister in the eyes of his audience betrayed his game.... The gall, which oozed from the whole speech, came from an embittered heart ... for reasons other that those allowed publicly. Mr. Bourassa said that ... the government doomed the people to the arbitrary views of a single man, the Attorney General.... Why then did Mr. Bourassa, this great, this unique Liberal, vote in favour of this law? He justified his vote by explaining that he did it because he knew that this law would remain a dead letter ... who says then that the Liberal party has not acted ... for the same reason? Mr. Bourassa, after having accused Sir Wilfrid of renouncing Papineau, dissociates himself from his grandfather by asserting that the ideas of Lafontaine ... were preferable to those of the last period of his grandfather's life.[6]

Later in his autobiography, Bouchard is far more moderate in his appreciation of Bourassa:

> Bourassa, surrounded by idolatrous admirers who sought to win him to their nationalist cause, hesitated to completely abandon the concepts he had adopted on Canadian unity. The narrow nationalism preached by separatists of the province of Quebec was far from pleasing to him ... I even doubt if he ever was a convinced partisan. His nationalism was rather Canadian than Québécois. He differed from the view of Sir Wilfrid Laurier who desired to make Canada an independent nation within the orbit of the autonomous nations of the Empire, while the member from Labelle proposed the same doctrine, but outside of framework of the Empire.[7]

Henri Bourassa reproached the Jean Prévost for not having accounted for an official trip in Europe, an account amounting to the sum of $2,000. The Liberal press took note that the nationalist leader—Bourassa himself—had refused to render an account of personal expenses of $2,200, incurred in his capacity as

---

6   *L'Union*, 11 août 1906.

7   T.-D.B., *Mémoires*, II, p. 134.

secretary of an international commission to define the borders of Alaska. In a speech on May 1, 1900, Bourassa announced that he was not obliged to provide any explanation on this subject.[8] The press accused him of hypocrisy.

In truth, the nationalists did have many legitimate complaints. D'Alton McCarthy, a Conservative member, later independent from 1876 to 1889, was the most explicit spokesperson for the idea that Canada should be a uniquely English, Protestant nation. Repeating some aspects of Lord Durham's famous report of 1840, he called the French Canadians a "bastard nationality." McCarthy stated: "The sooner we take up our French Canadians and make them British the less turmoil we will leave posterity."[9] The British connection remained a divisive factor in the relationship between Quebec and the rest of Canada. Unfortunately, as often as not, there was implicit in this conflict the idea of the superiority of the Anglo-Saxon race. Initially, French Canadians had strongly supported the suppression of the Riel Rebellion of 1885. In April of that year, the *Voltigers* Regiment was not only honoured upon leaving Quebec City and Montreal, but in Toronto as well. In Montreal, a large crowd led by Honoré Beaugrand, the mayor, sent off the sixty-fifth Regiment with a fanfare. On its return in the early summer, another celebration took place at the train station. But French Canadians were greatly insulted that in spite Riel's voluntary surrender the government hanged him. Louis Riel is probably the most controversial figure in Canadian history. Historiographical research shows diametrically opposed views on Riel and Métis rights.[10] In reviewing the historiographical literature on Riel, one could conclude

---

8   Ibid., p. 166.

9   O. D. Skelton, *Life and Letters of Sir Wilfrid Laurier,* Volume 1; (Toronto: Oxford, 1965), p. 129.

10   Thomas Flanagan holds that the Métis had and have no rights, and that Riel was a deluded scoundrel. Thomas Flanagan, *Louis 'David' Riel; 'Prophet of the New World'* Rev. ed. Toronto; University of Toronto Press, 1996, and Thomas Flanagan, *Riel and the Rebellion: 1885 reconsidered,* Toronto: University of Toronto Press, 2000. Most other historians find that the government was at fault in provoking the Métis both in the Red River area (Manitoba) in 1870 and in the 1885 rebellion in the future Saskatchewan and Alberta provinces. Most also see Riel as a delusional hero of the West. See also Frances W. Kaye, "Louis Riel in Sculpture: Any Important Form," *Prairie Forum,* 22, 1997, 103–133. Ramon Hathorn and Patrick Holland, *Images of Louis Riel in Canadian Culture,* Lewiston, Edwin Mellen Press, 1992. Donald McLean in *1885 and After—Métis Rebellion or Government Conspiracy?* p. 79–104. (Winnipeg, Man., Canada: Pemmican Publications, 1985). Todd Sauve, "[Louis Riel] may have been crazy, Prof. [Tom] Flanagan, but he did the West a lot of good," *Alberta Report,* 25, 1998, 9.

that he was indeed the Father of Manitoba in 1870, when he was a rational leader; but that in Saskatchewan fifteen years later, he had clearly become delusional. The French-Canadian members of the Macdonald cabinet, who reluctantly agreed to Riel's hanging, were viewed as traitors. The Conservatives dropped in popularity in Quebec, resulting in the election of Laurier in 1896. (Laurier was defeated in 1911 due to the collaboration of the Quebec nationalists led by Bourassa, and the federal Conservatives.) In 1897 the provincial Liberals won power and kept it for thirty-nine years, until Duplessis defeated them in 1936—once more after a combination of nationalist forces with the ultramontane Conservatives.

The Boer War strengthened the anti-British feelings of French Canadians. They did not want to participate in colonial wars to defend the Empire.[11] Laurier was very sensitive to the wishes of the whole nation while recognizing the reluctance of his own province to participate in the war. Thus, he refused the 1897 proposal to create an Imperial Council, which, directed from London, would only have served to entrench the colonial status of Canada (and the other dominions). This increased Laurier's popularity, even in English Canada, by appealing to its growing inclination towards independence. Moreover, Laurier refused to contribute directly to the defence of the Empire.[12]

Outside Quebec, the concept of an English and Protestant Canada was predominant. In 1871, the legislature of New Brunswick abolished separate schools

D.N. Sprague, *Canada and the Métis, 1869–1885,* (Watterloo, Ont., Wilfrid Laurier Press, 1988), p. 252, See also D.N. Sprague, "Deliberation and Accident in the Events of 1885," *Prairie Fire: A Manitoba Literary Review,* 6, 1985, p.102. Sarah Carter, *Aboriginal People and Colonizers of Western Canada to 1900,* (Toronto: University of Toronto Press, 1999). Desmond Morton, *Ministers and Generals; Politics and the Canadian Militia, 1868–1904* (Toronto: Univ. of Toronto, 1970), 74. Desmond Morton, "An Introduction," in *The Queen v Louis Riel. The Social History of Canada.* General Ed. Michael Bliss, (Toronto: Univ. Toronto, 1974). Desmond Morton, *The Last War Drum; the North West Campaign of 1885,* (Toronto: Hakkert, 1971). G. F. G. Stanley, in *1885 and After; Native Society in Transition,* ed. F. Laurie Barron and James B. Waldram, (Regina: University of Regina Press, 1986). Diane P. Payment, *"La vie en Rose?* Métis Women at Batoche, 1870–1920." From, *Rethinking Canada; The Promise of Women's History,* ed. Veronica Strong-Boag and Anita Clair Fellman, (Toronto, Oxford University Press, 1997). Nathalie Kermoal, *"Les femmes lors de la résistance de 1870 et de la Rebellion de 1885,"* *Prairie forum,* 19, 1997, 153. J.R. Miller, "From Riel to the Métis," *CHR,* 69, 1988, 11. and J.R. Miller, *Skyscrapers, Hide the Heavens, A History of Indian-White Relations in Canada,* 3rd Edition, (Toronto: University of Toronto Press, 2000).

11   Schull, p. 376–397.

12   Ibid., p. 382.

for the French-speaking Catholic population, the Acadians. In 1890, Manitoba abolished separate schools and cancelled French as an official language, betraying the original provincial mandate of 1870—obtained by Louis Riel in his first effort to procure justice for the Métis. English Canada refused Catholics the right to a school system in the new provinces of Saskatchewan and Alberta in 1905. In 1912 Ontario rendered the use of French as a language of instruction illegal, even in schools where the majority of the students were French Canadian. It severely limited French as a subject of study. "It seemed that French-Canadians would be allowed to remain French in Quebec," Joseph Levitt observed, "but in the rest of Canada, they would have to become English-speaking."[13]

The nationalists also rightfully complained about Ottawa's immigration policy. Between 1901 and 1911, more than 2,000,000 immigrants entered Canada. Only 30,000 were French-speaking. In Le Nationaliste Jules Fournier showed that in 1904, Ottawa had spent $200,000 in England to recruit immigrants, but only $13,000 in France and Belgium. He also informed the public that there were hundreds of agents in England, compared with only three in France. To counter the argument that the French did not emigrate, he noted that of the total French and Belgian emigration of 135,000, only 2,380 had come to Canada.[14] On the other hand, the nationalists did acknowledge the fierce opposition of the French government to emigration to Canada. In his memoirs, Senator Raoul Dandurand reveals how his efforts and those of the agent of Canada in France were frustrated by the president of the Council (and Minister of the Interior), Georges Clemenceau, who addressed a newsletter to all prefects warning against emigration to Canada, describing the dangers of relocating to a cold, infertile land. Moreover, he prohibited the activity of the recruitment agents.[15]

A serious problem arose for the nationalists, since from their viewpoint Laurier came to represent the lesser of two evils. The Conservatives were obviously more imperialistic than the Liberals. Even when the coalition of nationalists and Conservatives defeated Laurier in 1911, the election question was about Canada's direct contribution to the construction of British ships, versus the construction of a Canadian navy, which Laurier favoured. The Tory press pushed

13   Joseph Levitt, *Henri Bourassa and the Golden Calf,* (Ottawa:Les Éditions de l'Université d'Ottawa, 1972), p.6.

14   Jules Fournier, *Le Nationaliste,* 12 aôut 1906.

15   Raoul Dandurand, *Les Mémoires du Sénateur, édité par* Marcel Hamelin, (Quebec: *Les Presses de l'Université Laval,* 1967), p. 141–160.

for a direct Canadian contribution to "dreadnoughts" for the British fleet.[16] Bourassa was supporting the views of the Conservatives!

Faced with his anomalous position on the federal scene, Asselin, Fournier and Omer Héroux persuaded Bourassa to turn his attention to the province. On August 5, 1907, he convened a public meeting at Saint-Roch, at the centre of the riding represented by Sir Wilfrid Laurier, to initiate his campaign. The Liberals judged this a staggering provocation. Bouchard was incensed. "That the Saviour speaks in other counties, all right! But that he dares to profane the Holy Land of the Prime Minister by holding a meeting there in order to destroy him in the esteem of his fellow citizens, that is the absolute limit!"[17]

The Liberals organized a warm reception for Bourassa. Lavergne spoke for only ten minutes. When it was Bourassa's turn, the noise that greeted him became so vociferous that he was unable to speak. Then pebbles, tomatoes and rotten eggs replaced shouts. The people grouped on the dais had to flee. The demonstrators hoisted the organizer of this reception, Louis-Alexandre Taschereau, the MLA from Montmorency, on their shoulders. The supporters of the nationalists did the same with their leader, whom they delivered to his hotel.

Friends of Bourassa announced that their chief would avenge himself against the insults of Saint-Roch. Fifteen days later a meeting was organized in Saint-Hyacinthe. To keep the confidence of the voting public of the region, the Liberals decided to challenge Bourassa, and to do so with local speakers. The nationalists demonstrated their duplicity by printing two types of flyers. For the Liberal parishes, the phrase "By invitation of the Liberals of Saint-Hyacinthe" was included to give the impression that the Liberal leaders had invited Bourassa. For the Conservative parishes, the flyer did not have that subtitle. T.-D. denounced this skullduggery in his newspaper by publishing the two flyers side-by-side.[18]

The Liberals decided that Bouchard would speak for their side, before Bourassa. He prepared his address with care, by examining the texts of Bourassa's speeches. From a 1902 speech at the National Monument Theatre in Montreal, he discovered that the member from Labelle had expressed his views on the education of farm boys: "In our rural areas especially, studies should be reduced to the essential elements. It is useless and dangerous to keep the child who will

---

16   Wade, p. 563.

17   T.-D.B., *Mémoires,* II, p. 159.

18   *L'Union,* 20 *aôut* 1907.

have to continue to live from working on the land too long in school."[19] Facing an enormous crowd, T.-D. began his speech by refuting some of the allegations of the nationalist orator who had preceded him on the podium. He then charged that Bourassa had reneged on liberal principles, that he had himself advocated in Saint-Hyacinthe in 1897 during the election of his cousin Georges-Casimir Dessaulles. While reminding the audience of Bourassa's speech advocating less education for farm boys, Bouchard said:

> For us, public education is the most important question.... Before caring for the life of the cedar, larch, pine, spruce trees of our forests, it is necessary to pay attention to the intellectual life of our children; before dreaming of populating the north with colonists, it is necessary to think of filling the brains of the sons, of our workers, and our farmers with knowledge to keep them on an equal footing with those of other countries. That Mr. Bourassa and his friends shout on rooftops that education occupies too great a place in the program of our provincial government, is their affair, but they cannot claim, at the classic site of liberalism, that they are Liberals who follow the venerable program of our reformers.... Gentlemen, if the province of Quebec, if Liberals, if Conservatives can no longer produce honest men to govern us, it is high time to abolish the representative system. If our race is degraded to this level, let us have responsible government disappear. Stop the wheel of progress, put it in reverse. Let us leave the twentieth century, to sink into the darkness of the Middle Ages. Let us call quickly for the monarchy and create Mr. Bourassa, Marcelin-Albert the Second, French-Canadian King, because we are ripe for slavery![20]

This last sentence infuriated Bourassa, who followed Bouchard to the podium. However, Bouchard felt that he had achieved his goal. The time that Bourassa devoted to demolishing Bouchard's attack gave him less time to attack the members and ministers. Overall, Bourassa spoke for an hour and fifteen minutes. He was at the height of his oratorical power. Despite the torrent of insults and sarcastic insinuations that came from Bourassa's mouth, T.-D. remained happy to have drawn his fire.

---

19   T.-D. B., *Mémoires*, II, p. 157.

20   *L'Union*, 22 *août* 1907.

Despite the hostility of the majority of the audience, Aimé Beauparlant pointed out contradictions in several parts of Bourassa's speech. Beauparlant read a letter from Laurier to show how the opposition used lies, tricks and bad faith. Laurier wrote that he did not approve of Mr. Bourassa; that Mr. Bourassa was not one of his close political friends; and that he had never authorized anyone to use his name for the organization of this demonstration.[21] This letter counteracted the Bourassist story that the member from Labelle was a friend of Sir Wilfrid Laurier and that it was the Prime Minister himself who secretly asked Bourassa to challenge the Liberal cabinet in Quebec. *Le Nationaliste*, as could be expected, reported the meeting as a triumph for Bourassa: "Five to six thousand people cheered Bourassa at Saint-Hyacinthe."[22] *The Gazette* reported the meeting as a "Lively Debate in Saint-Hyacinthe."

> The debate was characterized by personal scurrilities and by acidulous epithets such as political acrobat, mangy animal, wolf in lamb's garb, political football, puppy, demagogue, St. Jean-Baptiste lambs, notorious rascal, thief, new messiah, and political adventurer.... The member of Labelle was set back, however, on the educational question. His opponents [sic—T.-D. Bouchard] quoted one of his speeches at the National Monument to show that he was against the education of the masses, particularly the rural population ... that although he was now opposed to the creation of a Minister of Public Instruction, he had voted in favour of the measure when introduced by the late Premier Marchand, and that his reasons for not supporting the measure now—namely because he did not want a Protestant minority subjected to the rule of a Catholic majority—could not stand, as the Protestant section of the Council of Public Instruction had already declared itself in favour of the creation of a Minister of Public Instruction.[23]

The speech put Bouchard on the national map. The Liberal newspaper *Le Canada* extensively quoted Bouchard's speech, noting that he was a journalist and Chairman of the Finance Committee of Saint-Hyacinthe. *The Globe* of Toronto quoted his speech on August 19. It was quoted in *The Montreal World*

---

21   Ibid.

22   *Le Nationaliste,* 16 aôut 1907.

23   *The Gazette,* Aug. 19, 1907.

on August 18, in *The Witness* on August 19, in *La Presse* on August 19, and in *The Star* on August 19. Rumilly describes Bouchard's intervention:[24]

> T.-D. Bouchard, who entered the municipal scene in the prime of his youth as alderman at the age of 25 years, [sic], was already the prototype of those advanced politicians, full of resources, soon indispensable.... He edited *L'Union* and advocated the municipalization of electricity and the taxation of religious property. Beauparlant and Bouchard were strong enough players. But their body blows to Bourassa only stimulated his witty eloquence and ended in their undoing.[25]

Bouchard wrote that there was no doubt that Bourassa had scored over his opponents in some ways. However, he emphasized that there was also no doubt also that on several points our friends had won, notably with respect to truthfulness.[26]

Many parishes invited Bourassa to speak after the St.-Roch meeting. The nationalists organized a grand tour for their leader, to stir up the troops and strike while the iron was hot. Indeed, invitations from counties, cities and parishes multiplied. Almost everyone wished to hear Bourassa. However, on August 19, the workers of Hull decided not to invite Bourassa to their Labour Day festivities, so as to avoid giving a political connotation to the day. Bourassa seemed prepared to accept the idea of founding a third party by invoking the example of Honoré Mercier, who had made an appeal to the "best elements" of the two parties in the 1880s, but had never delivered.[27]

A dramatic turn of events took place on October 17, 1907. The minister of lands and forests, Adélard Turgeon, resigned from the cabinet and from his seat in Bellechase, and invited Bourassa, the federal member from Labelle, to resign and chal-

---

24 Ibid.

25 Rumilly, *HPQ*, XIII, p. 82.

26 *L'Union*, 24 aôut 1907.

27 Gilles Gallichan, *Honoré Mercier, La politique et la culture*, (Sillery: Septentrion, 1994) p. 52. Mercier won the election in Quebec by appealing to the anti-clerical Conservatives and the Liberals, whipping up nationalist feelings after Riel's execution. The Conservatives were deeply divided by their ultramontane adherents and their anti-clerical elements. Joseph-Adolphe Chapleau led the major anti-clerical element of the Conservative Party. He tried to form a common front with the Liberals in 1879, and again, unsuccessfully, with Mercier in 1882. See J.A.A. Lovink, "The Politics of Quebec: Provincial Political Parties, 1897–1936." PhD Thesis, Duke University, 1967.

lenge him for the provincial seat. (See footnote 3 on the libel trial of Asselin.) Thus, the nationalist leader would be able to present the "proof" of his accusations of corruption against Turgeon, who declared: "They have maligned me in the eyes of my electors of Bellechase. I will be vindicated in my riding."[28] The leaders of the nationalists and the Liberals swarmed into the county. Numerous politicians endorsed Bourassa. The federal MPs Onésiphore Talbot and Ernest Lapointe (who would become the leader of the Quebec Liberals during Mackenzie King's tenure of office) supported Turgeon, as well as "that alderman of Saint-Hyacinthe who had already contradicted Bourassa: T.-D. Bouchard."[29] Bouchard notes: "The organizing committee for Mr. Turgeon charged me with the direction of the battle in the parish of Saint-Charles-de-Bellechase."[30] After a turbulent campaign, on the evening of November 4 Bourassa was crushed by a majority of more than seven hundred votes. He almost lost his deposit.[31] This happened in spite of the interference of the priest of Buckland, a small parish in the county of Bellechasse, who openly came out in favour of Bourassa in church on the Sunday before the election. The three other by-elections resulted in the selection of all three Liberal candidates. Thus, the population affirmed the government of Lomer Gouin in four by-elections—unheard-of results for a government in office.

In early June 1908 provincial general elections drew near. Henri Bourassa's supporters wanted him to stand for election in Saint-Hyacinthe. Joseph Morin, the sitting MLA, had lost the support of some Liberals. Local squabbles sowed discord among his friends. Some farmers were dissatisfied with him. Moreover, certain Liberals of Saint-Hyacinthe were in favour of Bourassa because they believed him to be a supporter of scholastic reforms. These sympathizers admitted that Morin was a staunch Liberal, but they wanted a more aggressive and more eloquent representative. Many saw an alternative in Télesphore-Damien Bouchard. They asked him to accept the nomination, and he acceded to their request, subject to Morin's approval. Bouchard said that he owed this courtesy to someone with whom he felt a close personal and political kinship. Morin agreed to step down in favour of Bouchard, but said that he would first consult the Liberal leaders. Among them were a certain number who were antipathetic to T.-D., Bouchard, perhaps because of his origin from the lower town, his fiery

---

28   R.Rumilly, *HPQ*, XIII, p. 105.

29   Ibid., p. 106.

30   T.-D.B., *Mémoires*, II, p. 166.

31   A candidate had to gain a certain percentage of the vote in order to keep his deposit.

nature, his poor French and his habit of swearing.[32] M. Rochefort recalled a 1912 visit MLA Bouchard made to the grade school he had attended:

> They never really accepted him.... He was never asked to dinner at the big houses in Saint-Hyacinthe.... He never forgot that he had been poor. When he came to have supper with us at l'Académie Girouard to make a speech, he was like a little boy. He ate like he was starved—he held the bowl up to his mouth with both hands, like a child—he had four bowls, and it made us kids laugh. He did it to put us at ease. Even later, when he was a Minister ... he never forgot the people he'd [sic] known when he was poor. He was proud of his ideas, but never of himself.[33]

The leaders consulted did not approve of Bouchard, and Morin so informed him.[34] They decided to hold a nomination convention, which took place on May 18, 1908. T.-D. Bouchard refused to present himself as a candidate. Senator Dessaulles announced that he favoured Morin, expressing the hope that their county, the Liberal fortress, would not pass into the hands of the enemy. He reminded the audience that since Confederation, the Liberals of Saint-Hyacinthe had known only two defeats. The first had followed a disastrous fire in 1876, which had deprived the city of a good number of electors; and the second was the result of a controversy caused by the settlement of the problem of the Jesuit property by Honoré Mercier in 1892. (Mercier had been blamed for consenting to this deal in order to gain the good graces of the clericals.)[35] The unanimous

32　Lovink points out that the political parties in Quebec from 1897 to 1936 were elitist. They chose a strong leader who often controlled the riding choices of candidates standing for elections. This was especially true of the party in power, and that was the Liberals during the period of his study. The leaders came from the *haut-bourgeoisie*.

33　M. Rochefort, personal communication to Chisholm, p. 80.

34　In April 1905, Lomer Gouin became the new provincial Liberal leader, succeeding Marchand. Gouin was the son-in-law of Honoré Mercier (from Saint-Hyacinthe), had investment property in Saint-Hyacinthe, and visited regularly. T.-D. accompanied Gouin to a celebration in honour of the curé of Sainte-Hélène and informed him about their projects of municipal reform. Somehow this early contact may have resulted in Gouin's negative estimation of Bouchard's ability.

35　Yvan Lamonde, *Louis-Antoine Dessaulle*, p. 49–50. At the time of the conquest the British military requisitioned the Jesuit Seminary. Several years later Pope Clément XIV abolished the Jesuit order. When the last Jesuit priest died in 1800, the Jesuits' assets became Crown property. Re-established in 1842, the Jesuits returned to Canada and claimed their properties,

choice of the delegates was Joseph Morin. As president of the Young Liberals, T.-D. assured Morin that they would remain united around him in spite of the fact that among young there were a number of strong, active nationalists. The opposition chose Bourassa as the candidate.

The election was scheduled for June 8, 1908. To challenge Gouin directly, Bourassa ran against the premier in his district of Saint-Jacques, in Montreal, as well as against Joseph Morin in the district of Saint-Hyacinthe. (At that time, double candidacies were allowed.) Gouin did the same, contesting in Saint-Jacques and in the county of Portneuf. In this pre-radio and pre-television age, *assemblées contradictoires*—public debates—were almost mandatory. The struggle in the riding of Saint-Hyacinthe was intense. Everywhere, in both the rural part of the county and in the City of Saint-Hyacinthe, the debates featured Bourassa facing off against Morin, Beauparlant and Bouchard. Later, the police forbade these debates in the larger cities because of fights in the course of which spectators were often hurt. According to Father Benoit Lacroix, the atmosphere was similar to that of today's hockey games.[36]

With the results swinging between Bourassa and Morin, an anxious crowd shuttled between the offices of the Liberals and the Conservatives. Early results gave a majority first to Morin, then to Bourassa. The reporting officer delivered the definitive announcement the following day. Each candidate received 2,027 votes. The reporting officer, Joseph Nault, had the right to cast a tie-breaking vote, and did so in favour of Morin. Bourassa requested a judicial recount, which resulted in victory for the nationalists by a thirty-nine-vote majority. Some scrutineers had inadvertently spoiled ballots by numbering them, thus theoretically eliminating the secret nature of the election. Nevertheless, in the province as a whole, the election resulted in an outstanding victory for the Liberals, who took fifty-five seats out of seventy. Premier Gouin won in the riding of Portneuf by a plurality of eight hundred votes, but he was undone in Saint-Jacques by Bourassa. Only two nationalists were elected: Bourassa, and Armand Lavergne

---

as did the Archbishop of Quebec. In addition, the question was complicated by the claims of the English of Quebec that the original aim of the seizure of assets had been to benefit education. Each successive government until Mercier avoided dealing with the problem. Mercier obtained permission from the Vatican to settle the problem. He gave $400,000 to the Church and allowed the Pope to decide how to distribute the money. He awarded $60,000 to the Protestant community for education.

36   Father Benoit Lacroix, personal communication.

in Montmagny. As for the Conservatives, they succeeded in only thirteen ridings. Perversely, Bourassa abandoned the seat of Saint-Jacques, where he had received a legitimate mandate, to take the Saint-Hyacinthe seat where his win was controversial.

Bouchard's attacks against the nationalists in *L'Union* had placed him within a hair's breadth of bankruptcy. He had borrowed a large amount of money on promissory notes signed in favour of the Bank of Saint-Hyacinthe, among whose directors were two of his worst political enemies, Doctor Ostiguy and L. P. Morin. Morin was a lumber merchant and owner of a door-and-frame factory. He was also one of those who had carried T.-D. on his shoulders eight months previously, after his re-election as alderman. In the meantime, he had become a fervent admirer of Bourassa. Therefore, when he read the denunciation of *Le Sauveur, leader du parti des purs*, (The Saviour, leader of the party of the pure) on the first page of *L'Union*, he became violently angry. He entered T.-D.'s office, showed him the newspaper, and threatened, "I'm going to close you down!"[37] Shaken, T.-D. responded, "You will never make me a *castor*." The two promissory notes that were due at the bank tormented him, but he resolved not to think about them and to prepare his speech for the meeting with the nationalists. Barely fifteen days after the election, the Bank of Saint-Hyacinthe declared bankruptcy. Bouchard's friend Joseph Morin was among the directors, and one of the most involved shareholders. Not only could Morin lose the capital he had invested; but as a director he was required by the law to refund clients' deposits up to double the amount of the worth of their shares. This caused Morin to face ruin.

Lewis Morison had the same financial problems. As well, his health was seriously affected, accentuated by his increasing blindness. T.-D. paid him a visit. Bouchard reports that he was greeted with Morison's wide smile of yesteryear, as though his own ruin was not presaged by the bank's failure. Morison noted: "I expected the closure some days after the elections." He remembered that Bouchard owed the bank a large sum of money. Forgetting his own precarious position, and thinking of his former editor, he continued, "I hope that you will come out unharmed from the claws of the liquidator and his attorney." Bouchard notes, "When saying good-bye, he wished me to have courage. A later year, he died completely bankrupt but with an intact reputation."[38]

---

37   T.-D.B., *Mémoires*. II p. 161.

38   Ibid., p. 181.

Bouchard was very anxious. L. P. Morin's threat to close down his newspaper and Morison's remarks haunted him for some days, and especially at night. Morin personally held one promissory note of $200, and the bank held another for fifteen hundred. The bank appointed Fabien Philie, a member of the Knights of Columbus, liquidator of the bankruptcy; and Louis Lussier, Bouchard's most persistent adversary on the municipal council, as attorney. Bouchard had to take immediate steps to avoid personal bankruptcy, since he did not have the money to redeem the two notes, the entire payment of which would be required immediately by these creditors. He thought of approaching his political friends. He thought of approaching Beauparlant, but he had not forgotten that Beauparlant had refused him $40 to pay his workers. Therefore, he did not dare to ask Beauparlant to lend two thousand. Even Joseph Morin, due to his own financial losses, was in no position to help. Bouchard was depressed. He informed his wife of his state of affairs. As a man of his time, he would have wanted to protect his wife from these financial concerns.

> I had to tell her that we were close to ruin.... Although solvable I was not in a position to lose some thousand dollars that I had succeeded in saving and investing in my printing presses. My financial embarrassment resulted from the bankruptcy of the bank, the liquidator and his attorney demanded payment ... I had no money and the family of my wife was just as poor as mine.[39]

Blanche-Corona suggested that he appeal to Louis-Philippe Brodeur, now Minister of the Navy. Brodeur lived in nearby Saint-Hilaire. She knew that he was very helpful and liked to oblige deserving people in need. T.-D. wrote to explain the situation, suggesting that if someone did not come to his rescue, the organ of the Liberal Party in his riding would cease publication. In response, Brodeur suggested that T.-D. approach one of his close friends, Marcellin Wilson, owner of a Montreal distillery, adding that he had informed Wilson of Bouchard's impending visit. Wilson received Bouchard in a friendly manner. After he explained his financial problems, Wilson lent him $2,000, to be guaranteed with shares that T.-D. possessed in the company that owned the press and his newspaper. Bouchard recounts: "Although he appeared to be a very prudent businessman, I began a friendship with him which ceased only at his death.

---

39   Ibid., p. 182.

And this friendship … was reciprocal."[40] The following day, he proceeded to the office of L. P. Morin to inform him that he would not have to obtain a legal writ to close his newspaper, since he had now paid up. He then presented himself at the office of the liquidator of the bank and paid the balance due on the other note, asking them to inform their attorney, Lussier, that he would not have the opportunity to sue his adversary on the municipal council.

Meanwhile, there was a renewed campaign of defamation by *La Tribune* and its publisher, Lieutenant-Colonel Denis. In order to ruin Bouchard's reputation, Denis made use of the pens of two ecclesiastics who attacked Bouchard under the pseudonyms of "Julien Brieux" and "Gustave Belvel."[41] Their goal was to take over the printing contracts for the publication of several religious newspapers such as *Le Petit Rosaire*—a Dominican monthly review with a large circulation—as well as the *L'Echo* of the Union of St. Joseph, a Catholic mutual insurance society. *L'Echo* did indeed cancel its contract. T.-D. replied in *L'Union*:

> For some years we have had religious peace in Saint-Hyacinthe …
> the clergy attended exclusively to things that concerned it and left the
> citizens to choose in the realm of politics … laity had stopped their
> criticism towards the interference of priests in the struggle between
> Liberals and Conservatives … the insults and the treacherous insinu-
> ations, filling pages, against leaders of the Liberal party of Ottawa, of
> Quebec, of Saint-Hyacinthe, and notably against our director had no
> other goal than to bring back the struggles of the past.[42]

Then Bouchard attacked the abbé who wrote under the pseudonym of Julien Brieux, who "should meditate on one of the three theological virtues: charity." Reproached for his support of the idea of taxing the religious sisters of the *Hôtel-Dieu*, Bouchard pointed out that the *Hôtel-Dieu* of Quebec annually paid $500 for its consumption of water, yet no one accused the City of Quebec of being administered by Freemasons, atheists or the heartless. He also wrote that the law on the taxation of all property (without excepting some religious communities), which he and his friends had wanted to pass in the municipal council two years previously with the aim of maintaining roads and sidewalks, was already law in

---

40   Ibid., p. 183.

41   Ibid., p. 182.

42   Ibid., p. 185.

almost all cities of the province, including Montreal, Trois-Rivières, Rimouski and Marieville. Bouchard demonstrated his social conscience and his concern for the poor, and directly attacked the Church's wealth:

> Julien Brieux sees the touching side of the life of the good Sisters of Charity, women exerting a devoted, noble and useful profession ... but if Julien Brieux took the trouble to look into the homes to appreciate the difficulty which a wife has to balance the daily budget.... If Julien Brieux could and wants to understand the miseries against which a father of a family has to struggle without end.... Should one call heartless those who ... wish to relieve families of taxes which crush them? Julie Brieux should not ignore the situation of our poor families.... If, to excite religious passions against us, he continues to declare that the city of Saint-Hyacinthe is indebted to religious communities, that the clergy is close to poverty, we will demonstrate right here, with numbers in hand, after having established an inventory of the property, land and mortgage loans due them, shares in banks or in manufacturing companies, owned by our clergy ... we will demonstrate that the pauper is not always the one who extends his hand, but very often he who has the hand extended to him.[43]

By drawing attention to the Church's wealth, this article resulted in much backlash. The clericals hoped to have the newspaper placed on the index of forbidden publications. Bouchard, however, had a friend in the person of the bishop of Saint-Hyacinthe, Alexis-Xyste Bernard, "a thoughtful man who did not involve himself in partisan politics."[44] Meeting Bouchard in the course of an election campaign, Bernard affectionately squeezed his hand and said: "I like to receive you. When you come to speak to me, you enter by the great front door of the bishopric, and not by the side door of the Cathedral, as those who came to see me yesterday evening, under cover of the fog."[45] Bouchard understood by this that his enemies had wanted to obtain the intervention of the bishop against him, and that this sneaky approach had displeased Bernard. The campaign to deprive T.-D. of his Catholic clientele did not achieve its goal. His establishment continued to thrive. His finances having improved, he could undertake the repair of the old building he had acquired in 1903. In addition, with the

---

43   T.-D.B., from *L'Union, Mémoires*, II, p. 188.

44   Ibid., p. 188.

45   Ibid., p. 188.

help of his friend Joseph Huette, he bought Doctor Ostiguy's adjoining house, as Ostiguy was leaving the city to establish himself in Montreal. The Knights of Columbus had held its secret meetings at Ostiguy's house. From his rooms in his adjoining building, Bouchard had been able to eavesdrop on the meetings of the Knights through some air vents connecting the two buildings. Thus, sitting comfortably in front of his fireplace, he was always aware of their attitudes and plans. They never suspected that the spy they anxiously sought among their ranks was none other than their main enemy.

A federal election took place in the autumn of 1908. Since Henri Bourassa represented the riding provincially, the Liberals organized themselves to obtain their revenge. Bourassa had met his equal in parliamentary debate in the person of Premier Lomer Gouin, an outstanding orator. In the Assembly, Bourassa had to prove his demagogic accusations against public figures. Gouin replied to the nationalist leader's first speech by bringing irrefutable evidence demonstrating that his denunciations of certain individuals were based on false reports provided by unprincipled people.

To face Aimé Beauparlant, the outgoing member, the Conservatives chose Doctor Cartier, a good physician from the countryside, who had already represented the county in the legislature. Nevertheless, Beauparlant was very popular. Bouchard reports: "His good nature, his contempt for ridiculous convention attracted the silly mockery of his adversaries; he has remained a child of the people."[46] At the request of the Liberal candidate, Bouchard undertook his share of a series of contradictory debates in the countryside, for a period of four weeks. He thus entered into contact with all the Liberal leaders and activists in the district. There were rumours that he would be the Liberal candidate in the next provincial election. Bourassa spoke at a meeting in Saint-Hyacinthe to support Cartier on October 17. The result was clear: Aimé Beauparlant took the county again, with a majority of 557 votes. Although Ontario and Manitoba produced weak majorities for Conservative candidates, Sir Wilfrid Laurier was re-elected Prime Minister of Canada, as the Liberals had won a strong overall majority of fifty-four seats.

At the end of December 1908, the town clerk resigned because of serious sickness. Some aldermen counseled Bouchard to replace him. T.-D. was well aware of the ins-and-outs of municipal administration. The city also possessed competent personnel. Blanche-Corona encouraged him to rest. He had not

---

46   Ibid., p. 191.

taken a holiday for several years due to his work, his political activity, and his efforts to augment his income. He decided to apply for the clerk position. His friends informed him that in their opinion, as head of the civic administration, he would be more useful to his fellow citizens than as the simple representative of a district. The salary for position of town clerk and superintendent of the water department came to a total of $1,500 per year. Again, with his characteristic concern for the opinion of his "enemies," Bouchard felt that nobody could accuse him of having abandoned the role of alderman for gain.

Before proceeding to nominate him, his friends realized that they lacked one vote, from an alderman who stated that he was uncertain. This man later came to see Bouchard in his office, and demanded $500 for his vote. Since this man worked for the manufacturer Payan and Duclos, Bouchard informed them about the offer. Duclos undertook responsibility to arrange things. Some hours later, the extortionist telephoned Bouchard to report that after having thought it over, he had decided to vote for him. Bouchard understood that Duclos had intervened. Thus on Friday, December 18, 1908, the municipal council of Saint-Hyacinthe accepted his resignation as alderman and approved his nomination as clerk of the city and superintendent of the water Department.[47]

Barely twenty-seven years of age, he states:

> My relatives and my friends, who counseled me to withdraw at least for some time from active political life, were not wrong. From the first days I perceived how heavy was the burden that I had borne on my shoulders … innumerable worries due to my turbulent career had weakened my nerves. Also, the assurance of a regular income and a peaceful life gave me the calm and the intellectual serenity that I so needed to preserve my health.[48]

Was his concern a sign of neurasthenia, or of hypochondria? It is certainly surprising to see such an admission from a man with so much energy, so much vigour. His immediate family was constantly concerned with issues of health. Of course, in the case of Mrs. Bouchard—with her pregnancies, and her children— these anxieties had proven to be legitimate. When one examines newspapers

47   Ibid., p. 192.

48   Ibid., p. 194.

of the period, it is fascinating to observe the quantity of advertisements for remedies to cure all illness and pain.[49]

Town council with the town clerk in the foreground, sporting a moustache, circa 1910

In 1909 there were many deaths among Bouchard's family, friends and enemies. In March 1909, Blanche-Corona's mother died. T.-D. had liked her very much, since she was an open-minded person. In his view she was a true Christian. Then, on May 21, 1909, two months later, the Bouchards lost their second child, Adelstan Blanchet, from the complications of whooping cough. In July, it was the turn of his dear master, Lewis Morison. Two of his adversaries also died: Colonel Denis, proprietor of *La Tribune*; and the veterinarian Tellier, the right-hand man of Ostiguy. As has been noted, on May 21, 1910—one year after Adelstan Blanchet Bouchard's death—they celebrated the birth of their second girl, named after her mother. She was their third child to be born alive—a happy event, followed by the baby's death

---

49   *L'Union*; Tablette Baby's Own; for babies who do not sleep and eat well; *Le Rémède de Famille*—pills from wild roots of Dr. Morse; Tablettes de Stuart against dyspepsia, Boils stopped in five days by the marvellous action of Stuart's Calcium powders. Hall Family pills to cure catarrh—acts directly on the blood and mucosa, etc.

on December 8, 1910, from dysentery. These were terrible events, depressing both Blanche-Corona and T.-D.

At the municipal council, people felt the presence of a socially aware administration. T.-D. could not participate in the municipal elections of January 1909 because of his official position. The aldermen in the first four districts were elected by acclamation, but in District 5 there was a battle. Unfortunately, the law was against the Liberals, since in order to vote it was necessary to pay one's municipal taxes beforehand. This law thus increased the chances of the rich. Rich candidates or their friends could pay their taxes to ensure votes. The reform of this unjust system had been part of the program of the progressives for a long time. The Conservative candidate won over the Liberal candidate by nine votes, a considerable advance compared to the election of 1907, when the Conservatives had a forty-vote majority.

Meanwhile, Bouchard's financial affairs continued to improve. When Joseph Morin came to see him to offer him his home on the grand Girouard Boulevard for approximately half the price it had cost, he first refused. He informed Morin of the poor state of his finances. His income would not permit him to maintain such a luxurious house. Morin had concluded an honourable arrangement with the liquidation office in the matter of the bank bankruptcy, thereby saving him from the total loss of his investments. However, he had to acquire some cash to conclude this agreement. Morin told Bouchard that he would accept a deposit of a thousand dollars with low repayments. In sum, "he asked me a favour, he who had helped me when he was wealthy."[50] Bouchard signed the note. He devised a plan to divide this residence into two apartments. By renting out the second flat, he could live with his family in one of the most elegant places in the city while not exceeding his limited budget.

---

50   T.-D. B., *Mémoires*, II p.196.

**The magnificent home of Joseph Morin on Girouard Blvd.—sold to
T.-D. Bouchard, who converted it into two dwellings.**
(From the collection Claude Morin, Saint-Hyacinthe.)

In 1910 Bouchard successfully sued Joseph de la Broquerie Taché, owner of *Le
Courrier*, the conservative paper, for defamation. *Le Courrier de Saint-Hyacinthe*
had accused Bouchard of being a denier of God: *un Renégat de Dieu*. In this
suit Bouchard testified about his faith, stating that he believed in a supreme
being, but not because of the elaborate proofs provided by the priests of his
time. His belief in God was based on faith, not reason. Judge Paul Martineau
awarded Bouchard $50 for damage to his reputation.[51] The victory represented
a feather in his cap, increasing his prestige in the eyes of many of his fellow
citizens. However, it did not bring an end to his squabbles with this newspaper.
In 1923 Harry Bernard, a French novelist and ultramontane, became the editor

---

51 *Jugement de la cour Supérieure, no.* 135, *le* 4 *avril* 1910. Delivered by the Honourable Paul G.
Martineau, J.C.S. D.-T. Bouchard plaintiff, J. de L. Taché, defendant.
Deposition of Mr. D.-T. Bouchard: Reproduced from a political pamphlet published by
an opponent in an election campaign in 1936. *Archives Soc. régionale d'histoire de Saint-
Hyacinthe*: sec. 13, Fig. 1, p. 70.

Q: Did you declare to Mr. H.G. Vaillant…that hell does not exist?
A: No.

and director of *Le Courrier de Saint-Hyacinthe*. Bernard and Bouchard often tangled with one another in their respective papers and in the courts.

LOCAL POLITICS

At the end of 1909, Doctor St. Jacques, the mayor of Saint-Hyacinthe, decided to retire at the completion of his mandate. In his place the Liberals chose Paul-Frédéric Payan, the owner of a large leather factory. He had been an alderman for several years. Payan differed from Samuel Casavant, his Conservative and Bourassist opponent not only in his general outlook, but also in his religion. Payan was a Protestant, a descendant of Huguenots, and dean of the Presbyterian Church of the city. Casavant had provoked the hostility of voters some months earlier by presiding at a public meeting to approve the sale of a private water-supply company to the village of La Providence. T.-D. had succeeded in having the council increase the ridiculously low tax the company had paid to the city. The company had passed this increase on to its consumers, who promptly organized a strike and obtained their water by sinking artesian wells. The enterprise went bankrupt. L. P. Morin purchased it for a sum of

---

Q: You swear that you never declared that there is no hell?

A: Yes, I never said that that place did not exist. As to how Hell is constructed or looks, if M. Vaillant knows, I don't. I never denied the existence of a place for future punishments.

Q: Did you deny in front of Mr. H.G. Vaillant or Mr. Rémi Guertin the existence of God or a Supreme Being?

A: No.

Q: You never denied...the existence of God, future punishments, or Hell?

A: Future punishments, I understand as Hell.

Q: You seem to object to the term Hell. Did you deny any of those things?

A: I never denied any. I discussed the value of proofs provided, and I was preoccupied by philosophic questions, but I never denied those things...I discussed but I never denied the existence of God, future punishments, or Hell.

Q: What proofs did you place in doubt?

A: Different proofs provided for those things. *For me, the belief in God is a matter of faith and not of reason.* [Emphasis added]

Several witnesses claimed that they had heard Bouchard say that he did not believe in miracles, in God, or in Hell. However, the Judge did not take their testimony very seriously since they were all revealed to be political enemies and they asserted that Bouchard's reputation as a non-believer was notorious. The Judge found for the plaintiff.

$8,300. With the agreement of Casavant, he hoped to sell the company to the city for the sum of $10,000. Council adopted this proposal, but it still required the approval of the voters. Towards this end, Casavant presided at a public meeting, hoping to gain approval of the populace. The proposal was defeated by 200 votes against 22. This did not bode well for Casavant's mayoral campaign.

Bouchard opened the mayoralty campaign by publishing an article announcing the retirement of Doctor St. Jacques and the candidacy of Payan, who would run against the candidate of the "blues" and the liberal-clericals, Samuel Casavant.[52] T.-D. urged the population to pay their taxes in order to be able to exercise their right to vote.[53] They heeded the call. On December 14, more than 400 taxpayers besieged the taxation office to pay their taxes. The thought that a Protestant could represent Saint-Hyacinthe at the upcoming Eucharistic Congress in Montreal, and at the centenary celebration of the foundation of the Seminary of Saint-Hyacinthe, scandalized *Le Courrier* and *La Tribune*. On Sunday, December 19, 1909, the priest of Notre-Dame parish preached a message urging electors to support the Catholic candidate. Bouchard protested in his newspaper against the undue influence of a Minister of Religion, and against the two newspapers: "We do not see what harm religion would suffer if a Protestant were to represent at religious celebrations a city with a majority of Catholic citizens."[54] He also noted that the Catholic clergy lived exclusively on money provided by Catholics, who earned their living partly in the enterprises of Protestants. Moreover, the clientele of such enterprises were largely Protestants. For example, the Casavant organ factory delivered half of its products to Protestant churches.

Payan was elected with a majority of 137 votes, the most ever obtained by a candidate for mayor, according to annals of the city, to that date. All five Liberal candidates for alderman were elected, including Messier in District 5. Of the 11 members of the council, there remained only a lone voice of the reactionary group. Bouchard rejoiced: "The old Huguenot, who the clericals had so reviled, is thus able to recognize that Catholic Canadians of French descent do not fear supporting leaders of value ... in spite of attempts to influence them based

---

52 *L'Union, 7 décembre* 1909.

53 *L'Union, 11 décembre* 1909.

54 Ibid., *18 décembre* 1909.

on religious and racial prejudice."[55] Disappointed, the Conservatives practically abandoned the struggle in the municipality to concentrate on the provincial and the federal realms. Thus, the population of Saint-Hyacinthe reaffirmed their liberal roots, demonstrating that their political orientation was more progressive than that held by the elites. Of course, Lovink and Frank Underhill have stressed that apart from party loyalty there was little to distinguish the Conservative Party from the Liberal Party. They both came to represent the business class, at least provincially and federally. But on the local level, on local issues, there seemed to be essential differences.[56]

Bouchard attributed the provincial Liberal victories from 1897 on to their energetic efforts to seek legal recourse when it concerned their integrity and honour. He blamed the defeat of the federal Liberals in 1911 on the absence of such efforts.[57]

---

55   T.-D.B., *Mémoires,* II, p. 210.

56   J.A.A. Lovink, "The Politics of Quebec: Provincial Political Parties 1897–1936," Doctoral thesis, Department of Political Science, Duke University, 1967. See also Frank Underhill, "The Development of National Political Parties in Canada," *CHR*, XVI, 367–387

57   T.-D.B., *Mémoires,* II, p.198.
   On May 19th, 1909, in the Legislative Assembly, Louis-Alexandre Taschereau, defended his colleague Turgeon, who had been blackened by *Le Nationaliste*: "I will say to Mr. Bourassa that he is surrounded by bandits for whom the reputation of a neighbour does not count." He continued by suggesting that Olivar Asselin was involved in sending a telegram signed, falsely, "Lomer Gouin," to the Baron de l'Épine, the sole witness in the Prevost-Asselin trial. (See footnote 3.) The telegram had the return address of Asselin in Montreal. Asselin confronted Taschereau at the exit from the Chamber and asked why he said that Asselin had received the telegram when he knew that Asselin was not in the city. Taschereau had not made this explicit accusation. Nevertheless, Asselin threw himself on Taschereau—striking him and making his lip bleed—without listening to Taschereau's explanation. Taschereau thought of returning blows to his far shorter opponent, but called the police instead. (Vigod, p. 45.) Asselin remained in custody during the night, in the basement of the legislature. According to Rumilly, Asselin fled before Taschereau had the time to put his books down.
   "Taschereau, tall and thin as a rake…left the Assembly hall with a large parcel of books under each arm. Asselin, small and thin, weighing 118 pounds, in an acute rage leaped onto Taschereau, hitting him on the mouth, causing bleeding. The Minister of Public Works had not time to put down his books, when Asselin ran away. Since the assault happened in the Legislature, Asselin was arrested by order of the Speaker. Judge Chauveau…condemned Olivar Asselin to fifteen days of prison." (Rumilly, *HPQ,* XIV, p. 52–56.)
   And in a different version, according to Pelletier-Baillergeon:

The people … often believe awful accusations against public men. The only means to protect against defamation of character is to prove that the accuser deceives … even when the accusation is so ridiculous that sensible people would recognize it … if in the province of Quebec the Liberal party has avoided the collapse that overtook Sir Wilfrid Laurier in 1911, it was thanks to the obstinate defence which the leaders mounted to oppose those who persist in wanting to destroy the party by evoking prejudice of race and religion, through lies and calumny.[58]

The nationalists, with Henri Bourassa as leader, played their role in the tragi-comedy, which resulted in the defeat of Sir Wilfrid Laurier in 1911. Bourassa appeared on stage surrounded by his new allies, giving the drama an ironic twist because at his side was Jean Prévost—ex-Minister of Colonization, Mines and Fisheries—whom he had dismissed in the past as *Jean-sans-tête* (witless John). The three leaders of the provincial Conservative Party also gathered around him. They had come to Saint-Hyacinthe on October 2, 1909, where an election meeting was held to support Bourassa's right-hand man N. K. Laflamme,

---

"The journalist in question reacted…"You know that it is not true." But his adversary maintained his insinuations, while stating in the same breath that he was being badly misinterpreted. This evasion, more than the accusation, placed Asselin into a rage. Quickly, supple as a cat, he leaped…and delivered a strong blow to his honourable accuser." (H.P.-B., p. 445.)

Some hours later, when the legislature had returned to work, Taschereau declared that Asselin's recourse to violence was not a surprise; but rather the ultimate argument for a disciple of Bourassa—the logical acme of a campaign to destroy the reputation of respectable people, of judges, politicians and opponents. Taschereau sat down, thinking that nobody would defend Asselin. But he was wrong. *Le Nationaliste*, and even some Conservatives, felt obliged to declare Asselin a martyr. They alluded to irregularities in his arrest and detention. (In fact, he was a sick man, suffering from a gastric ulcer.) They asserted that it was just revenge for the insult of the riot of Saint-Roch, when Bourassa was prevented from speaking, attributing the blame to the organizer, Taschereau. Dorion, in an editorial in *L'Action Sociale*, an ultramontane newspaper, suggested that Taschereau had deserved this thrashing. Taschereau denounced the newspaper and demanded to know if a newspaper that condoned violence should be distributed in classic colleges with the endorsement of the bishop.

In an article titled: "Prostitution of Justice," Jules Fournier alluded to the condemnation of his colleague Olivar Asselin. He was brought to court and condemned to three months of prison for contempt of court by Judge François Langelier. Liberated under restraint after some days of detention, he was again incarcerated in the prison of Quebec when his sentence was confirmed by the Court of Appeals.

58 Ibid., p. 201.

running in the district of Saint-Jacques, Montreal, against Clement Robillard. Bourassa scornfully called Robillard *un petit marchand d'épinette*—a small merchant of pine beer. The coalition of Conservatives, nationalists and reactionaries did not prevent Robillard from crushing his opponent, whom Bourassa had praised as the greatest attorney of the country. In his efforts to unseat Laurier, Bourassa became increasingly beholden to the Conservatives. Some explained the animosity underlying Bourassa's attitude by accusing him of being vengeful because he had not been appointed Minister of Posts, or chosen as Assistant Speaker of the House in Ottawa, or offered a diplomatic position as Canada's representative in Paris, which he so desired.[59]

Because of his official position Bouchard could not participate in the civic elections of January 1909. The aldermen in the first four districts were elected by acclamation, but in District 5 there was a battle. The Conservative candidate won over the Liberal in District 5 by nine votes. This nevertheless represented a considerable advance for the progressive forces when compared to the previous election of 1907, when the Conservatives had obtained a forty-vote majority. At the new municipal council, the people felt the presence of a socially aware administration. They initiated reforms that had been advocated for a long time. The first problem was the municipalization of electrical power. The contract for the lighting of streets, squares and public structures had run out. The council asked a professor of engineering from McGill University to formulate plans for a municipal plant run by gasoline, since the large companies controlled the local waterfalls. As superintendent of the Department of Water and Public Lighting, Bouchard spent long evenings verifying the submitted calculations. Mayor Payan, himself ex-president of the local electricity company and still its largest shareholder, had declared during the election that he would not be influenced by his interest in the company. Payan then visited T.-D. in his office, where he asked Bouchard if he was convinced that the plan could truly lighten the burden of the citizens. When Bouchard replied affirmatively, Payan himself introduced the motion to the Council, which approved it unanimously. A referendum of proprietors then approved the action of the council by a vote of 236 against thirty-eight.[60]

The struggle of the clerical group against those they accused of membership in or support of the Freemasons continued. In Montreal, three armed bandits robbed and assaulted Professor Larose, secretary of a Masonic lodge. The main

59   Ibid., p. 201.

60   *L'Union*, Articles supporting the motion appeared in June 25, 30 and July 14, 1910.

assailant was arrested. In spite of the positive identification of the assailant by Larose and by three witnesses who confirmed that he had admitted his crime to them, he was acquitted. Bouchard was incensed. "In our province where the occult power of the reactionary group reigns … it was not easy to bring thieves to justice when the crime serves a so-called sacred role."[61] The local clerical group decided to invite a lecturer from Montreal to speak against the Freemasons, naming T.-D. Bouchard and his friend Joseph Huette as members. They submitted to the city clerk a request to rent the public hall. Bouchard, aware that this was a potential trap, consented. On the evening of the conference, he arranged for the hall filled with his friends before the arrival of the ultramontanes. The orator, who became aware of the nature of his audience, began by declaring that it was at the request of Sir Wilfrid Laurier that he would unmask the Freemasons. This gratuitous affirmation exasperated Jean Plante Bigaré, who leaped from his seat and shouted, "You lie!" A huge clamour arose from the crowd. The Liberals invaded the stage. The lecturer escaped. Once calm was restored, Bouchard's friends hoisted him on their shoulders to the stage, where he became the orator of the evening. Nevertheless, the lie affected Huette's business. He lost much of his religious clientele and did not recover from the shock of being accused of Freemasonry. He confined himself to his bedroom despite having been re-elected as alderman at the beginning of the year. Huette died in March of 1911 at the age of only forty-five. T.-D. Bouchard was then elected president of the Board of Trade of Saint-Hyacinthe in his place.

In the meantime, defamation suits against *Le Nationaliste*, Henri Bourassa and Olivar Asselin continued. Mr. Roode of Montreal had two arrest warrants issued in police court against Asselin and Bourassa for a defamatory caricature, in addition to three suits in civil court against these same journalists and a fourth against *Le Nationaliste*. In 1910 Bourassa founded *Le Devoir* as an ultramontane nationalist newspaper, and launched a campaign encouraging French Canadians to boycott banks whose shareholders were English. O. S. Perreault, president of the Board of Trade of Montreal, declared that he regretted this appeal to prejudice, stating that such attitudes were harmful to French Canadians, delaying and even paralyzing their efforts to achieve and improve their position in the commercial world. Quoted in *L'Union*, Perrault stated: "No question of provincialism, parochialism, or chauvinism for businessmen."[62] This corroborates

61   T.-D.B., *Mémoires*, II, p. 219.

62   *L'Union*, 8 *octobre* 1910.

Frank Underhill's thesis that the French-Canadian business community joined with the Montreal-English business community to support industrialization.[63] It confirms Underhill's contention that not all the elite supported the promotion of French-Canadian society as rurally focused, as advocated by Canon Lionel Groulx and the ultramontane nationalists. The nationalists vainly attempted to arouse the public through an appeal against the rising spectre of war. The Navy Law, recently adopted by the federal government, served as the main theme in their campaign. *Le Devoir* began frantic attacks against Laurier and the Liberals. The Liberal press reacted:

> There are colleges where the reading of all newspapers except for *Le Devoir* is forbidden.... Fathers who send their sons ... see them return to the paternal home with ... a political deformation that converts them into fanatics believing that Laurier is a traitor, a renegade, a pleasure seeker, a vile politician, *"sinking in manure!"*; that Gouin is a public criminal; that Lemieux is unworthy and dishonours his race and his country; that Brodeur is thoughtless; that all Ministers are criminals; that all Members, except, of course, for the nationalists, are loose and bring shame to French Canadians; that all Liberals are grafters who put Canada and Religion in danger.[64] [Emphasis added]

The derogatory expression used by Bourassa—that Laurier was "sinking in manure"—caused more harm to the nationalist leader than all the usual exaggerations expected from him. In an editorial appearing in *L'Union*, T.-D. took on the *castors* and their newspapers, responding to their claims that the Liberal Party was in hands of radicals, Freemasons and enemies of the Church throughout the province.[65] The ultramontane press also directed its arrows against priests, against the Seminary of Quebec and against the Archbishop of Quebec. Bouchard reprinted Cardinal Taschereau's pastoral mandate of June 1, 1883, which denounced the overzealous use of the accusation of Freemasonry by the fanatics. The cardinal ordered Catholics, "after having consulted your confessor,

---

63   Frank Underhill, "The Development of National Political Parties in Canada," *CHR*, XVI, 1935, 367–387.

64   Jules-Edouard Prévost; Editor of *l'Avenir du Nord;* cited in T.-D.B., *Mémoires*, II, p. 232.

65   *L'Union*, 10 *février* 1910.

if you have some doubts, you are required to give your evidence to the competent authority."[66]

In 1910 there were foreboding signs of war. In England, one spoke of the "German peril." In Canada, the two great political parties agreed to ensure a common defence. However, Sir Wilfrid recommended the creation of a Canadian war fleet, while the Conservatives proposed a direct contribution of several million dollars to the English war chest. Deprived of his political role at the municipal council because of his official position as town clerk, Bouchard nevertheless, kept up his fierce attacks in his newspaper, castigating what he felt was the hypocrisy of the Conservative leader Robert Borden, and of Bourassa.[67] He reported that in a round of speeches in the Maritime provinces, Borden had declared that Laurier wanted to separate Canada from the mother country through the creation of a Canadian navy and thus was a traitor to England and the Empire. At the same time, his ally Bourassa preached, in French to the Acadians in the Maritimes, that Laurier was a traitor to his race because he was ready to sacrifice French-Canadian youth as cannon fodder for England. Laurier was an imperialist ready to sacrifice Canada to England. Sir Wilfrid Laurier denounced the "beavers" in a speech given at the *Monument National* in Montreal on October 10, 1910.

> These hot-tempered people … are the Pharisees of Canadian Catholicism, those who have appointed themselves as pretentious defenders of the religion which no one attacks … those who have assumed the monopoly of orthodoxy, those who excommunicate right and left, all whose height exceeds by a little their puny stature, those whose motive and instinct seems to be hatred and envy, base envy, those who insulted Cardinal Taschereau alive and now dead, and attack his memory.[68]

Laurier continued his speech by quoting from a recent talk given by Bourassa, who had maintained that he had approved of Laurier's attitude during the Colonial Conference held in London in 1902, when Laurier was alone among the leaders of the colonies to refuse to commit to supply soldiers for wars of

---

66 Ibid., 8 *février* 1910.

67 Ibid., 22 *avril* 1910.

68 Ibid., 13 *octobre* 1910, Bouchard ran an extract of Laurier's speech, and in the subsequent editions of October 15, 18, 20, 22, 25, 27 and 29, he ran the whole speech.

the Empire. Laurier remarked with irony that if this was indeed the opinion of Bourassa, "he kept it close to his chest." According to Laurier:

> Mr. Borden revives the old habits of stating in Ontario the opposite of what his partisans say in Quebec … that Mr. Bourassa and his followers shout abuse and insult the greatest of French Canadians surprises us little … both Borden and Bourassa are prime examples of those foaming at the mouth … they are fools and accomplices who differ only in their rigidity, the colour and the length of their hair.[69]

During the months of August and September, T.-D. continued his attacks against Bourassa, and now also against Prévost—the former enemy and current partner, *Jean-sans-tête*. The headlines of *L'Union* read: "Blue Hysteria" on August 13; "The Babies—*Les Crèchards*" on August 26; and "Do not Falsify History" on August 31. In an article entitled "Handful of Truths," Bouchard accused Bourassa of agreeing to renounce his opposition to a bill establishing the new Western provinces in 1905, if Laurier appointed him Assistant Speaker of the Parliament.[70] Beauparlant offered a challenge to Bourassa: if the latter could prove beyond doubt that by adopting the Canadian Navy Bill the autonomy of Canada would be diminished in any way, and if he could prove that according to the bill service in the navy would be compulsory, he would resign his seat and defy Bourassa to run against him.[71] Bourassa refused the challenge. Nevertheless, Bourassa's demagogic and inflammatory ability to move crowds was legendary and remained undiminished. He warned his flock:

> You will also pay a tax of blood. Each father who watches his child grow up, who hopes for a rosy future for him, who holds him dearly, and after having given him the best of his being, the best of his love, and who lives only for him, every mother can say that the fruit of her womb will be thrown into bloody battles, that he will run shivering between bullets, and that his brown or blonde head covered in blood, sliced off by a sword, with a moan, unheard, in a foreign land.[72]

And again:

---

69   Ibid., 22 *avril* 1910.

70   Ibid., 8 *septembre* 1910.

71   Ibid., 13 *octobre* 1910.

72   T.-D.B., *Mémoires*, II, p. 224.

Seven piastres for the child who will be born tomorrow and who will be sent to slaughter in China, to Japan, or elsewhere. But at the moment of harvest, the agent of this paternalistic government will come knocking at the door and will say to the robust father and to all his sons: leave your house because England, or a group of speculators, demands your flesh and blood to enlarge its territory or to promote an enterprise.[73]

During 1910 and 1911 this inflammatory rhetoric gave rise to passionate responses in the Liberal press. Bourassa and *Le Devoir* were regularly criticized: "Can anyone match the incomparable member of Saint-Hyacinthe, a prodigious speaker … who knows how to visualize cannon fodder and glimpse into the wombs of Canadian mothers?"[74] The violence of diatribes against Laurier increased with the approach of an expected federal election scheduled for September 21, 1911. "If Lavergne is a beaver, Sir Wilfrid should be classified in another category of rodents, those disgusting beasts."[75] In the Liberal newspaper's reply, entitled "Bourassa, There's the Enemy," "Ajax" comments on the by-election in Drummond-Arthabaska, where the Conservative-nationalist candidate had just won:

He [Bourassa] can be proud of his work … it is … a steep slide for the grandson of a seigneur, to become a bum…. They used the most shameful underhanded guile, the most dishonourable falsehoods … They appealed to the emotion of the voters by fantastic tales, the most atrocious lies…. He used the opportunity to take his revenge on the insult to his self esteem when Sir Wilfrid Laurier refused to allow him to eat at the ministerial table … he is, all at the same time, boastful, a liar, and a hypocrite.[76].

And, under the title "The Work of Bourassa," "Ajax" writes:

For 15 years French-Canadians have been able to consider political problems from the viewpoint of the whole of Canada and not from the viewpoint limited to their province alone. Bourassa has narrowed

---

73   *Le Devoir, 8 aôut* 1910.

74   Article signed "Ajax"; *De la Vigie;* cited in *L'Union,* 18 *octobre* 1910. (From the style, one might assume that "Ajax" was T.-D. Bouchard.)

75   Article in *Le Soleil; "Jugez-les";* cited in *L'Union,* 20 *octobre* 1910.

76   Article; De La Vigie cited in *L'Union,* 10 *novembre* 1910.

their public enthusiasm.... For 15 years Laurier worked towards the union of the races ... towards religious peace ... Bourassa has concentrated on race ... he has united Protestants against Catholics.... For 15 years, there was a spirit of respect and esteem between religious and civil authority ... Bourassa has spit into the eyes of our magistrates ... he has drooled on our Ministers ... he has dragged down in the mud some of our most remarkable men.... for 15 years our clergy, obeying the order of Our Holy Father, confined themselves to the exercise of holy functions and left the political arena. Bourassa led several members of the clergy onto this terrain, where their cassocks dirty the Church ... Bourassa spreads discord and disunion, he has created a considerable uneasiness between the English and French clergy ... he has kindled an internal war within the Church, fruitful only in ominous results for the Church and deplorable for the faithful. Here is the man whom it is necessary to crush to save our country from civil war, save our province from shame, save our religion from ruin.[77]

The quarrel between English and French Catholics in Ontario schools also contributed to inflame the thoughts of the peoples of Quebec and Ontario. Bishop Fallon of London, Ontario, did not believe in the effectiveness of bilingual schools. Bourassa accused the bishop of narrow-mindedness and fanaticism. The struggle against this prelate was keen. It provided nationalistic orators with a theme and served to revive hatred against all who did not speak the French language—even Catholics.[78] During the Eucharistic Congress of 1910 Bourassa addressed the crowd from the pulpit of the metropolitan church. In response to Monsignor Bourne, Archbishop of Westminster, Bourassa dramatically contested his approach to language. "Providence wished the principal group of this French Catholic colonization to constitute a corner of the earth where the social, religious, and political state approaches most closely that which the Roman and Apostolic Catholic Church teaches us is the most desirable state of societies." He then exclaimed: "For the love of God, do not take the French language away from us."[79]

---

77   Ibid., cited *in L'Union*, 15 *novembre* 1910.

78   There are many references in the clerical literature that the greatest threat to French-Canadian Catholicism was the English-speaking Irish Catholics. See Chapter ten, footnote 53.

79   Henri Bourassa, *Religion, Langue, Nationalité*, (Montréal: Le Devoir, 1910), p. 15.

While the federal election in Drummond-Arthabaska of October 1910 resulted in a victory for the nationalists, the provincial by-elections in the ridings of Drummondville in March 1910 and in Saint-Jean in December were victories for the provincial Liberals. Bourassa had taken an active part in the election campaigns. The Liberals, who had been despondent in November, regained their battle spirit when the December victory took place. The politico-religious group of the clergy was not content to work against Sir Wilfrid Laurier from the shadows. They carried out a campaign in which their presence was conspicuous. Clerical intervention was so evident that the brother of the Liberal candidate—one of the leaders of the Catholic Youth—complained bitterly of this undue influence.

The Nationalists/Conservatives of Saint-Hyacinthe announced that Ernest Guimond would be their candidate in December 1910 for the upcoming federal general elections. He had previously run against Beauparlant, the outgoing Liberal member. On August 6, 1911, Aimé Beauparlant delivered "one of the most fiery harangues of his life," to the cheers and applause of the crowd.[80] Beauparlant had not been feeling well before this meeting and caught a cold while on the platform. He then took to bed. A week later, before an enthusiastic crowd of thirty thousand, other local Liberal leaders held forth against the Nationalists/Conservatives. *Le Devoir* accused T.-D. Bouchard of organizing this slap in the face of the nationalists. Beauparlant died on August 19 of pulmonary complications from his cold. The Liberals hastily choose Louis-Joseph Gauthier, an ex-MP from Assumption, as his replacement. This was unfortunate for Bouchard because Gauthier was to become his secret enemy.

On August 1 Laurier launched a manifesto to the Canadian people in which he explained why the Liberal Party supported a policy of trade reciprocity. He outlined the long history of support for reciprocity in Canada—both before and after Confederation, both by Liberals and by Conservatives. Nevertheless, the elections of September 21, 1911, resulted in a victory for the Nationalists/Conservatives. Sir Robert Borden became Prime Minister. The irony is that it took the combined forces of the Orange Order in Ontario and the nationalists in Quebec to succeed in evicting Laurier after fifteen years in power. In Ontario the Conservatives won seventy of eighty-five seats. In Quebec the Nationalist/Conservative coalition won twenty-five of sixty-three seats, although in Saint-Hyacinthe the Liberal candidate Gauthier won. The results were a great

---

80 T.-D.B., *Mémoires,* II, p. 233.

disappointment for Laurier, the Liberals and Bouchard, who lamented: "All these fanatics, the nationalists, and the Tory jingoists obtained their goal."[81]

Towards the end of December 1911, Bourassa put out feelers to the new Conservative government, to obtain the post of Canadian commissioner in Paris, a post it was said he had solicited in vain during the reign of Laurier. In spite of the opposition of Samuel Hughes—Minister of Defence and spokesman for the jingoistic Orangemen—the cabinet ratified his request. The paradox is that the secularist French government flatly refused to ratify this nomination. Bourassa blamed the cabinet rather than the French government. *Le Soleil* declared that Bourassa "felt a such disappointment that he took after the ministers unfavourable to his application.... The great master, having no favours to hope for from the cabinet, declares war on it."[82]

After his provincial victory in 1908, Bourassa had disappeared in Europe for several months without communicating with his troops.[83] In 1911, he had the same reaction—withdrawal from active political life. His behaviour provoked disarray among the Conservative nationalists of Quebec. No one could understand Bourassa's strange silence. He refused a cabinet post and active leadership in the governing coalition. He also rejected calls to create a nationalist political party, a strategy that left his forces in a state of disorganization.[84] Bourassa declared that nationalism was not a political party, but a simple movement (*un mouvement vers la crèche*—a movement towards the crib, quipped Laurier). The imperialistic policy of the Borden government began to discredit the Conservative Party in Quebec. Later, as a result of the conscription crisis of 1917 the country became even more divided. The federal Conservatives became the English-Canadian party, and the Liberals became the French-Canadian party. By then Bourassa had been long denouncing those members from Quebec who had accepted posts in Borden's cabinet, calling them sellouts. Twenty-two nationalists won seats. Only five remained faithful to Bourassa. Bourassa claimed that the others attended to their personal interests by accepting cabinet posts. But what were his followers to do in the face of his strange refusal to lead them? It is an interesting thought

81   *L'Union*, 23 *septembre* 1911.

82   *Le Soleil* cited in T.-D.B., *Mémoires*, II, p. 266.

83   H.P.-B., p. 409–410.

84   L.-D.-R., p. 564.

to compare Louis-Joseph Papineau, Henri Bourassa and René Levesque—all charismatic nationalist leaders whose stars faded, seemingly before their time.

All the while, the local press continued its campaign against T.-D. He retaliated in his newspaper and brought suit against those who defamed him. At the beginning of 1911 he won two suits, against L. P. Morin and de la Broquerie Taché. As part of his duties as town clerk, Bouchard was also secretary of the evaluation office. In 1911 he had made new estimates of real estate values. G.-C. Dessaulles owned a property of 140 *arpents*. By virtue of old municipal laws, this area benefited from tax exemption. Bouchard, with the support of the reform group, decreed a special tax levy on all property. Not wanting to be accused of favouritism, they fixed the overall value of Dessaulles's property at $23,500. Dessaulles protested, finding this figure exaggerated. After public hearings, the municipal council approved Bouchard's decision. Dessaulles appealed to the Superior Court. Judge Martineau concluded that the evaluation was reasonable. In court T.-D. encouraged the city's attorney to ask if the plaintiff was willing to sell his property for a price less than that of the evaluation. He replied in the negative. T.-D. then had the lawyer ask if he would accept to sell for the price indicated on the roll, $23,500. This time he replied in the affirmative. Meeting Dessaulles in the hallway after the hearing, Bouchard asked him if he was serious when he had declared that he would accept this price. Receiving an affirmative reply, Bouchard told him that if he had enough money he would buy the property himself. Dessaulles responded in a cheerful way: "I don't need money. Find a friend who will advance you $2,500. I will wait for the payment of the balance. I have confidence in you." Bouchard, commenting on this incident, writes: "This perfect gentleman had understood that despite the esteem that I felt for him, I had not hesitated to do my duty. He forgot the personal wrong I had caused him."[85] T.-D. saw an exceptional opportunity to earn a small fortune. A more favourable site for an anticipated spread of housing in Saint-Hyacinthe did not exist. In partnership with both the protonotary Albini Beauregard and the notary Victor Morin of Montreal, he formed a company of equal shares, and bought the property. He then organized a contest to choose a name for the district, with concurrent publicity. On July 1, 1911, the partners proceeded to the distribution of prizes. The name selected was "Bourg-Joli." In a single afternoon their agents sold lots at a price totalling double what they had paid for the property. In addition, they still had four-fifths of the property remain-

---

85   T.-D.B., *Mémoires*, II, p. 241.

ing for future sales. Bouchard became a real estate entrepreneur, and remained one throughout his life. He cherished the concept of free enterprise and the independence permitted by wealth. "Later, I bought the shares of my two associates ... the property increased in value ... it became a real gold mine.... These worldly goods have allowed me to enjoy a certain independence of character and permit me to express my opinions without fearing to suffer materially ... I acquired them due to the open-handedness of the seigneur Dessaulles."[86] This event demonstrates the linkage that Bouchard made between financial security and political/journalistic independence.

In December Bouchard's newspaper became a weekly. The competition from daily metropolitan newspapers with large circulations had become too intense. At the same time, he changed the name of the newspaper: *L'Union* became *Le Clairon—The Bugle*—appearing for the first time on January 2, 1912. Bouchard announced the principles of the new newspaper, which were similar to those in his previous announcement made when taking over *L'Union* in 1904. "Our newspaper will be liberal. We have faith in true liberal principles for the safeguard of our national and religious rights, and we will be ready to fight for these principles, towards and against all."[87] Again, he repeats the themes of battle and fighting.

From the beginning of 1912, thoughts turned to the upcoming spring provincial elections. The Liberals were divided. The reformers had chosen Télesphore-Damien Bouchard as the candidate, but the elite—the "bourgeois" of the upper town—tried to block his nomination. His political attitudes in general, his policy in favour of the municipalization of public utilities, and his role in having the municipal council adopt measures to suppress graft and favouritism in the awarding of contracts for public works, alienated the support of those dealing with government. The Conservative-clerical nationalist coalition undertook a campaign of disparagement. In a humorous column in *La Tribune*, an editor reported that he had met Damien Bouchard on Girouard Blvd., holding a rosary in his hand and reciting prayers to St. Joseph. Father Laurence, a priest from the countryside around Saint-Hyacinthe, and a friend of T.-D., wrote a letter of protest to the editor of *La Tribune*. The newspaper retaliated in a violent article, calling the priest naive. Father Constant Doyon, after two years in Fall River, Massachusetts, returned to Saint-Hyacinthe and delivered a

---

86   Ibid., p. 242.

87   *Le Clairon, 2 janvier* 1912.

sermon at the Notre-Dame Church against the Knights of Colombus. This constituted a second clerical support for Bouchard. (Father Doyon was the priest who had officiated at his wedding in 1904.)

Henri Bourassa seemed ambivalent about returning as MLA representing Saint-Hyacinthe. He was disappointed by the behaviour of his troops, specifically in what he determined was the collaboration of twenty-two of the nationalist/ Conservative members with the Borden government. He was also annoyed by the hot reception he had received from the electorate of Saint-Hyacinthe during the meeting organized after the turbulent reception of Sir Wilfrid Laurier in Montreal. His popularity was in decline. All these factors played a role in his decision not to stand again. In April of 1912, Henri Bourassa declared that he had retired from politics because he was "disgusted with the greed of his compatriots." Some months later, he published a violent article in *Le Devoir* in which he explained what had incited him to proclaim his *Non-Serviam*. He decried the behaviour of politicians and was less than complimentary to the high clergy. This attracted a rebuke from Abbé Groulx's ultramontane *La Croix*, which had previously idolized him: "This journalist ... who accuses our spiritual superiors to be passive witnesses of the obliteration of morals ... We do not remember having read ... an insinuation as wicked towards the Bishops of the Province of Quebec."[88]

The Conservatives again choose Guimond as their candidate. L. J. Gauthier had just defeated him in the federal election. During the campaign, Bouchard's adversaries raised the issue of age. He was thirty years old. They also implied that his election would displease the Church. They whispered about his low birth in the lower town; of his being the son of a shoemaker and the grandson of a water-carrier. His enemies claimed that his candidacy should bring about a motion asking for his resignation as town clerk in the council. This placed him in a dilemma. The revenue from the newspaper and the presses was not sufficient to make ends meet. His salary from the city was the lone sure source of revenue. He had just moved into Morin's house with the concomitant expenses of converting it into two apartments. Therefore, because of the possibility that he might lose the election, he hesitated to resign his municipal position. Blanche-Corona advised him to be optimistic. He decided to resign if the party accepted him as the candidate.

---

88   T.-D.B, *Mémoires,* III, p 48–49.

At the last moment, the private electricity company used another ruse to oppose his candidacy. It spread the rumour that the motors of the municipal energy supply were not powerful enough to operate all the fire pumps. Bouchard rushed to disprove the rumour, organizing a general alarm on April 16. The regular and voluntary firemen turned on all eight lines of hose. All came into action at the same time. The new central pump had no difficulty in providing the necessary output. At a distance of one mile from the central pump, the pressure of water remained constant. The chief of the fire department declared that the system could even handle ten more hoses. This demonstration, carried out in front of many curious spectators, convinced the population that T.-D.'s calculations had been correct. The following Monday Télesphore-Damien Bouchard was unanimously chosen candidate of the Liberal Party for the seat in Saint-Hyacinthe, and he resigned his position as town clerk.

Senator Raoul Dandurand, a veteran Liberal Party leader, was the featured speaker at the first *assemblée contradictoire* for Bouchard. He declared that he was happy the party chose him to support Télesphore-Damien Bouchard. His presence disputed the claims of Bouchard's adversaries, who had circulated a rumour that no important personality would come to speak in his favour. The clergy were forced to curtail their comments because the bishop, Monsignor Bernard, was against the intervention of priests in temporal affairs. In fact, he seemed to be partial to Bouchard. The battle was extremely difficult, but on May 15, 1912, the riding of Saint-Hyacinthe elected Télesphore-Damien Bouchard as its representative to the Legislative Assembly with a majority of ninty votes. Overall, the Liberal government of Sir Lomar Gouin remained in power with a forty-two-seat majority. Bouchard proudly wrote: "Laurier was avenged … the water-carrier's grandson followed the grandson of the seigneur of Montebello to Parliament Hill."[89]

In this chapter, we have seen the rise and fall of the Bourassa nationalists on the national and provincial scenes from 1900 to 1912. Télesphore-Damien's political career advanced from alderman, to town clerk, to leader of the Liberal Party in Saint-Hyacinthe, and finally to MLA representing his native city.

---

89   T.-D. B., *Mémoires*, II, p. 281.

D. T. Bouchard, Candidat Liberal, 1912

(Note: This is the original campaign picture with his name as "D. T.")

Chapter V

MEMBER OF THE LEGISLATIVE ASSEMBLY

When the electors of Saint-Hyacinthe chose Télesphore-Damien Bouchard, then only thirty years old, to represent them at the Legislative Assembly of Quebec, he could not have been prouder. While congratulating him, his father, now fifty-nine, remembered the prediction made by Honoré Mercier when his son was a baby—that one day he would sit in the Legislative Assembly.[1] Bouchard would go on to represent his riding for almost thirty years. After this, his first provincial victory, the Liberal supporters of Saint-Hyacinthe celebrated on the great public square. He met a delirious crowd, which celebrated the return of the district to the party of the *rouges*. It was an unforgettable evening.

On July 1, 1912, Bouchard was the guest speaker of the Saint Jean-Baptiste Society. He called his speech *Vers les plus haut sommets*—"To the Greatest Heights."[2] He praised the French-Canadian people, their patron saint and the founder of the society, Ludger Duvernay. He paid tribute to the patriots of 1837–38, and to the vocation of "our race." With flowery imagery he declared; "This vocation is to maintain alight on the alabaster snow of our winters and the green emerald rug of our Canadian summers the sacred torch of French and Catholic civilization."[3] However, he cautioned the audience that there are people who ruin St. Jean-Baptiste celebrations by yielding to the inclination to exaggerate by voicing "outrageous praise" of the "race," creating falsehoods by embellishing its qualities without even making the least allusion to national weaknesses. He condemned chauvinism, a "hypertrophy of patriotism." In a

---

1   T.-D.B., *Mémoires*, III, p. 31.

2   Speech given for the celebration of St. Jean-Baptiste Day in Saint-Hyacinthe, July 1, 1912. *L'Imprimerie* Yamaska. ANQ, *Fonds* Bouchard, P-10/24.

3   T.-D. B., *Mémoires*, II, p.12. and ANQ, *Fonds* Bouchard, P-10/24.

comment that probably did not endear him to the majority of supporters of the society, he warned his compatriots that:

> We must be careful to avoid chauvinism, that hypertrophy of patrio-
> tism, which paralyses progress by making people believe that they
> have attained the summit of their greatness. It is true that we have
> a history about which we have the right to be proud. In spite of all
> adverse events we have succeeded in preserving our faith, our lan-
> guage, and our laws. But … we have weaknesses, which have cost a
> lot.[4]

Bouchard went on to blame lack of education as a cause of French-Canadian emigration to "foreign soil." He did congratulate the province on the recent improvements in education and ended his twenty-six-page speech by express-ing the wish that "a young nation coming from a proud race … will be … the luminous beacon guiding peoples to an increasingly perfect civilization."[5]

Bouchard began to fulfill his promises to take care of the underdog. He took on the cause of a delegation of barbers from Montreal who belonged to an international union. The legislature had adopted a law compelling all barbers in the province to join in an association controlled by a nationalist group by appealing to racial and religious prejudice against the international union. The law forced every barber in the province to pay an annual contribution of $2 pocketed directly by the union directors. With the authorization of the premier, Bouchard presented a bill abolishing the requirement of obligatory contribu-tions to this association. He received threats in an anonymous letter. Other letters followed to inform him that if his bill passed he could expect revenge. He paid no attention to these letters, but one morning he received an envelope on which the sender revealed his identity by writing the name "Bouchard" in a par-ticular way. Since one of the directors of this union was also named Bouchard, T.-D. compared the handwriting on the envelope with that which appeared in reports of the association, and found a perfect match. When informed of T.-D.'s detective work, the Members of the Legislative Assembly, not wishing to be associated with these threats, voted for the law by a strong majority. This episode remains a testimony to the intelligence of T.-D. Bouchard.

---

4   Ibid., p. 18.

5   Ibid., p. 26.

The *Daily Mail* scandal broke at the beginning of 1914. The proprietors of the *Daily Mail* had concocted a plot to discredit the Gouin government. Their particular goal was to prevent the adoption of a law concerning one of the most powerful trusts in Montreal. The plan involved engaging the services of a private detective agency to compromise ministers, members and legislative councilors by trying to bribe them to sponsor a bill establishing an imaginary association. They succeeded in bribing two legislative councilors and one MLA, using hidden listening devices to establish proof. (Possibly the first time such technology was used.) Bouchard noted: "This conspiracy to ruin the Liberal Party established that after spending fifty thousand dollars drawn from the reserves of the Conservative Party, they had succeeded in compromising only one lone Liberal member out of sixty-four."[6] Bouchard thought that this was an opportunity to convince the premier and the cabinet to end the practice, current at the time, of allowing "promoters of doubtful projects and agents of large organizations to benefit from excessive privileges."[7] Indeed, some members who were lawyers had legal associates who had free access to the Legislative Assembly floor. It was easy for unscrupulous member-lawyers to share their fees between them. This influence peddling took place almost openly, on a wide scale. The member-lawyer implicated in the *Daily Mail* affair was also the leader of the group that had opposed the abolition of the law on barbers. The government came out unharmed by this affair, but Bouchard determined that it was a propitious moment to institute a minor reform that would deny associates of member-lawyers free access and privileges in the Assembly Chamber. Accompanied by a member-lawyer sympathetic to the reform, Bouchard laid out his arguments to Gouin. He emphasized that the cabinet had been exposed to embarrassment due to some notoriously greedy members. Gouin agreed that their complaint was sound and authorized the presentation of the law, unanimously adopted.

Bouchard's views on the control of graft among representatives of the people alienated him from some of his colleagues. He consequently found it prudent to work behind the scenes in order not to compromise the odds of adopting laws on education, economic and social questions in the face of clerical opposition and that of his new adversaries among his fellow Liberals. An example of this strategy was the manner in which he dealt with the issue of school fees. The existing law stated that any local school commission that did not collect a monthly contribution from every

---

6   Ibid., p. 53.

7   Speech delivered to the Legislative Assembly. Feb. 13, 1914. Yamaska Press. ANQ, P 10/24.

pupil would not receive government support. This measure prevented poor people from educating their children. There were municipalities where citizens even chose to lose their governmental subsidies rather than impose a fee of this nature. He asked a Liberal member well regarded by the clerical element, Wenceslas Lévesque, to present a law in his own name to make the monthly educational payment optional for poor people. The house accepted the proposal without a hitch, to loud applause in the Chamber. T.-D. was convinced that if he had initiated the bill, it would have never been adopted.

Going back to the time of Honoré Mercier, representatives from Saint-Hyacinthe had promised to have the Assembly pass a law abolishing tolls on the three local bridges. The problem was complex. Two of the three bridges belonged to a private company, but a group of almost three hundred farmers owned the third. It was necessary for these owners to give up their shares in the public interest. T.-D. succeeded in convincing the majority of shareholders to ratify such a step. He then convinced the cabinet to grant the municipality $60,000 to cover expenses to repurchase the bridges, to defray the cost of repairing them, and to maintain them in perpetuity. By proclamation of the Lieutenant-Governor, Sir François Langelier, the three toll bridges of Saint-Hyacinthe became toll-free on February 14, 1913. Comparing Télesphore-Damien Bouchard's behaviour to the motto of Napoléon, Monsignor Choquette wrote: "*Si c'est possible, c'est fait, et si c'est impossible, ce sera fait.*"[8] ("If possible, it's done, if impossible, it will be done.") The local celebration was enthusiastic. "At the stroke of midnight, after parading through the streets of the city, led by a band, torches in hand, crowds of citizens gathered … to remove the barriers that in the memory of man, had prevented free circulation."[9]

THE EDUCATION ISSUE

During the nineteenth century and well into the twentieth, the Roman Catholic Church did not favour compulsory education or government interference in this field. A bill for compulsory education in Protestant schools was introduced into the Legislative Assembly in 1912. In order to understand the issues involved in the debate on, it is useful to review some of the history on education reforms from 1867-on. Among both Liberals and Conservatives

---

8   Msgr. Choquette, *Histoire de la Ville de Saint-Hyacinthe*. Richer et Fils. 1930, p. 437.

9   T.-D.B., *Mémoires*, III, p. 45.

were many who thought that the Church had no place in the educational system. Pierre-J.-O. Chauveau, a man close to George-Étienne Cartier, led the first Conservative provincial government after Confederation. Although a Conservative, Chauveau belonged to the anti-clerical faction of the party. He formed a ministry of public education (*L'Instruction publique*) in 1867.[10] In the next few years, the ultramontanes grew in power and in 1875, under premier de Boucherville, succeeded in abolishing the ministry. De Boucherville, an ultramontane, had the support of the Church.[11] As Rumilly remarks:

> He [de Boucherville] was himself of an ultramontane tendency and disposed to mark the Catholic seal of approval to French Canada's legislation. He thus prepared his reform with the bishops.... Neither the Gallicanism of George-Étienne Cartier nor the radicalism of Joseph Doutre disturbed the power of the clergy, but in 1875, under the government of de Boucherville, the state became subordinate to the Church.[12].

To replace the defunct ministry the government would appoint a superintendent to follow the directives of the separate councils of the Catholic and Protestant committees. The Catholic committee was composed of all the bishops and an equal number of laypersons appointed by the government. The catch was that the bishops had the right to name a stand-in, whereas the lay members did not have this right. This assured a majority for the bishops, thus reinforcing the power of the Church on the committee. Rumilly comments: "By decreasing the influence of the politicians on education, de Boucherville and the bishops saved the day."[13]

Education became an election issue again in 1897, when Félix-Gabriel Marchand won for the Liberal Party. He introduced a law establishing a ministry of public education, substantially altering the Quebec school system. The law would permit the government to appoint inspectors. The teachers, lay and clerical, would be required to obtain a certificate of competence; and the ministry would select the books and determine the curriculum recommended by the

---

10 L.-D.-R., p. 281.

11 R. R., *HPQ*, II. p 18.

12 Ibid., p. 18. In 1871 the ultramontane faction of the Conservative Party formulated "the Catholic program," which essentially gave the Church supremacy over the state.

13 Ibid., p.19.

appropriate committees. The law set Marchand on a collision course with the Church, and notably with Msgr. Paul Bruchési, the Archbishop of Montreal. Perhaps tongue-in-cheek, Bruchési declared: "If the laity are not satisfied with our education, which we consider perfect to accomplish our aim—the formation of priests—they should open their own secondary schools." (As an attestation to the success of the seminary system, there is a handwritten note in the Saint-Hyacinthe Seminary's yearbook of 1893 describing graduates' occupations at the time of their fifteenth reunion in 1908: ten priests; five lawyers; two doctors; one engineer; two journalists; three unknown—and no businessmen.)[14]

In spite of the repeated edicts from Rome concerning the separation between the state and religion, the quarrel persisted. Marchand explained to the bishops that the creation of a ministry of public education would not alter in any way the jurisdiction of the council controlled by the bishops. The role of the government minister would only to be that of an administrator and person responsible for the physical plant of schools. The young Archbishop of Montreal, regarded as being of an authoritarian and prickly nature, took it as an attempt to reduce the power of the Church. He thus left for Rome, where it would be easy, he thought, to oppose the proposed legislation. Marchand wrote a firm and measured letter to Rome, specifically to His Eminence Cardinal Rampolla. The letter, dated November 19, 1897, reviewed the history of the "miserable defiance" of the clergy of the province of Quebec towards public authority. Marchand explained that his intention in creating a ministry of education was not to change the jurisdiction of the council dominated by the bishops. On November 22, Bruchési sent a telegram from Rome to the premier: "Pope asks you to defer bill of public education. Letter sent today."[15] Marchand replied the same day that the proposed measure was already included in the Speech from the Throne to be read the following day, but that he would await Bruchési's letter before actually presenting the bill to the Assembly. On November 24, the Lieutenant-Governor, J.-A. Chapleau, replied to Bruchési, supporting Marchand's views concerning the division of church and state. He emphasized that the law contained many guarantees for complete supervision of all schools concerning religious authority, and therefore:

---

14   ASSH, class records.

15   Rumilly, *HPQ*, IX, p. 26.

> This measure in no manner contravenes the rights and privileges which the Church claims ... [they are] left, as previously, under the absolute control of the Council of Public Education ... the Church should not, it seems to me, refuse the effective participation of the State in the work of the public education ... the government ... will confirm by its declaration, these guarantees that the Church has always requested ... to ask for more from the Assembly ... would open the door to a reproach of trespassing on the constitutional authority of the State.[16]

Chapleau, a staunch Conservative, was nevertheless a leader of the Conservative anti-clericals. As H. Blair Neatby and John T. Saywell have noted, Chapleau led the Quebec wing of the Conservatives for many years, and opposed the *castor* faction of the party.[17]

Bruchési's letter arrived on December 7. In it he confessed that he had based his opposition to the bill solely on newspaper accounts. Marchand sent the letter immediately to Chapleau, accompanied by a letter threatening the resignation of his government. The Lieutenant-Governor dispatched a telegram to Cardinal Rampolla: "Convinced that this step would be ... a disaster for the peace and harmony of its citizens ... my Prime Minister believes, with reason, I believe, that he would have no other alternative but to deliver his resignation into my hands, if the demand of the Holy Father remains as has been transmitted by Msgr. Bruchési ... an absolute order to the Prime Minister, as a Catholic."[18]

Marchand answered Bruchési on December 11, stating that he was deeply distressed to learn that the Archbishop preferred the journalist's version to the declaration of good faith of the government. He noted that there were guarantees for religious teaching, the preservation of a separate school system, and the continuation of the authority of the Council of Public Instruction on the moral and religious direction of teaching. Although the government had made an effort to explain its plan to the bishops, no opposition was brought forward prior to the Speech from the Throne. As Raoul Dandurand remarks: "During the electoral period, several months had passed without any authorized voice

---

16 Ibid., p, 28.

17 H. Blair Neatby and John T. Saywell, "Chapleau and the Conservative Party in Quebec," *CHR*, XXXVII, 1956, 1–22.

18 Rumilly, *HPQ*, IX, p. 32.

heard to demonstrate that the measure in question would affect the moral and religious teaching in our schools."[19]

Finally, on December 11, a telegram arrived addressed to Sir Adolphe Chapleau from Cardinal Rampolla: "The Holy Father wanted to express His wish to avoid all innovation.... *He did not intend to exert such pressure which could bring the Minister to hand in his resignation.*"[20] [Emphasis added.] Dandurand writes: "It is clear that His Holiness Leo XIII and Cardinal Rampolla were as annoyed as the Marchand government ... at the bizarre action of Msgr. Bruchési."[21] Dandurand also quotes from a letter to Chapleau from Cardinal Merry del Val, (previously a papal delegate to Canada and thus very knowledgeable about Canadian affairs) where Merry del Val deplored Bruchési's manoeuvre: "I had knowledge of the letter and the dispatch ... after they already had been sent, and I confess that this manner of interpreting the thought of the Holy Father appeared to me very strange."[22]

The bill entitled "Law of Public Instruction" was introduced in the Legislative Assembly in a first reading on December 13, 1897, and adopted on January 5 following a vote of forty-eight for and nineteen against. The Conservatives, however, held the majority in the Legislative Council (the upper house) and on January 10 they rejected the bill. People regarded the Conservative victory as another intrusion by the clerics in temporal affairs. It took more than sixty years for Quebec to establish a ministry of education, during the government of Jean Lesage.

In 1912 Dr. John T. Finnie, the member from Saint-Laurent, presented this bill to establish compulsory education for Protestant children. All the Protestant school commissions declared themselves in favour of this legislation. T.-D. was happy to be able to express his views on this subject, to try to enlighten the public and to prepare the terrain for a future in which the same would apply to Catholic students.[23] In his powerful maiden speech to the Legislative Assembly on November 26, 1912, T.-D. declared himself to be in favour of the Finnie

---

19   Raoul Dandurand, *Les Mémoires du Sénateur,* Édités par Marcel Hamelin; (Québec: Les Presses de L'Université Laval, 1967), p. 93.

20   Ibid., p. 98.

21   Ibid., p. 110.

22   Ibid., p. 111.

23   Ibid., p. 58.

bill.[24] He demonstrated its necessity, its advantages, and its inoffensive character even for Catholics. At the beginning of this speech, he specified that he was a sincere champion of the religious school system, and repeated this affirmation towards the end of his speech. ("I am a supporter of the present school system.")[25] He added that he believed in the usefulness of the coexistence of lay teaching alongside religious instruction. "Education is the primary source of progress, happiness, and national prosperity."[26] Bouchard stressed that education is one of the main factors of social progress. He compared the economic situation and the morals of educated citizens with those who were uneducated. Social justice demanded that the state had the obligation to protect children by inculcating elements of science indispensable to all human beings in the modern world. Bouchard stressed that human capital is primordial and invoked the need and the interest of the state to increase the national wealth. There was no need to be a great philosopher to understand that an illiterate person is inferior to an educated one. The enormous emigration of French Canadians to the United States was partly due, he believed, to the lack of that education that he felt supplied the essential knowledge to make Quebec farms more productive. To adversaries, who saw in compulsory schooling a breach of individual liberty, he pointed out that state regulation was sometimes necessary. He cited as an example the law that the government had just adopted requiring butter and cheese manufacturers to obtain a diploma from the Provincial Dairy School. This piece of legislation demonstrated that state government had already recognized the principle of compulsory education. "One could ask the dairy school director," he said, "if it is easy to teach the calculation of the percentage of acidity, the richness of milk fat, or of casein to pupils who do not know that two and two makes four, who count on their fingers or with matches.... There are a great number of these persons in our province."[27] Bouchard ended his speech with a survey of the progress of education in the wider world. He noted the existence of compulsory education in Greece for children of five years to twelve years of age since 1833, in Turkey since 1869, in Serbia since 1882, in Romania

---

24   T.-D. Bouchard, *L'Instruction Obligatoire;* Speech before the Legislative Assembly. November 26, 1912, *L'Imprimerie* Yamaska, 35 pages. ANQ *Fonds* Bouchard, P-10/14.

25   Ibid., p. 8.

26   Ibid., p. 25.

27   Ibid., p.16.

since 1885—in short, in almost all the great countries of the world: England, France, Germany, Italy, Sweden, Japan, the United States and most Canadian provinces. Only Russia and Spain lacked a compulsory education law. Only one boy in eighteen and one girl in forty-three attended schools in Russia in 1906. In Spain, with a population of eighteen million, nine million were illiterate.

The Catholic newspaper *L'Action sociale* published an article against compulsory schooling by quoting a Frenchman, Father Duballet, who spoke against the famous maxim, "One school more, one prison less." Duballet's thesis was that this was far from being true when the school is not Christian, when moral values are not taught (i.e., in republican France). Bouchard pointed out that unlike those in France, Quebec schools were indeed Christian, and therefore Duballet's argument demonstrated the moral usefulness of compulsory schools rather than the contrary. In spite of his fiery defence of the proposed Finnie bill, T.-D. yielded to the arguments of his leader Lomer Gouin, who came out against the bill because he did not want to confront the clerical forces both inside and outside his party. In addition, some opponents of the bill argued that its adoption would serve to perpetuate the division between the Catholic and Protestant school systems. This line of thinking influenced the Protestants, most of whom abandoned Finnie. Not being able to count on the support of the Protestant members, Bouchard voted against the bill.

The people of the upper town underestimated Télesphore-Damien Bouchard's strengths. They felt that he would never do well because of his rough manners and vigorous reaction to criticism. When he spoke publicly, he could be graceful and tactful, as he was during his speech before the Reform Club of Montreal on March 19, 1916. In that speech, he praised Gouin, to whom he gave credit for the reformist policy on education.

Bouchard began his political career on the theme of education, and in 1918 he had another opportunity to express his views on this subject. The school commissions of Drummondville and Saint-Jérôme asked the government to authorise local school commissions of towns with over thousand inhabitants to impose obligatory education for children of seven to fourteen. T.-D. Bouchard again began a campaign in support of this idea—in articles in his newspaper, and in the Legislative Assembly.[28] He approved of the campaign in favour of compulsory education by MLA Langlois and Senator Dandurand, who finally convinced Bruchési to change his views on compulsory education in 1920. But

---

28   L.-D.-R., p. 531.

the majority of the other bishops on the education council did not agree at this time.[29]

PRIVATE AFFAIRS AND POLITICS

Meanwhile, T.-D. pursued his private enterprise. His parliamentary allowance was not sufficient to allow him to balance the family budget. He never felt that a representative of the people had to be condemned to live in poverty. In fact, he thought that without private sources of income the temptations of illegal acquisition of income would be strong, and that this was the cause of corruption and graft in public life. In 1909, he opened an automobile agency "for vehicles equipped with gas motors." He expanded this business in 1912. He declared his home a place of business, carrying out transactions of all sorts—especially real estate, selling lots and houses.

In reply to De la Broquerie Taché's accusations in *Le Courrier* that he was not a self-respecting MLA because of his commercial activities, Bouchard wrote in his newspaper that, yes, it was true. He was not proud. He worked honestly to earn his living, and did not enrich himself by illegal means, ending up in prison as some Conservative members. He did not use the "fictitious noble particle" on his name. He had not consulted Monsignor Tanguay's dictionary in the hope

---

29 Wade, p. 608. At the turn of the century, there were three major subjects of debate on schooling: the establishment of a ministry of education, compulsory schooling and the establishment of a separate Jewish school system. Although the massive immigration of 1880–1914 was predominately Christian, Irish and Eastern European, there were many Jews among the Eastern Europeans, who gravitated primarily to Montreal, although there were some found in most Quebec towns. By 1916, in some districts of Montreal, Protestant schools became almost entirely patronized by Jewish students. (In 1900, 20 percent of the student population of Protestant schools was Jewish; in 1910, 35 percent, and in 1916, 45 percent.) The Jewish community was bitterly divided on the issue of whether to have its own school system. In the end, the debate was moot because the bishops opposed the creation of a third religious school system. In 1917, it was agreed that the Jewish students were to be counted as Protestants.

The Jews of Quebec are often criticized for not integrating with the French majority, forgetting that they were excluded from educating their children in French until very recently. As Yvon Deschamps jokes, in the past it was easy to distinguish between French Canadians and others by their speech, but since all groups, especially immigrants from all over the world, are being educated in French, it is now impossible to tell who is who. Now, with one's back turned, one cannot tell the child of recent immigrants from those eleven or twelve generations back.

of finding among his ancestors *un comte De la Pelle ou un marquis du Broc* (a Count of Shovels or a Marquis of the Pitcher). He then reviewed all the types of work he had accomplished in his life: grocery delivery boy; leather-cutter, piano teacher and journalist. "I am not a proud member, it is true. The state pays an honest member so little, and as I do not want to become a dishonest member, I am obliged to engage in various professions."[30]

The new member from Saint-Hyacinthe was in his element in the Chamber. One often heard his speeches, always with the facts in hand, repetitious and long at times, in direct and pointed tones. He displayed a keen sense of debate. His new status brought prestige with it. When Sir Wilfrid Laurier visited his loyal troops in Saint-Hyacinthe, in August 1913, Mayor Payan introduced him, and T.-D. Bouchard wished Laurier welcome. He delivered his speech, full of military metaphors, from a platform in the centre of the city, before almost thirty thousand people according to the rival newspaper *Le Courrier,* or at least twelve thousand according to Monsignor Choquette.[31] T.-D. Bouchard—acquiring an early middle-age spread, with vivid, clear dark eyes, and now sporting a moustache—rose to render a graceful homage to his leader: "Saint-Hyacinthe has known Sir Wilfrid since he was a simple soldier in the Liberal army.... The vanquished Laurier is even greater than Laurier the victor ... waiting for the hour of revenge which will be not long coming."[32] The opposition newspapers noted that although Bouchard insisted that the nationalist movement was dead, he had devoted a major part of his speech to killing it.[33] However, this accusation is not true. A close examination of his seventeen-page speech reveals that six pages were devoted to praising Laurier, four attacked Borden and his Naval Law, and only four addressed the nationalists.[34]

With the threat of a war, Bouchard's enmity towards Bourassa increased. The nationalists preached against Canada's participation in an English war against Germany, even though they were responsible for the defeat of Laurier in 1911. Thus, they had facilitated the election of a Tory government with jingoist

---

30   T.-D.B., *Mémoires,* III, p. 43.

31   Msgr. C.P. Choquette, *L'Histoire de la Ville de Saint-Hyacinthe.*

32   T.-D.B., *Bienvenue à Laurier, 16 aôut* 1913. Imprimerie Yamaska. *Fonds* Bouchard; ANQ, P-10/14.

33   Rumilly, *HPQ,* XVIII, p. 87.

34   T.-D.B., *Bienvenue a Laurier,* ANQ, P-10/14.

Orangists as ministers (e.g., Sam Hughes). The nationalists' success was due in part to the fact that they controlled the biased (anti-English) teaching of history in the classic colleges.[35] For his support of the municipalization of electricity, Bouchard was called a socialist, a centralizer and a Freemason. The day that the nationalist dentist Philippe Hamel denounced the trusts and the abuse of private enterprise, according to Bouchard, "they hurried to support him because he was a nationalist and a Bourassist."[36] The outbreak of war in Europe on August 4, 1914, alarmed the population of Quebec and Canada. Following the example of Laurier, Bouchard became an apostle of the intervention of Canada in support of England faced with "the German assault." He travelled all over the province and harangued crowds by backing the war, without worrying about harming his chances for re-election. This may have contributed to his defeat in 1919.

At this time, Bouchard did not express views favouring a state monopoly in electricity. He did not wish to completely eliminate the existence of private companies. He simply wanted to create municipal electrical enterprises to force a reduction in rates through competition. "I wanted to protect the public against excessive prices which greedy capitalists extorted from their clients."[37] He was convinced that they sold electricity at ten times its cost, according to his calculations "as an amateur engineer." His campaign was successful. Electricity was municipalized by degrees in Saint-Hyacinthe; prices decreased in a dramatic manner.[38] Consumers saved millions of dollars and private companies could continue to operate, content with reasonable profits. In economic matters T.-D. believed in controlled capitalism. Bouchard was fundamentally an enlightened nineteenth-century man.

---

35   This nationalist anti-English presentation of Quebec history continued until at least the 1940s and perhaps later. See Catherine Pomeryol's book *Les intellectuels québécois: formation et engagements 1919–1939,* (Paris: L'Hartmattan, 1996.) See also Jean Lamarre, *Le devenir de la nation québécoise, selon Maurice Seguin, Guy Fregault, et Michel Brunet,* (Sillery: *Les éditions du Septentrion,* 1993).

36   T.-D.B., *Mémoires,* II, p. 18.

37   Ibid., p. 71.

38   Clarence Hogue, André Bolduc, Danièle Larouche, *Québec, un siècle d'électricité,* (Montréal: Libre Expression, 1979) p. 194. In 1934, when the new municipal plant was set up, it attracted 850 subscribers vs. 300 for Southern Power, which then reduced its price to compete.

In the Assembly, Bouchard succeeded in having a law passed which allowed municipalities to decide the rates of taxation of city properties, including those of religious communities. In Saint-Hyacinthe, these occupied more than half of the city and a large proportion of properties fronting on Girouard Blvd. In spite of the opposition of the Church and calls by the Vicar General of the Seminary of Saint-Hyacinthe, the bill passed by two votes. It became law before the dissolution of the Chamber on March 15, 1915. As a result, the Dominicans, who required a new building, accepted a contract with the city that included a tax on the sidewalk, the roads and water. Mayor Payan revised the city charter to conform to these new concepts, allowing taxation of the small Presbyterian community for the first time.

In September of 1916, T.-D. was to be judged by the people of Saint-Hyacinthe. The days preceding the election were peaceful. His opponents continued to vilify him. The reactionary press offered the usual gratuitous insults. Representing himself, he brought suit in court against the authors of libellous articles published about him. While addressing a meeting of parishioners in a rural parish, the priest ordered him to leave Church property. He refused to comply, and the audience approvingly broke out in applause. After a lively campaign, his voters remained faithful. He was re-elected MLA by a greater majority than he had received in the preceding election.

In 1917, Mayor Morin resigned his office. T.-D. gives two reasons for the resignation. First, an associate of his office, Armand Boisseau, embarrassed the mayor by promoting a local bill to grant a Montreal entrepreneur a "lavish" over-inflated contract.[39] In addition, Morin found himself in a very difficult position because in decreeing conscription, the federal government had given mayors the unpleasant task of granting exemptions to conscripts who had good reasons to be excused from service. A large delegation approached T.-D. to offer him the candidacy. He refused, stating that he did not feel solid-enough support in public opinion and that his enemies would ruin him because of the new unpleasant role of the mayor in granting exemptions. However, at the insistence of his petitioners, with all his arguments ineffective, he yielded. He accepted even though believing that he had signed his defeat as MLA. They replied that they would rather have him as mayor than as MLA. (That is what happened in

---

39   T.-D.B., *Mémoires*, III, p. 73. Boisseau was to become the independent Liberal candidate who defeated Bouchard in the provincial election of 1919, urged on by the federal MP, L.-J. Gauthier.

1919.) Some days later, he was elected the first citizen of Saint-Hyacinthe by acclamation, a position that he held—except for a brief interruption (1930–1932)—for twenty-seven years.

Télesphore-Damien's early career as MLA resulted in some positive results for his constituency. His maiden speech on education was remarkable for its depth, but its brilliance was spoiled by the lack of support for Finnie's bill. The amalgamation of the Quebec nationalists and the Ontario Conservatives, a strange alliance in that Bourassa campaigned for the Empire, caused the defeat of Laurier in 1911. In the next chapter, we will explore Bouchard's activities as mayor and as MLA from 1917 to 1935.

MLA Bouchard, circa 1916

Chapter VI

MR. MAYOR

As a member of the provincial legislature, Télesphore-Damien Bouchard had already acquired a reputation as a battler for reform. Now, in his new role as mayor of Saint-Hyacinthe, he was able to pursue his struggle on a second front. In his city he kept the contractors of garbage collection and of road repair to the strict terms of their contracts. He improved city finances through the levy of special taxes, which he had introduced with the new provincial charter. He decreed a uniform tax based on the annual or movable value of their property, for all citizens. Bouchard held that now the proprietors of heavy industry and the religious communities should no longer obtain water, protection against fires, and sidewalks, for "ridiculous sums."

Bouchard gave talks all over the province in favour of compulsory education. Before a predominantly English-speaking audience at the convention of the Union of Canadian Municipalities, he emphasized that there were progressives among the French Canadians whom the clerical element did not dare to attack openly, and that his compatriots were not all backward and anti-British.[1] He ended his speech on an optimistic note. He felt that one should not lose confidence because in the near future, thanks to progress in education, the politico-religious domination would be overcome. National unity would be achieved for the greatest well-being of the country. Thanks to this speech he was unanimously elected to the vice-presidency of the association, and the next year he became its president. Bouchard was also active in the formation of a group of farmers who first met in Saint-Hyacinthe in 1918. The *Union des Agriculteurs de la Province de Québec* elected him their first president at this meeting even though he was not a farmer. The historian Robert Migner holds that the minister

---

1   *Fonds* Bouchard, ANQ, P-10/24. Discours 1917.

of agriculture, who wanted to avoid an independent body—that is, one independent of the government—orchestrated Bouchard's election as president.[2]

Despite Bouchard's successes, the provincial elections of June 1919 showed that Bouchard's enemies had gained ground. Armand Boisseau stood for election as an independent Liberal candidate with the endorsement of the federal MP, Louis-Joseph Gauthier. (At first Boisseau had given up his candidacy after Bouchard won the official nomination of the Liberals of Saint-Hyacinthe. But then, when support appeared, he changed his mind.) A clerical group supporting Boisseau demanded that Lomer Gouin publicly disavow Bouchard. The president of the Association of Catholic Youth sent a telegram to the premier asking him to declare himself for one or the other candidate. Gouin's antipathy to Bouchard was manifest when he replied publicly that he would leave the choice to the electors of Saint-Hyacinthe. This lack of official endorsement was equivalent to telling the voters that T.-D. was not the authorized candidate of the party. As noted by Linteau, Durocher and Robert, the party wanted to teach Bouchard a lesson—to get him to moderate his views.[3] Although he was well-known, perhaps his modest origin from the working class, his reputation as an anti-clerical who saddled the Church with municipal taxes, or the municipalization of electricity worked in some combination against him. Especially irritating may have been his advocacy of major reforms in education. Bouchard had a prolonged stay on the back benches. The party leaders did not seem to like him, and regarded him as a maverick. While he had entered the Legislative Assembly at the age of thirty, he was denied promotion until 1928, when at the age of forty-six he was appointed deputy speaker. Named speaker two years later, he joined Taschereau's discredited cabinet in order to reinforce it and possibly save it in 1935. According to Bouchard, he received more applause than Boisseau at the public debate, since the latter was not much of an orator. However, oratory did not always result in votes. On the day of the election Bouchard was crushed by a majority of well over five hundred. The electoral mores of the period and for a long time in Quebec history—as well as of the rest of Canada—left much to be desired.[4] As Laurier had

---

2   Robert-Maurice Migner, *Le monde agricole québécois et les premières années de l'Union catholique des cultivateurs (1918–1930)*, thesis for PhD (history) Université de Montréal, 1975.

3   L.-D.-R., p. 557.

4   There are many books and articles on the electoral mores of Quebec politics. Beginning with Alfred Duclos DeCelles, *Scènes de moeurs électorales* (Montréal: Librairie Beauchemin,

noted in 1877, "telegraphed" votes were a current practice. The list of voters was full of dead people and fictitious names. The purchase of votes by outright gifts of money or alcohol was common. The job of strong-armed thugs was to destroy the premises and the files of the other party, and to frighten their scrutineers. The Union Nationale during Duplessis's years of power developed these measures to a fine point. Of course, both parties carried out these practices, with the party in power having the advantage. The practice picturesquely called "the deportation of the Acadians" consisted of sending known voters of the other party on a bus, far into the countryside, with offers of free drinks. They were then abandoned there, drunk, on the eve of the ballot. This practice was current even in the 1940s.[5]

Did the Liberal Party succeed in teaching Bouchard a lesson? Undoubtedly they did not. Bouchard discovered that Armand Boisseau had spent $72,000 during the election. Bouchard contested the election on grounds of fraud and corruption. Where had that enormous sum of money come from? He discovered that the seventy-two thousand (dollars) had come from money entrusted to Boisseau's law office—of which he was secretary—for placement as mortgages or for lending to small municipalities. Boisseau's lawyers succeeded in dragging the court case out for several years. Eventually Bouchard obtained satisfaction in the Appeal Court, which upheld the judgment of the Superior Court. The second court annulled Boisseau's election, and disqualified him from running for seven years. After consulting the new premier, Louis-Alexandre Taschereau, Bouchard's lawyer instituted criminal procedures against Boisseau. Finally, arrested for obtaining money under false pretexts, he resigned. Before his trial, "in pity for his wife and his children," T.-D. offered to drop his complaint if Boisseau left the county. Boisseau refused.[6] In his *Mémoires*, T.-D. refers to Armand and Louis-Joseph by their first names. He explains that this was in order to protect their descendants from shame, "so as to not throw discredit

---

1919); Jean and Marcel Hamelin, *Les mœurs électorales dans le Québec* (Montréal: Éditions du jour, 1962), Jean-Paul Desbiens, *Les insolences du frère untel* (Montréal: Les Éditions de l'Homme, 1960). See also the well-known article by the priests Gérard Dion and Louis O'Neil, *L'immoralité politique dans la province du Québec*, criticizing the régime of Duplessis, *Le Devoir*, 7 aôut 1956; and the editorial of Gérard Filion the next day in *Le Devoir, Réformes des lois et des mœurs électorales*. From 1875 to 1997 there were fifty-one elections cancelled because of fraudulent activity (thirty-nine from 1875 to 1897), www. assnat.qc.ca/fra/patrimesteroine/annulees/html+moeurs.

5   Judge Marcel Nichols, personal communication.

6   T.D.B., *Mémoires*, III, p. 78.

on their families."[7] However, forty years earlier he certainly attacked them publicly, vigorously and effectively. In May 1922, "Armand" was forced into bankruptcy, and in December, he was condemned to two years in prison. In February of 1923, the Liberals of Saint-Hyacinthe again chose Télesphore-Damien Bouchard as their candidate for the next provincial election.

During the period of 1919–23, Louis-Joseph and Armand's group succeeded in electing the majority of the aldermen on the city council. In the hope of discrediting the mayor, they opened an inquiry on his administration. Due to lack of evidence, the inquiry could not arrive at a conclusion. After a certain period, T.-D. summoned the person charged with the inquiry to make a preliminary report. Counseled by T.-D.'s adversaries, he refused to obey the mayor. By virtue of his discretionary power, Bouchard suspended the inquiry, "which put an end to this comedy … the inquiry came to an abrupt end."[8] T.-D. issued a critical pamphlet, *Lettre à Louis-Joseph* in a run of several thousand copies, distributed throughout the city and the rural parishes. Bouchard accused Louis-Joseph of hypocrisy—of pretending to be a Liberal when he was really a conservative pro-clerical who had spread slander about Bouchard, and had supported the candidacy of Armand Boisseau. In July 1919, the Liberal convention repudiated Louis-Joseph Gauthier in unequivocal terms: the delegates refused to renew his candidacy for the next election. The Liberal Party convention of 1921 chose René Morin, an ex-mayor, as the federal candidate. Several years later, at the request of the Liberal candidate for the county of l'Islet, Bouchard reissued the pamphlet in order to discredit Gauthier in another election. This reissued letter was even more critical than the previous one.[9] Sued for $10,000 by Gauthier, Bouchard declared that the facts were true and that the public interest was served. The judge accepted his plea and dismissed the case. In spite of a campaign in l'Islet in which the clericals and Louis-Joseph appealed to religious passions, the people remained deaf to their call. Gauthier lost by a majority of 4900 votes.

Mayor Bouchard remained a popular figure in the eyes of the workers and proprietors. During the shoemakers' strike at Ames-Holden, the two contending parties chose Bouchard as the sole arbitrator. He succeeded in obtaining an amicable agreement in what threatened to be a prolonged dispute in which each party stood to lose thousands of dollars. To help the poor people of the city he

---

7   Ibid., p. 73.

8   Ibid., p. 79.

9   T.-D.B., *Lettres à Louis-Joseph (Gauthier) Fonds* Bouchard; ANQ, P-10/24. 1926.

organized a co-operative bakery that for many years succeeded in keeping the price of bread lower in Saint-Hyacinthe than in all other cities of the province. He had also introduced lower taxes for the citizens of the city by reducing the rate of property evaluations.

The "little Sunday mass" continued to meet on the premises of *Le Clairon*, from ten o'clock until noon. This custom continued until the 1940s. Liberals and Conservatives could question their federal and provincial representatives, and exchange ideas. There were frank discussions, sometimes animated. In fact, for those who held politics to be a religion, the meetings could be great fun. According to Judge Victor Chabot, an admirer of Bouchard, Conservatives and opponents also attended the "little Sunday mass." It was open to everyone, even those who voted against Bouchard.[10] People attended in order to ascertain his opinion or to ask his help for a justifiable project. The "little mass" succeeded in uniting provincial and federal organizers, people of various opinions, radicals, free thinkers, moderate Catholic militants, and Protestants. Those attending, in general, shared the conviction that the Church did not belong in political affairs. The "little mass" contributed to maintaining the influence of the Liberals in Saint-Hyacinthe. It was the centre of information. In this way the leaders kept up their current knowledge of local party interests. If a problem arose somewhere, the leaders learned about it and worked to resolve it before it became worse.

The need to win the next election also preoccupied these leaders. Considering the questionable practices of the time, electoral victories did not come cheaply. Votes might have to be bought. Under these circumstances, at least according to one report—from what, it should be admitted, must be considered a dubious source—Bouchard determined that it was wasteful to seek to win by too large a majority. If he received more than a four-hundred-vote majority, he would call his organizers to task, telling them that this was unnecessary and too expensive. A majority of hundred was just as good as a majority of 2000. "When the majority exceeded the agreed-upon level, he banged his fist on the table and in an angry voice reminded them that he did not need a large majority ... that each superfluous vote cost him money." However, we should consider this anecdote questionable because Jean-Louis Gagnon, who reports it, cites Gérard Brady as the source of this story. Bouchard once sued Brady for falsely accusing him of graft. Brady then published a retraction.[11]

---

10   Judge Victor Chabot; oral communication cited in Chisholm, p. 90.

11   Jean-Louis Gagnon; *Les Apostasies* (Montréal: *Éditions La Presse*; 1985), I, p.208.

As mayor, Bouchard abolished door-to-door begging. This resulted in a campaign of abuse by the *Patronage Saint Vincent de Paul*, which had been benefiting especially from collecting from the market's butchers. Bouchard had already sued this institution for its refusal to pay taxes. His inflexibility worried some of his partisans. Bouchard claimed to have calmed these critics by saying that everyone would appreciate his impartial application of the law. "... by proving to them that the population agreed with the strict application of laws and regulations to all, without exception, and thus I would be justified when I would be called to account for it in the renewal of my mandate."[12] This faith in the population's capacity to judge fairly was somewhat unrealistic. In spite of this confidence in the people, Bouchard almost lost the next election for the mayoralty in 1921—his margin of victory was only thwenty-one votes. There were rumours of a recount. Taking the advice of the "little mass" he decided instead to request a new election. He was subsequently re-elected with a greater majority.[13] In the following three elections for mayor, Bouchard was elected by acclamation. At each election, he was re-elected with a greater majority until 1930. In the provincial election of 1923, the electorate once again gave him its confidence, sending him to the Legislative Assembly with a majority of 800 votes. He therefore avenged his defeat of 1919, when he had lost by 500 votes. He had picked up 1300 votes from one election to the next, and on July 2, 1923, celebrated his victory at a huge rally.

During this period, the higher clergy of Saint-Hyacinthe was sympathetic to Télesphore-Damien Bouchard. In 1924 Abbé Decelles, his ex-professor and superior of the seminary, was appointed bishop of Saint-Hyacinthe in the place of Monsignor Bernard. Both bishops had a good opinion of T.-D. A short while after his consecration, the new bishop (Decelles) had good words to say about T.-D. at a meeting with several members of the clergy. He had also approved the Grey Sisters, who had refused government funds—a veiled approval of the separation of ecclesiastical and civil power. This same year, for the first time in local history, there was a celebration with two orators to bless the occasion: a Catholic priest and a Protestant minister. In a provocative act some days later, the new town hall was inaugurated without the customary blessing. To those who accused him of not "making his Easter" (confessing and taking communion at Easter) or of not attending church, the young seminarian Rochefort declared, "They said that he did not attend church. This is not true. I remember, twice, to

---

12   T.D.B., *Mémoires*, III, p. 81.

13   Rochefort, personal communication to Chisholm, p. 91.

have followed him to the sacrament on Sunday."[14] Although not exactly proof of dedication to religious devotion, this admirer understood that T.-D.'s anticlericalism did not have anything to do with his personal religious convictions. Bouchard believed that the more money that the Church had available, the more temptation it had to mix into temporal affairs.[15]

In the educational field, the municipal council set up a radio station of limited range—the first municipal station in the province. In 1925, Bouchard introduced band concerts in the poor people's districts. Until then, open-air concerts took place only in the upper town. He beautified the city by establishing public parks on sites of abandoned factories. He encouraged agricultural fairs. In order to avoid spring floods he had cement support walls constructed at the edge of the river, thereby reclaiming land for parks and providing boat landings.

One of the spring floods in Saint-Hyacinthe

14   Ibid., p. 92.

15   T.-D.B., *Mémoires,* II, p. 21.

Although his wife, Blanche-Corona was happy to observe that T.-D. was no longer required to travel to Quebec City from 1919 to 1923, their family life was still rather gloomy. Mrs. Bouchard remained a semi-invalid, mostly confined to the house. Their daughter Cécile-Ena, having completed primary school, attended Trafalgar School, a private Montreal boarding school for girls of "good" families from Westmount (the district of the wealthy Montrealers). As noted, the relationship between mother and daughter was extremely close. Blanche-Corona greatly missed Cécile-Ena. When Cécile-Ena was in Saint-Hyacinthe she took on the role of political hostess, accompanying her father to various public functions. Mrs. Bouchard read many novels from her husband's huge library, and occasionally went out to see movies.

With the assistance of an architect and his own inventive mind, T.-D. made plans to construct a new house. This little fortress was designed to stand on a bank at an elbow of the Yamaska River which curved alongside Girouard Boulevard at this point. Built on landfill, it took years to complete. Bouchard strengthened the basement to prevent flooding and had extra, extremely well insulated electrical outlets installed. Since he was well-acquainted with all the local contractors, their workers and the sources of construction materials in the city, he could evaluate their work and materials. The opposition claimed that the retaining wall for his house was built with public funds. His friends replied that instead of defrauding the city, he had benefited it by constructing a wall that protected all of Girouard Boulevard, threatened by the erosion of floods. T.-D. himself was an enthusiastic swimmer. He had a swimming pool built in his new house. Always self-taught, he had learned how to swim from a book by a famous swimmer, Annette Kellerman.

Bouchard's home on the bank of the Yamaska River in winter

During 1926 and 1927 Bouchard continued his efforts to beautify the city, improve public health, and provide free recreation for the populace. The council established anti-tuberculosis clinics and a public health clinic. T.-D. favoured the creation of a modern hospital. From the provincial government he obtained $100,000 of the $500,000 necessary to build the hospital. The city purchased land in the lower town from the gas company, thus causing the disappearance of a disgraceful factory that stank, depreciating the property values of the neighbourhood. A public garden replaced it. Animal pens near the railroad station were replaced by playing fields alongside a park of planted ornamental trees. The council bought the Laframboise racetrack north of town for the Agriculture Society and converted it into a municipal park and an amuse-ment park. A section of it was reserved for the agricultural association's annual exhibitions. To the south of this property, the council voted funds to construct an enormous swimming pool with a spacious pavilion allowing bathers to change clothes and to take a shower. Built according to a new model, this oval basin of 250 feet in length was only six inches deep along its outer edge and eight feet deep at its centre. It was a pool built for safety and security. In 1926 Bouchard bought a building to house a theatre, and called it the Corona Theatre in honour of his wife.

Bouchard was re-elected mayor by acclamation in 1926, as was his team of aldermen. The court case that the city had brought against the religious communities for payment of taxes dragged on. The city lost in the Quebec courts. The council decided to submit the case to the Supreme Court and, if need be, to the Privy Council in London. This determined attitude stimulated the religious communities to begin negotiations for an amicable settlement. Thus, in 1927, after agreement with representatives of the bishop, the city signed a concordat in which the religious communities were committed to pay all imposed taxes for the duration of twenty years. It was the first time that such an act was signed in the province. In 1947 the Church renewed the concordat with the city for a new term. Bouchard defended himself against the accusation of being an extremist by noting the city's contributions to the religious communities. In spite of the opposition of some of the progressive aldermen, he provided some financial support from the city to meritorious works directed by ecclesiastical institutions. He re-established an annual grant of $600 for a poor-people's hospice. He also had the council agree to a sum of $10,000 to assist the seminary in constructing a new building to replace one that had been lost in a recent fire.

In the Legislative Assembly, Télesphore-Damien Bouchard introduced a bill to revise the law on work accidents, modelled on an existing law in the province of Ontario. For three years following the adoption of the standing legislation, he had argued that it left manufacturers and workers at the mercy of insurance companies. Finally, the government, convinced by his arguments, created a Commission of Work Accidents, which would rule on all cases of death or invalidity occurring accidentally to workers.[16]

In 1928, T.-D. registered a bill on the Chamber's calendar to allow the partial nationalization of electricity. Taschereau, who was against this discussion, instructed the Speaker to delay the debate until the last hour of the session, so that Bouchard would not have time to give his speech. T.-D. was one of the few MLA's who had written out his speech. When he presented his motion, the

---

16   T.-D.B., *La Suspension de la loi des accidents de travail,* 1926 Discours ANQ *Fonds* Bouchard, P-10/24.

premier, unaware that Bouchard had done so, stated that there were only a few minutes left for the debate, and in view of its importance, it should be postponed. To an explosion of laughter from his colleagues, T.-D. then moved that the Assembly adopt his written text, considering it to have been delivered orally. This tactic automatically introduced the issue and presented his views to the columns of the daily press, whose editors had already received advance copies of the text. The publication of this speech provided publicity for his opinions.[17] It prepared the way for changes in the Liberal government's approach to the power "trusts" in 1935 and the adoption of the Hydro-Quebec Law in 1944.

At the beginning of 1928 Taschereau appointed Bouchard assistant speaker of the Legislative Assembly, thereby increasing his salary of $2,500 by an additional $1,000. Contrary to Taschereau's expectation, T.-D.'s new function did not prevent him from continuing his campaign against the electricity trusts. Locally, he prevented the City of Saint-Hyacinthe from renewing a ten-year contract with the power company. The company had to be content with an annual agreement. Again, this did not exactly endear him to certain influential citizens.

During a joint meeting of the congress of the Union of Municipalities of Quebec and the Canadian Union of Municipalities, T.-D. was elected as a representative to the World Congress of Towns and Cities, to take place in Seville and Barcelona in Spain in 1929. He soon put himself to work to study Spanish. After several months, he was sufficiently familiar with the language to hold a conversation, and even to write his speech in Castellan. Before his departure for Seville, on February 21, 1929, his friends organized three dinners to wish him a happy journey. Despite efforts at pressuring Blanche-Corona to accompany him, she refused. To the sound of a fanfare, he left Saint-Hyacinthe accompanied by his daughter Cécile-Ena. He notes that he had paid for his daughter's trip himself.[18] Once again the family interdependence is demonstrated by their daily concerns about Mrs. Bouchard's health, expressed in their correspondence.[19] Bouchard and his daughter displayed their guilty feelings at having left Mrs. Bouchard alone for every day of their two-month trip. Before the train left Montreal for New York, on its arrival in New York, before the boat left the port, on arrival in Southampton, on arrival in London—at each stage of the trip they made

---

17 T.-D.B., *La régie publique et l'exploitation des forces hydro-électrique,* 1928 ANQ *Fonds* Bouchard, P-10/11.

18 T.-D.B., *Retour d'Espagne,* ANQ *Fonds* Bouchard, P-10/24.

19 Private letters. From the collection of family correspondence; Mme. Claire-Simard Odermatt.

efforts to communicate with her, by telephone, by telegram and by letter. All these communications dwelt on their concerns about having left her, and they repeated that they would return immediately if she wished.

London and Paris especially were discoveries for Cécile-Ena. She subsequently returned there frequently. The trip was a success for Bouchard. The congress enthusiastically received his speeches in Spanish as is usual when foreigners attempt to communicate in the local language. He made many new friends. On his return, he was the guest of the University Circle of the University of Montreal, to whom he gave a report on his Spanish experience (at a cost for dinner $5 per person).[20]

In contrast to his public persona, there was also a dour side to Bouchard, which disturbed his daughter and another observer, Doctor Segall, who reported that there were long silences at the dinner table.[21] On the other hand, Gerard Longtin, a cousin who had his education paid for by Cécile-Ena, found him to be an extremely affable and voluble person, although he admits that when he knew him in later life, one had to ask questions in order to obtain a response.[22] Certainly, Cécile-Ena had a most difficult relationship with her father. In her private papers she repeatedly refers to him as hard and cold. She blames him for interfering in several matrimonial possibilities,[23] although those who knew the family well describe Cécile-Ena as a spoiled, not very attractive person. Bouchard himself commented several times on the propensity of many members of the Bouchard family to be isolated and individualistic. Cécile-Ena also accuses her father of not understanding women, mainly his wife and his daughter. What with all his political activities, the newspaper and the mayoralty, he had little available time for them. Travelling often, he was rarely at home on weekends, leaving his women alone. Cécile-Ena attributed the suffering of her mother to her father's negligence. On the other hand, she adored her father. She was certainly his girl, as stubborn as he was. They fought often, especially about her spendthrift ways.[24] With tremendous determination, he was convinced that he

---

20   T.-D.B., *Retour d'Espagne,* ANQ *Fonds* Bouchard, P-10/24.

21   H.N. Segall, personal communication.

22   Gerard Longtin, personal communication.

23   Personal communication, C.-E. B. and Mémoires by CEB—in papers entrusted to Mme. Claire Simard-Odermatt.

24   Judge Marcel Nichols, personal communication, and Gerard Longtin, personal communication.

was always right. However, in time, he could admit that he was wrong. Margaret Laberge, the wife of a naval officer stationed in Saint-Hyacinthe, reported having been invited to Bouchard's home to play cards and finding him to be a poor loser: "He shrugged his shoulders and groused: 'These damned cards.'" As she notes he did not direct his anger towards her; he even succeeded in persuading her to teach English to the local female workers.[25]

On May 12, 1910, during a banquet given to celebrate the thirty-fifth birthday of "our nice mutual relief organization, *The Union of St.-Joseph,*" Bouchard toasted, "An answer to the health of Ladies," in the manner of a nineteenth-century man, praising the traditional view of the woman behind the throne. "He paid tribute to the French-Canadian woman and spoke about all the good that our wives do, called to further the well being of our race … see what influence that a woman can have for the good, that the great celebrities of history owed their success to the encouragement of a constant woman who understood their happy influence for the good."[26] This confirms Cécile-Ena's view of her father.

DEFEATED AS MAYOR; RE-ELECTED

In 1929, Bouchard's opponents began to attack him as a spendthrift with public money. They said he would drive the city to ruin with his innovations, the establishment of parks and playgrounds, and the improvement of traffic circulation in the town (specifically the introduction of one-way streets). Although the changing-rooms for men and women were at opposite ends of the swimming pool, his accusers decried the public scandal of mixed swimming, claiming that bathers displayed themselves publicly in indecent bathing suits. In Catholic Quebec, mixed swimming went contrary to the conventions of modesty. Clerical disapproval continued with the appearance of one-piece bathing suits and short skirts. A familiar scene at this time was a priest or a nun heading off a column of young children in order to prevent the view of tourists in shorts—or of the advertising of brassieres or naked babies in streetcars of the Montreal Tramways Company, even though the advertisements were discreetly covered. In a comment on clerical control of every aspect of life, one observer remarked that in Saint-Hyacinthe the clergy was very puritanical, like elsewhere in rural Quebec. The bishop forbade his parishioners to attend dances at the naval base. "He

---

25   Margaret Laberge, personal communication to Chisholm, p. 182.

26   Ibid., 12 *mai* 1910.

thought that it was a sin even to dance with your own husband!"[27] Once again Bouchard was ahead of his time. The council, which had voted for the pool, claimed that it was Bouchard's idea, and indeed it was. He was also criticized for many restrictive rules he introduced to increase traffic safety, to facilitate faster traffic on the roads, and to improve public health. His detractors characterized him as a dictator. The people called him "le boss."

Consequently, T.-D. Bouchard was narrowly defeated in the mayoralty election by Dr. J.-Henri Pagé on July 14, 1930. Although beaten, he retained a majority of aldermen on the council. He advised his friends on the council to allow the new administration all the necessary latitude to carry out its program. In his newspaper, he challenged the new administrators to modify his policies. His principal critics, who had promised to close the pool during the campaign, nevertheless joined in the celebration at its inauguration the day following their victory. Later they attempted to abrogate Bouchard's regulations, but the council would not agree to allow the changes. Moreover, unemployment resulting from the crash of 1929 was increasing at an alarming rate. The council could not reasonably stop public works. The mayor's friends convinced the council that it was necessary not only to continue work underway, but also to begin new projects, requiring an increase in public expenses. Bouchard felt that greedy contractors would exploit the situation. Forgetting that the city already possessed a sewer system to drain water overflow, the new mayor proposed the construction of a mile-long supporting wall along the river. This project was much ridiculed by the citizens, led by T.-D. They dubbed the author of the plan "Mayor of *Cuvetteville* (Basinville)" because this project would result in an immense basin, at the bottom of which would be the poor district in the lower town, where the majority of the population lived. In spite of this construction and Mayor Bouchard's efforts later, spring floods continued to occur in 1927, 1936, 1939, 1951 and even in 1976.[28]

In council, Mayor Pagé had a friend who was also secretary-treasurer of several smaller municipalities. This man "forgot" to deposit funds destined for public expenditure into corporate accounts, depositing the money into his own private account instead. This "forgetfulness" allowed him to profit from the interest. T.-D. exposed him, as this was the same individual who had accused him of dishonesty as mayor. Appearing before the council as a simple citizen,

---

27   Margaret Laberge, personal communication, to Chisholm, p. 150.

28   *Le Courrier de Saint-Hyacinthe* mentions these years of floods; see Soc.d'histoire régionale de Saint-Hyacinthe, *Saint-Hyacinthe 1748–1998*, p.16.

Bouchard challenged this man to submit his request for an inquiry into the Bouchard administration in writing, as the law required. While the audience jeered, this individual did not persist. At a meeting held in the Hay-Market, Mayor Pagé, declared, "The ex-mayor Bouchard is an honest man; he is even the most honest man to have served on the municipal council."[29]

In the 1931 council elections, all of Mayor Pagé's aldermen were defeated. From the month of January, the mayor sat but did not govern. He asked the town clerk to sound out T.-D. Bouchard as to whether he would consent to prepare the budget for the next financial period because, he confessed, he did not know enough about municipal administration. Bouchard remarks with some condescension, "Finally, Mayor Pagé was a good fellow. Before being indoctrinated by Henri Bourassa he was a Liberal."[30] This thought convinced Bouchard to accept. Thus, he prepared the budget for 1931 and Pagé presented it to council. In 1932, Télesphore-Damien was elected first magistrate of his city for the fifth time, without opposition. At his inauguration, he noted that aldermen sympathetic to his cause occupied all ten seats of the new council.

At the opening of the Quebec Legislative Assembly in January 1930, Premier Taschereau moved to appoint Bouchard as Speaker of the House. The promotion was perhaps a reflection of the favour Bouchard had found with the party, or perhaps it stemmed from the party bosses finding him too persistent and tedious, and was an effort to shut him up. But most probably it was because of his success and popularity at the local level. Bouchard occupied the Speaker's chair until June 1935, receiving $6,000 in addition to his salary as an ordinary member ($2,500). He had been a backbencher for twelve years and Assistant Speaker for two years; and now, as Speaker, he would continue to perfect his knowledge of parliamentary procedure. This knowledge was especially useful during his stint as House Leader of the Liberals facing Maurice Duplessis in his first term of office from 1936 to 1939. If Taschereau thought that Bouchard would cease campaigning for his causes, he was wrong. (During debates, the speaker is constrained to maintain strict neutrality.) He kept in close touch with developments and promoted his aims through similarly minded members willing to serve as intermediaries.

During this period, he was secretary-treasurer of the Union of Canadian Municipalities, a member of the Reform Club of Montreal, and director of a company called "Hydropeat." He was also president of the theatrical company of

---

29   T.-D.B., *Mémoires*, III, p. 93.

30   Ibid., p. 93.

Saint-Hyacinthe. His flair for making money in real estate continued. He bought inexpensive properties, subdividing them for sale at advantageous prices. He was very prudent and careful to keep his private fortune separate from his public affairs. In his position as mayor, Bouchard had to deal with the ever-present temptation to profit from inside information on land speculation. However, even his most persistent adversary could never discover a dishonest action, and no accusation of this sort was ever made. Eugene Payan, the son of the former mayor, put it this way: "He wasn't just a money-maker, not a grabber.... He was way ahead of everybody ... when there was a fire he would buy the place for a song ... he borrowed $25,000 to buy up land across the tracks ... subdivided it.... Today almost 10,000 people are living there."[31] However, T.-D. did boast to a close acquaintance—his physician—that he had been shrewd and sharp in his land dealings.[32]

Although the people had suffered from the Depression, they re-elected the Liberals under Taschereau in the provincial elections of 1931. The Conservatives led by Camillien Houde gained only eleven seats, including one occupied by the young Maurice Duplessis. In the new Taschereau cabinet, there was a young minister of agriculture, Adélard Godbout—a quiet gentleman who would later become Taschereau's replacement and then Bouchard's nemesis. At the end of the year another future foe was raised to the high office of cardinal—the Archbishop of Quebec, Msgr. J. Rodrigue Villeneuve.

Speaker of the Legislative Assembly, 1930–1935

---

31   Eugene Payan, personal communication to Chisholm, p. 100, no doubt referring to Bois Joli.

32   H.N. Segall, personal communication.

As speaker, Bouchard had to put a brake on his natural tendency to battle with his opponents. He devoted himself to the study of the complexities of parliamentary procedure. In addition to convincing some members to propose measures that he wished to see passed, he attempted to help applicants to find work. He would do this even for old enemies if he thought that they could be useful to the government and the people. He tried without success to find work for Harry Bernard, ex-publisher of *Le Courrier de Saint-Hyacinthe,* although he had gone to court against Bernard for defamation. As Bernard noted, "T.-D. Bouchard was always proud when good things happened to someone from Saint-Hyacinthe. He would have been happy to find me official work in Quebec, and at the same time maybe some of my friends or family would have voted for him instead of against him."[33]

In 1932, the economic crisis deepened. Unemployment increased, and governments were obliged to come to the assistance of municipalities to ease public misery. The newly reinstated mayor asked Judge Victor Chabot, a solid supporter, to help him by accepting the role of president of the finance committee. They had mutual respect for one another. Chabot found Bouchard energetic and brilliant.[34] They proposed municipal laws for the unemployed—laws unique in the province and based on legislation that had worked well in Paris. The province had established various work-sites where the work and salary conditions were more advantageous than in private industry. Workers deserted private jobs and flooded the state and municipal work-sites. To help the destitute, the state provided direct subsidies. Under the mayor's influence the municipal council refused to accept the policies of the provincial ministry. The council introduced a revolutionary plan. It abolished direct support and gave work to the *bona fide* unemployed, providing that they consented to donate a quarter of their work hours. Workers would receive pay for thirty-three hours, and work an additional eleven hours *gratis.* Bouchard noted that names of the "fraudulent" unemployed quickly disappeared from the municipal lists.[35]

In order to decrease the burden on the masses, council abolished the tax on tenants. It reduced property taxes 50 percent. This greatly eased the burden on the majority of taxpayers. Despite this decrease in tax collection, the administration succeeded in balancing the municipal budget. At the end of the fiscal

---

33   Harry Bernard, personal communication to Chisholm, p. 101.

34   Judge Victor Chabot, personal communication to Chisholm, p. 104.

35   T.-D.B., *Mémoires,* III, p. 94.

year, the town achieved a surplus, given that all useless expenses had been eliminated. The widely circulated metropolitan newspapers—even *Le Devoir*—published articles praising the city council of Saint-Hyacinthe.[36] It had accomplished what one could qualify as a miracle in civic administration in the face of the Depression. Bouchard's opponents, interpreting the prosperity of city finances, accused him of reducing the poor people to famine with the intention of filling the municipal coffers. There was hunger in Saint-Hyacinthe, like elsewhere in Quebec and the rest of Canada, but little famine. By reducing property taxes, eliminating taxes for tenants and reducing the municipal electricity rates, council helped the poor people.

Bouchard was now recognised as "king" by friend and foe. In his study he displayed a bust of Napoléon Bonaparte, whom he resembled in form—now rotund, nearing fifty years of age. He admired Napoléon not for his military conquests but for his talent as an administrator. Bouchard did not drink strong alcohol. He had a glass of wine with his evening meal, and a brandy after the meal. Called avaricious, especially when he continued to prosper during the Depression, he lived well. He would say that if it appeared that he adored money, it was in order to gain his objectives as a public servant and because he had known since his youth how difficult it was to earn money. He knew that after the next election, he could find himself without a seat. He was not free of debts; he kept his office walls covered with bank promissory notes, drawing visitors' attention to them. "You see, it is because of them that I have to earn money."[37]

The leaders of the party still did not trust Bouchard. When he publicly called for the rescinding of the law preventing the entry of children into movie houses, he was criticized by the premier himself, as well as by the cardinal's publication, *L'Action catholique*. Taschereau bluntly warned him: "I believe that you were wrong to make such a statement. You will stimulate protests, which will not advance your cause. Several bishops have written asking us not to change this law."[38]

The City of Saint-Hyacinthe had demonstrated as early as 1909 that it was possible to produce electrical power, powered by gas, at one-seventh the price asked by private companies. In the 1930s, modern, stronger internal-combustion motors were required to replace them. Bouchard hired Nicholas Sauer, a White Russian exile, as the city engineer. Sauer had left Moscow

---

36   *Le Devoir*, 25 mars 1936.

37   V. Chabot, personal communication to Chisholm, p. 104.

38   ANQ *Fonds* Bouchard, P-10/19. Letter from A.-L. Taschereau to T.-D.B., Dec. 28, 1932.

during the revolution of 1917. In Moscow, he had been director of the city's electrical plant, which had produced 66,000 kilowatts furnished with simple steam-engines. Sauer had contacts with several European metallurgic manufacturers, allowing the mayor and his engineer to obtain information to verify their own calculations. This information confirmed data that they had obtained from American establishments. They submitted the conclusions of their study to the municipal council. The aldermen approved the proposal and a loan of $310,000. A referendum of proprietors adopted the projet by a majority of 439 against 157, despite a tenacious battle directed by the local power company. This plant would challenge private industry, which charged exorbitant prices "which brought them millions."[39] Immediately, the local company offered a reduction in rates, even though it had claimed a month before that a reduction was impossible. Télesphore-Damien recommended that the council refuse the offer, and waited with some anxiety for the aldermen's reply. He was greatly pleased to learn that his colleagues had confidence in his judgment. They decided to proceed with the modernization of the plant.

After the adoption of the motion, Bouchard and Sauer left for Europe to visit factories in Germany and England to continue negotiations begun from Saint-Hyacinthe. They departed on December 13, 1933, on a trip lasting three weeks. On his return, arriving in New York, Bouchard received worrisome news by telephone. His wife was severely ill. Just after his departure, Blanche-Corona became sick with malaise and fever. Mrs. Bouchard and her local physician consulted Dr. Harold Segall, who examined her three days following the onset of her illness. Dr. Segall's notes suggest a possible diagnosis of typhoid fever.[40] With exemplary thoroughness he took two samples of blood. The sample sent to the laboratories of the Montreal General Hospital was negative, but the sample sent to the provincial laboratory was positive. No cure was available for typhoid fever in those days.[41] Doctor Segall travelled by train between Saint-Hyacinthe and Montreal every two or three days, and more often towards the end. Accompanied by Cécile-Ena he greeted Bouchard on his return at the beginning of January 1934, and informed him about the precarious state of his wife's health. She died ten days later, on January 14, 1934, with her husband, Cécile-Ena and Doctor Segall at her bedside.

---

39   T.-D.B., *Mémoires,* III, p. 97, see also Hogue, Bolduc and Larouche, p.194.

40   Frank M. Guttman, "The Bouchards of Saint-Hyacinthe and Dr. H. N. Segal," in *Festschrift for his 90th birthday.* (Montreal: McGill University Press, 1989), p. 322–332.

41   Ibid., p. 324.

Alas, she who had been the companion of my life was to expire ten days after my return. She died a victim of the negligence of our milkman who had bought cream from a farmer ... which was cooled in a contaminated artesian well. In spite of a municipal regulation demanding that all milkmen pasteurize their products, this cream had been distributed without having been submitted to usual examination. The inquiry ... revealed that this farmer's wife had also died due to this infectious fever a month previously, contracted from the same source of contamination. Underground infiltration coming from a cowshed situated nearby spread into the poisoned well.... My soul was in mourning for my immense loss. I found myself at home alone without she who had been my heart and joy for thirty years.[42]

Madly in love with Blanche-Corona since the age of nineteen and married at the age of twenty-two, he was shattered by the loss of his wife. The one consolation was his daughter, Cécile-Ena. She helped him to endure the cruel blow by replacing her mother in the home. "To keep house, and in order that nothing should change in our habits, she was required to make many sacrifices for which I am indebted. For my part, I resolutely turned to my work. For me, it was again the most efficient means to chase away dark thoughts, which sometimes came to haunt me."[43] Perhaps he had doubts about his one-sided relationship with his wife—doubts of whether the marriage had really been the best choice for Blanche-Corona.

Throughout his life T.-D. enjoyed the company of priests. He liked conversing with them, especially with Dominicans. He became an expert in Catholic Church dogma. Abbé J.A.M. Brousseau was often a guest in his home. Abbé Brousseau was the curé of the St. Jérôme parish, north of Montreal, and was an open-minded priest. He was relieved from his functions for unknown reasons—perhaps they were related to his free spirit. He had organized a theatre group in his parish. He also had a huge personal library (with banned books?), which ended up first in Bouchard's hands, and finally, after Bouchard's death, in the library of the Dominicans on Côte Ste. Catherine Road in Montreal and in the Seminary of Saint-Hyacinthe. Abbé Brousseau was a scientist, a man of independent spirit, and an ideal priest to be the confessor of T.-D. Bouchard. He was an earthy man who liked to tell suggestive stories about nuns

---

42   T.-D.B., *Mémoires,* III, p. 99.

43   Ibid., p. 100.

and priests, even in the presence of women.[44] He brought joy into T.-D.'s often-dreary house.[45] Abbé Brousseau's body rested in T.-D.'s home after his death, when the Church authorities in Montreal informed Bouchard that they were about to bury Brousseau in a common grave. In the end he was buried in the Saint-Hyacinthe cemetery, in same plot as Mrs. Bouchard—where eventually Télesphore-Damien and Cécile-Ena would be buried.[46] Bouchard and Cécile-Ena commissioned the memorial stone, designed and executed by the famous sculptor Émile Brunet.

Clouds accumulated over Europe with the arrival of Hitler in power in Germany. In Saint-Hyacinthe there were a few followers of Nazism. They were naturally Bouchard's enemies. When Bouchard favoured a motion granting a subsidy to the Jewish proprietors of a clothing factory, thereby allowing them to enlarge their establishment and create more work locally, the "black-shirts" placed placards in shop windows of the commercial district denouncing the proposed project by the mayor to "Judify our French city." The mayor congratulated the populace: "These calls for anti-Semitism receive the welcome they deserve. There were only 14 fanatics out of a population of 14,000."[47] However, it was not necessary in the '30s to be pro-Nazi to be anti-Semitic. Despite many people such as T.-D. Bouchard, anti-Semitism was widespread in Quebec, like everywhere in Canada and many places around the world. In Quebec it was prevalent among both major language groups. The years of agitation by right-wing and ultramontane Catholic newspapers such as *La Croix*, *La Croix de Montréal*, and *La Vérité*; and the activities of Jules-Paul Tardivel (influenced by Drumont and Maurras of France, where the Dreyfus affair had inflamed the country) favoured a climate of anti-Semitism.[48] During the 1930s the nationalistic *L'Achat chez nous*—"Buy at our own"—campaign promoted by Canon Groulx and the Order of Jacques Cartier was directed principally against Jewish storekeepers, with little success.[49]

---

44   Father Milot, in preface T.-D.B., *Mémoires* II, p. 9,10 and Chisholm, personal communication.

45   Dr. H.N. Segall, personal communication.

46   Dr. Segall and I attended Cécile-Ena's funeral in 1987.

47   T.-D.B., *Mémoires,* III, p. 95.

48   Jean-Denis Bredin. *The Affair; The Case of Alfred Dreyfus.* (Paris: George Brazillier Inc. 1986).

49   M. Oliver; *The Passionate Debate* (Montreal: Véhicle Press, 1991), p. 187.
     In Quebec, doing one's "steinberg," became a verb denoting shopping at Steinberg's, one of the first large, modern food stores. As an example of the anti-

We have seen the active role that Bouchard took in directing the affairs of his native city as mayor. He made many improvements to the lives of the inhabitants of Saint-Hyacinthe. During the Depression he sought to relieve the citizens of their heavy financial burdens, succeeding in making the city known throughout Canada as exemplary. In the Legislative Assembly he was finally recognized by Taschereau who appointed him assistant speaker, and then, in 1930, Speaker of the House. In the next chapter we will follow T.-D. in his battle against the hydro-electricity power companies, and to his entry into cabinet.

Dr. Harold Segall and T.-D. Bouchard in the living-room.
Note the portrait of Blanche-Corona over the fireplace. Circa 1953.

Semitism of the elites, there is the story of Dr. Samuel Rabinovitch. In 1934 the interns and residents of Notre-Dame Hospital in Montreal went out on strike to protest the hiring of Doctor Rabinovitch, a medical graduate (with distinction) of the University of Montreal. The strike spread to all five hospitals of the University of Montreal system, involving most of the interns and residents. Although the hospital board supported him, Doctor Rabinovitch withdrew. Olivar Asselin strongly condemned the strike as motivated by "racist hatred." Asselin wrote that *Le Devoir* was alone among the large daily newspapers in being in favour of this strike.

Chapter VII

CABINET MINISTER

Bouchard had won the battle in the Assembly authorizing municipalities to produce and distribute electricity. In the light of these events Sir Herbert Holt, head of the Montreal Light, Heat and Power Company—and also head of numerous banks and trust, insurance and power companies—cut prices to encourage smaller cities to renew their contracts. In Saint-Hyacinthe the Southern Power Company, owned in part by Montreal interests (Nesbitt-Thomson), also offered to reduce rates. Too late, replied the mayor and council. Rumilly commented, "Bouchard has won his efficiently managed battle, and his prestige increases."[1] The Maskoutain and the City of Sherbooke's efforts to reduce electricity costs seemed to be contagious. Several municipalities in the Eastern Townships followed their example. In Trois-Rivières the municipal council demanded a 40-percent reduction from the Shawinigan Water and Power Company. Mont-Laurier's council considered purchasing the local company. In Montreal a project to use the aqueduct canal to produce electricity was revived. Engineers evaluated the cost at $100,000, instead of the $630,000 paid to Montreal Light, Heat and Power. Father Cambron, a Jesuit, speaking on the radio under the auspices of the Union of Catholic Farmers, openly criticized the "trust." He held that the rate set for a given amount of electricity by the Montreal Light, Heat, and Power Company in February 1934 would be $108.20. In Sherbrooke, where the city sold the electricity, the same quantity would cost $56.36; and in Ottawa, it would cost $18.36—a difference of 83 percent.

Taschereau did not change his nineteenth century *laissez-faire* ideas despite the publication of the papal encyclical *Quadragesimo Anno* in 1931, which proclaimed the duty and the responsibility of the state to ease the burden of poor people. The *programme de restauration sociale (*Social Restoration Program)

---

1   Rumilly, *HPQ*, XXXIII, p. 235.

conceived by *les Semaines sociales*, a group financed by the Jesuits, was based on the papal encyclical. Later it was adopted in its entirety by the *Action libérale nationale*.[2] Olivar Asselin in *Le Canada* dismissed the *Programme de restauration sociale* as an "instrument of warfare created by the Jesuits against the Liberal Party ... [he] was sorry to see the Jesuits compromised in the political propaganda of the *Jeunes Canada*."[3] As Quinn suggests, this is rather harsh judgment because the Pope had criticized the capitalist system and had even recommended worker-employer co-operatives, and as well that "Certain forms of property must be reserved to the state, since they carry with them the opportunity of domination too great to be left to private individuals without injury to the community at large."[4] However, Taschereau did not pay any attention to the Pope's encyclical. In 1933, Premier Louis-Alexandre Taschereau declared old-age pensions and family allowances to be pernicious remedies that would financially and morally compromise society's future.[5] He accused supporters of these measures of promoting social revolution by encouraging the masses in their expectations of receiving everything from the state.[6] According to the premier, unemployment allowance was the most ominous doctrine that had invaded Canada. He acknowledged the state's obligation to intervene when there was an emergency, but he confused recipients of support with rebellious bourgeois youth who felt that the state (or their relatives) owed them everything. In short, Taschereau was not the only Canadian politician of the period who did not understand Keynesian economics or the United States' New Deal. One can understand Taschereau's rigid adhesion to old principles and beliefs. A man approaching his seventieth birthday does not change his ideas easily—although he did bend in 1935 by introducing the social reforms that he had previously condemned. Taschereau's philosophy was quite widespread. Even progressive liberals such as Athanase David supported him.

---

2   The ALN, *Action libérale nationale*, formed in 1935, was a coalition of the nationalists and dissident liberals dissatisfied with Taschereau's passivity. See p. 198.

3   Rumilly, *HPQI*, XXXIII, p. 214. *Jeunes Canada*, founded by André Laurendeau, was a nationalist-Catholic political group.

4   Pius XI, *Quadragesimo Anno*, (London, 1931), p. 51, cited in Quinn, p. 156.

5   *Le Devoir*, Jan. 13, 1933.

6   ANQ: *Fonds L.-A. Taschereau*, Letters to Father Henri Roy, Nov. 17, 1933 and Father Alexandre Dugré, November 24, 1933.

Taschereau's understanding of social security was analogous to his understanding of hydroelectric questions. As a nineteenth-century man, he did not foresee the rapid, overwhelming wave in public opinion against *laissez-faire* attitudes and in favour of the philosophy of state intervention. This was a conclusion that resulted from the Depression and growing expectations of the public. His critics could only explain his attitude as symptomatic of a man who was a protector of trusts, of the corporate elite; and indifferent to the needs of the population at large. Taschereau defended himself by insisting that he had sued the coal trusts—that he had passed a law extending the collective agreement, which allowed the government to protect the employer and the employees. This law was severely criticized by Bouchard, who felt that only the insurance companies benefited from the law. As noted, a more progressive law supported by Bouchard eventually replaced it.

Between 1930 and 1935 Bouchard continued to play a prominent role in the campaign to reduce electricity rates, even though he was speaker of the Legislative Assembly.[7] He gave talks in ten cities of the province on this subject.[8] His speeches were widely reported in the press. The inauguration of the giant power project in the Tennessee Valley by the president of the United States—the Tennessee Valley Authority (TVA)—increased public awareness of the question.[9] The "Beauharnois scandal" in 1931 decreased public confidence in the Liberal government. The

---

7   *Fonds* T.-D.B.: List of brochures (at first speeches) at the ANQ, P-10/11:
     La régie publique et l'exploitation des forces hydro-électrique, 1928.
     Règlement no. 446, 1933.
     L'Électricité dans la province de Québec, 1934.
     La domination des trusts électriques, 1934.
     La métropole commerciale et l'électricité, 1934.
     Les réformes qui s'imposent dans la régie de nos ressources hydro-électriques, 1935.
     La Municipalisation de l'électricité à Saint-Hyacinthe, 1938.

8   To note just two of these talks (reprinted as brochures as above):
     "La Domination des Trusts Électriques"—talk given at the Palais Montcalm. Quebec City.
     June 11, 1934 at the Invitation of La Ligue des Consommateurs d'Électricité, 53 pages.
     Fonds Bouchard, ANQ, P-10/11:
     "La metropole commerciale de l'électricité à l'École du Plateau," Montréal, June 20, 1934 at the
     invitation of the Ligue des Propriétaires, 55 pages.

9   The American power monopolies contested the project in court, accusing the state of competing with private industry and thereby violating the American Constitution. On the other hand, criticism of the TVA was partially muted by the extensive coverage of the famous criminal case in the "yellow press" involving the supposedly fraudulent dealings of the financier Samuel Insull, owner of electricity companies in the United States.

Beauharnois Power Company had provided enormous funds (over $900,000) to the federal and provincial Liberal governments, and to the Conservative Party, to obtain approval of their project to harness the Soulange portion of the St. Lawrence River. Both political parties received money, but the larger amount ($700,000) was given to the Liberals, who were in power. Prime Minister Mackenzie King was also involved in the scandal.[10]

Unrest concerning this question in Quebec created a propitious climate for a movement supporting public regulation of the power monopoly. The nationalists, led by Dr. Philippe Hamel, and other unhappy Liberals disappointed by Taschereau's authoritarian manner, his association with the "trusts," and his refusal to apply pressure to the power companies, began to think of joining forces. At the time, it was accepted practice for politicians to be members of company boards of directors. Taschereau was a director of many private companies.[11] Paul Gouin, son of Sir Lomer Gouin and grandson of Honoré Mercier, led the Young Liberal dissidents. Gouin and friends founded *l'Action libérale,* and were then joined by the nationalists of Quebec City, forming *l'Action libérale nationale* (ALN). Their goal was to provide an opposition to Taschereau that would also be an alternative to Duplessis's Conservatives. They advocated nationalization of electricity, as well as socio-economic reform allowing French Canadians to benefit from industrialisation without damaging the unique values they deemed necessary for group survival: the French language, the land and the devotion to the Church. Many Liberals shared the fears of the Nationalist-Liberal Oscar Drouin, MLA for Quebec East, and a protégé of Ernest Lapointe—fears that the Liberal Party would be ruined if it continued to follow the dictates of big business

---

10   T.D. Regehr, *The Beauharnois Scandal: A Story of Canadian Entrepreneurship and Politics,* (Toronto: University of Toronto Press, 1990). Both Senators Hadon and McDougald, heavily involved in the Liberal Party as well as in the Beauharnois Power Company, entertained King on a trip to Bermuda and then in New York at luxurious hotels. They were seeking special privileges for the company including rights to the St. Lawrence River. When the scandal broke, King denied that he was aware that McDougald intended to pay his bills, and paid him back, pp. 109–112.

11   Vigod. Vigod exposes the close association of many Ministers with industry, pp. 12–13, 139, 191. Taschereau accepted directorships in several major financial institutions: North American Life, Barclay's Bank, The Royal Trust Company, the Sun Life Assurance Company, the Title Guarantee and Trust Corporation, the Royal Liverpool Insurance Company, Canadian Investment Funds, and the Metropolitan Life. His Minister of Roads, Léonide Perron, was a major shareholder in the Canada Cement Company.

in this period of economic crisis.[12] These Liberals pressed for urgent changes in the policies of the Taschereau government, but to no avail. This contributed to the climate of distrust in the regime. The relationship between Paul Gouin and Taschereau was uneasy, especially after the death of Sir Lomer Gouin in 1929. Trained in law and gifted with a superior intelligence, Gouin preferred to write poetry and hold intellectual soirées. He requested a sinecure as assistant director of the Museum of Quebec. Taschereau refused, considering this position an insult to the memory of Gouin's father and his grandfather.

Following the publication of their manifesto, Bouchard began contact with the founders of the new movement. The dissidents took note of his campaigns against the trusts and for public ownership of electricity. They sought a more experienced and more dynamic leader in the Assembly than Gouin. The rumoured proposed leaders were Ernest Lapointe, T.-D. Bouchard and Athanase David.[13] In early August of 1934 a dinner was arranged to discuss the "politics of the day" with Paul Gouin and two federal Liberals, Cyrille Dumaine and Adélard Fontaine, at Bouchard's summer house at Pointe-aux-Fourches, just outside Saint-Hyacinthe.[14] According to some, T.-D. initiated the meeting, but according to Cécile-Ena the dissidents had done so.[15] Later, Gouin did not remember who had initiated it, but he confirmed that he considered Bouchard for the leadership.[16] "We never knew exactly why he named us delegates to that meeting," he explained. "He was a man attracted by progressive ideas. He may have hoped for the leadership of the movement, or he may have hoped to impress Mr. Taschereau."[17] This question is still open for debate. However, Rumilly also confirms that the ALN looked to Bouchard as leader. "The supporters of a re-liberalization of the Liberal party sought T.-D. Bouchard to accept the leadership of the party [the ALN] whose program advocated the nationalization of public services."[18]

---

12   Patricia Dirks, *The Failure of l'Action Libérale Nationale* (Montreal and Kingston: McGill-Queens University Press, 1991), p. 29.

13   B. Vigod, p. 204.

14   P. Dirks, p. 53.

15   C.-E. B., personal communication.

16   P. Gouin, personal communication in interview by Chisholm, CBC. AN Ottawa.

17   P. Gouin, personal communication to Chisholm, p. 113.

18   Rumilly, *HPQ*, XXXIV, p. 38.

Mr. Minister in the Taschereau and Godbout Cabinets, 1936

Mr. Mayor—sporting a cane—and the town council, circa 1938.

The close association of the liberal dissidents of Montreal with the clerical nationalists of Quebec City no doubt had an influence on Bouchard's decision to remain in the Liberal Party and not to move against Taschereau. He feared the narrow minds of the clericals more than he did the conduct of Taschereau. In his biography of Taschereau, Vigod attributes Bouchard's lack of confidence in the dissidents to this fact: "T.-D. Bouchard probably rallied to Taschereau because he feared the alternative was a regime of clerical reaction."[19] Bouchard was known to be hostile to the people surrounding Taschereau, particularly Charles Lanctôt, who had been implicated in corruption for years and who ended up being exposed by Duplessis in the hearings of the Committee of Accounts in 1936.[20] He was also unimpressed by Paul Gouin. Black describes Gouin as: "this timid champion of popular causes who never was elected except in literary circles."[21]

The association of the Montreal reformists and the Quebec City national-ists such as Hamel and Chaloult puzzled Taschereau. They were supported by *Jeune Canada*, a political group inspired by Abbé Groulx, editor of the *L'Action française*, which preached an oncoming conflict between the "races" and whose contributors had flirted with separatism in 1921, attacked modern industrialisation and urbanization, promoted agriculture as the only outlet for French-Canadian activity, and criticized the government directly. The founding fathers of *Jeune Canada* were Groulx's ex-students. Their first manifesto pro-claimed that the defeat of Taschereau was the number one item on their agenda. Gouin's friend the editor and writer Jean-Charles Harvey warned him that the enemies of the premier and his new friends included people of the extreme right: the *"Laurentiens, les supra-nationalistes, Fascistes, isolationistes, séparatistes et les cléricaux."*[22]

As we have noted, it is curious to observe that Lomar Gouin, and later Taschereau, kept a man of such energy and conviction as Bouchard from pro-motion to the cabinet. He had entered the Legislative Assembly in 1912, but despite his well-documented and well-studied speeches, he was not called to the inner sanctum until 1935—and even then it was an attempt to reinforce a

---

19   Vigod, p. 209.

20   Ibid., p.52–54.

21   Conrad Black, *Duplessis,* (Montréal: Les éditions de l'homme, 1977) p. 130. Note: I used the French version of this biography.

22   *Fonds* Jean-Charles Harvey, Bibliothèque de L'Université de Sherbrooke. *Mémoires,* Chapter 3, p.1. letter Harvey to Gouin July 16, 1936.

faltering cabinet. For leaders of the Liberal Party (and those of the ALN) who were essentially the representatives of the upper bourgeoisie, Bouchard was only a crafty small-town politician.[23] Alternatively, perhaps his extreme honesty in public affairs annoyed his colleagues. After his appointments as assistant speaker in 1928 and speaker in 1930, possibly in order to keep him quiet on the educational and energy issues—unsuccessfully—Taschereau then offered him the lucrative post of president of the Montreal Tramways Commission. Perhaps the premier was hoping to keep him quiet on the education and energy issues. If this was the case, he was unsuccessful (as he had been when Bouchard was appointed Speaker of the House). Taschereau said, "I know a man who would make an excellent president of this commission, if he was not so attached to his city and to politics."[24] But Bouchard did not bite. "As you say, I am too attached to political life to leave it."[25]

During the first session of the legislature in 1931, the premier's support for the Quebec Power Company against the City of Quebec contributed to discontent in the Liberal Party caucus. This battle went on for almost two years. The public demanded either that rates should be comparable to those of Ontario Hydro, or else that the city should municipalize electricity. In a private member's bill, the Quebec city council urged the Assembly to revise its city charter to remove all obstacles to the construction of a municipal system of electricity. Patricia Dirks notes that T.-D. Bouchard supported the City of Quebec's request: "[Bouchard] … that traditional Liberal critic of government policies on the electricity issue."[26]. To fight this move, the company submitted its own bill to the Assembly to protect its charter in case of expropriation. After a tumultuous debate, the Quebec Power Bill, protecting the trust, passed. Five Liberal members rebelled, voting against it (not Bouchard, who was still in the speaker's chair). Finally, to solve the problem, in exchange for a promise to submit the problem to a public service commission, Taschereau obtained the company's consent to withdraw its bill, and at the same time, the city's private bill was withdrawn. Bowing to Liberal critics, Taschereau appointed a commission of three members charged with the task of examining the problems of hydroelec-

---

23   Mme. Vautelet, personal communication to Chisholm, p. 2.

24   Rumilly, *HPQ*, XXXII, p. 235.

25   Ibid., p. 235.

26   Dirks, p. 31.

tricity. Cleverly, he chose Ernest Lapointe, the federal leader of the Quebec Liberals and a critic of his energy policy, as chairman of this commission.

Thus, in 1932, the first witness to appear before this commission in Montreal was T.-D. Bouchard, representative of the Union of Municipalities (secretary-treasurer), president of the League of Electricity Consumers, and special delegate from twenty-six municipalities. He spoke for six hours over a two-day period. At his own expense, he followed the commission's hearings throughout the province for four months. The Lapointe Commission began in Quebec, where Hamel and Bouchard testified. The commission returned to Montreal, where Bouchard gave evidence once more. The commission travelled on to Hull. Bouchard followed and bore witness again. The commission moved on to Rimouski. Bouchard appeared and testified. He also spoke in Chicoutimi and Three-Rivers, again in Quebec City, and again during the final hearings in Montreal. In total he gave eighteen hours of testimony. At each stop, Bouchard presented general and local arguments based on his extensive studies of the subject. According to the journalist Edmond Turcotte, "he had his facts and figures completely mobilized for the attack."[27] George Montgomery, the attorney representing the power company, remarked to Bouchard, "We would pay a man like you dearly." However, Bouchard pretended not to hear.[28] Vigod explained:

> The decisive presentation however, was a confidential memorandum from Bouchard to Lapointe. Setting out the results of his 18-month survey of municipal leaders, Bouchard reported universal complaints against domestic and commercial rates ... recommended that the province enable local councils to take over distribution facilities, to expand and operate them efficiently, and to purchase their electricity from the private suppliers at rates comparable to those charged by Ontario Hydro. The companies would retain valid titles ... but no further resources should be alienated to them ... undeveloped sites should be reintegrated into public domain at the original price—possibly for future public projects which could compete with private interests ... what he did hope was that the threat would be sufficient to induce reduction by private distributors.[29]

---

27 *Le Canada,* 14 *juin* 1934.

28 Rumilly, *HPQ,* XXXIV, p. 112.

29 Vigod, p. 197.

The Lapointe Commission did not adopt Bouchard's recommendations. However, it did recommend changes. Instead of provincial acquisition and provincial development of hydro power, it called for close control of the companies through the creation of a regulatory commission. On the whole the report pleased St. James Street (Montreal's Wall Street), which had feared a state monopoly.

Towards the end of 1934, the electrical plant of Saint-Hyacinthe opened, placing the city among those with the lowest rates in North America. In 1935, the Public Ownership League, an American association, invited Bouchard to speak on the subject in Washington. The invitation was to reciprocate for a talk given by its secretary—Carl Thompson, an American apostle of nationalization—which he had delivered to the Union of Municipalities in the autumn of 1933. In his address T.-D. Bouchard denounced the Lapointe report as "destined to cover up the errors of our barons of electricity and to prepare consumers to swallow the bitter pill of a new regulatory commission, aimed in reality not to save the poor consumer, but the authors of their woes."[30]

Taschereau, realizing that it was more necessary to obtain the co-operation of Bouchard than to enact the exact recommendations of the Lapointe Commission, sent Jacob Nicol, a Liberal Party leader, to negotiate an agreement with him. The result was a compromise between the report's and Bouchard's recommendations.[31] The fact that Taschereau agreed to a compromise with Bouchard, a frank critic of the government in economic matters for a long time and a rumoured candidate for the leadership of the ALN, was testimony to party fears concerning the growing influence of that new political formation.[32] It was a tribute to Taschereau's ability to bend with the wind when faced with no other choice. In March, Bouchard submitted three draft bills based on the compromise modifications. One created an electricity commission (*La Commission de l'eau courante*), the second authorized cities to municipalize electricity, and the third set up a plan of rural electrification—a sort of Hydro-Quebec—enabling it to acquire waterfalls. On April 25, 1935, before the General Committee of the Legislative Assembly studying the government bills, T.-D. delivered a long speech in support of the proposed legislation, consisting of fifty thousand words on 100 typed pages. He recalled his struggles to reduce the cost of power to the

---

30   T.-D.B.; speech given in Washington, before the Public Ownership League. *Le Moniteur*, published by the *Cercle d'étude de Gardenvale*, March, 1935.

31   *The Montreal Gazette*, March 17, 1935.

32   Dirks, p. 63.

consumer. He stated that the government and the opposition had always considered that private initiative was the best way of operating hydroelectric resources, but that he had never held this opinion. What paralyzed economic progress was the huge over-capitalization of the private companies, which required exorbitant profits.[33] Rates were raised too much and electricity was even less available in Quebec than in Ontario. The report of the Lapointe Commission was too timid, recommending only a partial remedy. The ideal would be a state authority. Bouchard then paid homage to Henri Bourassa, a supporter of state control of electricity. Nevertheless, he saw positive things in the report. In the absence of total nationalization, the competition of a public authority, whether national or municipal, would oblige companies to reduce their rates, as had been demonstrated in Westmount and in Saint-Hyacinthe. Adoption of the bills would allow the improvement of rural life, and thus keep people on the land—and even attract more of the population *to* it. Later appearing in pamphlet form, his talk was entitled "The Government has to Act,"[34] Bouchard concluded:

> I am a Liberal. I have fought inside the party. Twenty times I have refused to take the leadership of a new political party. It was said that I would never otherwise obtain the required reforms. However, the government grants me these reforms: that's progress. I accept the powerful help of the government with eagerness, which will help the recovery of the popular classes by saving them from the domination of the trusts. I remain with the leaders of the Liberal party.[35]

Rumilly conceded that it was a solid speech, and Maskoutains who attended, approved with pleasure. "In the imposing framework of the Assembly, [Bouchard] the courageous, the convinced, the stubborn, the persistent, and the incorruptible, who untiringly denounces the clericals …"[36]

In a flurry of activity, Taschereau also modified his long-standing opposition to old-age pensions, but as indicated by the Provincial Secretary in a memorandum to Prime Minister Bennett, he waited for the federal law to undergo some modi-

---

33   The Montreal Light and Heat and Power Company was said to be over-capitalised by $44 million in 1943. Gérard Boismenu, *Le Duplessisme, Politique économique et rapports de force*, 1944–1960, (Montreal: Les Presses de l'Université de Montréal, 1981) p. 182.

34   *Fonds* T.-D.B., ANQ, P-10/11.

35   Ibid.

36   Rumilly, HPQ, XXXIV, p.175.

fications. The Assembly rejected a bill on female suffrage, opposed by Taschereau, by a vote of forty-three to nineteen. Bouchard had informed Thérèse Casgrain (the leading feminist social democratic personality of Quebec) that in the event of a tie vote, he would break the tie, as is the prerogative of the Speaker of the House, and would do so by voting in favour of women's suffrage.[37] Taschereau accepted and allowed a vote on a bill prepared by Bouchard to repurchase seigneurial annuities by a national syndicate with loans guaranteed by municipalities and the provincial government. The session ended on May 18.

On June 6, 1935, Télesphore-Damien Bouchard finally entered the cabinet of Louis-Alexandre Taschereau as Minister of Municipal Affairs, Trade and Commerce. In agreeing to participate in the government, Bouchard laid himself open to the accusation by the Conservatives, and especially of the ALN, that he had been bought off for his co-operation on the electricity bill. However, in view of the clerical-nationalist nature of the ALN and the tone of his speech supporting the bill, there is logic to his action. He accepted a less-than-perfect plan because it would be passed, and it at least represented an improvement.

---

37   Chisholm, Thérèse Casgrain, personal communication to Chisholm. Thérèse Casgrain entered the public sphere during the federal election of 1921 when she conducted a highly successful campaign for her husband who was prevented from doing so by illness. She became sole president of the Provincial Franchise Committee (later the League for Women's Rights) in 1928—a position she held for fourteen years. In November 1929 she appeared before the Dorion Commission, which had been set up to look into such things as a woman's right to her own earnings, the right to bring lawsuits without her husband's consent, etc. One of the main obstacles to winning suffrage in Quebec was the lack of support from rural French women. She was able to reach many of them through her radio program, "Femina," which was broadcast over French and English networks, and by speaking at conventions.

Following the war and the final achievement of the vote in 1940, she continued faithfully to press for child-protection laws, prison reform, government appointments for women and amendments to the civil code. She became vice-president of the National Federation of Liberal Women, and in 1948 resigned to join the CCF Party. She soon became vice-chairperson of the national CCF executive and in 1951 was chosen Quebec Social Democratic Party leader, which post she held until 1957—she was the first woman party leader anywhere in Canada.

When the NDP succeeded the CCF in 1961, Casgrain continued her active support, holding the position of national vice-chairperson. "I can't imagine a woman who has the best interest of her children at heart not taking an interest in politics," she said: "**I am convinced that until we have more women in politics—openly, flagrantly and unashamedly committed to the struggle for the liberation of woman and determined to change traditional power politics to make it more responsive to the dispossessed of this earth—we as women are doomed to many more years of oppression and exploitation.**"

What is evident is that he does not appear to have been a man who could be easily bought off, especially on a question that he had held so dear to his heart for a long time. In accepting a cabinet post his income increased. As a minister he would receive $8,000 in addition to his member's salary. Accused of accepting the portfolio because of financial gain, Bouchard defended himself.[38] Before the Assembly on April 15, 1936, he explained:

> My adversaries, who belong to the groups of new Liberals, accuse me of abandoning my ideas to enter the cabinet. There is an essential difference between me and this group ... which prevented me from joining. When I campaigned against the electricity monopoly I looked for only two things: to stop the financial manipulation of the great companies ... and to insure ... reasonable prices to consumers.... My adversaries of today fight the trusts not with the aim of protecting the public but especially to destroy the government.[39]

Bouchard claimed that he had made history as the first journalist appointed to the cabinet in Quebec. The same day, the Liberals of Montreal, pleased to learn that one of their group had been promoted greeted him with a reception on his arrival at Windsor station. They proceeded to a celebration at the Reform Club, where Jacob Nicol, who had accompanied Bouchard on the train, declared: "We are at a turning point in our political and economic history, and this point is marked by the entry of Mr. Bouchard into the Taschereau cabinet."[40] Even Rumilly was enthusiastic:

> The entry of Bouchard into the Taschereau cabinet, proposed as an antidote by Nicol, can be, indeed, very significant. Thirty years earlier the young Bouchard had entered public life, in the municipal council of Saint-Hyacinthe with a very simple program of two points: the taxation of religious property and the municipalization of electricity. He belonged to the radical tradition of the "old red" Maskoutain. In the course of a career which carried him to the Mayoralty, to the Assembly, to the Speaker's chair of the Chamber, and finally in the provincial cabinet, T.-D. Bouchard has been able to play down, but

---

38   Robert Saint-Germain and Jacques Bibeau; M.A. thesis (History), *Télesphore-Damien Bouchard: Un chef du Parti Libéral; (1935–1944)* Université de Sherbrooke *novembre,* 1973, p. 22.

39   *Le Devoir,* 15 *avril* 1936.

40   *Sherbrooke Daily Record,* June 7, 1935.

indeed, not to renounce his ideas. *More than Paul Gouin and Jean Martineau himself, T.-D. Bouchard is the man to "re-liberalize" the Liberal party, that is, to give it a progressive orientation, an orientation "of the left." The radicals salute his rise with joy.*[41] [Emphasis added]

Edmond Turcotte, editor-in-chief of *Le Canada*, declared: "Progress is to the left and the Liberal party is to the left."[42] There was a general sigh of relief in the province—at last Taschereau was doing something to answer his critics. Perhaps it was the last chance for the government to save itself. For St. Germain and Bibeau, "From then on, Bouchard would remain one of the powerful men in the provincial Liberal Party."[43] His implacable enemy Harry Bernard, the editor of *Le Courrier* who closely followed Bouchard's political career, wrote: "A ministry was given to Mr. Bouchard because Mr. Taschereau feared him. Since his campaign against the electrical trust, Mr. Bouchard had become dangerous for the government, his prestige growing each day in the whole province."[44] The entry of Bouchard in Taschereau's government was seen as the last hope of a dying regime that had been in power for thirty-eight years and was rooted in inaction and corruption.

Saint-Hyacinthe gives a triumphant greeting to its new minister. (*Le Canada*)

41   Rumilly, *HPQ*, XXXIV, p. 185.

42   *Le Canada*, 19 *juin* 1935.

43   R. S.-G. and J. B., p. 16.

44   H. Bernard; *Le Courrier de Saint-Hyacinthe*, 29 *novembre* 1935.

On June 10, an enthusiastic crowd awaited Bouchard's arrival in Saint-Hyacinthe. His fellow citizens, including provincial and federal representatives of the region, and Athanase David, Secretary of State, warmly welcomed the new minister. In a speech at the reception following his welcome, he repeated that he had fought for reforms and not against a government, while the aim of some individuals was solely the defeat of the government. He always knew that the government would in the end accept the proposed reforms. The Taschereau government, he went on, had proved that it was not allied to the trusts. Bouchard maintained that the government had surpassed the Lapointe Commission:

> The government has gone farther than the Lapointe Commission. Not only has it formed the suggested regulatory commission, but also it has created a Hydro-Quebec by increasing the power of the Water Commission, which henceforth can develop hydraulic power, to buy, to sell, and to distribute electricity. Further, it has decreed that henceforth, only the government or municipalities will develop new water-power. The government has therefore made a complete revolution, which we requested in the provincial administration of our hydroelectric resources.[45]

The Taschereau government's demise had been delayed, but not for long. Winds of change were blowing over Quebec. In addition to the disaffection of many Liberals and their promise-filled speeches, the Taschereau government had to face the eloquent young leader of the Conservatives, Maurice Duplessis. The energetic efforts of Bouchard would not prove sufficient to stave off the upcoming defeat. In the months to come, Bouchard used all of his forcefulness to explain to the population his position and his continuing support of the government. At a meeting in the Saint-Jérôme arena on June 13, he resumed his argument. It was inconceivable for him to leave the Liberal Party. Those who had left the party (i.e., the ALN) were the real traitors, for they chose not to fight for their cause within the fold. He had entered the government because he was reassured that the reforms he had fought for would be adopted. On June 16 the minister spoke again, in the same vein, at a meeting held by the *Club Liberal Marchand* in the municipal park of Saint-Jean. He declared that had he wanted to be minister, he could have been chosen to be so fifteen years earlier—probably an unrealistic statement, unless he could have moderated his feistiness. Bouchard explained on the radio in November of 1935 that these energy laws gave the people the means to protect themselves against the excesses of the great corporations. He also stated that the premier had invited him

---

45 *Le Devoir,* 10 *juin* 1935.

into the cabinet to see to the proper application of the laws voted on by the government "at my suggestions and those of the Electricity Commission."[46]

Teddy (to Taschereau): "It was only an electric storm, boss."

Teddy (to Taschereau): "We tried a bunt, mother, and we were good for a home run."

---

46   T.-D.B.: *"Le gouvernement libéral, un vrai gouvernement de réformes Populaires."* Fonds Bouchard, ANQ, Collection de Brochures P-10/11, p. 15.

**Teddy: It's not to sing your praises Boss,
but you have just hired a man who knows the line.**

The opposition increased its support because of the economic situation of the population of Quebec in these years. The population paid close attention to the promises made by leaders of the ALN. At this time, radio began to play a role in politics, replacing public debates. Conservative leader Maurice Duplessis impressed the people with his witty eloquence and dynamism. A true demagogue, he was a great speaker who used malicious sarcasm to demolish his adversaries. To survive this wind of change, the Liberal Party had to present a more dynamic image, a more liberal spirit, and an attitude more open to reforms. The member from Saint-Hyacinthe represented these elements for the people of Quebec.

Claude-Henri Grignon, the author of many books, known for the radio and television dramatization of "A Man and his Sins" (*Les belles histoires des pays d'en haut*), and mayor of Ste.-Adèle, meeting Bouchard for the first time in this period, describes him:

> I see him rather round with a protuberant stomach, active, laughing on occasion, a good bourgeois with a clear eye, a mischievous smile, replying with lively repartee, sometimes colourful, often cruel. A formidable man. He made me think of the great Edouard Henriot of France.... A colourful personality this T.-D. Bouchard, who cursed opponents, and, even though liberal, of a very particular spirit which the leader, the somber Taschereau, did not always comprehend. Among these men, from 1880 to 1940, Bouchard was certainly the most popular, the most discussed, and the most original. I am not

the only one who has this opinion. All the facts go to prove it. A remarkable and curious thing is that when I was literary editor of his newspaper *En Avant,* Bouchard allowed me the most complete liberty to defend, to glorify precisely, those whom he firmly attacked … which shows an uncommon open-mindedness.… In the course of my lifetime I have known politics, politicians, political schemers, dreamers, jokers, pirates, gangsters, liars, the weak, the uncompromising, the corrupt, and corrupters. *I have never known a man more honest than T.-D. Bouchard. It went beyond the state of an admirable mania. He, so little clerically inclined, revealed himself scrupulous to a fault, embarrassing to those around him.*[47] [Emphasis added]

In the federal elections of October 14, 1935, the Liberals, led by William Lyon Mackenzie King, achieved a decisive victory. In Quebec, led by Ernest Lapointe, the federal Liberals swept the province. Taschereau, seeking to take advantage of the federal victory, announced elections for November 25. Although some ministers wanted to wait until the next spring, Taschereau counted on the division of the opposition forces—the Conservatives and the ALN—to free the Liberals from worry. There would be a three-way race against a divided opposition. However, on November 7, the Conservative Party and the ALN announced that Gouin and Duplessis had formed an alliance. The news stunned the Liberals. The combined opposition would present only one candidate in each district. The *Union Nationale* (UN) had been born. According to the agreement, if the UN formed the government, Duplessis would be premier and Gouin would choose the members of the cabinet. Bouchard, who thought little of Duplessis, was satisfied that he had made the right choice in not joining the dissident liberals. He had insight into Duplessis's autocratic nature.

Once again the low clergy intervened in this campaign, on the side of their traditional allies the "blues," who supported clerical control of life in Quebec. Father Archange, a Franciscan from Montreal, asked his parishioners to vote against the Liberal Party. In Thetford Mines, Abbé Gravel, chaplain of the union, urged people to vote for the candidate of the *Union Nationale.* Even Rumilly was shocked: "The prize goes to Abbé Lavergne, the robust priest thundering from the pulpit and numerating crimes which we have the duty

---

47   Claude-Henri Grignon in T.-D.B., *Mémoires,* III, pp. 9–13.

to punish, to stop."[48] In the absence of Cardinal Villeneuve, the auxiliary bishop of Quebec ordered Abbé Lavergne to be silent. Nevertheless, the *Union Nationale* printed his sermon and distributed it throughout the district. Abbé Lavergne continued to inveigh against the government in districts where he was not constrained by the Archbishop's prohibition.

On the evening of the elections, the extent of the disaster became apparent. Forty-eight Liberals and 42 *Union Nationale* members were elected, of whom 26 were ALN and 16 were Conservatives. The UN received 49 percent of the popular vote, and the Liberals 46. In the election of 1931, the Liberals had enjoyed a majority of 68 seats. Even in his own riding, Taschereau received a majority of only fifty votes. T.-D. Bouchard survived with a decreased majority of 463 votes, as compared to one of 931 votes in the previous election. During the difficult election campaign, Bouchard was the object of sustained attack. As always, the newspapers called attention to electoral fraud: the names of people of certain religions had been omitted from electoral lists; and some candidates obtained more votes than registered voters—especially in the Jewish districts of Saint-Louis and Saint-Laurent in Montreal, which led to anti-Semitic comments. *Le Devoir,* reacting to the election of Dr. Anatole Plante in the district of Mercier, noted that the Jewish votes had saved him.[49] The paper also commented on irregularities in the election of Athanase David, and wondered how many spruce trees had voted in some northern counties.[50]

The Liberals sought to replace Taschereau, but he remained imperial and proud: "I am able to hold our ground better than any of you."[51] Recognized as fundamentally honest, Bouchard emerged as one of the leaders of the party and the government. Accusations of corruption never did stick to him, although accusations about his religious beliefs and Freemasonry did. He took on all of the great problems: electricity; unemployment (which had been transferred from the public works ministry to his own municipal affairs ministry); the constitution of Montreal; and old-age pensions. He attempted to establish a province-wide program of public works, similar to his Saint-Hyacinthe municipal plan, to solve the unemployment and relief problems.

---

48   Rumilly, *Duplessis,* I, p. 204.

49   *Le Devoir,* 26–27 *novembre* 1935.

50   Ibid.

51   Ibid., 14 *février* 1936.

On April 14, 1936, Bouchard submitted a bill in favour of old-age pensions. A dreadful uproar in the Assembly greeted his four-hour speech (seven hours long according to Black). The confrontation with his old companions in the fight against the electricity trusts, Hamel and Drouin, was fierce. Bouchard defended himself as having introduced laws in the public interest concerning electricity. He castigated *la bonne presse* (the righteous press), namely *Le Devoir* and *L'Action catholique*. He declared that when the ALN had approached him with potential leadership, he was celebrated in the "Holy Press" as often as were the encyclicals. He spoke without a text, and replied directly to the numerous interruptions. Admiringly, Black notes: "His keen features scathingly swept systematically the opposition benches row by row, seat by seat. He denounced the 'two-headed' pirates of the *Union Nationale*, all of whose political experience was limited to disorderly meetings and acrimonious complaints."[52] Standing upright in the middle of the aisle, his powerful voice thundered against the opposition and filled the Chamber. Bouchard, with remarkable insight into the future, declared that, with the exception of Duplessis's naive allies, everyone could see that his reactionary schemes would ruin or neutralize the entire opposition. Bouchard affirmed that the heavy hand of this previously despotic conservative would reveal his true self, and the opposition would show its true colours.

Members of the opposition jumped from their seats and screamed at the incendiary nature of Bouchard's speech. He invited Drouin, who interrupted him continually, to complete his speech for him, saying that he should able to do so, because he had often accompanied Bouchard on the platform and applauded often when they had campaigned together against the electricity trusts. When Hamel interrupted him on the electricity question, Bouchard denounced him for his simplistic zeal, pointing out that the government had made several concessions in its law. He cited some remarks made by Hamel on the public ownership of basic industries, and malicious personal allusions that Hamel was supposed to have made about Taschereau. Bouchard went on to accuse Hamel of being an unlucky speculator in electricity, since he already owned shares in private companies—an accusation which embarrassed his opponent. He accused Grégoire, mayor of Quebec City, of corruption during the municipal elections—notably of having employed the services of a pimp and other low-life individuals. At the conclusion of the debate,

52   Black, *Duplessis,* p. 193.

T.-D. goaded Grégoire, stating that he would repeat his allegations outside the chambers face-to-face. Bouchard's barbs, launched amid cheers from the Liberal benches, silenced each attempt to block his remarks, to the extent that interruptions by the opposition gradually diminished in strength. Grégoire, Hamel and Drouin could no longer be heard. In his long parliamentary career, Taschereau had rarely seen such a performance. Again, Bouchard had won the admiration of Rumilly:

> T.-D. Bouchard, Minister of Municipal Affairs, Trade, and Commerce, formed a protective shield for the Liberal government. It is he who presented the first important measure—the bill of old-age pensions. He also takes on the question of unemployment under his responsibility. A parliamentary committee of 18 members, presided over by T.-D. Bouchard, will study the various modes of administration proposed for the city of Montreal. T.-D. Bouchard will settle the question of electricity, change the constitution of Montreal, and save the Liberal government.[53]

Bouchard went to work to solve the problem of unemployment on a provincial scale, by implementing the solution he had carried out with such success in Saint-Hyacinthe—that is, by replacing direct help with a public works program. This plan would oblige the unemployed to work for wages, thus using public money in a healthier way. The money would diminish the ranks of the unemployed, and also would eliminate from the public lists those who were content to receive help without working. Bouchard claimed that his plan could produce savings of $6 million a year for the City of Montreal and for the province. *Le Devoir,* not usually favourable to the interests of the Liberal Party, evaluated the Bouchard project in glowing terms: "In Saint-Hyacinthe, this regime has obtained the most complete success ... Mr. Bouchard has succeeded in not only saving his city from state-initiated idleness, but has arrived at a fruitful solution in the interest of the city."[54] The central committee of the Catholic Union of Montreal approved Bouchard's plan with some modifications.[55]

---

53   Rumilly, *HPQ,* XXXV, p.151.

54   *Le Devoir,* 25 *mars* 1936.

55   *Le Clairon,* 5 *juin* 1936.

Some days later, however, his political enemies organized a hostile welcome for Bouchard on his arrival in Montreal. The crowd shouted, "Down with the 'trusts'! Down with Taschereau! Down with Bouchard! Down with stealing elections!" This did not prevent Bouchard from speaking, and the assembled critics listened—and even applauded when he discussed the unemployment question.[56] In addition to obliging the unemployed to work, he advocated allocating $10 per month to those leaving the city to return to the rural areas—thereby potentially decreasing the number of unemployed in the city by forty thousand. He proposed offering a premium to housewives who created new jobs by hiring a maid. In addition, he announced that the government would defray 60 percent of the cost of renovating buildings. On April 7, 1936, the Montreal city council approved Bouchard's 23-point plan for municipal reform.[57]

In a dramatic turn of events, the opposition—taking advantage of the absence of several Liberal members on May 7—introduced a motion asking the Chamber to adopt its own old-age pension bill. Recognized by the speaker, Bouchard saved the day by holding the floor for forty minutes, allowing the party whips to gather the missing members to reject the motion.[58] The Legislative Assembly then adopted the government's version of the bill on June 11.

On June 1, when he tried to speak to a crowd in the Mount-Royal Arena, Bouchard did not receive the same warm reception as the one he experienced at the Montreal council. The crowd, led by the nationalist *Jeunes Laurentiens,* did not let him speak, and booed constantly. He was finally able to deliver his talk by radio from an adjoining room. In Quebec City, two thousand unemployed gathered in front of Parliament on June 4, demanding to see Bouchard. He came out of the legislature and quieted the crowd's booing.[59] The Hay-Market fighter had no fear of popular demonstrations. He informed the demonstrators that workers would have time to study the plan before its application. The crowd, more or less happy with Bouchard's reply, then demanded that Duplessis come out, but to no avail.

---

56   Ibid., 30 *mars* 1936.

57   Ibid., 1 *juin* 1936.

58   *Le Clairon,* 8 *mai* 1935.

59   R.S.-G. & J.B., p. 29.

During the intense debates of the first five weeks of the new Assembly, Paul Gouin was absent, as he was preparing his maiden speech. He thus left the leadership of the opposition to Duplessis alone. Gouin kept up with what was happening in the Assembly by inviting colleagues to dinner, where "one ate well and sometimes read poems."[60] On May 7, Duplessis exercised his prerogative as Leader of the Opposition to convene the Committee of Public Accounts, which had the mandate to examine the financial administration of the government. The committee had not sat for ten years. Duplessis had prepared an attack over a long period, secretly amassing information that would damn the government. With a sense of the dramatic, he announced in advance that there would be scandalous revelations. At first, Duplessis attacked the Minister of Colonization, Irenée Vautrin, by questioning his deputy minister, Richard. This high-ranking civil servant admitted to having made payments to friends and Liberal candidates who had not done any work, by order of the minister. Yes, he had hired the son of a Liberal organizer, even though there was no need for him. Yes, the minister had settled all sorts of personal accounts—extravagant repairs in his office, family holidays, hunting trips and golfing trips—at the expense of his ministry. Then came the turn of Oscar Bériau, a Liberal organizer who had employed his son and nieces in government stores. He had sold sign posts and registration plates at an exorbitant price. The expenses associated with these projects largely exceeded the authorized budget. Other witnesses revealed scandalous relationships between the government and suppliers of wood and other construction materials. Then J. O. Frechette, accountant of the department of the Attorney General, appeared. When questioned about the expenses of his boss Charles Lanctôt, the Attorney General, Frechette refused to give information stating that his department did not provide details on this subject. Therefore, Duplessis summoned Lanctôt himself, taking closer aim at Taschereau, Lanctôt's chief and friend.[61] Lanctôt, distinguished and arrogant, did not enjoy appearing in the witness box.[62] Duplessis and Lanctôt discussed whether Lanctôt considered

---

60   Black, p. 197.

61   Vigod questions why Taschereau kept the corrupt and hated Lanctôt in his cabinet, as a leftover of Gouin's cabinet, pp. 52–53.

62   The press followed the hearings closely. *La Presse* 9, 14, 29 *mai* and 2, 3, 4, *juin* 1936. A. Taschereau's defense was that every treasurer had done the same thing—*La Presse* 5.6.9, 10 *juin* 1936. *Le Devoir*, 6 aôut 1936.

himself a public servant. Duplessis wished to have him confess that while fully employed by the province, he was at the same time the attorney for paper companies and power companies that dealt with the province. Liberal MLA Peter Bercovitch came to the rescue, objecting that these questions concerned Lanctôt's personal affairs. "Are you Mister Lanctôt's attorney?" asked Duplessis. "I am a member of the committee, as you are," Bercovitch replied, "Article 390 of the regulations gives us the right to inquire about public expenses, not the personal business of Mr. Lanctôt."[63] In a heated cross-examination, Bercovitch opposed a series of objections. Duplessis accused Lanctôt of stealing. Lanctôt replied that Duplessis was a liar, and that he had gone beyond his rights as Leader of the Opposition.

Gouin rarely attended these sessions. He disapproved of Duplessis's accusatory, violent tone. Duplessis—always standing, always on the offensive—surprised the members and officials with unexpected questions, stupefied them with sarcasm and puns, and threw them off guard. With an immense prior build-up through leaked information, each session became more dramatic than the preceding one. With a majority on the committee, Bercovitch's objections were maintained by the chairman and upheld by a vote of the committee. However, the newspapers fanned public curiosity. Black notes the general *Schadenfreude* of the public, as does Rumilly: "The newspapers were obliged to print the complete hearings to satisfy public curiosity, and possibly public maliciousness."[64] *Le Devoir* headlined articles with such titles as: "Accounts of Mr. Vautrin's Trip," or "Mr. Bériau sells the province for $900,000"[65]

After Lanctôt, the premier's brother appeared—Antoine Taschereau, the accountant of the Assembly. He was responsible for the distribution of parliamentary paycheques. The first day, Duplessis laid a trap to get A. Taschereau to perjure himself. Antoine Taschereau denied knowledge that he had profited from the interest on parliamentary funds deposited in his name at two branches of the Canadian National Bank. A. Taschereau's son was the manager of one of these branches. Then Duplessis dropped a bombshell. He produced proof that not only did Antoine Taschereau profit from the interest on these

---

63   Rumilly, Duplessis, p. 230 "Bercovitch, the Jewish Member " according to Rumilly.

64   Ibid., p. 229.

65   *Le Devoir*, 14 *mai* 1936.

public funds, but that nine years previously, in 1926, he had written to the bank after it objected to this manner of proceeding. In that letter, he had written that these accounts were purely personal. The proof was that he alone signed the checks.

In the face of these scandalous revelations, the government could not organize a real defence. The federal Liberals were appalled, and put pressure on the provincial party. Taschereau would have to go. They felt that it was necessary to act with the utmost speed to prevent serious damage caused by Duplessis's revelations. On June 11, 1936, Taschereau dissolved the Assembly. "With such a dissolute government, dissolution was required," was Duplessis's barbed comment.[66] The members of the opposition surrounded Duplessis, congratulating him.

Louis-Alexandre Taschereau, humbled after a long thirty-six-year career of public service, had reached the end. Although he was never accused of having personally profited from his position, he was deeply humiliated and bitterly disappointed. He proceeded to Lieutenant-Governor E. Patenaude's office to hand in his resignation, suggesting as his successor either Edouard Lacroix—the candidate of MacKenzie King and Ernest Lapointe—or Adélard Godbout, whom he personally preferred.[67] Lacroix declined, stating that he did not like to have his hands tied, and so Godbout became the seventeenth premier of the province of Quebec. So that he would have a clear mandate, Godbout called for an election in August—a mistake, as it turned out.

Louis-Alexandre Taschereau's place in the history of Quebec has now been reassessed by the nationalists who have discovered Duplessis's hypocrisy in dealing with American big business—particularly the Ungava agreements dealing with the selling and leasing of land for iron ore mining at very low prices—and his anti-union, anti-worker behaviour in the Dominion Textile conflict, and in Asbestos (see below).[68] The Liberals also remembered Taschereau for his

---

66   *Le Devoir*, 13 *juin* 1936.

67   Lacroix, MP for the Beauce, later became a supporter and a major actor in the nationalist *Bloc Populaire*.

68   Eugène L'Heureux, a nationalist and a savage critic of Taschereau in the 1930s, revised his opinion after Duplessis's agreements on Ungava. Duplessis was severely criticized for his largesse in granting mining rights to big American and Canadian iron ore companies in Northern Quebec. *L'Événement*, 2, 4, *avril* 1949. The nationalist, René Chaloult also revised his opinion. *Mémoires Politiques*, p. 292.

positive social programs.[69] "The image of Taschereau as a reactionary, pure and simple, also ignores the substance of social and institutional reforms in the 1920s. The Public Charities, Public Health, and Adoption Acts, and various educational initiatives, come quickly to mind."[70] For all his defects, he was wholeheartedly dedicated to public duty, to the exercise of power in the public interest. He had "the courage to resist forces in French-Canadian society which were far less progressive and open than he was."[71] Without exception, Taschereau opposed nationalist ideology and prejudices, risked the anger of the clergy with social reforms that he considered necessary, and faced the interests of high finance and big business when their conduct threatened the economy of Quebec.

It is an irony of history that it was thanks to Taschereau's intervention that Duplessis was elected in 1931 in Trois-Rivières, with a majority of forty votes. The local Liberal organizers had begged "Chubby" Power, the provincial organizer, for some supplementary financial assistance, which would bring victory to the Liberal candidate.[72] Taschereau vetoed the funds, preventing Power from providing them. Taschereau wrote that it would be better to have to face Duplessis than to face Camillien Houde, at that time leader of the provincial Conservatives. "Houde is a naughty scamp and a rascal, while Duplessis is gentleman of good family, and would be a far more acceptable Leader of the Opposition as far as we are concerned."[73] What poor judgment! For all his faults, Houde did not have Duplessis's mean streak. Duplessis's election in 1931 allowed him to mount a campaign to unseat Houde as leader of the Conservatives.

For the coming 1936 election, Paul Gouin demanded the same proportion of ALN/Conservative candidates as those elected in the 1935 election. Duplessis did not agree. Many ALN members now looked to Duplessis as the true leader of a future government, in part because of Gouin's poor performance. Gouin announced that he was leaving the *Union Nationale*, as

---

69   Vigod, p. 250–252.

70   Ibid., p.252.

71   Ibid., p. 255.

72   N. Ward; *A Party Politician; The Memoirs of Chubby Power* (Toronto: Macmillan, 1966), p. 326.

73   Ibid., p. 326.

predicted by Bouchard. Locally, Bouchard once again contested the mayoralty election against Doctor Pagé, scheduled for July 13, 1936, just at the time of the provincial campaign. Despite the attempts of Harry Bernard to lead a smear campaign patterned after that of the Committee of Public Accounts in his newspaper,[74] T.-D. Bouchard was re-elected mayor, with four of his candidates as aldermen on the council. Conrad Black notes that Duplessis had repeated Bernard's "entirely false" accusations during the session of October 1936—that the government had remunerated some of Bouchard's employees. Again, Black stresses Bouchard's honesty: "It [the accusation] was entirely false, and the reputation of Bouchard thereby increased. This was not one of Duplessis's most brilliant outbursts."[75]

Despite the death of a man named Desjardins during the "deportation of the Acadians"[76] organized by the Liberals, the election of Bouchard as mayor gave courage and hope to the Liberal forces. Godbout opened his election campaign in Saint-Hyacinthe on the eve of the local mayoral election. The Liberals placed the emphasis on the revival of the Liberal Party. In an effort to deflate the effects of the inquiry into public accounts, Godbout promised a commission of royal inquiry. Bouchard declared that the split between Gouin and Duplessis showed that the old Conservatives could not be trusted. Essentially, the electoral programs of the two parties did not differ very much. The ALN program inspired both.

As Bouchard's adversary in the provincial election the *Union Nationale* chose Albert Rioux, ex-president of the Union of Catholic Farmers and editor of the newspaper *La Terre de chez-nous*. Although it was not the custom for ministers to participate in public debates, Bouchard accepted Rioux's challenge. Thus, on August 15, in front of a crowd of ten thousand people, Rioux repeated Bernard's accusations concerning the sum of money that Bouchard had received from the government between 1932 and 1935. Bouchard defended himself fiercely. *Le Courrier,* he protested, had combined his salary as deputy, his salary as speaker, and the salary of his secretary. It was true that his company, Yamaska Press, had benefited from government contracts—an

---

74   H. Bernard, *Le Courrier de Saint-Hyacinthe*, 19 *juin* 1936.

75   Black, p. 249.

76   "The deportation of the Acadians" is explained on page 131.

accepted practice—but he had never made a great profit on these contracts. An indescribable din accompanied the exchanges and speeches.[77]

An enormous 88 percent of eligible voters participated in the elections. Bouchard won his provincial seat by a slim majority of seventy-two votes, reduced to fifty-seven votes after a judicial recount on August 25. However, Godbout's government was defeated in a smashing victory for the *Union Nationale*. The *Union Nationale* obtained seventy-six seats. The Liberals obtained only 14 seats. Godbout was not elected in his riding. The newspapers were full of speculation concerning the choice of party leader. Would Godbout remain? Would a Liberal cede his seat for Godbout? Would Bouchard with his long parliamentary experience be chosen to head the party, or simply lead the troops in the Assembly? Even Harry Bernard, in *Le Courrier de Saint-Hyacinthe*, expressed the thought that Bouchard was a possible choice as leader.[78] At a meeting on September 24, the Liberal caucus asked Godbout to remain head of the party and gave Bouchard the job of acting House Leader of the opposition. Thus, the long reign (1897–1936) of the provincial Liberal Party ended. T.-D. Bouchard now prepared himself for the role of Leader of the Opposition in a dramatically changed house.

---

77   R. S.-G & J. B., p. 233.

78   *Le Courrier de Saint-Hyacinthe*, 28 *août* 1936.

Chapter VIII

LEADER OF THE OPPOSITION, 1936–1939

As Bouchard had predicted, Maurice Duplessis was merciless in his pursuit of power, taking over complete control of and dominating the *Union Nationale* party. Oscar Drouin was the lone representative of the defunct ALN chosen to participate in the cabinet. Duplessis kept the three fervent nationalists Hamel, Grégoire and Chaloult out of his first cabinet. Although Duplessis did offer them positions in the cabinet, each one set unacceptable conditions. Hamel demanded the immediate nationalization of the Beauharnois Power Company, and Grégoire's and Ouellet's entry into the cabinet. Duplessis refused. Years later, Duplessis confessed with a malicious smile to the provincial Liberal leader, George Marler: "I told them that they could all be in my cabinet, but I did not tell them that they would be ministers without portfolio."[1] Jean-Louis Gagnon remarks, "As with all manipulators Duplessis was distrustful by nature. He knew by instinct to surround himself with the incompetent and the colourless. Men are all the more trustworthy when they do not have the means of attaining their ambitions, and when they need money."[2] In an editorial, Bouchard strongly condemned Duplessis's arbitrary, wholesale firing of government employees.[3]

In Quebec City, there were popular demonstrations against the new government of Duplessis. Many people were indignant that members of the ALN who had contributed so much to the *Union Nationale* victory were virtually excluded from the new cabinet. A furious René Chaloult organized a protest meeting at the Montcalm Palace, from which the crowd moved on to the Château

---

1 Black, p. 234. See also René Chaloult; *Mémoires Politiques* (Montréal: Éditions du Jour, 1969), p. 79–83, and Hector Laferté, *Derrière le trône, Mémoires d'un parlementaire québécois 1936–1958* (Sillery: Septentrion, 1998), p. 35.

2 Jean-Louis Gagnon; *Les Apostasies, I; Les Coqs du Village* (Ottawa: *La Presse*, 1985), p. 160.

3 *Le Clairon, 25 septembre* 1936.

Frontenac to confront Duplessis. The demonstration ended with several arrests. Never had a political elite lost its prominence in so little time as had the leaders of the ALN. In a letter written to Chaloult, Abbé Groulx complains:

> This victory will be short-lived, alas. I am profoundly saddened. I have never been able to share ... neither the optimistic confidence of Dr. Hamel, nor the enthusiastic confidence of Mr. Drouin, in your leader. He [Duplessis] belongs to the old generation of men ... with all the liars advocating good relations and co-operation between the two great races. We will have ... some administrative reform, some timid trials in economic and social policy. We have to mourn the grand national policy. To have used the three men, to have paraded them from one end of the province to the other, as the greatest electoral asset, then the day of victory, to throw them overboard, I call that dirty politics.[4]

Duplessis opened a special session of the Assembly on October 7, 1936, in an effort to demonstrate to the province that the era of reforms had arrived. In his Throne Speech he indicated that the government would introduce several bills pertaining to agricultural credit, reform of the electoral law, an amendment to the proposal of old-age pensions, laws on work accidents and measures against abuse of over-capitalization. He asserted the pre-eminence of human capital over monetary capital.

In his reply to the Speech from the Throne on October 13, Bouchard first congratulated the new Speaker of the House and thanked his colleagues of the opposition who had chosen him as leader. He then thanked his electors. He declared that, in spite of the defeat of August 17, the Liberal Party was far from ruin, having obtained 41.8 percent of the vote.[5] Bouchard criticized Duplessis's repetitive insistence on human capital, qualifying it as a digression designed to pull the wool over the eyes of the public. Commenting on the dissension within the new governing party, he declared, "We are far from the Golden Age promised by the leader of the *Union Nationale*. The premier is far from eliminating 'one-man government.'" He then observed sarcastically that the Speech from the Throne had lamely concluded with the thought that

---

4   René Chaloult, *Mémoires Politiques,* Montréal, 1969, pp. 91–93.

5   T.-D.B., "Considérations sur l'adresse en réponse au discours du Trône", 1936, *Fonds Bouchard,* ANQ, P-10/24.

the government was not ready to propose all of its reforms. Duplessis had stated, "It is obvious that we would not be able … to propose at this session, all the economic or social reforms that we recommend."[6] Bouchard continued his attack: this indicated that the new government had no new plans. Through the services of the party treasurer, Ward Pittfield, the government had borrowed $50 million from the Provincial Bank and the Royal Bank, the latter whose president was Sir Herbert Holt, chief magnate of the electricity trust. He denounced Duplessis for continuing the colonial practice of appointing an English person as provincial treasurer, in spite of his previous criticism of this custom. In order to call attention to the discord between Duplessis and Hamel, Grégoire and Chaloult, Bouchard asked what had become of the promise to nationalize the Beauharnois Power Company. Moreover, he pointed out that the new speaker of the Legislative Assembly was A. Raymond, vice-president of the Provincial Bank. Bouchard questioned why the insurance policies of government employees were transferred from the Quebec companies Sun Life and La Sauvegarde, to the Dominion Life of Toronto. Concerning the promise of abolition of tolls on bridges, he underscored sarcastically that, yes, there had been abolition of the tolls—but effectively, only for members of the legislature.

> If voters complain that … they asked for the abolition of tolls for themselves, the ministers will be able to reply that there is a beginning to all things, that first the Members themselves are going to sample free passage on the bridges and if they find that it is really pleasing, ah well, they will be able to promise to abolish the tolls for everyone at the next election.[7]

Commenting on the bill dealing with provincial agricultural credit, Bouchard stated that he was opposed to the creation of this new program since there was already a federal program in place. He concluded by saying that the opposition was ready to support all useful reforms of the electoral system of Quebec.

Bouchard's first speech as Leader of the Opposition made a good impression.[8] Edmond Turcotte praised Bouchard and condemned Duplessis' "arrogance, arbitrariness, his meanness, megalomania and paranoia." Turcotte noted Duplessis'

---

6   Ibid., p. 10.

7   Ibid., p. 11.

8   Edmond Turcotte, editorial in *Le Canada*, praising the Reply to the Speech from the Throne, reprinted in *Le Clairon*, 20 *novembre* 1936.

obsession to crush the opposition and to prevent the Liberals from protesting against the frequent and systematic violations of parliamentary procedure. It was widely disseminated in the newspapers and on the radio. It raised the Liberals' spirits. Even *Le Devoir*, on November 2, 1936, evaluated the performance as excellent, under the title—"Mr Bouchard Hits Hard and Mr Duplessis Responds:"

> M. Bouchard, Leader of the Opposition, hurled himself into the fray pounding for all he was worth. Full of contempt, he attacked the new regime on all vulnerable points. Mr. Bouchard's character is aggressive. He enjoys the struggle for the sake of struggle. Of an average size, plump, he becomes animated at the least opportunity, to discuss an issue, metaphorically rolling up his sleeves. Then, his face, usually flushed, he becomes positively inflamed: his cheeks, ears, neck, and his bald scalp, flush violently. His voice rings in the tone of a bugle. Mr. Bouchard has the natural enunciation of a powerful orator and of vengeful indignation.[9]

Duplessis summoned the Committee of Public Accounts to sit on October 21, 1936. He wished to take further advantage of the spectacle that had been so successful in the spring. Duplessis recalled Antoine Taschereau to continue his public humiliation. After a sharp interchange between Duplessis and Welcome, Taschereau's attorney, the latter was expelled from the room by a vote of the Committee, now composed of a majority of Union Nationale members. Duplessis again took up the attack against the suppliers of construction materials, especially those destined for settlers in Northern Quebec. He was merciless towards witnesses. Bouchard described Duplessis as a hypocrite, a liar and a swine. He provoked Duplessis in order to sow disorder in the procedure. In this he often succeeded. The discussion degenerated into shouts and insults. Bouchard proposed calling important witnesses of his own choice before the Committee of Public Accounts. Duplessis refused. In the quarrelsome, uncertain atmosphere of contradictory testimony, and growing lack of public interest, the sessions of the Committee closed three weeks later.

The parliamentary debates continued until Christmas. The Leader of the Opposition fought some thirty of the fifty bills adopted by the Assembly, using parts of his reply to the Throne Speech for each proposal. Harry Bernard reluctantly recognized that the Member for Saint-Hyacinthe "spared neither his time,

---

9   *Le Devoir, 2 novembre* 1936.

nor his work."[10] Commenting on the revelations of the Committee of Public Accounts, Alexis Gagnon wrote in *Le Devoir*:

> The Opposition appears more aggressive and alert. Each day Mr. Bouchard familiarizes himself with his new parliamentary role. He quickly catches on to the opposition's role. He denounces autocracy, abuse of ministerial authority. He calls for close attention to regulations, etc., as if he had done it all his life. And then he has a sense of humour, absolutely necessary for a Leader of the Opposition.[11]

In reaction to Bouchard's aggressive attacks, the premier threatened to have him appear before the Committee of Public Accounts to examine his activities as Speaker of the House. Traditionally, the Speaker, acting for the House as a whole, gave gifts at the end of each session to all members—often luggage, travel bags, or suit-carriers. According to Duplessis, Bouchard, as Speaker of the Assembly from 1930 to 1935, bought suitcases, resold them to his Yamaska Presses, transferred them in the name of his daughter, and resold them at a great profit. In general, Bouchard's known integrity did not leave him open to attacks of this kind. After thirty years of public life his enemies had never been able to catch him in underhanded dealings. "To put a stop to my energetic attacks against the government, its leader had the idea of using fear. He undertook an inquiry into the administration of the various departments that I directed. As in the fable, instead of discovering a mountain of corrupt practices, he found only a molehill."[12]

In examining the correspondence in the Quebec National Archives (ANQ) concerning the acquisition of these valises by the Speaker via the Yamaska Press, there is no evidence of profiteering and none that Cécile-Ena was involved.[13] The prices charged do not support the accusation. In his speech before the Liberals in June 1937, entitled "A Discredited Government," Bouchard described his lawsuit against Gérard Brady, who had repeated Duplessis's accusations on the subject of the suitcases in his Saint-Hyacinthe newspaper, *L'Idée Ouvrière*.[14] Some weeks before the trial was scheduled to begin, Brady publicly retracted

---

10   H. Bernard, *Le Courrier de Saint-Hyacinthe*, 20 1936.

11   *Le Devoir, 2 octobre* 1936.

12   T.-D.B., *Mémoires*, III, p. 107.

13   *Fonds* Bouchard, ANQ, P-10/46.

14   ANQ *Fonds* Bouchard, P-10/15.

these accusations in his newspaper. Duplessis had a great opportunity to try to prove these accusations, but he abstained, preferring to continue his defamatory statements behind his parliamentary immunity in the Committee of Public Accounts. In fact, Duplessis was never able to make his accusation stick. In turn, Bouchard proposed a Royal Commission of Inquiry into the sources of the *Union Nationale's* electoral funds. This proposal was refused despite favourable press comments. He recommended calling Sévère Godin, Sir Herbert Holt's secretary and vice-president of the Montreal Light Heat and Power Company, as a witness to testify. Bouchard declared that Godin would have interesting information on the relationship between the Duplessis government and the trusts.

One of Duplessis's ex-companions in the ALN organized a large meeting to demand his explanation of his contacts with the trusts, and to ask him the source of $180,000 that had been poured into his electoral coffers to help to upset the previous government. The meeting passed a resolution asking for Duplessis's resignation, accusing him of having betrayed his mandate and no longer representing popular sentiment. In February of 1937 Drouin, minister from the Liberal dissidents, sent Duplessis a long and painful memo. In it, he reminded Duplessis of the Conservative Party program established in 1933, and of the 1935 memorandum of understanding between Gouin and Duplessis concerning the immediate creation of a provincial hydro commission in competition with the electricity trusts. Since he received no answer to his letter, on February 22, 1937—two days before the opening of the session—Drouin resigned as minister and as chief organizer of the *Union Nationale*. As Bouchard noted, "There was no delay in the onset of squabbles in the camp of the victors of yesterday. Politicians who previously walked hand-in-hand began to tear themselves apart just like starved wolves sharing prey."[15]

By now the public debt had almost doubled. Instead of finding Duplessis a defender of unions, workers discovered that he was a protector of the large corporations. In May—in the manner of U.S. Senator Joseph McCarthy—Premier Duplessis, who was also the Attorney General, holding up papers in his hand, announced that he had issued orders to arrest two labour leaders in Montreal. Duplessis accused them of having communist leanings. Bouchard demonstrated the falseness of these accusations in the Chamber. Then Duplessis reversed himself. He informed the House that the summons in question would not be served. Following this, Minister J. O. Gagné, member for Arthabaska and heretofore

---

15   T.-D.B., *Mémoires*, III, p. 107.

a faithful devotee of *le chef*, resigned because he was displeased with provisions of the labour law—provisions which were the opposite of the proposed changes which Duplessis had promised to adopt.

The newspaper *L'Action catholique* initially received publishing contracts from the *Union Nationale* government, contracts transferred from the Liberal paper *Le Canada*. Because *L'Action catholique* began to criticize Duplessis, he cancelled its printing contract.[16] There were widespread complaints about Duplessis's conduct in the House. René Chaloult also protested: "Serious people deplored the frequent degeneration of discussion of problems into fruitless argument and insults.... Dignity was often lost in the Assembly ... and the premier did not shine as an example, especially during the session of 1936–1939—[there were] personal slurs, accusations, and threats of all sorts."[17]

Duplessis claimed to have increased the salary of lumberjacks from $30 to $40 by an order-in-council, bypassing the Assembly. Indignant, Bouchard demanded to see this order-in-council. Duplessis refused his request. Bouchard affirmed that the previous government had raised the lumberjacks' salary to $37, and that Duplessis had lied to the population by claiming to have increased salaries by $10.

In fact, the sessions of the Assembly had become scenes of great theatre. All questions registered for discussion became colourful confrontations. The Assembly sat for periods of fifteen to twenty-three hours, interrupted by a two-hour intermission for dinner. One attended either in the morning, afternoon, or evening. The galleries were full of spectators. People lined up to find a good seat. Gagnon describes the scene:

> Always with a hoarse voice, his neck buried in his shoulders, his short arms extended like a standing bear, Damien Bouchard, the ritual prayer over, had his lance hot on the heels of Duplessis, not giving him an inch. The effect is instantaneous, the Prime Minister immediately instinctively becomes a firebrand and the Members, fascinated, believe they see the two leaders ... disputing over mastery of the ring.[18]

Maurice Duplessis and T.-D. Bouchard knew just how far to go. Both excelled in parliamentary procedure. Nevertheless, the confrontations rapidly

---

16   Louis-Philippe Roy, *L'Action Catholique*, 3 mai 1937.

17   Chaloult, p. 31.

18   Gagnon, I, p. 199.

turned to body blows. The premier accused the Leader of the Opposition of having enriched himself by cheating on the salaries of his workers, and of having added to Sunday prayers, the "little mass" of Damien. Bouchard hit back hard, calling into question Duplessis's drunkenness and adultery: "I am a man who is prosperous, although I am not the son of a judge. I have earned my money. When others spend, I save. I do not drink, and I do not run around. As for the little mass, when I leave, *it is not to go across to visit another man's wife!*"[19] (Emphasis added.) Bouchard was alluding to Duplessis's drinking problem and to rumours that Duplessis, who visited the Saint-Joseph Oratory in Montreal every Wednesday morning, then crossed the street to visit his mistress, a married woman. When the session was extended in November 1936, the Liberals knew for certain that in T.-D. Bouchard they had a formidable House Leader who demonstrated all the required qualities of an indomitable Leader of the Opposition. His role consisted of opposing most government decisions. As Gagnon states, "he made this traditional rule a sort of state duty, which completely fit his character."[20] The Liberals were encouraged.

Though occupied by his duties in the Assembly, Bouchard did not neglect his municipal activities. There, he continued his reform policies, which resulted in providing the citizens of Saint-Hyacinthe with what he claimed was the lowest cost of living in the country. The great financial newspapers of the country cited the City of Saint-Hyacinthe as a model in financial management. A healthy administration was the main reason for this prosperity. Taxes were light and the public debt insignificant. At the beginning of July, four of his partisans out of five were elected to the council. The population obviously approved of his reign. The mayor profited from this situation, asking homeowners to vote a hundred thousand dollars for the construction of a stadium with a running track, to be used also on public holidays. The proposed stadium in the *Parc Laframboise* would be adjacent to the largest public pool in the province, and a baseball field. A very strong majority approved the proposal.

Many Liberal associations invited Bouchard to give talks that greeted with much acclaim. At the end of October 1936, he spoke at a banquet of the Liberal Union of Laurier. In December, the Young Liberals of Saint-Hyacinthe celebrated his fifty-fifth birthday. In February, at a Reform Club dinner in Montreal, Godbout congratulated the House Leader of the Opposition for his outstanding

---

19   Ibid., p. 200.

20   Ibid., p. 203.

job. Bouchard explained that some Liberals wanted him to refrain from comment on Duplessis's policies—to maintain silence, as a sort of strike. However, he felt that direct confrontation stood a better chance of rekindling the spirit of their supporters—a view that readily conformed to the philosophy of life, which he had expressed ever since his youth in the seminary. Before the Young Liberals of Saint-Hyacinthe, he announced the agreement of Godbout and Lapointe for the upcoming publication of a weekly Liberal newspaper.[21] The newspaper *En avant* saw the light of day on January 15, 1937, with editions in Montreal, Quebec, and Saint-Hyacinthe. It was printed at the Yamaska Press Company, with T.-D. Bouchard in charge of political articles and Claude-Henri Grignon in charge of the literary articles. Bouchard undertook the financial support of the newspaper for one year.[22]

The "virtuous press" began to publish (or originate) rumours suggesting discord between Bouchard and Godbout. They claimed that Bouchard was after the position of party leader, not just leader in the Assembly. Nevertheless, wherever he spoke, Bouchard paid homage to Godbout, whom he recognized as the sole head of the Liberal Party. It is true that Bouchard always felt that his enemies would not give him proper credit. He had misgivings about Godbout's past—Godbout was an ex-seminarian originally bound for the priesthood. But he also admired Godbout, whom everyone agreed had an extraordinary command of language, and who was the only parliamentarian capable of improvising long, well-phrased sentences punctuated with parentheses and digressions, always knowing how to end them with the appropriate verb, noun, and tense. He appreciated Godbout's affability, his frankness, his openness, his courage and his liberal convictions.

Duplessis repeated the Taschereau government's practice in his relations with big business. He awarded concessions of provincial resources to large companies such as the Ontario Paper Company, registered in Quebec as Quebec North Shore Ltd., assured of an almost inexhaustible forest reserve. Duplessis and Doctor Leclerc, the member for Charlevoix, proposed legislation regarding this transaction. Drouin protested, and Bouchard observed, "The Prime Minister spends his time fulminating against the large companies, but each time it is a

---

21   Bouchard states that he had the approval of the party leaders, but Laferté claims that they were uncomfortable with Bouchard's initiative and planned to start another liberal newspaper in Quebec. Laferté, p. 46.

22   *Fonds* Bouchard, ANQ, P-10/14.

question of his favourites, he votes for them."[23] In fact, each member requested exemptions for companies in his own district. Duplessis himself tabled two bills granting municipal tax exemptions to an electrical trust and to a grain elevator company in Trois-Rivières. The Assembly approved, without difficulty, pensions for the blind and for needy mothers. These measures were warmly welcomed in the province of Quebec, represented a visible, tangible credit for the government, and viewed as ahead of their time.

During this second session of the Assembly, Duplessis passed the famous Padlock Law, which allowed the Attorney General (Duplessis himself) to order a house or office padlocked when suspected of harbouring communist propaganda. Bouchard declared that he was not opposed to the fight against communists, but he deplored the arbitrary nature of the new law, and remarked that he believed that the greatest danger in Quebec came from fascist groups rather than from the communists, who after all had a small following.[24]

Duplessis introduced a new law on electricity. According to Bouchard, it was similar to the one introduced in 1935 by the previous government. He opposed the new law, with the support of the nationalists and some Liberal dissidents, since it contained an added twist that hindered municipalization rather than promoting it. Indeed, this legislation obliged municipalities that had decided to municipalize electricity to purchase the private electricity companies instead of competing with them, thereby rendering municipalization of electricity too onerous a project.

The law governing work-related accidents, according to the Leader of the Opposition, gave the government the arbitrary right to appoint and dismiss the members of the Work Accident Board, thus interfering with its independence.[25] Despite having previously criticized the municipal sales tax, once in office Duplessis elected to maintain it. Without consulting the unions, he introduced two labour laws. The government claimed that these measures would remedy

---

23   Rumilly, *Duplessis*, p. 332.

24   Yves Lavertu. *Jean-Charles Harvey, Le Combattant* (Montréal: Les Édtions Boréal, 2000). In this recent biography, Lavertu emphasizes the Fascist leanings of the French-Canadian elite—the nationalists—before, during and even after the war. In his book on de Bernonville he demonstrates the depth of Pétainist support even into the 1950s. The influence of the ultramontane Maurist, *Action française* priests in the colleges on the elite in the pre-war era is also well described in Catherine Pomeryol's book *Les intellectuals Québécois: formation et engagements 1919–1939,* (Paris: L'Hartmattan, 1996).

25   *Le Devoir*, 12 *mai* 1937.

the intimidation of union members revealed by a committee of inquiry on international union activities. This measure established union autonomy, but at the same time outlawed the closed shop. Of course, these labour laws did not apply to government employees, who had no right to organize or strike. Duplessis defended this state of affairs by invoking the particular nature of public service. The international unions denounced the legislation as that of a corporate state, claiming that a "Fascist" government had adopted it.

The 1937 session was extended until May 27 and only resumed eight months later in January of 1938. In J.-L. Gagnon's judgment, "It was with relief that the *Union Nationale* welcomed an end to the spring session of 1937. These three months had been so painful for Maurice Duplessis, who was not yet on orange juice, that he decided that the next return of Parliament would only take place in 1938."[26] (The orange juice remark referred to Duplessis's drinking problems. He became a teetotaller in 1943—when he was discovered to be diabetic—and drank only orange juice from then on.)

On June 17, 1937, T.-D. Bouchard and his faithful lieutenant in the House, Cléophas Bastien, were honoured at a banquet at Montreal's Windsor Hotel for the work they had accomplished during the previous session. Delegates and members from all over the province came to hear their leader and the Leader of the Opposition. Bouchard praised Godbout and described the Duplessis government as the *gouvernement de la déception* (government of disappointment) and *le règne du cosaque* (the rule of the Cossacks).[27] He described Duplessis's pitiful conduct in the Assembly, reminding the audience about the resignation of the member for Arthabaska—which had been tabled in the Speaker's office, then withdrawn. The premier had destroyed the MLA's written statement and then denied its existence, resulting in accusations of lying to the House and of not following parliamentary procedure. Bouchard then criticized the laws passed by the Assembly. He concluded his remarks by calling on the audience to celebrate the centenary of the Rebellion of 1837 by bringing about the fall of the Duplessis government, because the constitutional liberties for which the patriots of 1837 gave their lives were being suppressed. Godbout expressed his admiration and gratitude to Bouchard for a job well done.

In Montreal Jean-Charles Harvey, the ex-editor-in-chief of *Le Soleil* of Quebec City, began publishing a new newspaper, *Le Jour*, a radical liberal weekly dedi-

---

26   Gagnon, I, p. 219.

27   *Fonds* Bouchard, ANQ, P-10/15.

cated to "resolutely combat all anti-democratic ideology." It was published until 1946. According to Rumilly, Samuel Bronfman "the wealthy distiller, whose lawyer Samuel Smiley (his real name is Smilovitz)" secretly financed *Le Jour* and Smiley wrote the newspaper's charter.[28] Rumilly thus repeated the canard printed in *Le Devoir* that Jews financed *Le Jour*.[29] However, Yves Lavertu, in his recent biography of J.-C. Harvey, reveals that the secret source of funds was mainly Ray Edwin Powell, head of the Aluminium Company of Canada. Support came as well from Thérèse Casgrain, and Albin Janin, who supplied Harvey with the subscription list from his newspaper *L'Ordre*.[30] Smiley, an old acquaintance of Harvey's from Quebec City, agreed to be the *pro bono* lawyer, and he did write the paper's charter. Harvey was also a novelist. *Les demi-civilisés* was published in 1934, and banned by the Church because of its sexual frankness. This resulted in his dismissal from *Le Soleil*. Edmund Wilson, the eminent American literary critic, describes *Les demi-civilisés* as the first great modern French-Canadian novel: "The first audacious blow that was struck to let air into this closed French-Canadian world was by an unconventional journalist, Jean-Charles Harvey.... [the] novel called *Les demi-civilisés*.... caused a scandal and now stands as a landmark."[31] After his dismissal, Taschereau and Bouchard helped Harvey to find work in the government office of statistics, which he found distasteful. He was thus happy to become a newspaperman again. (Actually, Bouchard had suggested that Harvey become librarian of the Legislative Assembly, but Archbishop Villeneuve vetoed this idea.)[32]

In the fall of 1937, Bouchard gave numerous speeches. At the Congress of the Union of Property-Owners in Trois-Rivières, he called for a fair distribution of the tax burden among all citizens. He also urged the government to impose a limit on mortgage rates. On November 26, at the Adélard Godbout Liberal Club of Quebec, he denounced a scandal involving the Saint-Jérôme sandpits.[33] An organizer of the *Union Nationale* had bought a gravel pit from a widow for

---

28   Rumilly, *Duplessis,* p. 358.

29   *Le Devoir,* 11 aôut 1937. Harvey confronted George Pelletier in person the next day and a retraction was then printed.

30   Lavertu, p. 64.

31   Edmund Wilson, *O Canada* (Toronto: Ambassador Books, 1964), p. 136.

32   Lavertu, p. 17.

33   *Fonds* Bouchard, ANQ, P-10/46.

$400 and sold it a month later to the government for $4,050. During the period of 1936 to 1939, Bouchard received many letters from all over the province denouncing local examples of corruption.[34] At the celebration of the twenty-fifth anniversary of the Young Liberals at the Windsor Hotel on December 6, he warned that the party's enemies would try to associate it with doctrinaire liberalism (from France), as they had in the 1870s. As a *rouge* of yesteryear, he denounced the schemes "of a certain occult organization" (without naming it), that infiltrated all areas of Quebec society, battling against liberals and advocating a corporatist Catholic state. Without a doubt he was referring to the "Order of Jacques Cartier." He attacked Duplessis for destroying the Liberal-Conservative Party *(L'Union Nationale)* for his own personal advantage. He reminded his audience that it was the nationalists, in alliance with the Conservatives, who had caused the downfall of Sir Wilfrid Laurier. He was overjoyed to note that the public attitude towards the Liberals had changed for the better after barely a year of the Duplessis administration.[35] The Liberal performance in the legislature under Bouchard's leadership had resulted in renewed hope within the party.

In Quebec the Catholic Church was beginning to change its views on social issues. In Sorel, Bishop Philippe Desranleau supported the Catholic unions in their struggle against Marine Industries Ltd., owned by the Simard family. Joseph Simard was a leading Liberal Party boss and a good friend of T.-D. Bouchard. On August 2, the National Catholic Federation of Textile Workers went on strike in nine factories of Dominion Textiles and its affiliate, the Montreal Cotton Company. This involved ten thousand workers from four factories in Montreal, and factories in Valleyfield, Magog, Sherbrooke, Drummondville and Quebec. With the assistance of Cardinal Villeneuve, Duplessis succeeded in settling this strike, which lasted almost four weeks.

The third session of Parliament opened in Quebec on January 26, 1938. The Throne Speech feebly suggested that since the major proposals were adopted during the first two sessions, the Assembly would work on the completion of those laws. Other salient points were support for agriculture, technical and commercial education, the development of the road system, the struggle against Communism, and Duplessis's appeal to the nationalists, for provincial autonomy by blaming Ottawa for all ills. The budget contained some peculiar accounting practices, designed to cover up the disastrous state of public finances. Expenses

---

34   Ibid.

35   *Fonds* Bouchard, ANQ P-10/24.

were divided into three categories: regular expenses, exceptional expenses and capital expenses. The Minister of Finance proudly announced a surplus of $4 million in the regular expense account—thanks, he claimed, to the efficiency, honesty, and vigilance of the government. Bouchard and Bercovitch ridiculed this claim of a government that had accumulated an unprecedented debt of $73 million.

Bouchard began his Reply to the Throne Speech, entitled "A Government Which Mocks Parliamentary Rules,"[36] by offering his condolences to the Congregation of Sacred Heart Brothers and to the numerous families affected by a disastrous fire at Sacred Heart College in Saint-Hyacinthe. Forty-one pupils and five Brothers had perished in the catastrophe. The Coroner's inquiry had concluded that there was no evidence of a criminal act. Nevertheless, *Le Canada* blamed the Brothers for negligence. The night watchman had not set off the fire alarm, the firemen were slow to respond to the call, and some water pumps did not function. Rumours spread in Saint-Hyacinthe that the mayor himself had been the author of the alleged crime, although there was no evidence for this claim. The origin of this notion was Bouchard's open disapproval of the members of this religious order after an incident on Christmas, 1936, when a Nazi group, dressed in their parade uniforms, was allowed to approach the Holy Communion table in military formation. As mayor, Bouchard had disapproved of this fascist demonstration, and of the Brothers who had granted the hospitality of their church to Hitler's followers. According to Saint-Germain and Bibeau, many citizens of Saint-Hyacinthe remained convinced for a long time that Bouchard had played a role in the fire.[37] Although the accusation was "both absurd and untrue, Duplessis ordered a secret inquiry."[38]

In his speech, Bouchard also noted that only one new law was proposed: the establishment of a mining school at the University of Laval. The rest was rather vague. He went on to denounce the Duplessis government for making the provincial agricultural credit system into an electoral machine that favoured his party. He criticized Duplessis's policy in the field of colonization, declaring that it was nothing more than a continuation of the policies instituted by the Liberal government before 1936, especially in demanding work in return for

---

36   *Fonds* Bouchard, ANQ P-10/15, *"Un gouvernement qui méprise les usages parlementaires."*

37   S.-G. &B., p. 98.

38   T.-D.B., *Mémoires*, III, p. 111.

allocations. He reminded the House that the Duplessis government did not establish old-age pensions, as claimed by Antonio Barette, member for Joliette. Rather, the Liberals did, in 1935. He asked why pensions to needy mothers and to the blind approved more than eight months before, in the last session, had not yet been distributed. Finally, he thundered against both his local opponents and Duplessis, who had appealed to religious prejudices by accusing Bouchard of imposing a 10-percent tax on churches and the real estate of the religious institutions—a tax that would go towards fire protection, water, and sidewalk and road work in Saint-Hyacinthe. Bouchard questioned Duplessis's mathematics, explaining that he had omitted to mention that the Bishop himself had suggested the tithe of 10 cents per $100 (not 10 percent but 0.1 percent) and had signed a concordat with the City in 1927.

The March 1938 by-election in Bagot was a challenge for Godbout, who had taken up permanent residence in the riding in order to run the campaign. Duplessis, speaking in Acton Vale in support of the *Union Nationale* candidate, Adam, slyly alluded to government funding policies: "A vote for Adam is a vote for farm loans.... A vote against Adam is a vote against farm loans.... If you are against the loans ... you are free to oppose it. That is your affair and *you may be sure that we will respect your opinion.*"[39] (Emphasis added.) Quinn remarks that this undemocratic attitude was widely accepted as normal in Quebec. It represents a profound misunderstanding of the true nature of a democracy, in which the building of roads or farm loans should not depend on how the county votes, but rather should be the right of all tax-paying citizens. A benefit should not be a reward for voting correctly.[40] Bouchard saw the loss of this by-election as a response to Duplessis's campaign of vituperation and blackmail in Acton Vale.

The Bagot election disappointed the federal Liberals and dismayed the provincial Liberals. Godbout's star faded to such a degree that the Liberals discussed the replacement of their leader. Ernest Lapointe, the Quebec federal leader, supported Godbout. Neither the federal nor the provincial Liberals wished to see Télesphore-Damien Bouchard head up the party. It became increasingly urgent to summon a Liberal convention to confirm Godbout's leadership. The newspapers continued to report rumours of a struggle between Godbout and Bouchard, encouraging speculation. According to *Le Devoir*:

---

39   *Le Clairon*, 26 *février* 1938.

40   Quinn, p. 196.

> While we recognize that Mr. Adélard Godbout has great qualities, one begins to wonder if he is truly the chief capable of leading the party to victory. Against him is the fact that he and his colleagues shared responsibility for Taschereau's last years, which this province is not ready to forget. That also goes for Mr. T.-D. Bouchard, who hardly has enthusiastic support among the federal caucus.... As for Mr. Bouchard, one knows that the vast majority of Liberals would firmly oppose his candidacy to the direction of the party. As temporary parliamentary leader, he is acceptable, as leader of the party, never.[41]

Bouchard denied that he sought the leadership:

> I do not aspire, not in the least, to become leader of the Liberal Party. We are happy with the current head of the party and, unless he resigns, he will remain in this position until he replaces the current premier. It is wrong to claim that I aspire to the leadership. I am not to be compared to the present premier, who has gotten rid of all those who brought him to power ... I will continue ... to do my duty. It would perhaps be better for the well-being of the province for the leader of the Liberal Party to be present in this House, but I will do my best to represent him well.[42]

There were rumours that the party had tried to entice former Liberal dissidents. Some even suggested Paul Gouin as a candidate for the leadership race. Gouin posed too many conditions for a party that would not think of making major concessions to those who left the fold in 1935, thus contributing so much to the *Union Nationale* victory of 1936. Meanwhile, the nationalists such as Hamel, Chaloult, Grégoire and others, had regrouped into the National Party.

Bouchard knew that his odds of becoming leader were slim. Party stalwarts thought that he was a small-town politician. Perhaps his integrity annoyed them. In Taschereau's cabinet, in 1935 and 1936, as we have seen, his fellow ministers had found Bouchard's honesty and stiff-necked attitudes difficult to digest, and they complained. Bouchard defended himself by emphasizing that he had always been a loyal Liberal, alluding to his service as Leader of the Opposition. But the backroom boys of the convention did not consider him qualified to be at the helm of the party. Some said, "Godbout is

---

41   *Le Devoir,* 18 *février* 1938.

42   Ibid., 11 *mars* 1938.

clean. He is manageable. Don't panic if on nomination day Bouchard is named. We have persuaded him to refuse the nomination, but he insists on this gesture as an appreciation for his work. It was a critical moment because he could have accepted, but after a long hesitation he refused."[43] Thus, Godbout was chosen unanimously by the convention. Bouchard's refusal evoked Godbout's praise in his acceptance speech on Saturday night, when he spoke openly and surprisingly about his fear of Bouchard.

> I feared a battle so much that I trembled when I learned that a petition was circulating in favour of Mr. T.-D. Bouchard. With his gener-ous heart, he refused the honour of being a candidate, and possibly emerging victorious. If there was someone who deserves your con-gratulations today, it is T.-D. Bouchard. During this combat he not only had the courage to support the soldiers who weakened, but also to strengthen those who pretended to defend the cause while shoot-ing the soldiers in the back. Should I describe Bouchard's loyalty? He has made every sacrifice in order to continue to wave the flag. Mr. Bouchard, this meeting of Liberals has given you vivid testimony of our esteem, unequivocal esteem. If my words cannot express to you all my appreciation, these feelings are nevertheless sincere in someone to whom you express so much loyalty.[44]

Among the resolutions adopted by the congress were the abolition of the provincial Legislative Council (the upper House); the abolition of the Office of Minimum Wage; the standardization of school books and their free distribution; voting rights for women; and the nationalization of hydroelectric power. The influence of Bouchard on these resolutions is clear, although Godbout also had very strong feelings about them, and, as we shall see, he carried them to fruition in spite of tremendous opposition.

The Eucharistic Congress took place in Quebec City in June of 1938 where Duplessis achieved a small diplomatic victory over Lapointe. In a dramatic ges-ture, he offered Cardinal Villeneuve a magnificent ring—a purple (the colour of a cardinal) amethyst, surrounded by diamonds and engraved with the cardinal's coat of arms, the emblem of the Legislative Assembly, and the inscription, "in respectful homage." After a flattering speech, the premier took the ring from

---

43   Vautelet, personal communication to Chisholm, p. 128.

44   *Le Devoir,* 13 *juin* 1938.

his pocket. Villeneuve invited Duplessis to climb the steps to his throne and to slip the ring on his finger himself. While advancing, Duplessis dramatically proclaimed, "Please see in this act the sentiment of my filial affection. I believe!" Advancing again, he added with religious fervour, "I believe in God and in the Catholic religion!" The cardinal held the premier by his arm and said: "I recognize in this ring the symbol of the union of religious authority and civil authority."[45] Lapointe followed this presentation. In spite of a speech full of praise, he was unable to match Duplessis's dramatic gesture and his material generosity. A pontifical mass celebrated by Pope Pius XI from his summer residence, Castel Gandolfo, and broadcast by radio, consummated the congress. The celebrations had been an enormous success and resulted in increasing the prestige of both Cardinal Villeneuve and of Duplessis.

During the summer, Godbout and Bouchard criticized the Padlock Law, stressing that the real danger to democracy came from the Fascist movement. Duplessis called Bouchard a communist, quoting a letter addressed to a communist of Trois-Rivières in which the author expressed his approval of Godbout and Bouchard promoting an anti-fascist campaign. Bouchard expressed the hope that Duplessis would not "come to put a padlock on his door."[46] The premier and the Leader of the Opposition then carried on a debate on the respective dangers of fascism and communism. Bouchard wrote: "The important thing to note at present is that the Fascist Party exists. It is a menace and it is apparently tolerated by Premier Duplessis, this opportunist who used Paul Gouin to gain power and could also use gangs of fascists to carry out a *coup d'état*."[47]

Meanwhile, Duplessis tried once again to gain support by reconvening the hearings of the Committee of Public Accounts. Hearings began with Charles Lanctôt and Antoine Taschereau on the hot seat. The public, however, had lost interest. Duplessis promised imminent "stunning arrests," and indeed, he issued an arrest warrant for Lanctôt, a seventy-five-year-old man in poor health. He was deterred by public sympathy for Lanctôt and by Father Laflamme of the Quebec Basilica, who often gave Duplessis communion. Bouchard observed that once again the inquiry had come to an abrupt end. He expressed

---

45   Black, I, p. 302.

46   S.-G. & B., p. 104.

47   T.-D. Bouchard, *Le Clairon*, 3 décembre 1937.

a widespread opinion: "All thoughtful people in this province disapprove of this inquiry, which they consider a disgrace for the province."[48]

Duplessis's difficulties increased. In his cabinet, Minister of Roads François Leduc had the reputation of handing out contracts only after public tender, similar to Bouchard's habit in the Taschereau and Godbout cabinets. An engineer by training and a technocrat, he took his job seriously and never hesitated to contradict his colleagues or to challenge Duplessis himself. After all, he had received the largest majority in the provincial elections of 1936, and thus felt entitled to do as he pleased. In a cabinet where each contract was synonymous with graft (for the electoral coffers or personal enrichment), Leduc was not popular. To get rid of this recalcitrant minister who refused to resign, Duplessis was obliged to resign as premier. This was the first time in the history of Quebec that a premier had to resign in order to change his cabinet. Apparently he did not have the power to simply fire Leduc. The Lieutenant-Governor reappointed him premier, so that he could reconstitute a new cabinet without Leduc.[49] According to Black, Leduc was not sufficiently humble towards the cult of personality developing around *le chef.*[50]

Henceforth, Duplessis followed a procedure introduced by Mackenzie King, which required that each minister appointed to the cabinet submit an undated letter of resignation before being sworn in. Leduc called Duplessis a dictator. At the congress for the renewal of the ALN in Sorel, Paul Gouin accused Duplessis of having betrayed the Holy Alliance that had carried him to power. In all, five dissident MLA's—Hamel, Drouin, Chaloult, Marcoux, Gouin—and two legislative counsellors, Thériault and Ouellet, announced the founding of the *Parti National* on June 26, 1937. They demanded the application of the previously accepted program that Duplessis had abandoned. Duplessis's autocratic manner of governing had become notorious throughout the province. The Catholic union leader Philippe Girard stated, "there is only one Minister, Mr. Duplessis; the others sweep the floor."[51]

Was Duplessis a fascist or simply a right-wing authoritarian? Although he adopted some fascist practices—the Padlock Law, keeping secret files on many people in the province, an autocratic manner—he certainly could not be com-

---

48 *Le Devoir,* 5 *avril* 1938.

49 Gagnon, p. 225.

50 Black, I, p. 310.

51 *Le Devoir,* 2 *août* 1938.

pared to Mussolini, Salazar, Franco or Hitler. The latter outlawed other parties, destroyed democratic structures, instituted a secret police organization, and carried out arbitrary arrests of the opposition. In his second period of government, from 1944 to 1959, Duplessis used some very high-handed and vindictive methods to punish his enemies. (See below.) Nevertheless, he destroyed neither the fundamental parliamentary system nor the courts. Therefore, we must conclude that he was simply an authoritarian, right-wing politician.

During the 1930s there was disturbing news from Europe and Asia. The Japanese had launched their aggressive expansion towards Manchuria and China. The population of Quebec closely followed the war of the loyalists—the legitimate government of Spain—against the rebellious forces of the army and the Church. The forces of the right—fascists, the clergy, the nationalist parties and the corporatists—all supported Franco.[52] Catherine Pomeroyls has analysed the content of Le Devoir's borrowings from the French right-wing press during the Spanish Civil War—content which demonstrated support for the rebellious forces of Franco. She also noted "the silences and unspoken comments" in these borrowings.[53] Local admirers of Mussolini did not protest his invasion of Ethiopia. In 1936 Hitler began his successive seizures of adjacent lands by taking the Saar, and then the Sudetenland. In 1938 it was Austria's turn. After that came the ill-fated Munich accord and the dismemberment of Czechoslovakia. At each stage, Canadians suspected that war was imminent, but the passivity of France and England tended to convince them otherwise.

---

52 Hugh Thomas, *The Spanish Civil War*, 3rd edition (New York: Harper and Row, 1977). Tension was created in France by the decision to commit substantial resources to rearmament in response to German remilitarization of the Rhineland and over the question of whether to support the embattled Spanish Republic. Léon Blum, early in the Front Populaire government, began efforts to help the legitimate government of Spain, but was threatened by the British that in the event of a war, the UK would not support France. See Jean Lacouture, *Léon Blum*, (Paris: Éditions du Seuil, 1977), Roger Price, *A Concise History of France*, (Cambridge: Cambridge Univ. Press, 1993), Max Tacel, *La France et le monde au XXe siècle*, (Paris: Masson, 1989).

Philippe Bernard and Henri Dubrief, *The Decline of the Third Republic, 1914–1938*, translated by Anthony Forster, (Cambridge, Cambridge Univ. Press, 1985).

Jacques Chastenet, *Déclin de la Troisième 1931–1938*, (Paris: Hachette, 1962).

53 Catherine Pomeroyls, *"Le Devoir et la guerre d'Espagne. Les usages de la référence française,"* *RHAF*, 58, 2005, 347–387.

King George VI's and Queen Elizabeth's trip to Canada in the spring of 1939 was seen as an exercise in pro-British patriotism. Its goal was to mobilize public opinion and to underscore, in case of war, the close connection between the two countries. It emphasized the unspoken understanding that the day England declared war, Canada would be called upon to participate. The official explanation that the invitation to visit had dated from King George's 1936 coronation was not taken seriously. Mackenzie King and Ernest Lapointe saluted the King and Queen on their arrival in Quebec City on a steamship of the Canadian Pacific Steamship Lines. At the Legislative Assembly, Maurice Duplessis, greeted them in French: "Our province has always been faithful to the British Crown … we remain French, which British statesmen allowed us in 1791 and again in the Confederation Act of 1867. We cherish this past, and we will never cease to consider the Throne as the way of supporting our democratic institutions and our constitutional liberties."[54]

The King replied in French, praising the spirit of tolerance prevailing between the two great races living together. The welcome was extremely cordial. Thousands of onlookers had massed along the streets of the old capital, shouting cheers. Again, in Montreal, enthusiastic crowds saluted the King and Queen not only in the English districts but also in the French quarters of the city. At Delorimier Stadium, at Molson Stadium, to the assembled religious personnel in front of the Cathedral, at Dominion Square, and in front of the Windsor Hotel, where a crowd of more than hundred thousand had gathered—everywhere, the welcome was one of great enthusiasm. Even Camillien Houde, mayor of Montreal, charmed his royal visitors at dinner and made them laugh with flashes of his irresistible *bonhomie*.

The fourth session of the twentieth legislature opened in January of 1939 with another colourless Speech from the Throne. Even *Le Devoir* reported that eight *Union Nationale* MLAs did not participate in the customary ovation to the premier.[55] In a long reply to the Speech from the Throne, Bouchard was once again brilliant and witty. He entitled his address *Le sabotage de la représentation Populaire*.[56] Black describes it as a "splendid speech."[57] Bouchard criticized all aspects of the government program. He wanted to know why there were still communists in Quebec a year after the adoption of the Padlock Law. He again

---

54   Rumilly, *Duplessis,* I, p.513.

55   *Le Devoir*, 20 *janvier* 1939.

56   *Fonds* Bouchard, ANQ P-10/15.

57   Black, I, p. 316.

reminded the Assembly that the Liberal government of Taschereau had instituted social legislation not the present government. He reproached the government for anti-democratic procedures: arbitrary arrests of labour leaders; a nocturnal office search of the Unemployment Commission in Montreal; and the firing of employees appointed by the Montreal city council without just cause.

As in his previous replies to throne speeches, Bouchard upbraided the government for its autonomist bent, and for what he felt were its anti-federal distortions. The government had never mentioned federal government contributions of 75 percent of the budget in the areas of mining, railroads and pensions. He also decried increasing government interference in the settlement of labour conflicts. He accused the Dufresne Construction Company of having poured a sum of $650,000 into the electoral coffers of the *Union Nationale*. In return, it had obtained substantial contracts from the government for the construction of an electrical plant in the far north, and for the construction of bridges on Pie IX Boulevard and Charlemagne Street in Montreal. In addition, the Dufresne Construction Company had cancelled a $20,443.24 debt owed by *Le Devoir*, thus connecting the *Union Nationale* with this newspaper. Bouchard reviewed the Duplessis administration's record since 1936, and he found:

> … Promises not kept, shameless patronage, millions lost, dishonest elections, purchase of votes, electoral fraud, forced subscriptions to the coffers of the *Union Nationale*, a plethora of ministers, laws voted in haste, contracts without submission, loans favouring friendly brokers, undue influence on newspapers, a plethora of commissions, administration by ministerial orders-in-council, arbitrary measures, disdain of members' privileges, [and] unfair dismissals.[58]

On March 7, Bouchard delivered another impressive speech analyzing the budget, entitled: *Le régime du gaspillage*—"The Wasteful Government."[59] Examining the figures quoted by the provincial treasurer in detail, he agreed that income had been growing considerably, but said that this was due to the resumption of business. He cited federal figures to show that income had been rising everywhere in the country, and therefore it was not due to the good administration of the Duplessis government. Bouchard noted that while income had increased, the debt had increased by $131,000,000 during the three years of the Duplessis govern-

---

58   *The Montreal Gazette*, January 20, 1939.

59   *Fonds* Bouchard, ANQ, P-10/15.

ment. Instead of fulfilling its promise to decrease taxes, the government had spent wastefully. The surplus announced by the government had never existed. It was nothing more than accounting sleight-of-hand. In fact, the Duplessis government had driven the province into bankruptcy. The session of 1939 that ended on April 28 had been a letdown. The government had presented no worthwhile plans. Even Duplessis's fan Conrad Black has found that in less than three years, its performance was "disappointing. The government had not presented any valuable projects. In less than three years, [Duplessis] had increased parliamentary casualness to a breathtaking height, and showed arrogance of power."[60]

Since the Liberal convention in 1938, rumours had circulated that Bouchard would be appointed to one of the five vacant Senate seats, to get him out of the way. The newspapers continued to fan the flames of the purported conflict between him and Godbout. During the summer of 1939, Bouchard and Godbout travelled the province, criticizing the Duplessis regime and paying no attention to these rumours. Knowing the precarious state of provincial finances, they did not ignore the possibility of an early election. The theme of their speeches was so frequently repeated that it became a familiar refrain: "Every time your heart beats, Mr. Duplessis gets you into debt by two dollars … $125 a minute, $7,500 an hour, $180,000 a day, $1,250,000 a week, $5,625,000 a month and $67,500,000 a year … your children and your grandchildren will have to pay back this debt!"[61]

The news from Europe became more disturbing. The suspense ended on August 23, 1939, when Nazi Germany and the Soviet Union signed a pact of non-aggression. The Hitler-Stalin agreement allowed for the dismemberment of Poland. The wait was brief. On September 1, panzer divisions occupied Danzig and the blitzkreig of Poland began. On September 3, France and England declared war on Germany, too late to save Poland. In Canada, Mackenzie King summoned Parliament and proclaimed the War Measures Act; and on September 9, Canada declared war against Germany. The nationalists also spread out across the province during the summer to declare their opposition to a foreign war. Paul Gouin quoted the words spoken by King and Lapointe in 1935: "Ottawa does not have the right to get Canada into a foreign war without a plebiscite"[62] Paul Bouchard, the nationalist-separatist, editor of *La Nation*, declared: "I am resolutely … opposed to Canada's participation in the European war, because I

---

60   Black, I, p. 316.

61   *The Gazette,* August 17, 1939.

62   *Le Canada*, 9 *septembre* 1935.

do not want thousands of young Canadians to give their life beyond the seas to save international Jewish finance."[63] René Chaloult expressed himself in more rebellious terms; "We have to employ all constitutional and legal means to resist participation, voluntary or by conscription.... But after the exhaustion of all legal means ... I fear that French Canadians, rather than going to fight on the battlefields of Europe, would prefer to fight on the streets of Montreal."[64] T.-D. Bouchard had already announced his opposition to conscription. He maintained this position throughout the war, but wholeheartedly supported the war itself.[65] He agreed with the views of the party leaders, notably Ernest Lapointe, that Canada should participate in the war with an army of volunteers, but both disagreed with conscription. At the *Monument National* in Montreal on September 5, André Laurendeau presided over a demonstration of youths against the war, with the participation of union leaders, the Catholic unions, and the Union of Catholic Farmers.[66] Lapointe spoke out for the war but against the idea of conscription. He raised the fear of a civil war if Parliament did not follow the wish of the majority of Canadians to see Canada fight alongside England and France. However, he also criticized those who were already demanding conscription.

On a personal level during this period, Bouchard initiated improvements to his beautiful home on the edge of the river. In order to be able to carry on with his favourite exercise, swimming, even in winter, he constructed an indoor pool in addition to the one he had on the outside. The pool was combined with a greenhouse containing many plants, including cacti. He installed coloured fluorescent lighting, giving a festive air to the room. The project was expensive—$36,000 in all—and was completed on the day of the declaration of war. T.-D. and Cécile thought that they would not use it at all, but in fact it became the ideal place for patriotic receptions for the next four years, and even later. Five months after the death of Bouchard's wife in 1934, Joseph-Edouard Nichol, the husband of Annette Saint-Jacques, died. Some time in the following years, Télesphore-Damien began a relationship with the widow, which

---

63   *Le Devoir,* 5 *septembre* 1939.

64   Ibid., 5 *septembre* 1939. See Michael D. Behiels, *Prelude to Quebec's Quiet Revolution, 1945–1960,* (Montreal & Kingston: McGill-Queen's University Press, 1985). And Donald J. Horton, *André Laurendeau, French-Canadian Nationalist, 1912–1968,* (Toronto: Oxford University Press, 1992).

65   *Le Devoir,* 29 *mars* 1939.

66   Horton, pp. 89–111. See also Paul-André Comeau, *Le Bloc Populaire 1942–1948,* (Montréal: Québec/Amérique, 1982) pp. 170–175 for an analysis of the anti-Semitism of the Bloc in spite of Laurendeau's efforts against this illness.

lasted until her death in 1944. While they did not live together, he spent vacations at her Laurentian home, and they travelled together. In the late 1940s and 1950s, he was also friendly with a Mme. Morel, who often stayed overnight after the onset of Bouchard's illness, when nursing care was not available. During the same period he sometimes spent afternoons at a woman's home in Outremont.[67]

A gathering of the Liberal Party at Bouchard's country home, La Pointe des Fourches. From left to right: Peter Bercovitch, Cléophas Bastien, Jacob Nicol, Charles de la Grave, Félix Messier, J. A. C. Turcotte, Cyrille Dumaine, Frank Conners, Mme. Charles delaGrave, Télesphore-Damien Bouchard, Adélard Godbout, Charles-Auguste Bertrand, E. C. Lawn, Elie Beauregard, Léon Casgrain.

---

67   Judge Marcel Nicols, personal communication.

Chisholm reports a conversation with Cécile-Ena in which she states that she knew her father's mistress and even gave her some personal gifts after his death—probably referring to Mme. Morel. Dr. Segall spoke about Mrs. Bouchard being "a neglected woman" in 1930, but there is no evidence that he was unfaithful during her life.

On the provincial scene, Godbout's and Bouchard's predictions about the financial state of the government became a reality. Financial institutions demanded that the bankrupt government first obtain a new mandate from the electorate, before the banks would grant it loans. King refused Duplessis's request for a loan of $40 million from the Bank of Canada. Having won five by-elections since his accession to power, Duplessis felt that victory was probable. He was especially persuaded to go to the population since he felt that he had found a Liberal weak point—his rhetoric immediately took an anti-war direction. On September 24, 1939, Duplessis announced the dissolution of the legislature, calling an election for October 25. He denounced the increase of federal power, and the War Measures Act, which would result, he predicted, in the centralization of power in Ottawa, and in the assimilation of the French-Canadian people.

On the other hand, the Liberals—without forgetting that conscription was a very delicate issue in French Canada—declared themselves favourable to participation in the conflict. They reminded the public that it was the Conservative Borden, the political predecessor of the Leader of the *Union Nationale* (the former leader of the provincial Conservatives) who had decreed obligatory military service for overseas service in 1917, and that it was the Liberal Laurier who opposed conscription. The Liberals adopted a self-congratulatory posture. "Happily, King and Lapointe are there." Maurice Duplessis was first to attack on this issue, and thus was drawn into a battle with the federal Liberals because of his choice of issues. To combat the provincial Liberals, he tackled King and Lapointe. This gave the federal forces a mandate to participate fully in the struggle. Lapointe and the federal Liberals put their prestige on the line. A vote for Duplessis, they warned, would result in a loss of French-Canadian ability to defend their interest in Ottawa. In *Le Clairon*, Bouchard wrote:

> If the controversy had remained purely provincial, we would have strictly abstained from all intervention. But the Honourable Mr. Duplessis has not only precipitated an election in a critical period to sow discord, [but he has done so] at a moment when national union is challenged by a sacred duty. He is using this election as a pretext to criticize the federal government and particularly measures taken to insure efficiency and success of Canada's effort in the present conflict. A verdict in his favour would be a verdict against us. In such circumstances we cannot remain indifferent and our duty is to take note of the challenge that has been launched without any provoca-

tion ... [we] need the confidence and the support of our compatriots to maintain the authority necessary for the defence of their ideas and to safeguard their interests.[68]

Indeed Lapointe, Cardin and Power, continuing in this line of thought, threatened to resign if Duplessis was re-elected. They said that they alone could guarantee that there would be no conscription, and that they alone could protect Quebec's particularism against the latent hostility of the English provinces where imperial sentiment had been stirred. A vote against Duplessis would be a vote for the commitment of Lapointe-Cardin-Power against conscription. The Prime Minister of Canada, Mackenzie King, also made this commitment. A vote for Duplessis was a vote for conscription, disorder, disunion, and the incomprehension and anger of the English.

Speaking without notes on the campaign trail.
Note the sleeping clergyman.

---

68   *Le Clairon, 6 octobre* 1939.

While Godbout used the radio to open his campaign to many listeners, Duplessis, to his detriment, refused to broadcast his message because he would have had to submit his texts to the federal censor. He had thus deprived himself of a tremendous weapon. Godbout ridiculed Duplessis's attitude, underlining that the Liberals had nothing to fear from the censor whose unique function was to insure that no remark liable to serve the cause of the enemy would be transmitted. So while Duplessis debated with federal Liberals on the question of provincial autonomy, the provincial Liberals were able to attack the Duplessis government on its poor performance after three years of administration.

Duplessis opened his campaign before a huge crowd in Trois-Rivières, delivering one of the most famous speeches of his entire career. To the great satisfaction of his audience, he energetically replied to points raised by Liberals. But it seems that the premier was quite literally drunk during this speech: "There is no agreement about what he said. The session was hardly rendered more intelligible by the fact, known only to intimate friends, that the ideas of the Prime Minister had been tangled and deformed by an unfortunate excess of gin and champagne. The diction was clear, the voice strong, but he was nonetheless completely drunk."[69]

At the Liberal convention in the riding of Saint-Hyacinthe, T.-D. Bouchard was unanimously chosen as the candidate. He again attacked the government on its performance over the previous three years, and repeated his analysis of the poor financial situation. In *Le Clairon* he stressed this point:

> The real reason for elections at this time is the fact that the Duplessis government has $60 million to pay, that it cannot borrow anywhere. All provincial banks no longer want to place their confidence in this government, which leads to ruin and to bankruptcy.... We are going to pay attention more particularly to the rotten regime that oppressed us for three years.... Many scandals have marked its administration.[70]

Godbout and the federal Liberals proclaimed their dedication to provincial autonomy. Duplessis declared that he alone was able to safeguard the rights of the province, and was the only one who could prevent conscription. The Liberals said that in the event of Duplessis's re-election—and the subsequent resignation of Lapointe, Cardin and Power—there would certainly be conscription, since

---

69   Black, p. 346 citing R.J. Clark and Edouard Asselin.

70   *Le Clairon,* 6 *octobre* 1939.

there would be no opposition in Ottawa. Jean-Louis Gagnon thought that this tactic was a monumental error, since it linked the Liberals to an impossible promise, which they should have anticipated. Gagnon writes that it should have been apparent to all serious-thinking people—as it was to him on September 3, 1939—that this was a serious war that would end up requiring conscription and the sending of troops overseas. He based his judgment on the length and intensity of the First World War. This Liberal strategy ensured their eventual undoing at the subsequent election in 1944.

> These words [of Lapointe on conscription] disturbed me at that time. I found them stupid in the short run. Could one account for them on the grounds of naivety? On this point, Laurendeau was not wrong in seeing duplicity ... I immediately wondered how men, supposedly informed, could underestimate the German army at this point, when it had been necessary in 1914–18 to mobilize Europe, America, the Empire, and Japan to arrive at a successful conclusion.[71]

Gagnon was not alone in this view. The recruitment of volunteers for the war, in Quebec as in Ontario, continued even during the election campaign. Duplessis accused the Liberals of being linked to the communists. Bouchard called the *Union Nationale* fascist. *Le Clairon* reported the commentary of a German radio station on the political situation in Quebec.[72] *Le Soleil* wrote: "How happy Hitler would be to see a Nazi party win in French Canada."[73] This was, of course, a gross exaggeration. The *Union Nationale* was in no way a Nazi party, but Duplessis's non-support of the war was seen by Germany as aiding its cause. Both the Liberals and the *Union Nationale* presented candidates in all ridings. *Action liberale nationale* (the *Parti National*) presented candidates in fifty counties. Godbout and Duplessis held large meetings all over the province. Lapointe too was always present, supporting Godbout. Adélard Godbout had made the commitment to give voting rights to women and finally to institute compulsory free education. Both party campaigns ended with enthusiasm. Those surrounding Maurice Duplessis were happy and confident.

On Election Day, October 25, 1939, to the surprise of both parties, there was a complete reversal in the party standing in the legislature. The previous

---

71   Gagnon, p. 235.

72   *Le Clairon, 20 octobre* 1939.

73   Rumilly, *Duplessis,* I, p. 549.

Assembly of 1936 had contained, before subsequent defections, 76 members from the *Union Nationale*, and 14 Liberals. The new election gave 69 seats to the Liberals, and only 14 to the *Union Nationale*. The independent national-ist René Chaloult and the independent Camillien Houde, mayor of Montreal, also were elected. Duplessis was re-elected in Trois-Rivières by a majority of 1,713 votes as compared to one of 3,176 votes in 1936. The ALN did not gain one seat, and most of their candidates lost their deposits. Godbout once again became Member of the Legislative Assembly and premier of Quebec. Bouchard was decisively re-elected in his riding with a majority of 702 votes. The Liberal victory put an end to his role as Leader of the Opposition, which had been a heavy strain, but a task he had filled successfully and with honour. Here are three evaluations of his performance as House Leader: first, Alexis Gagnon, writing in *Le Devoir*, acknowledged:

> On the day following the sweeping victory of 1936, while the dis-oriented provincial Liberals, exhausted and debilitated by a very long struggle, felt somewhat adrift, Mr. Bouchard along with Messers Bastien and Casgrain took on the task of raising the morale of the failing troops. From the beginning of the first session, Bouchard attacked vigorously, he struck back at Mr. Duplessis with all he could muster. The latter … replied vigorously, by blows which would have definitively stunned any other adversary…. The task was not always easy because Mr. Bouchard and his colleagues were obliged to carry the weight of the previous administrations and to take on their backs the sins of Israël.[74]

In the same vein, *La Patrie* declared:

> One knows with what vigour, at the head of a few opposition mem-bers, Damien Bouchard led the struggle. Always in the breach, he was able to gain the advantage even in difficult conditions, some-times damning when it was necessary to fight. In addition, in his courageous newspaper *En Avant*, he has not stopped writing in sup-port of the Liberal party policy, such that by the pen as well as by the word, he has constantly fought for the cause which has so brilliantly triumphed at the polls last Wednesday.[75]

---

74   Cited in R.S.-G. & J.B., pp. 137–139—*Le Devoir*, 7 *février* 1939.

75   Ibid., p. 138—*La Patrie*—cited in *Le Clairon*, 3 *novembre* 1939.

In his political memoirs, René Chaloult, the ultramontane nationalist, describing Duplessis's rough style in the Assembly, reported that T.-D. Bouchard was the only one able to confront him successfully:

> Often implacable in debate, Maurice Duplessis was without pity for his adversary. All arguments were good if they could be used to destroy his enemy. He sought to annihilate his opponent. Tenacious, inflexible, on occasion in bad faith … he was a fearsome adversary and dangerous … most preferred to avoid him and to be quiet. Damien Bouchard, tough old fighter, did not care and gave back vigorous responses himself … I was in the Assembly one day when Duplessis attacked Bouchard in this manner.… The Member for Saint-Hyacinthe, with a rough hide, replied tit for tat: "I do not know it for certain, because nobody suspects the depth of the Prime Minister's malice, but if he pours a bucket of salt water on my head, then I will pour two on him." What do you say? That is how it was necessary to reply to Maurice Duplessis to gain his respect and to silence him.[76]

The *Union Nationale* obtained 39 percent of the vote, the Liberals 54 percent. These results were received thankfully by English Canada and the United Kingdom. They celebrated French-Canadian loyalty and common sense. King declared, "Victory for Mr. Duplessis would have been received … with joy in Nazi Germany."[77] The London and New York newspapers commented favourably on the Quebec choice. During the twentieth legislature, Bouchard carried out his task in an outstanding fashion. As Harry Bernard wrote, he had spared neither his time nor his efforts in the constant battle that he led against the Duplessis government. He was the candle of light that allowed the Liberal Party to restore its full flame. As St. Germain and Bibeau remark, "The struggle led by the opposition during these three years had been the roughest. If the son of the Hay-Market had lost some of his hide, he emerged nevertheless the great victor, and can claim his share of glory in the victory of the provincial Liberal party of October 25, 1939."[78] Bouchard had indeed led the Liberal team in the Assembly in such a vigorous manner that he deserved much credit for the

---

76   R. Chaloult, *Mémoires Politiques,* p. 31.

77   *Le Devoir* and *The Gazette,* October 26, 1939.

78   S.-G. & B., p. 140.

turnaround in Liberal fortunes. This was implicit in Godbout's fine tribute to him at the convention of 1938.

Télesphore-Damien Bouchard, Mayor of Saint-Hyacinthe, Member of the Legislative Assembly, previously Speaker, Minister in Taschereau's last cabinet, and Minister in the first cabinet of the short-lived Godbout government of 1936, entered Godbout's second cabinet with the title of Minister of Roads and Public Works.

Chapter IX

MR. MINISTER, 1939–1944

The new Godbout government initiated its program by reducing the size of the cabinet. The goal was to cut administrative expenses as much as possible, and to re-establish the province's credit in the financial world. T.-D. Bouchard, dean of the ministers, was appointed Minister of Roads and Public Works. Godbout had wanted Bouchard to be the first French Canadian to be provincial treasurer—that is, the Minister of Finance. Ernest Lapointe, demonstrating the tight interconnection between the federal and the provincial Liberals, vetoed this proposal, with the excuse that financial circles would feel less confident with a French Canadian in this post.[1] On December 15, 1939, Adélard Godbout went on vacation. Bouchard replaced him during his absence. He notes with pride, "Thus, the grandson of the water-carrier, after 30 years of struggle against the wickedness of men and adverse events, could celebrate his 48th birthday [sic—he was then 58 years of age] while he occupied the high post of acting premier of his province."[2]

When Godbout returned, during the Christmas holidays, the Minister of Roads left on a self-financed field-trip to Mexico, accompanied by his daughter Cécile-Ena as secretary. Employing fifty of the best American engineers to carry out some of the most modern methods of highway construction, Mexico had built terraced super-highways through mountains and across cliffs, filling in ravines and bridging rivers. Thanks both to the Mexican government authorities' willingness and to his knowledge of Spanish and English, Bouchard learned a lot. "I returned to the country with a mass of useful information which did not cost the government of the province a penny, since I had undertaken this

---

1   Laferté, p. 111.

2   T.-D.B., *Mémoires*, III, p. 115.

trip at my own expense."[3] Before returning, Bouchard and his daughter paid a visit to Los Angeles and San Francisco. While in Los Angeles Louis B. Mayer received the Bouchards in the studios of Metro-Goldwyn-Mayer, which had just completed the film "Gone with the Wind." [Bouchard was president of the Cinema Association of Montreal.] Mayer, a Canadian by birth, was very hospitable, providing a limousine and chauffeur. They met several movie stars, such as Robert Taylor and Lew Ayres, and had cocktails with Greer Garson and Mayer. It was a memorable visit. They then travelled by boat to Seattle.

On his return from Mexico, the Minister of Roads announced his intention to undertake large-scale projects. He gave instructions to the director of his ministry to prepare plans for province-wide super-highway construction. Quebec also would have modern roads. In June the newspaper of the Order of Jacques Cartier, *La Boussole,* congratulated him at awarding work only to Quebec contractors, and not to their competitors from other provinces.[4] Bouchard explained that this was not extraordinary, since his policy was to award contracts to the lowest bidder. "Contractors from outside Quebec formerly raised their prices exorbitantly.... Because they were required to subscribe important sums of money to the electoral coffers.... Nevertheless, the public was surprised by the praise given me by this reactionary organ."[5] To the dismay of the Liberals, Bouchard maintained a Duplessis nominee, the Conservative organizer Ernest Goyer, at the ministry as Director of Public Works, because of his competence.[6]

Jacques Nichols, son of his close friend and political associate Ernest Nichols, tells a story exemplifying Bouchard's integrity. Bouchard maintained an open door for Jacques and his brother, Marcel, now a judge of the appeals court. They called T.-D. *pépère*—"grandpa." As a young man, Jacques served as Bouchard's chauffeur, since, surprisingly, T.-D. had never learned to drive. One evening in the early 1940s, Bouchard told Jacques: "Prepare yourself to go out at eleven o'clock this evening!" They drove to the new turnpike under construction and parked in the forest, where they hid. The minister had calculated that the quantity of concrete used by the

---

3   Ibid., p. 116.

4   T.-D.B., *Mémoires*, III, p. 116.

5   T.-D.B., *Mémoires*, III p. 118.

6   Laferté, p. 135.

contractor was much more than what was required for the job, and he suspected theft. Indeed, in the small hours of the morning, the same trucks that had delivered the concrete during the day returned to reload their precious cargo. Having confirmed his suspicions, Bouchard alerted the police.[7]

The Minister supervising road construction.

As Minister of Roads, Bouchard received some unusual titles. The Algonquins honoured him, as did the Iroquois, appointing him honorary chief of their tribe. He was invited to smoke the peace pipe with the Mohawks of Caugnawaga [sic—it is now called Kahnawake], where he was presented with a beautiful helmet of eagle-feathers and baptized with the name "Io Ha Hi Ho," which means "Beautiful Path." The Algonquins called him *Ena Konen Enenko Kakina*, which means "the Greatest Builder of the Greatest Roadways." In November, the Canadian Association of Good Roads elected him president.

---

7   Jacques Nichols, personal communication.

The Greatest Builder of the Greatest Roadways.

Some time later, as Public Works Minister, he looked into the cost of the Botanical Garden project in Montreal—the brainchild of a great scientist, the botanist Brother Marie-Victorin. Duplessis had allocated $5 million for this project. Bouchard thought that the entire scheme was too expensive and too lavish.[8] He wanted to requisition the buildings of the garden for government use. He discussed the transfer of the property to the province with the Montreal alderman in charge, George Marler, who refused him outright. "It is ridiculous," Bouchard replied, "that your botanical garden takes so much place to grow 150 varieties of the same plant." Marler explained that this was essential for world-class scientific botanical research, and added that he was strongly convinced that the garden was an extraordinary educational resource. Futhermore, the city insisted on keeping the buildings and the grounds intact. All Bouchard had to hear were the words "educational resource," and he acquiesced. He calculated rapidly that it would cost the city $75,000. Marler quickly replied that although the city was in financial distress, it had reserved the necessary funds. Bouchard then responded, "All right, you will have the keys tomorrow morning."[9] He

8   Rumilly, *Duplessis*, I, p. 559.

9   George Marler, personal communication to Chisholm, p.113.

thereby showed that he was able to change his mind when presented with convincing arguments based on the benefit to the population as a whole.

The war in Europe was going badly for the allies. The Germans had easily overrun France. After the miracle rescue of British troops at Dunkirk, the fall of France was a severe blow to Canadian morale. Fascist elements and even pro-Nazi groups in Quebec carried on a campaign of defeatism and against enlistment into the armed forces. The Bouchards went on the air to broadcast words of faith and hope. Cécile-Ena organized Red Cross activities in Saint-Hyacinthe. General de Gaulle's broadcast from London in August 1940, announcing his continued resistance—to the Nazis, to Pétain's government, and the founding of the *France Libre* movement—were immediately supported by Bouchard, in contrast to the nationalist elites. From Quebec came a telegram of support from the mayor of Saint-Hyacinthe. Cécile-Ena, who was to join the armed forces, worked with Colonel Pierrené, a close associate of de Gaulle, and with the great-granddaughter of Marshal MacMahon, Elisabeth de Miribel, who was well-known in Canada.[10] De Miribel had moved to Canada from the Free French office in London, since she had family in Quebec. Cécile-Ena helped these representatives of Free France to understand the Canadian and Quebec state of mind. She organized the French National Committee, which would grow to ninety chapters strong throughout Canada before the end of the war. Bouchard's Windsor Hotel suite was the site of many meetings and soirées in support of the Free French. But as the influence of the pro-Free-French movement increased during the war, so did the movement of Vichy sympathizers also increase, as did the resistance to participation in the war—especially among the Quebec nationalists, the elite and the low clergy. As Eric Amyot points out, it is difficult to accurately assess the extent of support of the Pétainists or the Gaullists among the French-Canadian population of Quebec.[11] Certainly, among the elite, support for the Pétainists was strong, especially early in the war. However, once again, the support for Vichy among the people is uncertain. The people may not have followed the elite and *Le Devoir*. Cardinal Villeneuve and the high clergy energetically preached patriotism and loyalty to the home-

---

10   Marshall MacMahon was one of the leaders of the French army in the 1870 Franco-Prussian War. Unable to break through German lines to rejoin the forces of Marshall Bazaine, the French lost the Battle of Sedan, and the Prussians took Emperor Napoleon III prisoner.

11   Eric Amyot, *Le Québec entre Pétain et de Gaulle, Vichy, La France Libre et les Canadiens Français, 1940–1945*, (Montréal: Fides, 1999).

lands—both France and England. They strongly supported and encouraged the population to subscribe to the war loan drive. The cardinal delivered a special message by radio calling for support for a general subscription campaign for victory bonds. He had prayers read in all Catholic churches of the province, decreeing sacrifices and fasts in support of the Allies. Monsignor Gauthier, the Archbishop of Montreal, kept silent about registration for a possible mobilization announced by the federal government on the day following the collapse of France. Villeneuve, however, displeased with Gauthier, intervened in Montreal with a pastoral letter read in all parishes. The letter read: "His Eminence, the Cardinal invites all priests to greatly facilitate national registration, as much as possible, by providing their people with the necessary information, in a manner in which those who depend on them may accomplish with precision and submission that which is rightfully requested by the public authorities."[12]

Captain (later Major) Cécile-Ena Bouchard

However, some of the low clergy promoted the anti-war and anti-conscriptionist movements. National registration was the first step towards conscription, they said. They were not wrong, despite the protestations of the governments to the con-

12   Collection of Pastoral Letters, *Archvêché de Québec*, 2 aôut 1940.

trary. This was just as Gagnon had expected. In the 1939 election campaign Gagnon had predicted that the war would be protracted and would eventually require conscription. He felt that the Liberals made a tragic mistake in promising that there would be no conscription.[13] A repetition of the scene that took place in Saint-Hyacinthe in 1936 occurred. In Montreal's Notre-Dame Church a platoon of hooded Nazis invaded the centre of the church during Midnight Mass. As Bouchard noted, these fanatics were a tiny but noisy fringe of the population.[14]

On January 18, 1940, Mitchell Hepburn, the premier of Ontario, presented a motion in the provincial legislature of Ontario condemning the federal government of Mackenzie King because, he claimed, it was not pursuing the war with sufficient vigour. King, he said, had to go. The Prime Minister replied that he would consult the people, and he called an election. Thus, on March 25, 1940, Mackenzie King achieved the greatest victory of his career with 144 Liberals elected as opposed to only thirty-seven Conservatives. Only one Conservative was elected in the province of Quebec. In the riding of Saint-Hyacinthe-Bagot, Liberal Adélard Fontaine received a huge majority of 10,600 votes, the largest ever recorded in the history of the riding.

The first legislative session of the new provincial government opened on February 20, 1940. The Lieutenant-Governor, Maj.-Gen. Sir Eugène Fiset, gave the Speech from the Throne. The government promised to adopt female suffrage; to balance the budget; to propose a less expensive distribution of electrical power; to undertake a vast program of road building; to centralize all the work on roads (until then road work was spread out among the ministries of roads, mines and colonization); to replace Duplessis's fair wage law by a minimum wage law; to improve forest and mining legislation; and to encourage new directions in agriculture, including the planting of linseed and sugar beet.

The question of female suffrage was the most outstanding innovation. Presented unsuccessfully as a private member's bill in each session since 1925, and opposed by Taschereau, its inclusion in the government's program was a triumph for Bouchard and Godbout. Cardinal Villeneuve expressed his disapproval in a pastoral letter on March 2, 1940, asserting that he was not in favour of female suffrage because it went against family unity and hierarchy—that it would expose women to all the passions and to all the excitement of the electoral

13   See p. 251.

14   T.D.B., *Mémoires,* III, p. 117.

process. In the Assembly, answering the opposition leader's sly inquiry as to how he intended to act in the face of the cardinal's disapproval, Godbout replied that, perhaps to Duplessis's surprise, there were still men in the province who kept their word. Then, privately, he threatened the cardinal with his resignation and the promotion of Bouchard as premier in his place, if Villeneuve persisted in his opposition to the bill. No further sound was heard from that quarter.[15] This historic legislation was adopted on April 11, 1940, by a vote of sixty-seven yeas versus nine nays. Quebec thus joined the other provinces and the federal jurisdiction in extending the franchise to women.

In the spring, municipal elections in Saint-Hyacinthe confirmed Bouchard's team in power. The mayor himself was re-elected by acclamation, and all his candidates for council seats were voted in. On the provincial scene Bouchard resumed his plan of assistance for the unemployed, which he had inaugurated with such success in Saint-Hyacinthe in 1934 and 1935. The minister explained that there were now some new aspects to the plan. Public works would be divided into two categories: those reserved for workers receiving direct government support; and those open to all workers. His program was subject to controversy. The mayors of several cities, including Quebec, opposed the plan, describing it as inhuman. While Harry Bernard, in *Le Courrier de Saint-Hyacinthe,* was happy to see the plan contested, Alexis Gagnon in *Le Devoir* approved of the program:

> This project, even though extremely reasonable, has raised a violent clamour in some milieus. The fact that mayors, aldermen, and MLAs are scandalized because a courageous minister wants to make the unemployed work for regular wages in exchange for direct support, shows just how deep the gangrene has set in.[16]

Bouchard answered his critics on May 3 by noting that creating work was the only cure for unemployment. The cost of unemployment totaled almost $226 million as of March 31, 1940, comprising $82 million in work projects and $144 million in direct assistance. Bouchard deemed this a wasteful expenditure. In the face of such large amounts, he felt obliged to do something. He announced that the government was going to place $20 million at his disposal

---

15   Genest, *Godbout,* p. 154. With Taschereau, and most likely against his own personal conviction, Godbout had voted against female suffrage in 1935.

16   *Le Devoir,* 10 *avril* 1940.

to distribute to workers. The international and Catholic labour unions submitted a resolution to the municipal authorities of Montreal, asking for a study of the Bouchard plan by a competent commission before its application. Despite this opposition, Bouchard could claim that after the plan's first four months of implementation, in Montreal alone, the number of workers needing direct relief had decreased from 45,000 to 13,000; and the province had saved $4,200,000. He again received the approval of Louis Dupire, the municipal affairs expert of *Le Devoir,* who called those who denounced this plan "myopic." For Dupire, the results were apparent. After just a few weeks there were no more than 64,302 persons in Montreal on the list of direct allocations, compared to 102,039 during the same period of 1939.[17] Dupire wrote that the whole province gained from work carried out by the unemployed. He also emphasized that American tourists wanted to travel on a good road system.

On November 19, before the members of the Kiwanis-St-Laurent Club at the Ritz-Carlton Hotel, the Minister of Roads gave a talk on the damage done by unemployment. Again he argued that direct support often resulted in making the victim's lot worse:

> The institution of direct support has been a misfortune for our people, known up to now for its qualities of valour, courage and dignity. One can never condemn enough the demoralization and disintegration that has accompanied this institution. Because, if we owe charity to the infirm, to invalids, and to all those without defence, it is the worst service, and I would say almost an outrage, to give money that he has not earned to a healthy-bodied man, to a man who has good legs, a good arm, and a good eye, money to do nothing … it is an outrageous scandal and almost a crime against those helped, a crime against their families.[18]

Bouchard described direct support as a cancer that grows and spreads by feeding on the "social cells" which it devours. In his opinion, direct support results in more unemployed. For example, in three cities—Saint-Joseph-d'Alma, Chicoutimi, and Cap-de-la-Madeleine—direct support became a real industry. He concluded by repeating that if the state continued to pour in allocations

---

17   *Le Devoir,* 20 *novembre* 1940. There is an obvious discrepancy between Bouchard's figures and those of Dupire; however, in each the impressive reduction of the welfare list is striking.

18   T.-D.B., *Le Clairon,* 22 *novembre* 1940.

without demanding anything in return, people would have no incentive to resume work; and once adopted, the bad habit would result in chronic laziness and falling prey to the worst physical and moral degeneration. "By restoring the taste and dignity of work," he stated, "we believe that we have benefited our race, our province, and our country."[19] Louis Dupire continued to approve of Bouchard's policy:

> It is Mr. Bouchard who has attempted, by taking the bull by the horns, according to his own expression, the second purge of the lists. We have to admit that he has succeeded.... If the City had not been put under tutelage, the operation would have failed once more.... We do not judge from narrow-minded considerations; we have not condemned, but on the contrary approved.[20]

Unable to pay back its loans, the City of Montreal declared bankruptcy on May 15, 1940. Under the legislation adopted in 1935 by the Taschereau government, the city fell under the tutelage of the Municipal Commission. According to Black, the 1935 bill was passed to mollify Bouchard and prevent his resignation as minister.[21] Thus, in 1940, Godbout appointed his expert in municipal affairs, T.-D. Bouchard, as Receiver for the City of Montreal. Bouchard's plan for the reorganization of the city council, which he had developed five years earlier, was put into operation.[22] This plan divided the city into eleven districts. Each would send six representatives to the city council—three designated by property owners and three by the public at large. In spite of his democratic convictions, Bouchard had adopted a corporatist plan by proposing that, in addition to these sixty-six representatives, eleven corporate associations appoint thirty-three aldermen. He wanted to have the mayor elected by the aldermen. Houde protested and succeeded in convincing Godbout to preserve the election of the mayor by popular vote. Duplessis denounced the anti-democratic nature of the law, which though inspired by a "documented democrat," created, in his view, classes of privileged electors. Bouchard replied that after three years of dictatorial administration, Duplessis was not in a position to call for democracy. For those aware of Bouchard's opinions on the corporatism of Mussolini or

---

19 Ibid., p. 6.

20 *Le Devoir,* 21 *novembre* 1940.

21 Black, p. 373.

22 Ibid., p. 373.

Salazar, his plan was indeed surprising. He reasoned that the huge number of aldermen (ninety-nine) would guard against the creation of blocs, and would prevent corruption and the use of public funds for private interest. In the end the scheme wound up being the first notable failure in municipal administration for Bouchard—probably because of its ineffective and clumsy conception.

The Assembly resumed the discussion once again on the construction of new buildings to house the University of Montreal—a project that had been put on hold by the Duplessis administration due to lack of funds. To reassure the bishops, Provincial Secretary Henri Groulx presented a bill that increased the board of directors of the University from seven to eight members, all appointed by the bishops. One of Bouchard's old professors, Msgr. Émile Chartier, an intellectual whom he held in high regard, was then secretary of the University. Acquainted with Bouchard for many years and familiar with his dedication to education, Chartier convinced his colleagues to appeal to this radical—this anti-clerical—for funding to complete the buildings. Bouchard writes with delight about his meeting with the delegation:

> They were wrong about my true feelings. Most of them expected to be disappointed, but they soon realized their error. Instead of dismissing some members of the delegation whom I had recognized as having worked in the shadows to destroy me, I warned them that if I accepted to settle the problem.... It was on the strict condition that those concerned would limit their request to the purposes of education only. I evaluated the amount that would be required, three million dollars ... I informed my old professor of rhetoric ... I would gladly consent to subscribe from my own budget one million of dollars annually for a period of three years, so as to complete the construction of their buildings.... Except for Monsignor Chartier, few of the delegation expected that the grandson of the water-porter, the kid from the Hay Market, would be called on one day to authorize the resumption of construction of the ... university, which had been threatened with ruin by the Depression.[23]

Moreover, he offered to buy the old university building on St. Denis Street to use for government offices. On June 3, 1943, at the inauguration of the new University of Montreal building overlooking Outremont, Bouchard was

---

23   T.-D.B., *Mémoires*, III, p. 120–121. See also Black, p. 378.

awarded an honorary doctorate for his services. At the same time, Canon Groulx and Louis Saint-Laurent also acquired honorary degrees.

In the summer of 1940 Mackenzie King attempted to increase the centralizing power of Ottawa, seizing upon unemployment insurance as a federal prerogative. King wrote to Godbout that the state of war greatly intensified the need for a national unemployment insurance plan. Godbout gave his consent without any public discussion. On July 10, 1940, the British Parliament in London, without debate, passed the constitutional amendment permitting this federal incursion into provincial jurisdiction. As a prelude to the federal program to erode provincial authority, in 1937 King had established the Rowell-Sirois Commission. It issued its report in 1940, recommending a more centralized national system with adjusted federal grants. All laws concerning—but not limited to—labour, minimum wage and working conditions, would henceforth fall under federal jurisdiction. To cover these increased expenses, the report suggested modifying tax-collection in favour of the federal government.[24] In the early part of 1941, a federal-provincial conference was convened to discuss the Rowell-Sirois Commission report. King tried without success to get the provinces to agree to more changes to the British North America Act. Mitchell Hepburn of Ontario and the premiers of the other provinces refused even to discuss the Rowell-Sirois report. The conference ended suddenly. Godbout delivered a brief, ambiguous speech asserting his goodwill, stating that he had not come to the conference as a Quebecer but as a Canadian. In response Duplessis issued a declaration defending the cause of provincial autonomy. He did not name his rival even once.

As president of the newly created Office of Economic Reconstruction—created following Roosevelt's example in the United States—and as Minister of Roads and Public Works, Bouchard was the subject of many rumours concerning his domineering style. His increasingly prominent place in public view resulted in much gossip. Some of his colleagues in the cabinet and in the caucus began to find that he had too much power, and that Godbout seemed more like a lieutenant of the Member for Saint-Hyacinthe, rather than his chief. Harry Bernard was happy to fan the flames: "If one believes some of the rumours ... Mr. Adélard Godbout is not really in control to a great extent in the capital. If he

---

24   L.-D.-R., II, p. 160–165. The report did note many anomalies with the system in place. Montreal was the least-compensated city in the country when it came to provincial funds. The Quebec contribution to unemployment support, direct, and public works, was almost double that of the federal contribution from 1930 to 1940. See Table 1, p. 47.

has the title of premier, it only for appearance's sake…. Nothing is accomplished in Quebec … without the acquiescence of Mr. Bouchard."[25]

Bouchard was also a target for caricaturists. Gratien Gélinas's *Fridolin Review* devoted a whole issue to the Minister of Roads.[26] In a satirical play, instead of a statue erected to the glory of La Vérendrye, there was an immense portrait of Bouchard with the title: *"Moi."* On the wall there was a map of Canada with all parts shaded except for a large red dot marking Bouchard's home city. At the bottom of the map one read, "All roads lead to Saint-Hyacinthe." Another sketch described Bouchard's secretary on the telephone responding to the premier: "Mr. Godbout, you will have to wait your turn for an appointment—in 15 days, just like the others."

Nevertheless, in Saint-Hyacinthe, Bouchard remained a trusted figure. In July of 1941, once again, his five candidates were all elected to the council by acclamation. However, in Quebec City he was not as popular. Members of the Liberal caucus complained bitterly about his policy on unemployment, his rigidity about patronage in government contracts, and his support for educational reforms. The discussion became heated, and again some suggested that he be appointed to the Senate. Godbout supported Bouchard and declared that he continued to approve these reforms because they were necessary for provincial progress. Bouchard comments:

> I expected these Liberal caucus manoeuvres influenced by clerical agitators and contractors, interested only in themselves, who I had not satisfied. Secure in the justice of my cause and with the support of my leader, I looked at the small clouds that appeared on the horizon with serenity. Perhaps they were the foreboding signs of a storm, more or less distant, in which I could be swept away. However, they did not scare me, and I did not intend to retreat.[27]

In analyzing the reported cabinet conflict, Alexis Gagnon in *Le Devoir* pointed to Bouchard's approach towards unemployment as the cause. He admired the tenacity with which Bouchard tackled the sore of direct support even at the price of his popularity. According to Gagnon, Bouchard had real difficulties

---

25   *Le Courrier de Saint-Hyacinthe*, 29 *septembre* 1940.

26   Library of the Université de Montréal, EPC—biomedia—AVDOC Filo 972.

27   T.-D.B., *Mémoires*, III, p. 123.

with the leaders of his own party, who feared disastrous results at the polls. Alexis Gagnon wrote:

> Therefore, a good number of besieged Members have demonstrated their displeasure, declaring that Liberal prestige is disintegrating and that the unemployed and the people growl. And they hold Mr. Bouchard's policies responsible for this uneasiness. Also for some time people contrive to want to place him in a golden sinecure [the Senate], far from unemployment and roads.[28]

During debates in the Assembly, in February 1941, after a long argument between Duplessis and Bouchard, about the construction of a bridge in Abitibi, Duplessis teased Bouchard and Godbout, to the great amusement of the Chamber. In a sarcastic tone, the Leader of the Opposition stated:

> There is something unfair here. It is the campaign of defamation against the Minister of Roads conducted by ministerial delegates. They accuse Mr. Bouchard of having imposed toll-rates, multiplied taxes, and demanded about $20 million more in taxes each year. One accuses Mr. Bouchard of having done all that, saying that it is his fault, and not that of Mr. Godbout. I protest in the name of Mr. Bouchard, and I want to defend him against these unjust attacks.[29]

Nevertheless, the fiery Member for Saint-Hyacinthe received two minutes of applause from his caucus and his fellow cabinet ministers after energetically intervening in a debate on the budget with an hour-long speech. *Le Devoir* reported that he was alone in reaching the one-hour limit fixed by House regulations.

> This speech, and the success that followed it, had a significant influence. It is a secret for no one that during the past two weeks, a group of ministers has formed which is hostile to Mr. Bouchard, because the latter holds the provincial purse-strings tightly and in an unfeeling manner; and dismisses various solicitations for small favours without beating around the bush. Yesterday afternoon, Mr. Bouchard insisted strongly on the fact that favours are not distributed to the right and

---

28   *Le Devoir,* 11 *février* 1941.

29   Ibid., 7 *février* 1941.

to the left—it is not patronage which elects members, but the results of good public financial administration.[30]

This conviction—that conscientious public administration and not patronage is the source of popularity—is certainly open to question. It was not the belief of the Liberal organizers throughout the province at that time, nor perhaps now.

In February and March, there were two main questions before the Assembly: the Saint Lawrence Seaway; and the nationalization of the Beauharnois Light, Heat, and Power Company. Duplessis took the opportunity of a visit of the Montreal Chamber of Commerce to Quebec City to try to raise the Seaway question, but Godbout blocked this attempt. The Chamber of Commerce was naturally opposed to the Seaway project—as were most Montrealers, who considered it a serious threat to the prosperity of their port. Mackenzie King announced the signing of an agreement on the Seaway with the Americans in the House of Commons on March 20. Godbout described the advantages of the seaway project for the province of Quebec: "Here is a government [the U.S.A.] which feeds the British Empire with war material. This government said to us: 'I need the Saint Lawrence to help us defend you.' Can we really refuse to cooperate?"[31] By submitting to federal pressure in agreeing to the Seaway, Godbout once again allowed the harmful conclusion to stand that he had not attempted in any way to protect the interests of the province. Duplessis exploited this argument vigorously.

In the Assembly, Bouchard was violently attacked on the question of nationalization of the Beauharnois Company, since he had been against it in 1937. He explained that he had never been against nationalization but against expropriation, which implied a price consented to by outside evaluators. These prices, he felt, had always been favourable to private interests. "For the past forty years," he declared, "I have never preached against nationalization. But I have always expressed myself against the forced expropriation of the Beauharnois."[32] Bouchard cited the example of the Montreal Streetcar Company, worth only $9 million according to his calculations, but for which a court of arbitration had fixed the amount to be compensated at thirty-five million. He explained

---

30   Ibid., 13 *mars* 1941.

31   Rumilly, *Duplessis,* I, p. 590.

32   *Le Devoir,* 15 *mai* 1941.

that the government was going to proceed in two stages: first it would study the Beauharnois Company's capitalization; and then study the effects of its nationalization—all done by an independent body. Subsequently, the government would enter into discussion with the proprietors. If they agreed on the price, the government would acquire the company. If not, the government would expropriate the company at a price fixed by a court, limited by the amount fixed by its own experts. Louis Depire's favourable opinion changed on this issue. "Mr. Bouchard has long fought the electrical trusts with courage and brio. One of the processes that he denounced with the utmost virulence is the 'watering down,' the dishonest inflation, of the capital. However, it is precisely this method which he applies to the evaluation of Montreal."[33]

In September T.-D. Bouchard gave an important talk to the Citizens Committee of Montreal on the *New Administrative Mode of the City of Montreal.* He repeated all his favourite themes on municipal democracy, healthy administration, the avoidance of corruption and favouritism. He called the direct-support policy of the governments of Taschereau and Duplessis between 1930 and 1940 as the greatest scandal of the decade. He said that his policy had saved Montreal alone $2 million. While approving of Bouchard's social policy and his plan to reduce direct support for unemployment, Dupire doubted the efficiency of the new regime and questioned Bouchard's democratic ideas.

> In order that the aldermen take their task seriously … it would be necessary that they be paid or that they have power…. The error the government has committed is in not proceeding in two stages: during the first, frank tutelage, in order to solidly re-establish the financial aspects and to research seriously an administrative system that had solid grounds for survival. Instead, a tainted, camouflaged form of tutelage has been formed that does not deceive anyone.[34]

A year before Canada's entry into the war and the fall of Maurice Duplessis, Father Georges-Henri Lévesque presided over the introduction of economic and social courses at the School of Social Sciences at Laval University.[35] Established at the express demand of Cardinal Villeneuve, chancellor of the university, the school would become a faculty in 1943. Welcomed with open arms by the

---

33   Ibid., 28 *mars* 1941.

34   Ibid., 23 *septembre* 1941.

35   Dickinson and Young, p. 285, see also Rudin, p. 131.

Quebec seminary and the university, the program was a popular one. Father Lévesque had been born in the Lac-Saint-Jean area, where people were described as "… gutsy, that is to say that they truly belonged to the country in the heart of Quebec where one expresses oneself directly and usually with eloquence."[36] Later, the enlightened middle class supporting the school was called leftist, and Father Lévesque himself became the object of a campaign of defamation. Antoine Rivard, a lecturer in the Faculty of Law at Laval University, struck the first blow in this campaign. During a press conference in mid-autumn, Rivard stated that he did not see the need to train sociologists when lawyers filled this role in Quebec. "Sociologists for what purpose? Everything is in the Civil Code." Later, when Father Lévesque recommended that the co-operative movement be non-sectarian—not divided into religious denominations—some bishops took him to the ecclesiastical court in Rome. This court, however, found in his favour—that is, Rome refused to condemn him.

Antoine Rivard replied to this change in climate when he gave a lecture at the Château Frontenac entitled "He Is Born to a Proud Race." In addition to his remarks on the study of sociology, Rivard had this explanation of French-Canadian history: "*We French-Canadians, we stem from a long tradition of ignorance and poverty, a tradition that we have to preserve.*"[37] (Emphasis added.) This affirmation resembles Henri Bourassa's thoughts at the beginning of the century, when he counselled against education for sons of farmers. According to Rivard, "They [our ancestors] made their choice: they have accepted economic inferiority … they preferred the rags of the pauper, miseries, hunger, and cold; they wanted all that in order to remain true to their faith, to their language, and to their laws." Then Rivard cited Léopold Richer, a nationalist journalist from *Le Devoir*, who wrote: "*To be faithful and to remain true to themselves, the French of Canada have taken the heroic route of ignorance, rural labour, the daily combat against the forest.*" Rivard concluded: "*We have to continue in the difficult, tedious and painful way that our forefathers have chosen and to which they have been committed.*"[38] (Emphasis added.) These views were those of Henri Bourassa and Lionel Groulx—nationalists who advocated a rural, agrarian, simple life for the French-Canadian people. They fought against the growing industrialisation

---

36   Gagnon, II, p. 31.

37   T.-D.B., *Mémoires,* III p. 137.

38   T.-D.B., *Mémoires,* III p. 137.

and urbanization of Quebec that they felt would destroy the French-Canadian way of life.[39]

Bouchard answered Rivard in a Montreal talk before the Saint Lawrence branch of the Kiwanis Club. His speech was entitled "If We Want to be True Patriots."[40] He described Rivard's talk as "in the true tradition of our worst Saint-Jean-Baptiste speeches."[41] Bouchard had spent a long time in preparing this speech, and had sent copies all around. Robert Saint-Germain and Jacques Bibeau remark, "Sensational words from the fiery member-mayor of Saint-Hyacinthe were expected."[42] Someone wrote Bouchard anonymously, warning him about his position on education: "Those who hate you and whom you hate are going to find so many bad things, that this will be your loss."[43] As usual, he ignored this warning. As we have noted, Bouchard was a long-time advocate of educational reform. In 1905 he had written in his newspaper that Quebec needed a bilingual, compulsory and free education system. Commenting on a compulsory school bill in his in his 1912 maiden speech to the Legislative Assembly, he had linked education to the national advancement of French Canadians. According to Bouchard, French-Canadian backwardness in education explained their backwardness in the economic area. In his *Mémoires*, T.-D. Bouchard devotes fifteen pages to direct quotation from his speech—which had been sixty pages long in total—given to the Kiwanis Club. This speech, he confesses, had been inspired by the recent talk of Rivard. He condemned those who continued to live in the past, those who held the false idea that French Canadians monopolize Catholicism. He remarked that there are more Catholics that speak a language foreign "to ours" than those who speak French.

> This fact seems to be ignored in the province of Quebec, especially by people who … confuse religion with language, and language with religion. Just as if millions and millions of human beings who do not express themselves in French would not know how to be good

---

39   Most figures on the rate of urbanization do not take into account the enormous emigration of French Canadians to U.S. cities. If these were to be included, then Quebec might have had an even greater rate of urbanization than most other provinces and states.

40   *Fonds* Bouchard, *Si nous voulons être de véritable des patriotes*, ANQ, P-10/25.

41   *Fonds* Bouchard, ANQ, P-10/42 p. 7.

42   S.-G. & B., p. 178.

43   Letter signed M. B. *Fonds* Bouchard, ANQ, P-10/14.

Catholics.... It is that one can not be a good Catholic without believing that some priests in cassocks or in pants preach social credit, family allowances, corporatism, separatism, the error of economic liberalism, the perversity of democracy, the dangers of bilingualism.[44]

He denounced the idea that those who preach bilingualism to French Canadians are erroneous, poor patriots, bad Catholics, "Anglicisers," and promoters of Protestantism.[45] He condemned the hypocrisy of the ruling classes. He saw that the French Canadians of Outremont and Westmount of his day (like those of today) educated their children in bilingual schools and summer camps, and at American or English Universities. Like many of the elite on the political scene today, including many prominent separatists, Maître Rivard had studied law at Oxford University in England. Bouchard was ahead of his time:

> These isolationists, that is to say, those who want French-Canadians to be a separate group on the American continent, admit … that English can be useful to our ruling class but they do not recognize that the knowledge of this useful language is indispensable to the great mass of people. There is a prejudice by virtue of which those of the past who confuse our minds hope to reserve education for the sons of rich families without caring for children of the working class.... It is nevertheless true that … whatever class one belongs to and whatever is the profession or trade that one plies, the knowledge of English is necessary, I believe even indispensable. Some say … that the child of the farmer or the worker does not need English. What an error … Only those who are for French-Canadian isolation and who wish to deprive them of the essential ways to improve their lives … have the right to preach against bilingualism at home.[46]

According to Bouchard, isolationists were true to their belief when preaching against bilingualism, since to be bilingual is an ingredient of Canadian unity. "They have aroused public opinion by giving people the impression that if they acquired an education, French Canadians would lose their language and their

---

44   T.-D.B., Speech, *Si Nous Voulons être de véritable patriote,* p. 5 *Fonds* Bouchard, ANQ, P-10/42 and *Mémoires,* III, p. 125.

45   Ibid., p. 19.

46   Ibid., p. 19.

religion."[47] Bouchard stated that the authorities no longer dared to preach the complete banishment of English from the schools. Instead, they carried out a slowdown strike. It had begun by suppressing the teaching of English in the lower grades. (During the Duplessis regime of 1936–39 the teaching of English was delayed by two years in primary schools.) When the teaching began, it was taught poorly, according to the dictum of Monsignor Laflèche. ("Teach English, all right, but teach it poorly.") Bouchard noted, "In our grade schools the teaching of a little English begins when it is too late to learn it correctly.... Why is there resistance to changing obsolete teaching methods?" Bouchard maintained his support for a Catholic and French education with a general curriculum—history, arithmetic, physics, chemistry—and held that English should be taught as a language, with study of the vocabulary and grammar. He pointed out that barely five million French Canadians lived on a continent that was home to two hundred million English-speakers. He wished to see bilingualism in Canada, from coast to coast, although he admitted that this was a difficult undertaking.[48] Castigating the separatist forces of his day, he emphasized that their opposition to English language education was driven by their desire to keep French Canadians isolated, and that French-Canadian "backwardness" was not due to the English.

> The separatists perpetuate the myth that if French-Canadians have remained a poor people, it is because the English would have consented to enrich us on condition that we abandoned our language and our religion.... The delay is really due to the ominous influence of those who have opposed ... the spread of popular education ... they have aroused public opinion by creating ... the impression that if French Canadians became educated they would lose their language and their religion.[49]

For Bouchard the privileged classes held the people back not to save their culture's religion and language, but rather to save their own money and preserve their ascendancy over their co-religionists. "Now that we have had mass educa-

---

47   Ibid., p. 19.

48   Bilingualism in Canada must be credited to Pierre Elliot Trudeau. Proir to Trudeau no MPs from the West or Ontario spoke French. Even English-speakers from Quebec did not bother to learn French.

49   Ibid., p. 19.

tion for a generation … tell me, you who belong to the elite of French-Canadian society, are we worse Catholics and worse patriots than those indoctrinated and counselled by our spoilsports of the past who once burned down the rural schools that progressive citizens of 1850 built in our countryside?" Bouchard reminded the audience that in 1853 Étienne Parent had proposed a plan of education including free primary instruction. Parent advocated free education at higher levels for those judged deserving by virtue of their talents and their good conduct, and the establishment of institutions appropriate to all types of higher studies necessary for civilization: schools for higher business administration and industry; colleges for the liberal arts; and universities for higher sciences. Bouchard stated that it had required seventy-five years to realize this program, and that the English had not caused this delay. Bouchard sardonically comments, "Ours is a singular vocation! To remain eternally ignorant, a poor and destitute people! Coming from a lawyer [Rivard] who preaches this while speaking of national pride is disturbing!"[50] He concluded by urging his listeners to push for the reforms recommended by distinguished laymen and by eminent members of the French-Canadian clergy. He called on all citizens of Quebec to support those who work for the economic advancement of their own and for the greatest harmony between the two great peoples of Canada.

Bouchard's speech provoked a violent controversy in the nationalist newspapers. He was accused of speaking and writing French poorly. He defended himself again by explaining that he spoke French like a Canadian, as taught by his good professors at the Seminary of Saint-Hyacinthe, to the best of their abilities. But at the same time, he admitted that he spoke and wrote French poorly: "No one more regrets my deficiency in the knowledge of our two beautiful living languages than I do." Humorously, he found it striking that Rivard's supporters also reproached him for not speaking English well. While Rivard recommended that his fellow citizens follow the advice of Monsignor Laflèche, Bouchard claimed that for once he was an obedient and submissive son.

As expected, *Le Devoir, L'Action catholique,* and of course *Le Courrier de Saint-Hyacinthe* criticized Bouchard for this speech. *Le Devoir* published a series of seven editorials on the teaching of English. Harry Bernard asserted that the 36 percent of the Irish in Quebec had abandoned Catholicism, as had 73 percent in Ontario. Bouchard made a clarification of his speech in *La Presse.*[51]

---

50   T.-D.B., *Si Nous Voulons…* p. 22.

51   *La Presse,* 22 *décembre* 1941.

Omer Héroux continued the battle in *Le Devoir* on December 26. A second clarification was added as an appendix to the pamphlet published by Bouchard on December 30. Rivard delivered an answer before the same Saint-Laurent Kiwanis Club at the Ritz-Carlton on January 21, 1942, and on radio, entitled: "We Hold True"—*Nous maintiendrons*. *Le Devoir* reproduced Rivard's talk under the caption "Mr. Antoine Rivard replied to Mr. T.-D. Bouchard, Public Works Minister of the Godbout cabinet, who attacked him without provocation." In fact, Rivard repeated his argument while specifying that he did not want to eliminate the teaching of English, but wanted to be sure that it was not introduced too soon in school—that is, before the age of twelve.

In 1939 Hector Perrier was the Provincial Secretary of the Liberal Cabinet, and therefore responsible for the Department of Public Education. He, Godbout, and Bouchard had all held progressive opinions on educational reform for many years. Jean-Charles Harvey wrote Bouchard on 13 December:

> How can I congratulate you enough for the common sense, which shines through this magnificent document and the courage that you show in the affirmation of the truth? This speech will be famous. It will produce shouts of panic from our cretins, but it will have the unanimous approval of all those who think and see clearly. You have without doubt followed my campaign regarding the OJC [Order of Jacques Cartier]. I persist. My documents become increasingly numerous and precise.[52]

Bouchard replied in a series of articles in *Le Clairon* from a hospital bed, where he was recovering from a severe bout of bronchopneumonia at the end of December. Because he coughed blood during this illness, he was convinced that he had tuberculosis, about which he had an intimate knowledge. As has been noted by several of his childhood friends, his uncle and a cousin had all died of tuberculosis. He thought that he would soon die. Doctor Segall assured him that he did not have tuberculosis—that blood in the sputum could equally be a sign of severe bronchopneumonia. He even bet T.-D. a hundred dollars that he would be alive in ten years; but ten years later Segall did not have the heart to remind Bouchard of the wager.[53] Almost at the same time, the same sickness (bronchopneumonia) brought Maurice Duplessis to the hospital, where diabe-

---

52   J.-C. Harvey letter, *Fonds* Bouchard, ANQ, P-10/14.

53   H.N. Segall, personal communication.

tes was discovered. It was an opportunity for his doctors and friends to finally convince him to give up alcohol. For the rest of his life he would never touch a drop, drinking only orange juice.

On his release from hospital, Bouchard decided to take a true leave of convalescence in Florida, where he remained for two months. On the way to Delray Beach, he stopped in Washington to see his cousin Abbé Edmond Fontaine, whom he visited each time he passed through the U.S. capital. His cousin informed him that during his recent visits to Canada, he had discovered that a certain number of clergy had modified their sentiments with regard to Bouchard; that they considered him more sympathetically.[54] This made Bouchard smile, since he had not forgotten "that absurd propaganda directed against me had been received as the Gospel by the unknowing and the stupid."[55]

Convalescence in Miami–1941

Convalescing in Florida, 1941

From Florida he sent regular contributions to his newspaper on his philosophy of life: "On a Trip of Convalescence"; "The Art of Resting"; "The Frenchman, a Born Moralist"; "On the Beach"; "To the Country of the Sun"; and "Away, in a

---

54   *Le Clairon,* "Vers le pays du soleil," 9 *février* 1942.

55   Ibid., and T.-D.B., *Mémoires,* III, p. 158.

Hospital." The last, dated March 1, 1942, tells about his urgent hospitalization for an acute urinary-tract obstruction. Even though he had suffered during the preceding night, he waited until morning to ask for the help and advice of his friend in Miami, Joseph Simard. One hour later Simard appeared in his hotel room accompanied by a physician. Bouchard was immediately hospitalized in the Saint-François Hospital, an establishment directed by the Franciscan religious order. After consultation with his physicians in Montreal, Bouchard agreed to be operated on by a specialist of great renown. On the eve of the surgery, Bouchard called for Abbé J. A. Girard of Saint-Hyacinthe, priest of the parish of Christ-Roi, who was visiting Coral Beach, to take his confession and administer last rites.[56] In those days a prostate operation was carried out in two stages. He underwent the first stage, to relieve the obstruction, in Florida. He then returned to Montreal, where he underwent the second stage at the Hôtel-Dieu Hospital in Montreal.

During his stay at the Hôtel-Dieu he met a young seminarian, Ambroise Lafortune. Father Lafortune sported a beard at a time when this practice was unusual. He would later become known as Father Ambroise of Radio-Canada Television. He was an independent soul, and the two men held lively discussions and established a lasting friendship. At the seminary Lafortune had been told that T.-D. had been excommunicated and that his anti-clericalism had developed into agnosticism. To his surprise he discovered the contrary: that T.-D. Bouchard was a practising, believing Catholic—nevertheless a liberal—with the same reformist ideas that he himself held. There had been a misunderstanding at their first meeting, on the Monday of the Holy Week of Easter. The young seminarian had been dressed in a cassock and Bouchard mistook him for a priest, sending him a gift of brains for his supper, with a note: "Here, Father, you will need these as a priest." To thank him, Father Ambroise visited, and they spoke on all safe subjects except religion.

Bouchard's surgeon Doctor Mercier had asked the sister in charge if she knew the name T.-D. Bouchard. She replied that yes, everyone knew his reputation. The physician forbade her to speak to him about religion or Christ. She was offended, saying that she was a professional nurse and of course would not speak to the patient about religion. On Good Friday, Father Ambroise, passing by Bouchard's room, heard loud swearing coming from within. "You damned nuns!" hollered the patient, "What kind of establishment are you running here? Where is the priest? I thought that this was a Catholic hospital! Where is the

---

56   *Le Clairon,* 1 *mars* 1942.

priest?"[57] The sister told him that the doctor had forbidden them to speak about religion with him. "But why?" he exclaimed. The sister hurried to find a priest to hear Bouchard's confession and to prepare him for Easter communion. Father Lafortune noted, "Bouchard was really a practising Catholic. There was always a priest in his life. I agreed with him that priests should deal with spiritual matters only. He was ahead of his time, and that is why he was attacked so viciously."[58]

T.-D. Bouchard was absent from Quebec during the height of the conscription crisis. Mackenzie King had tried to stick to his promise not to divide Canada by imposing compulsory military service as the Conservatives had done in 1917. He sincerely believed that conscription would not be necessary and that a volunteer army would suffice. In 1940 he introduced national registration, promising that it was not the first phase of conscription. This was precisely the contention of the nationalists, who held that it was the first stage of conscription, which turned out to be correct. Camillien Houde was imprisoned for four years for encouraging youth not to register. In 1939 the provincial Liberal victory had been based on the promise of no conscription. Ernest Lapointe, King's right-hand man for French Canada, who along with his Quebec colleagues in cabinet had threatened to resign in the event of a Duplessis re-election in 1939, died in November of 1941. His death came at a bad moment, since the war was going poorly and English Canada was demanding a more energetic commitment.

To solve this dilemma, King decided to consult the people by calling a plebiscite asking all Canadians to free him from his promise not to introduce conscription—*a promise really made only to the French Canadians to soothe their apprehension.* Godbout made a huge effort, often speaking alone to empty auditoriums in favour of the "Yes" side.[59] Pierre-Arthur Cardin, a senior Liberal leader, decided to resign from the cabinet, but put off his resignation until May in order not to harm the federal campaign for the release from King's promise. In fact, with his usual ambiguity, King announced that he would use the release from his promise only in case things got worse, but "not necessarily." ("Conscription if necessary, but not necessarily conscription.") However, since Cardin was reputed to be the best speaker in the metropolitan region, his silence during the campaign was eloquent. To be mute was equivalent of supporting anti-conscription views.

---

57   Father Ambroise Lafortune, personal communication to Chisholm, pp.145–146.

58   Ibid.

59   Gagnon, II, p.157.

In Quebec City, there was Louis Saint-Laurent, of whom Gagnon lamented, "[He] seems unable to plead a cause as soon as the audience becomes larger than a jury."[60] The other powerful Minister from Quebec, Chubby Power, no longer had the heart to work in the campaign. Against Groulx, Laurendeau, Filion and Drapeau, Adélard Godbout fought with the fire of a crusader.[61] Jean-Louis Gagnon describes how he was often alone with Godbout in several smaller provincial cities, where there were few listeners and where he was the only other person on the platform to warm up the audience. Gagnon, however, was wrong to criticize Bouchard: "Even Bouchard, hurt by the departure of Cardin, made only a symbolic gesture."[62] Since Bouchard was in Florida, and then in the Hôtel Dieu Hospital, for the months of February, March and April of 1942, he was not able to participate actively in the debate. Nevertheless, his newspaper came out strongly for the "Yes" side. On April 24, three days before the referendum, a long article of "Questions and Answers" appeared, explaining why the electorate should trust Mackenzie King and vote "Yes." The war was difficult and Canada had to prevent the collapse of Great Britain—otherwise, Canada itself could be threatened. In an editorial on May 1, Bouchard lamented the results that expressed the division of the two peoples of Canada.[63]

On February 11, the League for the Defence of Canada, a precursor of the *Bloc Populaire*, held a huge demonstration at the Saint-Jacques market. Jean Drapeau, Gérard Filion and Maxime Raymond spoke to a crowd of twenty thousand people. Henri Bourassa, now seventy-four years old, rose to address

60 Ibid., p. 157.

61 As noted, most of the elites were pro-Vichy and anti-conscriptionist. "On September 12, 1996, the Federal government of Jean Chrétien appointed Jean-Louis Roux as Lieutenant-Governor of Quebec....In the course of an interview, Roux admitted that in 1942, while aged 19 and a student at the Université de Montreal, he had decorated his lab coat with a swastika. This was done at the time of the plebiscite on conscription, as a lark, in defiance of the Canadian authorities that were about to introduce conscription....On November 5, Jean-Louis Roux resigned and presented his apology publicly." Claude Bélanger, www.marianopolis.edu/quebechistory/events/roux.htm.
    While sitting next to J.-L. Roux at a dinner in Ottawa, he told me that what he did was nothing in comparison with Trudeau, who, while dressed as a Nazi storm trooper on a motorcycle, visited several summer homes in Trout Lake, a Jewish summer resort, asking for "vasser". personal communication.

62 Gagnon, II, p. 157.

63 *Le Clairon*, 1 *mai* 1942.

the crowd, and predicted that conscription would be imposed within the next two years no matter what the results of the referendum. He denounced the "plots of Ottawa." A riot then erupted. Bourassa did not succeed in re-establishing order and an excited crowd made its way to Boulevard Saint-Laurent, where the demonstrators expressed their anti-Semitism by breaking Jewish shopkeepers' windows.[64] Godbout commented that the speakers wanted to incite the crowd to treason.

In 1942, the nationalists, the anti-conscriptionists, and the anti-Duplessis forces organized again under the banner of the *Bloc Populaire Canadien,* electing André Laurendeau as general secretary. With the active participation of Maxime Raymond, Phillipe Hamel, René Chaloult, Édouard Lacroix, Jean Drapeau, Henri Bourassa, and, of course, Abbé Groulx, this party announced its birth, both provincially and federally. Black suggests that:

> The cause [the Bloc] attracted the adherence of disciples as different as the prolific Abbé Groulx and that ancient monk of backward opinions, Michel Chartrand ... Groulx counseled Chartrand to discuss the project with André Laurendeau and Paul Gouin. The usual groups were interested in the project: the Saint-Jean-Baptiste Society of Montreal; the Association of Students of the University of Montreal; the Canadian Association of Catholic youth and the Junior Chamber of Commerce of Montreal.[65]

---

64 Monière, pp. 281–285. Monière claims that xenophobia and anti-Semitism were absent from Quebec life in the early nineteenth century. Papineau's Patriots gave the Jews their civil rights in 1832, a first for the British Empire—even prior to Great Britain. Monière blames the outbreak of anti-Semitism of the 1930s on the Depression. The Jews became the scapegoat for all the ills of society, the power structure and class divisions. The large influx of Jews, competing with the lower middle class for advancement in trade and the professions, resulted in French-Canadian displacement of their difficulties onto the Jews. The new biography of P.E. Trudeau by Max and Monique Nemni reveals that in his youth he was anti-Semitic and wrote in support of an independent Catholic French-Canadian state. As noted by Pomeryols, the young elites were raised to be pro-fascist, and *democratic* and *liberal* were terms of criticism. The model leaders to be admired were good Catholic dictators like Mussolini in Italy, Salazar in Portugal and Franco in Spain. *Young Trudeau: 1919–1944 Son of Quebec, Father of Canada*, Translated by William Johnson, (Toronto: Douglas Gibson Books, 2006).

65 Black, *Duplessis*, I p. 409.

The campaign was bitter. Gagnon cites Laurendeau: "A majority vote will suffice to tear French Canadians away from their country and to deliver them up to death against their will, in one of the five parts of the world where British interest places the interest of Canada."[66] Jean-Louis Gagnon was incensed : "To speak of dying to defend British interests at a moment when Russians were being killed by the hundred thousands and at the moment when Americans were called on to pay the bill, that borders on obsession!"[67] The referendum took place on April 27, 1942, with the expected results. English Canada voted yes, and Quebec voted, no. In Canada, 63 percent approved the proposition and 36 percent disapproved. On the other hand, only an estimated 15 percent of French Canadians had voted yes, as had nine of sixty-five Quebec ridings. But King, fearing a repeat of the riots of 1917, in wonderfully ambiguous language announced that conscripts would be limited to military service within Canada. Conscription for overseas service would never be necessary, but if it *did* become necessary, the government would now feel free to impose it. During the summer, the debate continued to rage on the Conscription Bill.

Bouchard returned to the Legislative Assembly on May 19 to prolonged applause from both sides of the House. He remained there only a few moments, just long enough to thank all his friends and his colleagues who had wished him well. Duplessis also extended a welcome, declaring: "We do not want the sinner's death, but his conversion."[68] In spite of Bouchard's absence, the government had passed two laws which he treasured: a bill eliminating tolls on thirteen provincial bridges; and a bill establishing a Higher Institute of Technology in Saint-Hyacinthe. Early in the century, Lomer Gouin had succeeded in lessening the hold of the Church on technical education by establishing similar schools in Montreal and in Quebec City, explaining to the bishops that he did not have the funds to establish two separate technical schools, one Catholic and the other Protestant. Bouchard had recommended the establishment of a technical school in Saint-Hyacinthe, where in addition to technical subjects, higher education would be taught. The clergy and *Le Courrier de Saint-Hyacinthe,* who saw in this endeavour an opening to non-denominational schools and the teaching of English, opposed the project. Godbout, like his predecessor Gouin, explained to the cardinal that the province

---

66   André Laurendeau cited in J.-L. Gagnon, II, p.160.

67   Gagnon, Ibid., p. 160.

68   *Le Devoir,* 20 *mai* 1942.

could not afford to establish separate schools based on religion. The law autho-rized three hundred thousand dollars for the construction of the school and an annual subsidy of $30,000 for its maintenance. Bouchard noted that after the Liberals were defeated in 1944, the school was changed from an institute of higher learning into a simple textile trade school.[69]

Captain Cécile Bouchard, of the Canadian Women's Army Corps, offered the services of her father to King through the intervention her friend Princess Alice, the wife of the Governor General, the Duke of Athlone. After all, T.-D. Bouchard had been well-acquainted with political affairs in the province of Quebec for many years. At the beginning of June, Cécile-Ena had an appoint-ment with Prime Minister King, with T.-D. waiting nearby in Ottawa in case of a call. What the Bouchards did not know is that King already had a very negative opinion of T.-D. Bouchard. During discussions between King and Godbout on the appointment of Lapointe's successor, Godbout mentioned Bouchard's name. Godbout himself refused to become King's federal lieutenant, feeling that his duty lay provincially, and also perhaps fearing that Bouchard would be his suc-cessor in Quebec. In his private diary King wrote, on December 4, 1941: "The only thing that I did not like and which occasioned me disappointment was his suggestion that I might take Bouchard into the government. False note!"[70]

King was polite with Captain Bouchard. She quickly understood that he was not inclined to request the services of her father. In spite of this reception, with a remarkable lack of pride or perhaps with little insight, Bouchard wrote to King, ostensibly to thank him for having accepted to meet with his daughter. "This difficult time created by the plebiscite vote ... I have lately had two seri-ous operations ... I am now very well, and ready to do my small share to help you in the hard and wonderful work you are doing."[71] The Roads and Public Works Minister did not even receive an appointment with King. He did receive a courteous note with wishes that his health would continue to remain good. And then, with his typical obfuscation, King wrote: "Until the present debate on conscription is concluded, it is going to be very difficult to do other than fol-low the proceedings very closely."[72] He was the master of not saying anything!

---

69   T.-D.B., *Mémoires,* III, p. 70.

70   J.W. Pickerskill, *The Mackenzie King Record,* Vol 1, p. 292, cited in Chisholm, p. 147.

71   T.-D.B., letter to King, June 9, 1941 cited in Chisholm, p. 147.

72   Ibid., p. 148.

Unfortunately, Bouchard's reputation of possessing a certain prickly rectitude, taking principled stands, and creating turmoil disturbed King, who was a master of dodging confrontational situations. Consequently, the Prime Minister of Canada refused to enlist the fiery politician from Saint-Hyacinthe.

In Ottawa there was one person who thought highly of Bouchard: Georges Benoit, a journalist attached to the War Information Board. He felt that Bouchard had much to contribute. He was impressed by the clear views of *Le Clairon* and travelled to Saint-Hyacinthe to meet its publisher. Benoit commented on the high degree of morale and working spirit among the employees of the newspaper. From then on, he often consulted with Bouchard on problems of war propaganda for his work. They got along well. "Like me, he did not mince words," remarked Benoit. "There was a bond of common thought between us."[73]

Often in the late nineteenth and early twentieth centuries, the banks of the Yamaska River would flood the town during the ice breakup of spring. On August 1, 1941, in his capacity as Minister of Roads and Public Works in the Godbout government, Télesphore-Damien Bouchard found himself a few steps from the house in which he had been born on St. Antoine Street in the poor district of Saint-Hyacinthe almost sixty years earlier.[74] Bouchard inspected the progress on a new "handsome and sturdy" new bridge, named in his honour, spanning the Yamaska River. As mayor of Saint-Hyacinthe and senior minister of the provincial government, he was influential in arranging joint financing for this project.[75] Photographs from this period reveal a short, stocky, balding man with bright dark eyes, a square jaw, and a determined, serious gaze. Almost all pictures throughout his career show him in an unsmiling, stern pose. The only picture showing him smiling is a portrait that was in the hall of Hydro-Quebec headquarters in Montreal, which depicts him as its first president.[76]

The Minister of Roads and Public Works regained his strength after his illness. At the beginning of July he was re-elected mayor by acclamation for the thirteenth time. His team of aldermen was again elected. The new council proposed a celebration of his twenty-fifth anniversary as mayor of the city. To commemorate this event, the council adopted a resolution naming the

73   Georges Benoit, personal communication to Chisholm, p. 148.

74   T.-D.B., *Mémoires*, I, p. 12.

75   T.-D.B., *Memoirs*, Chapter 1, p. 1. in *Fonds* T.-D.B., ANQ, P-10/18.

76   The portrait is no longer in the main hall of Hydro-Quebec.

new bridge the T.-D. Bouchard Bridge. Among the personalities who spoke at the proceedings were Premier Adélard Godbout and Senator Léon Mercier-Gouin. T.-A. Fontaine, Member for Saint-Hyacinthe-Bagot in the House of Commons, read a telegram of congratulation from the Prime Minister of Canada. Joseph Beaubien, mayor of Outremont and president of the Union of Municipalities of the Province, delivered a vigorous plea in favour of the teaching of English, paying homage to T.-D. as having been an untiring champion of this reform. He was also thanked for his contribution towards the resumption and completion of the University of Montreal building. On this day, the water-carrier's grandson was the focus of all Quebec. Senator Mercier-Gouin reviewed the main stages of the mayor's public life, ending with these remarks:

> Yes, these are heroic pages of history, which grandly honour him who has had the courage to write them with the sweat of his brave plebeian brow, unfailingly attached to democratic principles. Good Liberal, good citizen, good patriot, T.-D. Bouchard is a great Canadian; this old fighter is a fearsome, terrible adversary when he enters the battle, but in his private life, my dear friends, what a heart of gold! We are all so happy to honour today the popular Captain Cécile-Ena Bouchard by honouring her dear father.[77]

The celebration also included the inauguration and blessing of Télesphore-Damien Bouchard Park, that of the new bridge on Cascade Street, the official opening of the tunnel on Sainte-Anne Street, and the digging of the first spade of earth at the site of the future building of the Technical School of Saint-Hyacinthe. After these presentations, the crowd proceeded to the Hotel-Dieu hall, where a great dinner was held for a thousand guests. Again there were a number of speeches, among which were those of Msgr. Arthur Douville, bishop of the diocese; Adélard Godbout; Maîtres Fontaine; and Émile Boucher, Member for Saint-Henri. Despite the hopes of his enemies and some Liberal colleagues, Bouchard did not announce his retirement. On the contrary, this demonstration of confidence gave him more energy to continue his struggle. He said: "I have to continue to advance towards goals not yet reached; it is you who will give me sufficient moral force to conquer the difficulties of the last steep slope."[78]

---

77   T.-D.B., *En marge des fêtes du 16 octobre 1942, Fonds* Bouchard, ANQ, P-10/25.

78   T.-D.B., *Le Clairon, 16 octobre* 1942.

PROBLEMS IN THE CABINET

On November 5, 1942, the premier announced the most important cabinet shuffle since the election of 1939. Bouchard would give up Public Works to Georges Dansereau, and Godbout himself would give up the Colonisation portfolio to Cléophas Bastien. Bouchard hotly contested the change. The Quebec correspondent of *Le Courrier de Saint-Hyacinthe* assured his readers that the employees of the Department of Public Works celebrated their delivery from Bouchard's rule by collecting money to pay for a mass of thanks.

> Here again we find the influence of Mr. Bouchard, the fighter in the cabinet, who stood up to Mr. Godbout for months ... [He] refused to have Mr. Bastien as his successor. And then, he refused to give up altogether. Finally, in order to appease him, Mr. Godbout had to abandon one of the two ministerial posts he held himself. Even with this concession, Mr. Bouchard still was refusing several minutes before the swearing in ceremony.[79]

In view of the long time enmity between *Le Courrier* and Bouchard, one might question the veracity of this gossip. However, the disagreements between Godbout and Bouchard were now well-known in Quebec. Although Bouchard's loyalty to the party and to Godbout was undoubtedly sincere in the view of J.-L. Gagnon, there was a background of resentment:

> His loyalty [Bouchard's] was accompanied by a real resentment because of the old regime, which had feared his ideas. As Speaker of the House, therefore reduced to silence until the time Mr. Taschereau himself resigned, in extremis, to give him the portfolio of Municipal Affairs, he felt that he had been had. Yesterday, Leader of the Opposition, today number two of the party machine, strong in parliamentary experience and a good manager, he sees himself even more to be the head of finance and the conscience of the Godbout party. Promote Damien Bouchard to vice-Premier? Never! A good Catholic, one who never openly advocated anti-clericalism, Godbout went ahead on his own, without worrying at all about the Church's reactions. Certainly he came from far, very far; did he not enter the orders to hide during the First World War? Initiated into the Order of Jacques Cartier, he succumbed to the temptation of nationalism before shedding it in later life. Free from these constraints, the Premier

---

79   *Le Courrier de Saint-Hyacinthe*, 13 *novembre* 1942.

now intended to carry out fundamental reforms, indifferent to fear and protests. Bouchard openly admitted that there were no ideological conflicts between them, as he liked to say. Nothing separated them except for an obvious incompatibility of temperament. If there was a "watch-me" in Bouchard, the ecclesiastic in Godbout remained touchy. Coming out of a quarrel Bouchard—unshakeable in his bad mood—searched to justify himself, lifting his arms to heaven: "What do you want, it smells of the sacristy!" It was a concession on his part. I can remember, in 1936, after Mr. Taschereau preferred Adélard Godbout to him, on that day he said, "It stank of the sacristan.[80]

Gagnon's allegation that Godbout had studied for the priesthood in order to avoid conscription in the First World War is erroneous. It had been with sincere conviction that Godbout decided to enter the priesthood, at the Grand Seminary of Rimouski, in 1913.[81] During his studies, he suffered from terrible knee pain, a recurring problem since his younger days, which immobilized him for some time. Since the bishop absolutely refused to ordain any but the perfectly healthy, Godbout was forced to give up the idea of becoming a priest. He chose to study agronomy. He thus escaped military service for medical reasons, not because of religious orders.

The Cabinet, 1939. Note T.-D. Bouchard's position—at Godbout's right hand, almost at the head of the table.

80   Gagnon, II, p. 23.

81   Genest, p. 21.

In spite of a papal proscription against Catholics belonging to secret organizations, the priest-teachers in seminaries all over Quebec actively recruited members for the Order of Jacques Cartier from among their charges. For example, Ghislain Dufour was recruited at the age of fifteen at his seminary.[82] He was an inactive member, but when he arrived at university, he was again contacted to renew his membership.[83] We can therefore also question Gagnon's affirmation that Godbout was a member. If he was, he certainly was recruited in a similar manner to Dufour, and during his adult life never took his possible membership in *La Patente* seriously. (*La Patente* means "the thing" or "gimmick"—really "the license"—the nickname given to the OJC.) Godbout was a Liberal of the same school as Bouchard, but with a different temperament. He was labelled as being under the influence of the Church. As with Bouchard, the label, though different, stuck, although it was completely untrue. When questioned about the relationship between her father and Godbout, Cécile-Ena exclaimed: *"Qu'est que vous voulez, il était un ancien frère!"*[84] (What do you want? He was a former brother.) Nevertheless, Godbout deserves credit for the vast social changes enacted by his government between 1939 and 1944. Without his active intervention, none of Bouchard's preferred programs would have been adopted.

At the end of 1942 we find T.-D. Bouchard embroiled in a polemic with Monsignor Desranleau, the bishop of Sherbrooke. In a pastoral letter to his clergy, the bishop asked his congregants not to join organizations such as the Rotary, Kiwanis, and Lions clubs; or to resign if they were already members. Bouchard replied in his newspaper that the Pope had not condemned these societies, which had worldwide appeal.[85] Furthermore, he noted that these associations were neither anti-religious nor anti-Catholic. They brought together members of several religious and language groups for the purpose of social and charitable advancement. At the same time, Bouchard violently attacked those he called isolationists.

> It is those who complain loudly against organizations with mixed racial membership ... because they fear that contact with citizens of different languages will help us to understand those in each of the

---

82   Ghislain Dufour, personal communication.

83   Ibid.

84   C.-E. B., personal communication, 1975.

85   T.-D.B., *Le Clairon*, 4 *décembre* 1942.

two camps, to dissipate the feelings of distrust and the warnings, which come from the gospel of hate preached until the present by political schemers and fanatics eager to serve their prejudices or their personal interest before that of each of the great races who constitute the Canadian nation.[86]

For his sixty-first birthday, T.-D. Bouchard received an unexpected gift: the news that by a vote of twenty to six, the bishop-controlled Catholic committee of the Council of Public Education had approved compulsory education for children aged six to fourteen. After so many years of battle, his editorials in *L'Union* dating from 1905, his editorials in *Le Clairon*, his maiden speech in the Legislative Assembly in 1912, and his private member's bill of January 29, 1919, in favour of compulsory education, the principle of compulsory education had finally been approved by the ecclesiastical authorities on December 17, 1942. Harry Bernard commented on the issue of compulsory education in the December 18 edition of his newspaper. His article, however, went to press on the seventeenth, just before to the declaration of the Catholic committee. Bernard repeated all the old arguments that the Church had been making for over a century: that the education of children was the responsibility of parents; that the state should intervene only to support parents; and that compulsory schooling was a violation of the liberty of Catholic conscience. Bernard opined:

> Tomorrow they will shout that the people want compulsory education and will try to impose it. Note for the moment that all problems relating to schooling are the responsibility of the Council of Public Education composed of the *ex officio* bishops of the province, and that its opinion counts more, on this subject, than those of Messrs Bouchard, Bastien, and Paul-Émile [sic] Poirier.[87]

During a speech on December 19 at a large gathering to honour the president of the Federation of Chambers of Commerce of Quebec, Bouchard gloated: "… this achievement was crowned by putting the *Courrier de Saint-Hyacinthe* and its editor, Harry Bernard, in their place."[88] And on the twenty-fifth, revelling maliciously, Bouchard rejoiced that he was able to make a fool of Bernard. In an editorial entitled: "Compulsory Education: A Journalist Behind the Times," he

---

86   Ibid.

87   *Le Courrier de Saint-Hyacinthe*, 18 *décembre* 1942.

88   S.-G. & B., p.198.

declared that *Le Courrier* (and Harry Bernard) were senile, and that the newspaper had been established to defend backward ideas. "He has not even become aware," declared Bouchard, "... that in the course the last 20 years there has been an upheaval in the Episcopate's opinion on this question in our province."[89] Some days later, Bernard feebly replied, admitting that: "this council [the Catholic committee] having taken the decision which one knows, we have nothing to add."[90]

In the House, Bouchard gave a speech in support of the law on compulsory education, now approved by the bishops. He reviewed the history of education, reminding the audience that the early colony, by order of both Louis XIV and Louis XV, had established compulsory school attendance in 1661 and 1724. It was regrettable that religious quarrels had intervened to suppress this principle dear to all civilized nations and to all Catholic countries. He paid tribute to Honoré Mercier for having supported the idea against the opposition of the ultramontanes, who confused neutrality and secularism in schools with the idea of compulsory education. He recalled his two speeches in favour of compulsory education in 1912 and 1919, and the efforts of Senator Dandurand, Edouard Monpetit and a hundred other French Canadians who in 1919 begged Bruchési to intervene in this question, and finally met with success. Bruchesi finally agreed, but then the bishop of Montreal was not successful in transmitting his change in attitude to the Committee. Bouchard pointed out that the Church had now changed, and cited the names of all those bishops who approved of compulsory education.

According to Eugène Payan, son of the one-time mayor of Saint-Hyacinthe, T.-D. Bouchard fought in vain to have French-speaking schools for Protestants. Although Eugène Payan had become a prominent merchant in the city, owning a share in the Southern Power Company—and thus was someone who stood to lose by Bouchard's hydroelectric policies—he recognized the debt owed by the Protestants of Quebec to this man. His family had a problem: although originally French-speaking, they had to become Anglophone since they were not admitted to Catholic schools. They were sent to private English Protestant schools. "We have lost a lot of industry," said Eugène Payan, "because there were no places where Protestants could send their children to [French] school."[91]

---

89   *Le Clairon*, 25 *décembre* 1942.

90   *Le Courrier de Saint-Hyacinthe*, 13 *décembre* 1942.

91   Eugene Payan, personal Communication to Chisholm, p. 80.

In January of 1943, Bouchard thought that the time had come to introduce a reform which he held dear to his heart since the death of his wife, who had succumbed to typhoid fever from drinking unpasteurized milk ten years earlier. He submitted a proposal to municipalize and pasteurize milk, stating that centralization was necessary in order to obtain standard and reliable sterilization. Saint-Hyacinthe had the advantage of being the site of the Provincial Dairy School. He was convinced that the adoption of this project would result in similar benefits to the people as had come from the creation of a co-operative bakery in Saint-Hyacinthe. Since its foundation, the bakery had kept the price of the bread lower in Saint-Hyacinthe than elsewhere in the country. Bouchard introduced a bill in the Legislative Assembly to enforce obligatory pasteurization centralized in Saint-Hyacinthe. The milk monopolies in the larger cities opposed this legislation. The debate in the Assembly attracted widespread public attention. The Montreal city council adopted a proposal to study methods to control the sale of milk similar to those suggested for Saint-Hyacinthe. At that time, the industry received a subsidy of two cents per pint of milk. Because municipalization would deprive them of this increase in profit, the milk lobby initiated a protest campaign against the legislation. Bouchard published a free, widely distributed brochure entitled "Why it is Necessary to Municipalize Pasteurization and the Control of Distribution of Milk in Saint-Hyacinthe."[92] He outlined the medical benefits of pasteurization and the necessity of centralization in order to insure strict hygienic control. For Bouchard, the construction of a modern factory and a model of pasteurization would protect children and adults, and would result in a reasonable price for milk. His adversaries—*Le Courrier,* the Saint-Jean-Baptiste-Society, and the Chamber of Commerce—while advocating pasteurization, opposed municipalization. "Mr. Bouchard has grafted municipalization onto the idea of pasteurisation. This spoils things. Why municipalize and hinder liberty of trade when one knows that all forms of nationalization cost more than private initiatives."[93] However, the mayor had misjudged his fellow citizens in thinking they were ready to accept this reform.

In March, because of the provincial scale of the campaign against the bill, Godbout announced that pasteurization would not become compulsory in 1943. Nonetheless, on June 23, 1943, the House adopted a law concerning the Dairy School of the province of Quebec and the Pasteurization and Control Commission

---

92   *Fonds* T.-D.B., ANQ, P-10/11. Brochure, *"Pourquoi il faut municipaliser la pasteurisation et contrôler la distribution du lait à Saint-Hyacinthe.*

93   *Le Courrier de Saint-Hyacinthe, 12 février* 1943.

of Milk in Saint-Hyacinthe. The commission would be composed of seven members including the mayor as president, the director of the Dairy School, a person appointed by the Lieutenant-Governor, and four persons appointed by the city council. The campaign against this project spread to the municipal elections fixed for July 12. In four districts out of five, there was opposition to the sitting aldermen, contrary to previous years where Bouchard's team was often elected by acclamation. At least seven newsletters from the presses of *Le Courrier* were widely distributed to the population. They proclaimed that a vote for the opposition candidates was a vote against the municipalization of milk and thus a vote for free trade. Margaret Laberge, a historian and wife of a naval officer stationed in Saint-Hyacinthe, observed: "It was first political demonstration that I have seen led by a cow."[94] The elections were a net setback for Bouchard's team. The four sitting aldermen lost the election, with a tally of 1563 votes against 727. Political realist that he was, Mayor Bouchard concluded: "The result of the municipal elections … clearly indicate that our population is far from being prepared to approve compulsory pasteurisation."[95] Even though the local company stated that it would not put the new law into application, it was forced to pasteurize its milk because the Canadian naval training base in Saint-Hyacinthe threatened to boycott the local company's milk if it was not pasteurized, and to obtain their milk from a neighbouring city for their five thousand servicemen. The local company then complied.

Lasting four months, the 1943 parliamentary sessions were among the longest. Godbout was away at the bedside of his dying father, and so Bouchard as acting leader defended party policy with his usual vigour and determination. The opposition attacked the government for having concluded a contract with the province of Ontario to exchange hydraulic power sources on the Ottawa River, closer to Ontario than to Quebec. St. Germain and Bibeau remark that Bouchard was "cut to the quick," and quickly responded.[96] He defended the government by pointing out that Canada was at war, and that Ontario needed electricity for its war effort. In addition, Ontario had agreed to an exchange of power from the Carillon River, situated forty miles from Montreal and therefore more available for the needs of Quebec. To those of the opposition who spoke of treason, he replied: "Those who spread bitterness … are not patriots. They work for the fifth column."[97]

---

94   M. Laberge, personal communication to Chisholm, p. 150.

95   T.-D.B. in *Le Devoir*, 13 *juillet* 1943.

96   S.-G. & B., p. 208.

97   *Le Clairon*, 26 *mars* 1943.

This fourth session of the Godbout government was marked by an uninterrupted session of sixteen hours, and by an all-night session that focussed on the establishment of a beet-sugar refinery in Saint-Hilaire—a project dear to the premier. Two days before the end of the session, Bouchard had to defend the budget of his ministry. Duplessis badgered the Minister of Roads, asserting that the Sir Wilfrid Laurier highway between Montreal and Saint-Hyacinthe constituted a monumental waste. The anonymous *Le Devoir* columnist (or columnists) writing under the pseudonym *Le grincheux* ("Grumpy") declared: "For M. Bouchard, sixty years equals one hundred. It is with arithmetic like this that M. Bouchard ... has shortened the highway and stretched it to Saint-Hyacinthe."[98] *Le grincheux* also made fun of Bouchard's portly build, stating that since he had such a beautiful Athenian figure, "one could see him in the pose of the Discobolos."[99]

Generally, a deputy minister accompanied a minister in the Chamber. The former, being more aware of the details, would whisper answers to questions that the opposition directed to the minister. Bouchard, however, defended himself without this assistance, keenly aware of all details and figures himself. Yes, Bouchard admitted, this road was constructed on swamps, but they had been drained, and a vast area of land had been recovered for agriculture. He favourably compared costs of the four-lane Queen Elizabeth highway in Ontario with those of the six-lane [sic] Sir Wilfrid Laurier highway. The price of the Quebec project was $74,000 lower.[100]

On April 28, he explained his policy as Minister of Roads to the members of the Reform Club of Quebec. He condemned the previous system of patronage practised by the *Union Nationale* and claimed that with the new public tender system he had saved the province between 25 and 33 percent in costs.[101] He emphasized the importance of providing Quebec with a modern system of super-highways. In reply to his critics, who accused him of unduly favouring his riding, he stated that this road on the south shore of the Saint Lawrence

---

98   *Le Devoir,* 18 *décembre* 1941. This daily column was most probably the work of Gerald Fillion, the editor-in-chief, and several of his fellow journalists, composed as they sat for lunch. The column is cited many times for its anti-Semitic content in Esther Delisle's book on *Le Devoir.*

99   Discobolos: an ancient statue of a Greek discus thrower.

100 The Sir Wilfrid Laurier highway still only has four lanes. Perhaps six lanes were planned?

101 T.-D.B., brochure, *Progrès de la voirie provinciale depuis trois ans; Fonds* Bouchard, ANQ, P-10/11.

River from Montreal to Quebec was the same route taken by the Canadian National and Grand Trunk railroads. It had shortened the distance of the route from 173 miles to 153 miles, a great saving of time and gasoline. The north shore route is longer due to a northerly bulge of the river. Thus, the founders of Saint-Hyacinthe had the wisdom to situate the Maskoutain City on the most favourable line from Montreal to Quebec.

Before a distinguished handpicked audience at the Windsor Hotel in Montreal, on May 8, 1943, Bouchard held forth on his idea of establishing a liberal association called the Canadian Democratic Institute. The aim of the institute would be to counter the Order of Jacques Cartier. "Eminent French-Canadians," he explained, "have asked me to found an association whose principal objective, if not its sole goal, would be the defence of free speech."[102] The objective of this society would be French-Canadian progress in all spheres of private or public activity, in a spirit of freedom of opinion, a belief in science, and with broad-minded views on questions of race and nationality. Bouchard expanded on the two great streams of political ideology, taking up the theme of Laurier's great speech of 1876. Conservatives have faith only in established rules; liberals have the spirit of experimentation, believe in evolution, and do not fear experimental reforms in any sphere of intellectual, economic, or social activity. According to Bouchard, Quebec had been almost completely dominated by the conservative view, and had paid dearly for this blindness. However, in recent times, those who believed in the necessity of reform had obtained some breathing room. Some members of the clergy had now concluded that the teaching in primary schools in Quebec was far from perfect, and laymen were being admitted to teaching positions without the threat of being called bad French Canadians or bad Catholics. They suggested and promoted reforms in the schools. Priests could say and write that it is far from clear that the English had mistreated the French Canadians. They even went as far as to condemn the gospel of hatred that some educators preached against their compatriots of the other language, and to replace it by recommending a sincere understanding of them. In addition, the great majority of bishops now said that they were in favour of compulsory education. "Evidently," he concluded, "something has changed in our mentality in the province of Quebec, and happily so. Let us give thanks to broad-minded people and to the events that have produced this

---

102 T.-D.B., *Mémoires*, III, p. 162.

upheaval in ideas."[103] Despite these signs of changes, he warned of threats to democratic life in Quebec, and denounced a secret society without naming it (no doubt the Order of Jacques Cartier). This society aimed at the creation of a French, Catholic and independent state outside or inside the Canadian Confederation, as modelled after Ireland, Spain or Portugal.[104]

The emblem of the Democratic Institute would be a star of four points representing the four objectives of the Atlantic Charter: freedom of speech, freedom of religion, freedom from fear and freedom from poverty. Bouchard defended his decision to limit membership to French Canadians by saying that he did not want to allow his adversaries to call the Institute a creature of "foreigners." Finally, the constitution of the Canadian Democratic Institute would allow for three groups: governors, local study circles of active members who would be obliged to pay a sum of $50 per year for ten years, and a third category—members committed to give their moral support to the association, but who did not belong to the study circles. As expected, André Laurendeau vigorously attacked the Democratic Institute, calling it *"L'Institut plutocratique."*

> .... his new arm of war launched against the Bloc.... At the Windsor Hotel, grouped around him [Bouchard] there were "Liberal" ministers, members, and senators; "Liberal" journalists such as Mr. Jean-Charles Harvey; "liberal" thinkers such as Mr. J.A. Leclair; "liberal" businessmen such as M.M. Paulus and Armand Daigle; the director of the Sûreté [Police] "liberal," pardon, of the Sûreté provincial, Mr. Marcel Gaboury; "liberal" opportunists; red "liberals," with a small clever group who play the innocent and innocents who play the clever. To be a governor it is necessary to be committed to pour in an amount of $500 over ten years. Oh! What a dangerous democratic beginning ... instead of launching a liberal democracy, he has founded a liberal plutocracy![105]

The first session of the Institute took place on August 13, 1943, again in a reception room at the Windsor Hotel. T.-D. Bouchard was elected Supreme Governor. Dr. Oscar Mercier, former president of the Association of French Language Physicians and president of the University Circle, was elected second-in-command; and Senator

---

103 Ibid., p. 12.

104 See Chapter ten, footnote 52, p. 231.

105 *Le Devoir, 26 mai* 1943.

Léon Mercier-Gouin was chosen as honorary secretary. The second speaker on the program organized for January 17, 1944, was Father Arthur Maheux of Laval University. Some people tried to prevent Abbé Maheux from speaking to the members of the Institute. Called an assimilationist by the nationalists since the appearance of his book *Ton histoire est une épopée* in 1941, the Abbé knew that it was necessary to obtain permission from the Archbishop of Montreal to deliver a lecture in his diocese.[106] He requested this authorization but did not receive a reply. The evening before the day he was slated to appear, Maheux informed Bouchard that since he had not heard from the Archbishop, he could not hold to his commitment. Bouchard decided to speak in his name and to resign from the cabinet so as not to embarrass the government, and communicated his decision to the secretary. The secretary, Mercier-Gouin, went to the Archbishop's Palace in Montreal and learned from the mouth of Monsignor Charbonneau that his staff had kept him in the dark concerning Abbé Maheux's request. Authorization was granted immediately and sent to Quebec by telegram. Maheux's speech disappointed members of the audience sent to heckle—disappointed perhaps because of its academic nature or perhaps because he had softened its tone. They wondered why they had been sent to question this harmless speech.[107]

The federal government proposed to appoint Abbé Maheux assistant commissioner of a federal sub-committee for a new program for the teaching of history. This was a proposal for the publication of a text that would be acceptable to Canadians of all origins. This work was to be written by a committee composed of historians chosen by the various groups. *Le Devoir* launched a campaign against Abbé Maheux. Various sections of the Saint-Jean-Baptiste Society adopted resolutions repudiating his qualifications to serve as a French-Canadian representative on the committee. "Our history is not for sale. By naivety or by ruse, there are surely people to serve their purposes, who are ready to 'Sell us out in Quebec.'"[108] On December 18, *Le Devoir* renewed its attack and Bouchard reacted: "The dirty *Le Devoir* has begun a campaign against our lecturer. Aided by the secret society of the Order of Jacques Cartier and its multiple branches, they organized to sabotage our conference."[109] Léopold Allard, president of the Saint-Jean-Baptiste Society of Saint-Hyacinthe, suggested that Abbé

---

106 This title is a line from the French version of O Canada.

107 Maheux, personal communication to Chisholm, p. 157.

108 *Le Devoir*, 11 *décembre* 1943.

109 T.-D.B., ANQ, P-10/14.

Maheux could represent the Anglophone element of the country but that it would be an injustice to choose him as a representative the "real French-Canadian mentality."[110] Bouchard retaliated in an unsigned editorial, but one in which his style is clearly recognizable, asserting that Abbé Maheux was an eminent priest who believed that a separatist or isolationist policy would be disastrous. He accused the SSJB (and the OJC) of being "an electoral agency in the service of the *Bloc Populaire*, the nationalists and the reactionaries of Quebec. The SSJB, whose goal at first was the progress of French Canada, has become an organization devoted to suffocate modern progress, liberty of opinion, liberalism, and democracy."[111]

In 1943 the *Bloc Populaire* held meetings everywhere in the province with impressive turnouts. Duplessis denounced the Bloc as a Liberal plot to divide the nationalist vote. Nevertheless, in the Stanstead federal by-election of August 9, 1943, the Bloc's candidate emerged victorious. This showed the strength of isolationist and nationalist feeling. According to Rumilly, "A battalion of 'Brothers' of the Order of Jacques Cartier spread out through the county of Stanstead to support the *Bloc Populaire*."[112]

Locally, the majority of municipal aldermen remained hostile to Bouchard. Some even accused him, once again, of being responsible for a fire that had razed a city district. It was claimed that because of the municipalization of electricity, the water pressure of the fire hoses was insufficient. An inquiry requested by his friends on the council revealed that these claims were false. The electrical plant had not ceased to function for a moment, and delivered a maximum water output, with a reserve of 1,200 horsepower.

Bouchard's greatest satisfaction in 1943 was progress towards the public control of electricity. After a long inquiry into electricity trusts, through the action of the Public Service Authority six companies were forced to reduce their rates—including Southern Power, which distributed electricity to Saint-Hyacinthe industry. "It was … the triumph," Bouchard declared, "of a reform to which I was dedicated from my entry into the political arena. I was one of the fiercest protagonists."[113] Meanwhile, however, his adversaries in the *Union Nationale* and the Liberal Party, strengthened by the defeat of his municipal

---

110 Letter reproduced in *Le Clairon*, 25 *février* 1943.

111 *Le Clairon*, 25 *février* 1943.

112 Rumilly, Duplessis I, p. 645.

113 T.-D.B., *Mémoires,* III, p.166.

team, renewed their efforts to be to rid of Bouchard. In spite of the ferocious opposition of the party treasury, Godbout courageously decided to proceed with the expropriation of the Montreal Light, Heat and Power Company. At the same time, he strove to distance Bouchard from the cabinet. The majority of the Liberal caucus judged that the Member from Saint-Hyacinthe's behaviour bordered on disobedience. As we have seen, Bouchard could not accept that his ministerial responsibility and his budget was cut in half. Previously the minister of two departments accounting for 50 percent of the provincial budget, he was not content to be reduced to responsibility only for the road system. He did not let pass any opportunity to take on the premier, and often forgot to attend sessions of the cabinet. Although there was opposition from influential elements of the party, Godbout refused to cancel the expropriation of the Montreal Light, Heat and Power Company. "Adélard Godbout," Bouchard noted, "did not allow himself to be intimidated by the watchdogs of the Caisse [the Banks] by those he called 'guardian angels' because, in his words: 'Although they are supposed to be invisible and often unknown, they are very much present.'"[114]

The premier reached the conclusion that the unity of the party was at stake. It was necessary to obtain the support of the caucus. But in order to obtain this support, he had to secure T.-D. Bouchard's resignation. He would thereby decrease opposition within the caucus, and the opposition of Saint James Street. First, it was necessary to convince the fiery Bouchard. Early in 1944, Godbout summoned Bouchard to discuss the nationalization of the Montreal Light, Heat and Power Company. In the course of their conversation, Godbout asked him to accept the presidency of the commission created to administer Hydro-Quebec, with an annual salary of eighteen thousand dollars. Bouchard refused, affirming that he could still be useful to his fellow citizens by "promoting the ideas dear to me." They arranged to see each other the following day. Entering the premier's office, Bouchard exclaimed: "In all of this, I see the hand of the clergy seeking to drive me from public life!" Godbout responded: "How can you say such a thing? Far from wanting to distance you from public life, I intend to ask Mackenzie King to appoint you Senator."[115] He stated that Bouchard's attitude frustrated him considerably. He explained that he considered Bouchard to be the sole person who possessed the technical knowledge and the experience required to lead the Hydro-Quebec enterprise to fruition. Bouchard still refused. Godbout gave him

114 Ibid., p.166.

115 Gagnon, II, p. 243.

twenty-four hours to think about it, informing him that if his reply remained negative, Godbout would not have the law adopted before having secured the services of an administrator in whom he had absolute confidence—that is to say, he would withdraw the legislation. Bouchard then proposed to accept the offer of the presidency of Hydro-Quebec, without salary, but to remain in the cabinet. In this manner, he hoped to deprive his adversaries of an insidious pretext to discredit him by speaking about his pecuniary interest. Godbout did not bite. Bouchard had to accept the offer, or give up the adoption of the bill. Godbout ominously pointed out that nothing could guarantee that the Liberals would win the upcoming election. Considering this sobering thought—and the prospect that as a senator he would have a platform to continue his struggle in favour of freedom to think and propose education reforms—he accepted, stressing that he accepted reluctantly and that he would not modify his attitude on ideological questions. This was a portent of his speech before the Senate on June 21, 1944.

In the Assembly, on February 23, Duplessis alluded to rumours of the retirement of T.-D. Bouchard from public life in the House. Godbout replied:

> When the Leader of the Opposition will have carried out, for his province and his native city, a tenth of what the Minister of Roads has accomplished, he will be able to leave public life with the satisfaction of having accomplished his duty, his whole duty. The Minister of Roads is a model of a public servant. He has always had the courage of his ideas and he has many achievements to his credit.... He can say that he has always served his compatriots well.[116]

On March 3, 1944, the federal government appointed Télesphore-Damien Bouchard to the Canadian Senate. On April 14, Premier Godbout introduced a law establishing the Hydroelectric Commission of Quebec; nationalizing the Montreal Heat, Light, and Power Company and the Beauharnois Power Corporation; installing a vast rural electrification system; and creating a provincial hydroelectric system. On April 21, the provincial cabinet announced Bouchard's appointment as the first president of the Hydroelectric Commission of Quebec. In general the press reacted favourably to the news—with the exception, of course, of Harry Bernard, who continued his hateful comments, and *Le*

---

116 T.-D.B., *Mémoires*, III, p.169.

Devoir, which did not comment on the appointment. *Le Devoir* did nevertheless complain that two out of four commissioners were English.[117]

When the nomination was confirmed, Duplessis behaved decently and delivered an eloquent homage to his long-time enemy: "I have seen the Honourable Mr. Bouchard at work for years, and nobody can contest his love of work and his sincerity, even if one does not share all his ideas. The ex-member for Saint-Hyacinthe has worked so hard that his health has been compromised. It is with a unanimous voice that the House wishes him good health in his new functions."[118] Duplessis, though, was to change his tune three months later. The press generally congratulated him, except for snide remarks in *Le Courrier de Saint-Hyacinthe.*[119]

Adélard Godbout and Télesphore-Damien Bouchard at a political meeting.

117 The members of the commission were: Eugène Potvin, J.W. McCammon, George C. McDonald and Raymond Latreille.

118 *Le Clairon,* 10 *mars* 1944.

119 *La Presse,* 6 *mars,* 1944 and *Le Courrier de Saint-Hyacinthe* 10 *mars* 1944.

In this chapter, we have seen how the former acting House Leader of the Opposition evolved into the most powerful and effective minister of the Godbout cabinet. Clearly, none of the social advances of the government could have been adopted without the strong leadership of Godbout. However, on his left, there was Télesphore-Damien Bouchard always pushing for reforms in education, women's suffrage, labour laws and municipal issues. Bouchard's integrity and rigid approach to the awarding of government contracts—based on closed bidding instead of patronage—led to profound disaffection on the part of regional Liberal *apparatchiks*. This led ultimately to Godbout's decision to sack Bouchard from the government. The question in Godbout's mind was: would the new senator use his position to advance the cause of Quebec, or might he lash out against his "enemies" in his inimitable way and alienate himself from mainstream liberalism in Quebec?

Taking over the Montreal Light, Heat, and Power Corporation, 1944.

Chapter X

THE SENATE SPEECH

When the news of the creation of Hydro-Quebec became known, J.-L. Gagnon deliberated on how to present the story in *Le Canada*, the newspaper of the Liberal Party.[1] He had to choose between two words: expropriation or nationalization. In the end, he said: "a spade is a spade!" He continued, however, to search for a way to say the same thing less explosively. "By dint of thinking about the problem," he reports, "I happily arrived at a solution to get balance in a headline of eight columns on two lines: ELECTRICITY BECOMES A NATIONAL TREASURE." When Arthur Fontaine, a Liberal Party leader, anxiously called to learn how Gagnon was going to announce the news, Fontaine was delighted: "You have gilded the lily, but it will go better with a scotch … come to my house. Godbout awaits my telephone call."[2]

Just one month after his appointment, Bouchard announced a large reduction of between 18 and 20 percent on the electricity rates for the metropolitan region. On an annual basis, this amounted to a total of $2,210,000. He decreased the rate for hundred kilowatt-hours from $3.11 to $2.60. Godbout, however, remained anxious. Bouchard, appointed two months earlier, had not yet delivered his maiden speech. Rumour had it that he was working hard on a major, well-documented denunciation of the Order of Jacques Cartier. Adélard Godbout, who mistrusted the populist eloquence of his fiery colleague, asked Fontaine to request the help of Mackenzie King. King agreed to scrutinize Bouchard's speech before delivery. Therefore, Bouchard received the message that King wanted to see his text.

Even though he was out of the provincial government, Bouchard still caused Godbout a headache. On May 19, *Le Devoir* reported that employees of Hydro-

---

1   Gagnon, II, p. 251–252.

2   Ibid., p. 252.

Quebec had worked on Ascension Day, registered as a paid holiday for government employees. The employees, the report noted, had received the order to be at work under the threat of not receiving their salary.[3] Bouchard retaliated through his attorney Léon Mercier-Gouin, with a claim for $300 in damages, plus interest, calling the article clearly defamatory and demanding both a retraction and the publication of Bouchard's reply. In his response, published in *Le Devoir* on May 25, he clarified that his notice to employees on the eve of Ascension Day left them free to work or not to work, but that those who did not work would not be paid. Those who turned up at work could attend mass, being given a free hour to do so without loss of pay. This explanation was not enough for *Le Devoir*. To embarrass the government, the newspaper published the minutes of the Legislative Assembly debates in which Godbout had asserted that no government employee had worked on Ascension Day, along with several letters from employees of Hydro testifying that they had indeed worked on that day. On May 30 Godbout undermined his president of Hydro-Quebec by declaring that the employees in question who had not worked on Ascension Day would nevertheless receive their pay. "Having finally sent his unmanageable minister to the Senate," wrote Saint-Germain and Bibeau, "Godbout could not allow him to endanger the re-election of his government."[4] The following day, not to be outdone Bouchard announced that he would submit to the decision of the premier, but that employees who had worked on Ascension Day would receive double their salary for that day. The whole episode constituted a public humiliation for Bouchard, one that he blamed on Catholic groups stirred up by the Order of Jacques Cartier. He promised revenge.

Godbout continued to be concerned about the fiery senator. On May 4, Athanase David, formerly Provincial Secretary and now senator from Sorel, introduced a bill calling for the creation of a commission of historians from each province to prepare a standard textbook on the history of Canada, one that would be acceptable to all provincial governments. Many people supported this idea. Constance Garneau, president of the Civic Rights League of Montreal and a great admirer of T.-D., described examples of the education her children were receiving while attending French and English schools. A teacher in her son's English school insinuated that the French regime was not associated with any act of bravery, except for … "that little pimpled-faced pea-soup Madeleine de

---

3   *Le Devoir*, 19 *mai* 1944.

4   S.-G. & B., p. 237.

Verchères."[5] All the children laughed, including Garneau's son. This scandalized his mother. On the other hand, her two girls at convent school brought home frequent allusions to the perfidy of the English. For example, they heard the following in their arithmetic class: "General Winthrop burned down two churches, four stables and three houses. How many buildings did he burn down?"[6]

Senator David's motion aroused the nationalists. Léopold Richer wrote (with some confusion) against the motion: "What is the aim of a single history text, and who will benefit, which theory, and in whose interest would we have to put an end to the sterile struggles, that is to say, to the unceasing and splendid struggles that weave the framework of our history."[7] André Laurendeau, secretary-general of the *Bloc Populaire*, denounced what he considered an attempt to alter the French-Canadian past. During a meeting in Assomption, he declared: "They are trying to steal our history from us."[8] Allard, in *Le Courrier de Saint-Hyacinthe,* wrote: "We oppose the concept of a history manual that, just like a bank-note, is acceptable from one ocean to the other."[9]

Bouchard announced his participation in the debate on Senator David's motion. Godbout himself, still anxious, telephoned Bouchard himself to warn of the danger in attacking Cardinal Villeneuve, reputed to have been associated with the formation of the OJC when he was teaching in the order of the Oblats in Ottawa.[10] Godbout reminded Bouchard that the cardinal could influence the results of the next election. He even threatened that the speech could raise such discord that it would force him to dismiss Bouchard as president of Hydro-Quebec.[11] Bouchard replied that even if Godbout fired him, Godbout would still lose the election. Cécile-Ena, now a major in the Canadian Women's Army Corps, received a telephone call from her friend Sir Eugène Fiset, Lieutenant-Governor of Quebec. Fiset repeated Godbout's warning to her father. Meeting an eminent Liberal in the corridor of Parliament the day before his speech, Bouchard urged him to attend the following day, boasting: "I am going to bash

5   Constance Garneau, personal communication to Chisholm, p. 171.

6   Ibid.

7   *Le Devoir,* 8 *mai* 1944.

8   Ibid., p. 5.

9   *Le Courrier de Saint-Hyacinthe,* 28 *avril* 1944.

10   Father Milot, personal communication to Chisholm p. 167.

11   Ibid., p. 167.

this little jerk Godbout. I will show him that he cannot do without me."[12] The Liberal replied, "Don't be an idiot, T.-D. If you attack your people, no one will forgive you."[13] This practical advice did not stop him. He was determined. Some held that, now that he had obtained a lifetime seat in the Senate, he wanted to get his revenge, and he wanted to get it with all of Canada as his audience. Senator Vaillancourt, appointed on the same day as Bouchard and sharing his office in the Senate, also warned him: "Here the audience is larger. In Quebec we can discuss everything, but here it is necessary to watch our words."[14] Vaillancourt had been Godbout's assistant in the ministry of agriculture, and his personal and political friend. His was also one of the names quoted by Harvey in *Le Jour* in 1941 as a member of the OJC—but once again we might presume an adolescent indiscretion. Vaillancourt knew Bouchard's opinions, as did everyone in Quebec, and feared the aftermath of his speech.

Following another communication from the postmaster-general, Arthur Fontaine, Bertrand rushed over to remind Bouchard to submit his text to King. Bouchard, cunning at times, did not hesitate to play the village idiot when necessary. He seemed to accept Fontaine's repeated order. He would indeed submit his text to King, he said. However, instead of delivering it to the office of the Prime Minister, he brought it, in its French version only, to Senator James King, Liberal leader in the Senate. Since James King did not read French and did not really understand Quebec politics, he took Bouchard's gesture to be a manifestation of French-Canadian politeness.[15]

On a mild Wednesday, June 21, 1944, the newly appointed Senator Télesphore-Damien Bouchard waited his turn to present his maiden speech in the Red Chamber in Ottawa. At the same time, a Eucharistic Congress was being organized in his native City of Saint-Hyacinthe with the participation of the Pope's legate, and with all the French-Canadian clergy in attendance. The congress was to reach its climax on Saturday, following the festivities of Saint-Jean-Baptiste Day. Cardinal Villeneuve would deliver the final sermon to the congressional closing session. Everywhere in the province, officers of the *Société*

---

12   D'Hont, personal communication to Chisholm, p.167.

13   Mme. Vautelet, personal communication, reporting a conversation of her father Senator Geoffrion with Bouchard, to Chisholm, p. 167.

14   Senator Vaillencourt, Ibid., p. 167.

15   Gagnon, II, p. 253.

Saint-Jean-Baptiste organized festivities and parades. The newspapers were full of stories and photographs of the officers of the organization.

The senators and the press gallery were not surprised to see Senator Bouchard rise to support a motion by Senator Athanase David to create a commission to consider a standardized text for the teaching of Canadian history across Canada. The public expected a dramatic speech full of fierce flashes, but not one "soaked in vitriol."[16] Bouchard began his speech in French, but in order for his colleagues to fully understand it, he switched to English early on. However, he pointed out that in Parliament the French language was officially recognized, and he emphasized that those who really wished to follow the proceedings should have command of both languages.

Senator Bouchard began by denouncing the poor teaching of history, not only in Quebec but everywhere in Canada. However, since he was most familiar with the situation in Quebec, he would limit his remarks to teaching in that province. "If every province would correct its own errors," he declared, "the nation at large would be healthier."[17] Bouchard quoted examples of the contradictions in the history textbooks in Quebec, especially those regarding misdeeds related to the British conquest of 1759. On page 72, paragraph 134 of a text entitled *History of Canada* one reads: "The English ... abolished French laws.... All Canadians were compelled, under penalty of banishment, to swear the Oath of the Test."[18] (The Test was an oath of allegiance to the King. It denied the authority of the Pope and banned Catholics from Parliament and in the public service.) In contrast, on page 72, paragraph 135, the same text stated: "General Murray, named Governor General (1763) mitigated the rigour of the new regulations and did not exact the "Test Oath." In fact, Murray, as Military Governor from 1759 on, had allowed the "Canadiens" their language, freedom of religion and civil law—disobeying Colonial office instructions. Bouchard pointed out that one could read, on page 74, paragraph 137, in which Guy Carleton replaces Murray in 1766: "Guy Carleton, who replaced him, adopted towards French Canadians the wise and impartial policy of his predecessor." Nevertheless, on page 73 it said: "The clergy gave direction to the courage and the goodwill of

16   Genest, p. 278.

17   T.-D.B., *Mémoires,* III, p. 234.
      Also; ANQ, *Fonds* Bouchard, P-10/13; "The Teaching of Canadian History," p. 9 speech delivered in the Senate, June 21, 1944. Yamaska Printing Ltd., Saint-Hyacinthe.

18   Ibid., p.12.

the still-inexperienced French Canadians; it helped them to withstand oppression and injustice, and inspired a loyalty which forced England to give back to French Canada all the privileges conceded by the Treaty of Paris."

Bouchard observed that the Treaty of Paris (1763) had in fact preserved some important privileges of the people: religion, language and civil law. (These privileges were accorded as part of the Quebec Act of 1774. Earlier, from 1759 on, James Murray and Guy Carlton had simply ignored the instructions from London.)[19] The author of the text then asserted on page 75: "Since 1763 the Canadians had to complain of a government which did not do justice to their rights.... The Test Oath was keeping them away from state business: even their religion was hardly tolerated." And finally, "England ended by granting to the French Canadians all privileges possessed by free and independent peoples."[20] Bouchard concluded: "It is clear that the writer was forced by necessity to add these two lines ... because even a child of ten would not understand how it came about that after so many years of tyranny and oppression of his race and religion, the French Canadians had been as free and prosperous as he found them in his own time." And he summarized this section of his speech:

> The contradictory statements I have quoted clearly demonstrate that this teaching cannot be following the facts, but is intended to prejudice young minds against our compatriots of a different tongue and creed. It is un-Canadian, even un-Christian ... taught to divide the Canadian nation on racial and religious lines ... the permeation of the souls of our past and present generations of school children, college pupils, and students with false Canadian history, a still more erroneous interpretation.... has led many to wish for an independent form of government, seeing only the wrongs.... The task of changing the form of a government is not an easy one, so our secessionists have called for help from all the forces that appeal most to the popular masses—religion, race, and greed. The new state would be Catholic, French and corporate.[21]

---

19 James Murray, the first British Military Governor of Quebec was the son of a Scottish Jacobite father. His father and brother had been imprisoned for their support of the French and Scottish Catholic cause. Linda Colley, *Britons, Forging the Nation, 1707–1837,* (New Haven and London: Yale University Press, 1992), p.131.

20 Senate speech, "The Teaching of Canadian History," p.13.

21 Ibid., p. 15.

Now he diverted from the first component of his speech to the more controversial part: his attack on the ultra-nationalists of the Order of Jacques Cartier. Among those whom he accused of teaching and promoting this distorted history, he named the organization known as the Order of Jacques Cartier (OJC), a secret society established with the support of the clergy. It was founded in Ottawa in 1926, in order to defend and promote the interests of French Canadians in the federal civil service—a laudable aim. However, he went on to say, it quickly became the instrument of a narrow-minded, religious, Rome-oriented, nationalist elite.

Bouchard qualified his remarks by expressing his belief that more than 75 percent of the eighteen thousand members of the OJC did not suspect in any way where the directors of this secret society were leading them. Nevertheless, he felt that it was necessary to reveal its existence, "since most revolutions have had their beginnings in secret societies." He went on to repeat Jean-Charles Harvey's accusations, which had appeared in his newspaper *Le Jour* in November 1941. In a headline exposé on the front page, Harvey had called the Order "the Ku Klux Klan of French Canada." The Order's purpose, according to Harvey's exposé and based on quoted documents, was to infiltrate and secretly take over the political arena, and to control patriotic societies, governments and public administrations of all description, thereby advancing its narrow-minded, nationalistic and ultramontane Catholic views.[22] "The edict was well received, and nearly all Saint-Jean-Baptiste societies, Catholic syndicates, city school commissions, municipal councils, Junior Boards of Trade are under the direct influence of this secret order."[23]

The *Union Nationale* takeover of the government in 1936 had been thanks to the occult influence of the OJC. The leaders of the *Bloc Populaire* were also under its influence. It advocated an independent French Catholic state. Bouchard revealed the existence of two publications of the Order: *La Boussole (The Compass)*, the official organ; and *L'Émerillon (The Merlin)*, its secret publication. He quoted extracts from *L'Émerillon* that recommended a division of the province of Ontario, with its northern portion becoming a French Catholic state. Bouchard continued by quoting the advice of *L'Émerillon* to members of XC—that is, the *commanderies* (cells) of Ontario:

---

22 *Le Jour.* J.-C. Harvey; 15 *novembre* 1941 Front page headline: "The Ku Klux Klan of French Canada. Sectarian Nationalists, anti-Britannic, anti-Semitic, prohibitionists, Vichyards, colonists form a secret society, the Order of Jacques Cartier." This series of exposés continued weekly on November 22, 29, December 6, 13, and 20 in *Le Jour*. See Appendix, p.367

23 T.-D.B., The Senate speech, p. 16.

Our goal is to take over the leadership of all patriotic movements, organizations, celebrations, etc., to exclude from them everything smelling of the good understanding *[la bonne entente]*.... Economic decline started the very same moment that English methods were taught to us.... We are the lone race to copy others; result—failure everywhere. The Englishman does business as an Englishman, the Jew as a Jew.... Our school program anglicizes and renders [our children] stupid. Those who must learn the tongue of an overbearing neighbour, stimulate the arrogance of the neighbour.... The maxims are not to be questioned. It is the general good which inspires the maxims. Do not change their meaning without authorization from Ottawa (seat of the chancery).[24]

Bouchard noted that these instructions were published in 1937, at the time the German Nazis and Italian Fascists were helping Franco's insurrection against the democratic government of Spain. "The totalitarian progress in Europe in the decade that preceded the last war," he warned, "has given a new impetus to that backward movement tending to bring us back to the social and economic status of the Middle Ages."[25] He drew attention to a long article in the same edition of *L'Émerillon* in favour of the adoption of a national flag for French Canadians, to feature a royal blue background with a great white cross, and *fleurs-de-lis* in the four corners—a return to the flag of Louis XV. The Order had succeeded in convincing the authorities of the University of Montreal to hoist this flag atop its tower on a holiday. After the adoption of the present flag of Quebec by the Duplessis government in 1948, *L'Émerillon* proclaimed: "The flag, this *fleur-de-lis* flag, which our Order has recommended for twenty years, becomes the emblem of the province of Quebec ... one of the most beautiful victories of our Order ... an unprecedented victory."[26]

Unfortunately, the senator further shot himself in the foot by attacking the Church proper, quoting the words of the *chargé d'affaires* of the apostolic delegation to Canada, his Excellency, Monsignor Mazzoni. (Some years earlier, Mazzoni had recommended a Catholic state: "A Catholic peoplehood has the right and duty to organize itself socially and politically according to the teachings of its faith.") The fiery senator continued his indictment by defending Abbé

---

24 *L'Émerillon, mai-juin* 1937.

25 T.-D.B., Senate speech, p. 17.

26 *L'Émerillon, février* 1948.

Maheux, a Laval University historian who had been attacked by the Order and by the *Jeunes Laurentiens.*

> Distortions ... have gone so far that those who want to correct facts of our history that have been misrepresented are treated like traitors to their race and religion. One of our most eminent historians, Abbé Arthur Maheux, a member of the Royal Society of Canada and professor of Canadian history at Laval University ... has written a book entitled *What Keeps Us Apart?* This volume followed one bearing the title *Our Beginnings Under the English Regime....* Because Abbé Maheux wanted to be honest ... because his philosophy is that we should be good neighbours with our compatriots ... he has ... been at the centre of an unparalleled storm of abuse by our separatists and isolationists ... this most respectable priest was banned as a traitor to his race because he spoke the truth.[27]

Bouchard ripped into the *Jeunes Laurentiens* by quoting a message from its president, which declared that "this revolution that we want shall be practical, efficient, calm, and good, because it calls for pure, fundamentally Catholic and French men. *It is the revolution of liberated Spain, Portugal, of France under Pétain.*"[28] (Emphasis added.) And he linked the two organizations, *Jeunes Laurentiens* and the Order of Jacques Cartier, by quoting this passage: "... and especially Discretion! Do not commit the error of proclaiming that you are a Young Laurentian."[29] This was exactly the *modus operandi* of the Order. Members were instructed repeatedly to use discretion, discretion and discretion. Bouchard went on to say that the distorted teaching of Canadian history had already created nearly all of the harm hoped-for by those who were in favour of the breakup of the country. Their ultimate aim was not only to divide the people on linguistic and religious matters, but also to disrupt Confederation:

> To abandon the more human North American concept of a large nation composed of people of different religious beliefs and racial origins, and to revert to the old European concept of smaller nations of the same religious and racial descent.... These deceitful workers

27   T.-D.B., Senate speech, p. 21.

28   Ibid., p. 22.

29   Ibid., p. 22, see also Paul-André Comeau, *Le 1942–1948 Bloc Populaire*, (Montréal: Québec/ Amérique, 1982).

have already succeeded in destroying ... the former association of Liberal-Conservatives with the *castors* ... [This has been] easy ... for the leaders of our hidden fascists.[30]

Bouchard named the *Bloc Populaire*, led by the ex-president of the *Jeunes Laurentiens* (André Laurendeau), as "the open political tool" of the Order of Jacques Cartier. He warned that if liberty-loving people did not open their eyes in good time, they would see to what extent this sneaky work had undermined their free institutions. Bouchard concluded by acknowledging that some would denounce him for having openly expressed his thoughts on Canadian history and for having shown what was going on in "our upper and lower classes on the political situation." And with perhaps foolish stoicism, he spoke ominously of a situation in which "actors are rehearsing what some believe will be a farce, but which to my mind will eventually turn out to be a national tragedy.... In a mounting storm I like to face the wind and not be caught by it in the back. I am not a pessimist, but when I hear distant rumblings of thunder I am aware that the dark clouds are liable to burst over my head."[31] Here again we note a repetition of his youthful justification for an aggressive response to his opponents. He will save his honour, although he might suffer harm.

The clouds did burst over his head. Why did he choose the eve of the Saint-Jean-Baptiste celebrations to condemn the OJC—the right wing of Quebec politics—and its association with the Church? Warned of the consequences, Bouchard had nevertheless opted to commit political suicide, prompting almost universal denunciation. Why did he speak in English, complained the nationalists? On entering his shared office after his speech, Senator Vaillancourt told him how angry he was: *Un oiseau propre ne souille pas son nid*—"a clean bird does not soil its own nest." Bouchard was allowed to say such things in Quebec, said Vaillancourt, but not when the audience is the whole of Canada.[32] Yet, it is interesting to note that eighteen years later, Senator Cyrille Vaillancourt was one of T.-D. Bouchard's honorary pallbearers at his funeral. Following his speech, Bouchard went up to the Château Laurier Hotel. He was now uncertain that he would manage to weather the storm as easily as he had in the past. He telephoned Montreal to warn Cécile-Ena: "Well, I have made my speech." She

---

30   Ibid., p. 22.

31   Ibid., p. 23.

32   C. Vaillancourt, personal communication to Chisholm, p. 169.

replied bluntly, "It is what you wanted. Now you have to accept the consequences." Then he asked her what she would do if he had to go into exile. "Well,
I will accompany you," she replied.[33]

Rarely has a political speech made so many waves, and never had a Senate
speech had such a resounding impact. On the following day *L'Action catholique*
demanded his dismissal from Hydro-Quebec. Maurice Duplessis, who on March
3 had praised the new Senator, accused him of treason on June 22. He demanded
his head as president of Hydro-Quebec—in spite of the fact that Duplessis himself
did not like *la patente* (the OJC), this secret organization in which one blindly
obeyed an unknown leader in Ottawa, and which served as the nursery of supporters and even of future candidates for his enemy on the right, the *Bloc Populaire*.
"Still," Duplessis said, "these supremely unjust and unworthy declarations by a
public figure ... do not surprise me coming from him because for several years
already we have denounced and fought the anti-Canadian and anticlerical tendencies of Mr. Bouchard, tendencies which he has never had the courage to display as
cynically when he was obliged to submit to an election."[34]

Léopold Richer of *Le Devoir* wrote from Ottawa that it was the most surprising speech ever delivered in the Senate in the fifteen years he had been covering
the news.[35] According to Richer, Bouchard had contributed exactly what it took
to bring about a resounding defeat of the Liberals, both federally and provincially. The English press throughout the country treated Bouchard's speech as
a warning of a harmful secession movement, an allusion to a possible civil war.
The World War by then had lasted over four years. It was a time of great stress
for the population. The lists of the dead and injured published in newspapers
grew longer, and increasingly included French-Canadian names. The Orange
Protestants of Ontario approved of his speech. The Liberal press—Jean-Charles
Harvey's *Le Jour* and Edmond Turcotte's *Le Canada*—supported him.

The premier of Quebec, who had been getting ready to call elections, since
his term of office was almost over, declared that Senator Bouchard's speech
"... does not represent, in any manner, the opinion of any member of the provincial government."[36] Godbout went to Ottawa and made a scene with his

---

33   C.-E. B., personal communication to Chisholm, p. 169.

34   *Le Devoir*, 22 *juin* 1944.

35   Ibid.

36   Ibid., 23 *juin* 1944.

ex-minister. Bouchard was not willing to retract anything. Godbout summoned a special session of the cabinet on June 23. All the ministers feared the electoral repercussions of Bouchard's address. They adopted an order-in-council dismissing Bouchard from his position as president of the Hydroelectric Commission of Quebec. He was appointed to that role on April 21, barely nine weeks before. Although he was losing a job that was to be the crowning height of his career, the justification for his campaign for cheaper electricity rates, and a salary of eighteen thousand dollars, he took the news with good grace. "I suspected what might happen, but that does not modify in any way my convictions. My dismissal is of no importance. However, it is a confirmation of my declarations to the Senate. I have always spoken frankly, and I do not intend to change my style. What has happened only illustrates the futility of my speech to the Senate."[37]

Two days later, addressing a huge crowd from the pulpit of the Saint-Hyacinthe Cathedral—a crowd including eleven bishops attending the Eucharistic Congress—His Eminence Cardinal Villeneuve lashed out at Bouchard without naming him, asking what was the author's real purpose? He described Bouchard's words as unjust, abusive, thoughtless, and not grounded in truth. He asserted that "the insulter" had made "an unintelligent, if not treacherous, interpretation" of Monsignor Mazzoni's speech, which Villeneuve defended by explaining that Monsignor Mazzoni had only wanted to express "… the wish that a social doctrine fully inspired by pontifical teachings should be established among us."[38] In his *Mémoires* Bouchard explains that his reference to the words of Monsignor Mazzoni regarding church-state relations caused the cardinal's furious reaction. However, it is also possible that Villeneuve's intense reaction was linked to revelations concerning the OJC. The cardinal said, *Je laisse à d'autres de réfuter ses accusations d'ordre politique et racial.* ("I leave it to others to refute his political and racial accusations.") The cardinal also condemned Bouchard's newspaper. This damaged the senator the most. Many subscribers obeyed the injunction to boycott the newspaper, and circulation fell by half.

Although the cardinal's sermon impressed many, some Liberals were shocked by his words, especially when he spoke of a snake having appeared in Saint-Hyacinthe—a phrase not included in the published text.[39] The cardinal's words

---

37   *La Presse*, 24 *juin* 1944.

38   T.-D.B., *Mémoires*, III, p.176–178.

39   Yves Michaud, personal communication to Chisholm, p. 180. Michaud was a young journalist who began his career in Saint-Hyacinthe at Bouchard's newspaper, *Le Clairon*.

horrified Yves Michaud: "It shocked me that a member of the Church as important as Cardinal Villeneuve would take part in a political debate.... My two uncles, who were organizers for Senator Bouchard ... also criticized the cardinal. They were devout Catholics, but for them, to be Liberal was also a religion."[40] *The Montreal Gazette* declared that the majority of citizens of the province were unbelievably shocked by Bouchard's dismissal.[41] Even though opposed for a long time to the establishment of Hydro-Quebec, the *Gazette* objected to firing a capable administrator for political reasons. It asserted that this act exposed as false the pretence that the Hydro Commission was an independent body, and not influenced by politics. *The Montreal Star*, without even commenting on the speech, asserted that the premier had allowed himself to be influenced and had made a capable civil servant a political victim, doing himself harm in the process.[42] *La Presse* published the results of an inquiry: "A torrent of protest. All of Mr. Bouchard's compatriots condemn him," which was not entirely true.[43] At the end of this article, several exceptions were mentioned—for example, the historian and Conservative ultramontane Senator Sir Thomas Chapais, author of several historical works, who was quoted as stating that he did not immediately condemn the whole speech. Chapais felt that it was open to criticism, as were all other speeches given in Parliament. As far as he could judge, "the speech was regrettable from a certain point of view, although it contained some justifiable elements."[44] Constance Garneau supported the new senator: "He is too intelligent a man to advance such thoughts without knowing of what he speaks. He has demonstrated much courage. I hope that some one on the English side would have the same courage to denounce the prejudiced teaching in English schools against French Canadians."[45]

He later became a minister in the Lesage government, a minister in the *Parti Québecois* Lévesque government, and more recently a "Robin Hood" attacking the large banks and corporations. See also Laferté, p.43. Laferté reports that in 1936 Villeneuve had expressed negative thoughts about Bouchard to Godbout—that he should not be a member of the Liberal Party.

40   Ibid.

41   *The Montreal Gazette*, June 24, 1944.

42   *The Montreal Star*, June 26, 1944.

43   *La Presse, 23 juin* 1944.

44   Ibid.

45   Constance Garneau, personal communication to Chisholm, p. 171.

Bouchard asserts that his dismissal from his job as president of Hydro-Quebec came some days after the cardinal's sermon, but he is wrong.[46] It was not the cardinal's public statement that motivated Godbout, since the cabinet order-in-council was proclaimed on June 23, and the cardinal's sermon took place a day later. (Of course, there probably was direct private communication between Villeneuve and Godbout immediately after the speech, but there is no record of it.) Maxime Raymond of the *Bloc Populaire*, Antoine Rivard of the *Union Nationale,* and Harry Bernard also attacked Bouchard from the right. Louis St. Laurent, Minister of Justice in the King cabinet and the federal French-Canadian leader, minimized Senator Bouchard's speech by laying the blame for his deviant language on his fiery nature. St. Laurent asserted that *la Patente* was not an important organization, and that the Royal Canadian Mounted Police were aware of all subversive organizations in the country. He admitted to the existence of the Order, which had been organized several years previously for the purpose of increasing the numbers and influence of French Canadians in the federal civil service. He asserted that its annual report to the government listed its directors, and journalists could easily discover their names.[47] When journalists followed St. Laurent's suggestion, they discovered only denials. The list of directors consisted of three laymen and two priests. Four of these men refused comment, denying membership in the Order; and one had moved, not leaving a forwarding address.[48] Bouchard commented on this information by saying that he was not surprised: "The reaction proves the existence and the power of the Order."[49] Among the letters received by the Prime Minister of Canada was one from a correspondent who felt that history would prove Senator Bouchard right, and that if Mr. St. Laurent was as ignorant as he pretended to be, he did not deserve to remain Minister of Justice. The correspondent wrote that it was well-known that the Order existed in the form described by Bouchard.[50] Curiously, Bouchard's newspaper, *Le Clairon*, was silent on the subject of the controversy following his speech. In his *Mémoires* he asserts that he had received more than one thousand letters of congratulation.[51]

---

46   T.-D.B., *Mémoires,* III, p.178.

47   *The Montreal Star,* June 23 1944.

48   Ibid.

49   *La Presse,* 23 *juin* 1944.

50   King Papers; PAC.Mg 26–13, S-300-B Letter of J.S. Edgar, June 30, 1944.

51   T.-D.B., ANQ, there are about 100 saved letters.

What is the true history of the OJC? In his book on the OJC, G.-Raymond Laliberté describes the birth and development of the Order—an ultra-nationalist, secret, and xenophobic movement.[52] It linked its xenophobic message of narrow-minded Catholicism to the promotion of the French language—in itself desirable—but also to the promotion of a Catholic corporate state, thus expressing the ideas of Canon Groulx, who, according to some rumours, was at one time the chaplain of the Order. There were also rumours that at the Order's inception its chaplain in Ottawa had been none other than the future cardinal who reacted so strongly to Bouchard's 1944 Senate speech, the then-Abbé Villeneuve.

Bouchard claimed to have received the news of his dismissal from a journalist after being informed on the telephone by Godbout that the subject was under discussion at an urgent afternoon cabinet meeting. When so informed, Bouchard stubbornly reminded the premier "that he had accepted the presidency on condition that there would be no political interference, and that the administration of Hydro-Quebec would not have anything to do with my ideas concerning our intellectual and national life."[53]

According to Bouchard, Godbout replied that he would submit these views to the cabinet, even though he had already obtained the order-in-council signed by the Lieutenant-Governor. Objectively, with all the warnings we have noted, it seems that he was given enough advance notification. In any event, he made a graceful declaration the following day:

> My first reaction was one of sympathy for my old chief in battle, Mr. Godbout, who must be far more affected than me by the situation.... Once, the mass of fanatics threw Christians to the lions; today they allow those who want to maintain their freedom of opinion to die of hunger ... I love Canadians of French origin far more than do those who flatter and exploit their religious beliefs in order to better dominate them in the political arena. Liberated now from the heavy strain and the long hours of work, I am going to take up my journalistic pen and to continue the struggle, begun 45 years ago now, for the intellectual, economic, and social advancement of the descendants of

---

52   G.-Raymond Laliberté; *Une Société secrète: L'Ordre de Jacques Cartier*, (Montréal: Hurtubise 1983). See appendix, p. 367.

53   *Le Devoir,* 26 *juin* 1944.

those two great races that populate our country of such vast and so promising horizons.[54]

On the day following the cardinal's diatribe, members and friends of the *Garde de Protection Civile de Saint-Hyacinthe* met in the *Bosquet des Pins* for their annual picnic. Bouchard, having been invited to participate long before, bravely joined the crowd to assess the damage the cardinal's sermon had caused amongst "the people." "I addressed the crowd," he writes, "since I was asked to do so, and the applause that punctuated my speech proved to me that I had not lost the esteem of my friends."[55]

Cécile-Ena, recently promoted to the rank of Major, wanted to resign from the army, but her commanding officer would not accept her resignation, saying that it would be thought to be a punishment for her father's recent behaviour. Bouchard's daughter, therefore, remained in the service for another year. Bouchard was capable of a remarkable generosity of spirit. Again in his *Mémoires*, he has nice words to say about Cardinal Villeneuve: "one of the greatest figures of the Canadian Episcopate." Bouchard claimed that Cardinal Villeneuve died of a heart attack caused by the attacks of those "old companions of arms" who had undermined him. The cardinal, he reminded his readers, had given his whole support to the war and struggled against isolationist views, against the anti-conscriptionists, and against the ultra-nationalists.

> [He was] no longer sympathetic to the subversive isolationists and the Fascist French Canadians. The generous contribution of the Primate of the Canadian Church to our war effort paralyzed the work of the Fascists.... This sociologist and eminent theologian was the son of a shoemaker, as I was. We both loved the people and wanted to be useful. We have confronted each other in intense struggles. For my part, I have never felt resentment against him because I am convinced that by treating me with rigour, he listened only to his conscience.[56]

Bouchard continues with what one could perhaps qualify as a singular lack of perspicacity or understanding. "I do not believe that, for his part, he maintained his resentment against me. He knew me to be sincere and did know that if,

---

54   Ibid., 26 *juin* 1944.

55   T.-D.B., *Mémoires*, III, p. 181.

56   Ibid., pp.192–193.

sometimes, I exposed myself to receiving slaps in the face it was because my only concern was to remain faithful to my convictions."[57]

Godbout dissolved the Legislative Assembly on June 28 and immediately called an election for August 8. He again dissociated himself and the Liberal government from Bouchard's speech in the Senate. Nobody denied that Bouchard had chosen a terrible moment to take on *la Patente* and the Church. But to claim that he had wanted "to stab Godbout in the back," even if partly true, played against the Liberal Party. In fact Gagnon, one of the principal leaders of the Liberals, recognized in 1944 that by denying what Bouchard had said, Godbout and company justified the clericalism of Duplessis and the nationalism of Laurendeau. With opponents such as these, Duplessis had no need for other friends.[58]

Godbout asked the voters to judge his government on its achievements, and not on federal questions. He denounced Duplessis as a corrupt tyrant, who between 1936 and 1939 had demonstrated that he was incapable of governing. But the Liberal Party underestimated Duplessis's electoral common sense. He had been campaigning since leaving hospital in 1942. The ex-premier attacked the poor judgment of the provincial government, which he held responsible for federal intrusion into provincial autonomy. This, he claimed, was demonstrated by Godbout's weak reaction to the federal-provincial conference in Ottawa in 1941, by the transfer of taxation rights to federal jurisdiction without protest, and by the easily obtained agreement to changes in the Maritime Act pertaining to the Saint Lawrence Seaway. Godbout was even blamed for the 1940 imprisonment of the popular Montreal mayor Camillien Houde for sedition, and was condemned for his acquiescence in the matter of delaying the federal electoral map revision— which would have increased Quebec's representation based on the 1941 census. He also was blamed for the conscription issue. Duplessis played on these themes, emphasizing that all these policies undermined the autonomy of Quebec.

Both Duplessis and the *Bloc* used the Bouchard issue in the election campaign, describing him as the leader of the heretics and Liberals who wanted to assimilate into English Canada. The Liberals in turn directed their attacks almost exclusively against the *Bloc*, ignoring the danger from the *Union Nationale*. Without the benefit of polls to indicate voter intention, the Liberals were so confident that they would win because of the division of the right-wing vote that they thought they were going to elect too many members and thus would

---

57   Ibid., pp. 192–193.

58   Gagnon, II, p. 256.

have some trouble choosing a cabinet.[59] The *Bloc* continued to link Godbout and Bouchard, quoting the senator's words in support of the Liberal Party. As Bouchard declared in *Le Devoir*, the issue was that "Clericalism is the corruption of religion as nationalism is the corruption of patriotism."[60] André Laurendeau answered: "Mr. Godbout dismissed him [Bouchard] for electoral reasons.... The proof? A declaration from Mr. Bouchard himself ... that he continues to count on Mr. Godbout, to consider him the best representative in provincial politics.... A vote for the Godbout regime, says Mr. Bouchard, will be the best way to vote for my speech to the Senate."[61]

Another weakness in the Liberal front was that, in addition to Bouchard, eight ministers had left the cabinet since 1939, including the powerful Hector Perrier, who had introduced education reforms but was forced to resign for health reasons; Drouin, who had left for the presidency of the Municipal Commission; and Rochette, who had become a judge. In contrast to Gouin and Taschereau, who kept their cabinet members for a long time, thus strengthening their electoral teams, Godbout weakened his electoral team by allowing experienced, young, and well-known ministers to resign. He thus placed himself at a disadvantage in the campaign. Generally, people considered that representation by a cabinet minister was an advantage—it led to more patronage. Moreover, these departures left him open to suggestions that those leaving feared the impending election results. War casualties were also attributed to Godbout. More than three hundred Canadian soldiers had died in the first fifteen days of the invasion of Europe. The resentment provoked in Quebec by the war and forced conscription increased during the election campaign in the wake of the death of an army deserter, René Guenette, who was killed by a member of the Royal Canadian Mounted Police

The Liberal based its campaign on the government's considerable and impressive achievements. The Godbout administration had passed legislation on women's suffrage, compulsory education, and free schoolbooks. It had restructured the labour code, created Hydro-Quebec, and reduced electricity rates. It had adopted rural electrification plans and established a beet-sugar industry in Saint-Hilaire. It had displayed a rigorous control of expenses by requiring the

---

59   Ibid., II, p. 257.

60   *Le Devoir*, 25 *juin* 1944.

61   Ibid., 26 *juin* 1944.

submission of contract tenders and setting up a Public Service Commission. René Chaloult, the ultra-nationalist chauvinist, sheepishly admitted, "I seek an opportunity to vote against the government and I do not find any."[62] Bouchard, and Adélard Godbout, of course, had strongly supported these bills. Without their support, none of this legislation would have been passed. In opposition to the slogan, "Our master, the past"—that is to say, the doctrine of the *Bloc* and Canon Groulx—the Liberals had adopted a rallying cry which very well summarized Godbout's political activity: "Our master, the future!"

The nationalization of the Montreal Heat, Light, and Power Company had marked Godbout as a "socialist" and deprived him of electoral contributions from the big Saint James Street contributors. Liberal activists, especially in outlying regions, refused to participate in the campaign because they resented a government that favoured the lowest bidders, and mimimized patronage. The campaign was difficult for Godbout, booed as he was by crowds of demonstrators at meetings in Montreal, in Hull, and especially in Chicoutimi, where he had to leave under the protection of the police, without having uttered a single word. The demonstrators screamed, "Conscription!" or "Bouchard!" or "Guenette!" Godbout himself later admitted that the explanation for his defeat might in part have resulted from the fact that the Liberals had "ignored their friends."[63] In *Le Clairon*, Bouchard tried to help the Liberal campaign by naming commanders of the OJC, describing Canon Groulx as their leader. He also fingered some *Union Nationale* candidates as members of the OJC. No one sued him for libel.

On the evening of August 8, 1944, Maurice Duplessis's *Union Nationale* won the election with 48 seats. The Liberals won only 39 seats, and the *Bloc Populaire* elected 4 members. The *Bloc* received 15 percent of the vote, the Liberals 37 percent, and the *Union Nationale* 36 percent. Thus, the Liberals had received a higher percentage of the popular vote than the *UN*. Adélard Godbout, elected personally, spent the day in his constituency of l'Islet. Most of the old members of the *Union Nationale* caucus were elected, including Paul Sauvé, who was serving in France as Lieutenant-Colonel of the Fusiliers of Mount-Royal. Jean Drapeau was just barely defeated in Jeanne Mance. Montreal-Laurier elected André Laurendeau of the *Bloc*.

During the month of July, Senator Bouchard seemed for the first time in his life to accept the contempt he had aroused with his attacks against the Church

---

62 Ibid., 26 *mai* 1944.

63 Genest, p. 286.

and the ultramontanes. The fire of his youth and his adult life was going out. Because of remarks and resignations of some of the governors of the Canadian Democratic Institute after his speech, he submitted a letter of resignation in order, he said, not to embarrass the organization. In *Le Clairon* he explained to the voters of Saint-Hyacinthe the reason for his decision not to be a candidate during the next mayoralty race. It would soon be forty years, he said, since he had entered public life, and he had seen a considerable number of his reforms implemented. Together with a group of intelligent and devoted aldermen, he had succeeded in turning Saint-Hyacinthe into what was reputed to be a model city. He added that a group of "agitators," elected to the town council in the past year, had reversed progress and returned to political patronage. They succeeded in driving municipal affairs into a wasteful state. For a man such as Bouchard, who understood the importance of public affairs, it was impossible to submit to these changes. He stated that his duty as a citizen called him to a greater and far more important task. With some self-dramatization he declared: "We are entering … into a new era, possibly the most troubled of our history as a people, if some do not make the sacrifices necessary to warn of the danger before it is too late. Knowing full well the consequences of my action, I have offered myself as the first victim."[64] He asserted that he had acted only in the interest of his compatriots—both French and English Canadians. He then concluded his article:

> Thus, I have helped my city and my province to progress. This is even admitted to by my most persistent adversaries, and thus, in the new struggle which will be very difficult for your old Mayor, I will continue to serve in a higher but more dangerous sphere.… True Canadians of all origins desire to make their great country a common homeland, in which the four freedoms for which our ancestors have fought, and for which our sons fight on land, on the oceans, and in the air—freedom of speech, freedom of the press, freedom of religion and freedom from poverty—will reign.[65]

One must question why Bouchard had decided, in spite of ample warnings, to deliver his maiden speech in the Senate on such a controversial subject. We have seen how he wanted to get even with Godbout. We have seen how the defeat of his municipal team in 1944, for which he blamed the OJC, surprised and

---

64   *Le Clairon, 7 juillet* 1944.

65   Ibid.

discouraged him. But more important than these factors was the burning belief that the Right—the clerical, nationalist, isolationist and separatist forces—were gaining ground and would ruin the Canada he loved. Conrad Langlois states that this was the reason for his falling-out with Godbout. He wanted a frontal attack on the OJC, whereas Godbout favoured infiltrating the ranks of the OJC with Liberal workers.[66] Since his youth in the seminary—where Bouchard had never accepted real or perceived insults from other students—neither during his years as alderman, when he battled against his "adversaries" who plotted against his election, nor when nominated as Town Clerk, nor during his struggles to be elected as Member of the Legislative Assembly, nor as mayor of his native city. The implacable Télesphore-Damien Bouchard consistently remained faithful to his principles: always attack, since to do otherwise would be a sign of weakness. "[My] honour," he exclaimed, "was vindicated … had I crawled before an insult or a challenge neither side would ever have forgiven it."[67]

At the age of sixty-three, after forty years of public life, he had just delivered the most virulent speech of his eventful career, and probably the speech that caused the greatest storm on a national scale of any speech pronounced in the Senate, before or after his time. For the first time in his life, he seemed to have accepted the verdict of his fellow citizens, and, like a good Christian, to turn the other cheek, without bitterness. For many years, his enemies on the right, the clericals and the separatists had been his pet hates. His recent defeat at the municipal level had to weigh heavily on his heart. To be able to make speeches on the Senate floor—the highest political platform in Canada—was an irresistible temptation. Despite the unavoidable condemnation of the highest religious and civil authorities, the obstinate Télesphore-Damien Bouchard, convinced of the justice his cause, felt compelled to deliver his message.

Another question arising from the election victory of the *Union Nationale* is that posed by Herbert F. Quinn in his book on the *Union Nationale*. In it, he asks why the working classes and farmers vote against their economic interests and support conservative parties.[68] He points out that this is so not only in Quebec, but in Germany, France, and England as well. In the case of Quebec he writes:

---

66   Conrad Langlois. *La Patrie,* Semaine du 22–28 *novembre* 1962.

67   T.-D.B., *Memoirs,* Chapter IX, pp. 4–5 in *Fonds* Bouchard, ANQ, P-10/18.

68   Herbert F. Quinn, *The Union Nationale, a Study in Quebec Nationalism,* (Toronto: University of Toronto Press, 1963).

In a society where an ethnic minority has reason to believe that its interests as a distinct cultural group are threatened, the struggle to defend and protect those interests tends to become the dominant issue in politics and encourages the growth of strong nationalistic sentiments. As a result, purely economic issues, which ordinarily play an important role in any capitalist society, are likely to be pushed into the background. The average voter in this ethnic group may be more interested in the problem of maintaining the right to speak and use his language in everyday life than in the enactment of social legislation. His ability to retain the particular set of values found in his educational system may be more important to him than the struggle for higher scales. He may be more concerned about the possibility of the dominant group forcing upon him some policy in the realm of foreign affairs to which he is opposed, such as participation in a war, than with the question of introducing reforms in the capitalist system.[69]

There is no doubt that Bouchard's speech did not help the Liberal Party. However, the main issue was most probably Duplessis's effective campaign for several years on the autonomy issue. Godbout allowed the population to believe Duplessis's accusations on this score by his statement at the Rowell-Sirois Commission, by his acquiescence to King's amendment to the BNA Act, by his agreement to the changes in the Maritime Law that allowed for St. Lawrence Seaway development, and by his agreement to put off the census changes to the electoral map. As Quinn points out, if their autonomy is perceived to be threatened people will sometimes vote against their economic interests. We will now examine how Bouchard dealt with his political downfall and how he continued on his path in the days following his speech.

---

69   Quinn, pp.192–193.

Chapter XI

THE FOLLOWING DAYS

In the days following Bouchard's speech in the Senate, other provinces honoured T.-D. Bouchard. Invitations to speak arrived from many organizations throughout Canada—in Vancouver, Calgary, Regina and Winnipeg, for example. He was the guest of the Canadian Institute of Public Affairs in Couchiching. In the Senate he was rather silent when debate resumed on Senator David's motion. David made no comment on Bouchard's speech except when speaking in favour of his bill on July 19, when he stated that outside the Quebec family, he had always defended his province.[1] Bouchard got up on a point of privilege to reply to this oblique reproach. He said that when a French Canadian speaks in the Senate, he speaks in his own house and that the Canadian family is very much his national family. When he addresses the Senate, he is speaking to his own brothers.[2]

While visiting Toronto, a journalist asked Bouchard if he truly feared a civil war. Bouchard replied that the situation was serious and caused him a lot of anxiety—a reply that resulted in *Le Devoir's* accusation that he was the victim of an obsession.[3] Nevertheless, two weeks later, the same newspaper published an article that warned the population in headlines: "TAKE CARE! To burn or tear the Union Jack does not serve any good and can only cause harm. The young should beware of *agents provocateurs*. We should remember the experience of 1917."[4] Indeed, shortly after this, anti-war and anti-British demonstrators in Rimouski and Chicoutimi did burn the Union Jack. A manifesto of the *Bloc Populaire* in November 1944 declared that the response to conscription is inde-

---

1   David; Senate Debates, July 19, 1944, p. 317.

2   T.-D.B., Ibid., p. 319.

3   *Le Devoir,* 9 *novembre* 1944.

4   Ibid., 23 *novembre* 1944.

pendence. Therefore, the intrepid senator had not been far off in his fears of civil disturbance and of separatists.

The secretary of the Canadian Democratic Institute, Maurice d'Hont, was travelling on holiday in June of 1944, when he received a telegram from a friend telling him to return immediately to Montreal. Born in Belgium, d'Hont was not too familiar with Quebec politics. The furor caused by a speech that he considered harmless, surprised him.[5] He returned to Saint-Hyacinthe, where, on entering Bouchard's office at *Le Clairon,* Bouchard got up and asked if he was with him or against him. D'Hont replied, "But what do you think? Why would I have come to see you if I were not with you?"[6] Here again is an example of Bouchard's defensiveness. D'Hont had returned to try to save the Institute. Several members of the panicky business community had tendered their resignations, as had Bouchard. With delicate diplomacy—by first approaching the most sympathetic governors, then the less sympathetic, and finally the most recalcitrant—d'Hont was able to assert that the majority wanted to keep Bouchard as Supreme Governor and to refuse his offer of resignation. Bouchard was thus re-elected Supreme Governor of the Institute in September 1944, to the great relief of the more liberal governors.[7]

That summer was a difficult period for the senator. Many people who had sought him out during his years in power had deserted him. Aside from a few friends, he was abandoned, and even shunned. In admiration, Maurice d'Hont declared, "I was always at his side, and I never heard him complain about this."[8] D'Hont accompanied Bouchard on his travels in the other provinces, and helped him with his English. At the Empire Club in Toronto, against his secretary's advice, Bouchard insisted on reading some chapters from his memoirs and, as always when he read a prepared text instead of speaking spontaneously, he bored his audience. The following day, at the Couchiching conference, he again read chapters from his memoirs, despite the repeated advice of his secretary. He believed that a more intellectual audience would better understand the background of the opinions of a French Canadian. He immodestly confessed that his style was a fusion of the styles of Victor Hugo and Tolstoy. D'Hont

---

5   D'Hont, personal communication, to Chisholm, p. 188.

6   Ibid.

7   D'Hont and Therese Casgrain, to Chisholm, p. 188.

8   Ibid., p. 88.

explained: "Again, there was a disaster. Therefore, I asked the historian Mason Wade, who was there, to explain to Mr. Bouchard that he should only speak on politics, and not recount stories from his childhood. He must have been a powerful influence since, henceforth, Mr. Bouchard no longer read stories from his memoirs."[9]

In his address at Couchiching, Bouchard spoke about the considerable progress in educational reforms in Quebec. He spoke of his hope of seeing a uniform history text for Canada, and praised Quebec's economic progress and the change in attitude of the clergy concerning education and social affairs. He again criticized "a small but active group that sought the creation of an independent state, a racist and totalitarian state."[10] In spite of his qualification that these nationalists were just a small minority, English audiences simplified and generalized his remarks. He then gave a press conference to correct these misunderstandings. When he spoke of the danger of subversion by the OJC, many concluded that he was anti-Catholic. In *Maclean's Magazine* he tried to correct these false assumptions, but the headline of his article was sensationalized: "The Struggle for Quebec; Bouchard; His Dream Fights a Nightmare." This headline disturbed him.[11]

The Ottawa Citizen translated and reprinted some of his articles from *Le Clairon*. B. K. Sandwell, the editor of *Saturday Night,* commented on Bouchard's speech on July 1 stating that it was a dispute of concern only to French Canadians. However, on July 8 after having read the speech carefully, he revised his opinion; he was now aware that there truly was a danger coming from the Laurentian movement of Canon Groulx and the *Bloc Populaire.* On July 8 Sandwell wrote:

> Several eminent French Canadians [Louis St. Laurent?] have declared that they know nothing about it, and apparently supposed that therefore it does not exist. But Mr. Bouchard named its open or popular organ (*La Bousole*), which certainly does exist, for I have seen plenty of copies of it, and it teaches the precise doctrines which he has described.[12]

---

9   Ibid., p. 199.

10   *Canadian Press,* August 25, 1944.

11   *Maclean's Magazine,* October 1, 1944.

12   *Saturday Night,* July 1 and 8, 1944.

The editorialist of the *Ottawa Citizen* described Bouchard sympathetically, comparing him to Edouard Herriot of France, and declared that the name of Bouchard would be as important as that of Laurier in the histories of Quebec and Canada.[13]

Paul Gouin, former leader of the Liberal-Nationalists *(Action libérale nationale)*, who quit Taschereau in 1934 and then betrayed by Duplessis in *l'Union Nationale*, criticized Bouchard for having said to the English that Quebec was under the influence of priests and especially of the OJC. Nevertheless, he described their attempt to influence him: "It was a joke. I belonged myself for a short period of time." Then, he added a thought lending credence to Bouchard's claims: "Some of the leaders of the OJC were very narrow-minded—a small group. I never liked them at all. They tried to influence me in 1936, when I was a Member of the Legislative Assembly. They wished to dictate my policy towards Duplessis. Of course, I refused."[14]

The liberation of Paris on August 25, 1944, increased the sympathy of Quebec towards the Allies. Final victory was in sight, including the restoration of a free France. The Pétainists and the isolationists became more discreet. General de Gaulle received a warm reception in Quebec City, just before the opening of the Quebec Conference attended by Franklin D. Roosevelt and Winston Churchill. During Bouchard's trip to Western Canada, a bitter riot occurred in Montreal (as was the case in other Canadian cities). A fight broke out between sailors and the "Zombies." ("Zombie" was a name given to a conscript who refused to volunteer for overseas duty.) There was a wave of Orangist, anti-French-Canadian propaganda in the rest of Canada. Commenting on the supposedly high percentage of Zombies coming from Quebec, in a well-balanced article in *MacLean's Magazine* Blair Fraser noted that there were 150,000 soldiers in active service overseas from Quebec. Because of a lack of information about the true origins of the conscripts—as well as the many English names belonging to those who were French Canadian—allowed only for rough estimates. Fraser reckoned that one-third of the Zombies were of French-Canadian origin, a third English, and a third Italian or German. In addition, Blair insisted that Zombies existed everywhere throughout the country.[15]

---

13   Editorial, *The Ottawa Citizen,* July 17, 1944.

14   Paul Gouin, personal communication to Chisholm, p. 192.

15   Blair Fraser, *Maclean's Magazine*, August 15, 1944.

More recently, Serge-Mark Durflinger and Daniel Byers have exploded some myths about the Zombies.[16] Colonel Ralston, Minister of Defence, had just returned from a round of inspection in Europe in October of 1944, and presented his report to the cabinet. In it, he recommended the immediate dispatch of sixty thousand conscripts already mobilized under the National Resource Mobilization Act. Mackenzie King, aghast, could not accept this recommendation, and accepted instead Ralston's resignation—in fact, he encouraged it. In Ralston's place he appointed the popular General MacNaughton. Less than a month later, General MacNaughton had to recognize his failure, as most of the conscripts refused to volunteer for overseas duty. King profited from this period by making the public and Parliament understand that he no longer had a choice, in spite of his years of opposition to overseas conscription. Indeed, one can safely say that without King's resistance, overseas conscription would have been adopted long before 1944. The government decided to dispatch sixteen thousand conscripts to Europe, but only 2,463 of them participated in the last battles before the surrender of the Germans on May 8, 1945.

C. G. Power resigned his position as Deputy Minister of Defence because of the vote against conscription in his riding, which result had been in conflict with his personal views. P. J. A. Cardin, who had resigned earlier, announced his intention to fight the Liberal Party after having been one its most influential members for thirty years. L.-Philippe Picard, the MP from Bellechase, presented an amendment to the government Conscription Bill declaring the House's opposition to overseas service. He reviewed the opposition to conscription in the history of Canada and pointed out that in Great Britain, Northern Ireland, Australia, New Zealand and South Africa there was no overseas conscription. His amendment was seconded by a veteran of the First and the Second World Wars and a representative of Western Canada, Walter Tucker, who criticized the Conservatives for "wrapping the flag around themselves" and for reneging on their promises of 1940.[17] Tucker also pointed out that anti-conscription riots

---

16   Serge-Marc Durflinge, *"Bagarres entre militaires et "Zoot suiters" survenues à Montréal et à Verdun en juin,* 1944; *Problème de langue, de relations entre civils et militaires ou de rébellion juvénile?" Le 4e colloque en histoire militaire, Université de Québec à Montréal; le 7–8 novembre,* 1997.
      See also Daniel Byers; "Canada's Zombies; A Portrait of Canadian Conscripts and their Experience during the Second World War"; *Le 4e Colloque en Histoire militaire, novembre* 7–8 1997.

17   Commons Debates, November 29, 1944, cited in Wade, p. 1051.

had occurred in Vancouver, and were certainly not due to French-Canadian agitation. Cardin supported the amendment and declared, "Where are your concessions, you British Canadians, in favour of the French Canadians? What have you ever done to preserve the unity between the two great races of Canada? Unity has been maintained owing to concessions made by French Canadians."[18] The speaker ruled the amendment out of order. The *Bloc Populaire* held a meeting in the Saint-Jacques Market in Montreal on November 29. André Laurendeau and Jean Drapeau spoke of separation as the reply to conscription. For his part, Duplessis declined to convene the Legislative Assembly, in order to avoid giving the nationalists a forum, but as a compromise sent a telegram to Ottawa protesting King's decision.

At this time, Senator Bouchard and his secretary Maurice d'Hont were still travelling through the West. In Winnipeg, before the Empire Club on December 1, 1944, Bouchard admitted for the first time that if he had known how politically disastrous his words would be, he would have delayed his speech until after his death. Stubbornly, he then qualified this statement with the thought that he had felt a duty to persist. "I have even been accused of being mentally ill by a politician whom I have helped a great deal," he reported. He was referring to Godbout's reaction to his allegations about the OJC. His former leader had opined, "If Senator Bouchard has really said that, we should have pity for him, and wish him a return to health."[19]

The train continued its trip, transporting the senator and his secretary to Calgary, Victoria and Vancouver. D'Hont, while recognising his boss's faults, respected him for his courage; and as did the journalists of *Le Clairon*, d'Hont admired him for his frank, constructive criticism and his insistence on hard work for himself and his colleagues. Moreover, d'Hont found Bouchard incapable of malice and never impolite nor disagreeable. This constitutes a remarkable testimony from a young man keeping very long hours with his boss. What d'Hont disliked most about the senator, however, was his lack of table manners and his choice of card-playing companions on the train—two men "of humble origin." D'Hont found Bouchard's most difficult characteristic to be his persistence. "Sometimes you thought that you had convinced him; he seemed to have given in, but at the next meeting he came back with the same arguments and soon he

---

18   Ibid.

19   T.-D.B., *Fonds* Bouchard; ANQ, P-10/2, December 10, 1944.

would win his point by the exhaustion of others who had become too tired to argue with him."[20]

When they were apart on this occasion, as on all trips, T.-D. remained in contact with Cécile-Ena by telegram or, when feasible, by telephone. He was becoming increasingly dependent upon his daughter. Although still in the army, she was his hostess at evenings in Saint-Hyacinthe, at the Windsor Hotel in Montreal, or when he travelled to Ottawa for a dinner in the parliamentary restaurant at the Chateau Laurier. It was not easy to be the only child of T.-D. Bouchard, especially considering that the two shared the same stubborn character. Nevertheless, he did not dominate her completely. She never married. Daddy was always critical of prospective husbands.[21] At one time, an engagement was announced, but it fizzled out and was not mentioned again.[22] Cécile-Ena received recognition for her activities during the war. Her friend the Lieutenant-Governor of Quebec, Sir Eugène Fiset presented her with Membership of the British Empire, (MBE).

In the Montreal mayorality election of December 11, 1944, Adhémar Raynault, an old member of the ALN, opposed Camillien Houde, who had just returned from prison. Houde was elected. It is ironic that Raynault, a nationalist, attributed his defeat to what he perceived was a whisper campaign on the part of Houde's activists accusing him of being a member of the Order of Jacques Cartier (and a Freemason to boot), and that this caused him considerable harm.[23]

On his return to power, Duplessis demonstrated his vindictive and authoritarian nature.[24] He annulled the hotel and alcohol license permits of one of Bouchard's cousins, who rented his premises from T.-D.[25] This act deprived

---

20   M. d'Hont, personal communication to Chisholm, pp. 193–194.

21   Jacques and Judge Marcel Nichols, personal communication.

22   Ibid.

23   Adhémar Raynault; *Témoin d'une époque*. Éditions du jour, Montréal, 1970; pp. 174–179.

24   As Attorney General, "The Chief" used his absolute power to cancel licences permitting the sale of alcohol by "enemies." Frank Roncarelli, a Jehovah's Witness, took Duplessis to court for cancellation of his liquor license. Many years later Roncarelli obtained justice from the Supreme Court of Canada and Duplessis personally had to pay a large sum of money. Roncarelli's lawyer had been the eminent professor and poet Frank Scott.

25   Laferté reports meeting four citizens of Saint-Hyacinthe in October of 1944 who were indignant at Duplessis's action. They said that both Liberals and Conservatives were outraged that Duplessis's vengeance went so far as to cancel a liquor license of one particular person because she was related to Bouchard. p. 238.

Bouchard of eight thousand dollars a year in rent. Nor was this the first time that Duplessis had revoked the license of one of Bouchard's tenants. The first occasion had been in 1936 and involved the widow of Bouchard's election campaign manager. In order to relieve the widow of her debt, Bouchard had repurchased her lease. Bouchard commented on the new premier's tactic:

> It is certain that I will suffer great financial loss from this act of brutal vengeance. But if people think that I will renounce speaking my mind by using such low means, such people are sadly mistaken. Citizens will find it strange … that one can seize goods without a court order. This incident is another proof of the urgent need to denounce these devious methods, which have brought about the reign of terror under which we suffer.[26]

Just as he had refused to submit to attacks in the Assembly between 1936 and 1939, T.-D. Bouchard again refused to bow down to Duplessis's jibes. He defended himself vigorously. But his self-esteem was strongly affected. As with many self-made men, he felt himself judged in part by the amount of money that he earned. He had lost his lucrative position as president of Hydro-Quebec, and he lost money from the cancellations of newspaper subscriptions stemming from the cardinal's condemnation. He was not poor, having invested well. In spite of financial setbacks, he retained a chauffeur to drive him from Saint-Hyacinthe to his office in Montreal, near the corner of Guy and Ste. Catherine Streets. From his office he often walked the few blocks to lunch or dinner at the Mount Stephen Club, on the corner of Drummond and Burnside (now de Maisonneuve) Streets. While strolling between the two, he would often catch sight of old friends slipping into stores in order to avoid him.[27] Apropos of this, Bouchard said to Jean-Louis Gagnon, "Everything is allowed in love and war. I think that it is necessary to add, in politics!"[28]

In Saint-Hyacinthe, a clerical leader and former alderman, Victor Sylvestre, replaced Bouchard as mayor for one year. Hardly having been sworn in, he was arrested for perjury. He pleaded guilty and sentenced to pay a nominal fine, which aroused popular indignation. After the new mayor's resignation, a Bouchard supporter, Ernest-O. Picard, replaced him, obtaining the largest majority ever

---

26   *The Montreal Gazette,* October 14, 1944.

27   M. d'Hont, personal communication to Chisholm, p.189.

28   Gagnon, personal communication to Chisholm, p. 189.

gained until then in a municipal election. A month later, five of Bouchard's faction were elected aldermen. On May 11 Mackenzie King achieved a great federal victory, especially in Quebec: the Liberal Party elected 127 members, against 67 Conservatives and 28 CCF (The Co-operative Commonwealth Federation was a social-democratic party, and was precursor of the New Democratic Party). The *Bloc Populaire* collapsed, having only two anti-war candidates elected. Following his western tour, Bouchard spoke in his native city before a crowd of friends who had come together to show their support and approval. He discussed his successor as mayor, Sylvestre, contrasting his performance with Bouchard's own efficient economic management of the city's affairs, as well as his personal integrity.[29] In spite of his loss of power he retained many friends in Quebec and across Canada, where he had become a hero.

With the spring came the good news of Allied successes. The death of Roosevelt in April was mourned everywhere in the world. In San Francisco the allies united to form the United Nations. Later, Mussolini was executed, and the death of Hitler was announced. On May 8, 1945, victory was declared in Europe. In Quebec, as in the rest of Canada, wild jubilation reigned. Only *Le Devoir* declared that the victory was illusory and, with some perspicacity, warned of the danger of Communism, which was beginning to take hold in Eastern Europe. *Le Clairon* published this headline: "A Celebration For Peace."[30] During a Liberal meeting, Bouchard praised King's understanding attitude and delicate manner in easing tensions during the war. He reminded the audience that his own attitude on conscription had been entirely consistent: "I have never changed my opinion.… During my western tour, at the height of the crisis on the question of sending sixty thousand men overseas, T.-D. Bouchard did not fear to speak against conscription—not only in Montreal and Saint-Hyacinthe; but also in Winnipeg, in Regina, in Vancouver and all the cities of the west."[31]

In order to promote better understanding between the various peoples residing in Canada, in 1945 Bouchard founded the Canadian Unity Alliance, this time for all Canadians—unlike its sister association the Democratic Institute, which was limited to French Canadians. In July of 1945, Cécile-Ena, released from the army, and made a westward tour to promote the Alliance, visiting all

---

29   *Le Clairon, 2 février* 1945.

30   *Le Clairon, 8 mai* 1945.

31   Ibid., 11 *mai* 1945.

the main cities. The secretary of the new association, Maurice d'Hont—always efficient, intelligent and loyal—had made the arrangements. He spoke and wrote English fluently, and edited out most of the errors in Bouchard's speeches. Bouchard received the support of the Montreal financial community for the Canadian Unity Alliance. One representative of this group, J. B. MacDougald, wrote, "You certainly are indefatigable in your almost one-man crusade against the virus which has been and is still being fostered in this province to its detriment."[32]

The atomic bombs fell on Hiroshima on August 6 and on Nagasaki on August 9, 1945. Six days later Japan surrendered, and the Second World War ended. That same day, Marshal Pétain, leader of Vichy France, was condemned to death for collaboration. General de Gaulle later commuted his sentence to lifetime imprisonment. Pierre Laval, the Vichy Prime Minister (whom Bouchard called "another hero of our hooded ones,"[33]) was executed for collaboration with the enemy. Among those who spoke on the radio to the citizens of the old France to salute their new liberty, was Senator Télesphore-Damien Bouchard, still not forgotten.[34]

In late 1945 the Liberals celebrated the fifty-third birthday of Adélard Godbout with a huge banquet. Far from being excluded from this celebration, T.-D. Bouchard received a personal letter from the secretary insisting that he take part in what the senator deemed to be "a political picnic." Thus, the man unceremoniously dismissed sixteen months previously, attended without bitterness, along with Prime Minister King and the Federal Justice Minister, St. Laurent. "Thus the old *rouges* had not abandoned me," Bouchard recalls, "Only some rare Liberals saturated with clericalism were surprised by my presence at this meeting of party leaders. Was I not right to face the storm?"[35]

Bouchard returned the favour by inviting Godbout to be the guest of honour at an oyster-fest hosted by the Liberals of Saint-Hyacinthe. It was important not to nurture personal bitterness. He took his dismissal with much dignity and equanimity. Senator Bouchard delivered his second speech to the Upper

---

32   *Fonds* T.-D. B, ANQ, 115 P-10/3. Letter October 11, 1945.

33   T.-D.B., *Mémoires,* III, p.186. See also *Le Clairon,* 24 *avril* 1942 where Bouchard calls Laval *un homme sinistre, le* Quisling *français.*

34   *Le Clairon,* 13 *aôut* 1945.

35   T.-D.B., *Mémoires,* III, p. 187.

Chamber in October of 1945. As always, his address was well-prepared and too long. He denounced corporatism and socialism, and compared the Duplessis regime to that of Salazar in Portugal. He did not mention the Order of Jacques Cartier. The Democratic Institute continued to offer to the Montreal public lecturers chosen "of preference from among Catholic orators so as to not provide material for criticism from the reactionaries."[36] One of the invitees was the Catholic labour leader from France, Paul Vignault, who expounded upon the dangers of clerical interference in political affairs. He quoted the words of Monsignor Saliège, Archbishop of Toulouse, recently appointed cardinal and who was a representative of the left-wing Catholic movement in France:

> The future of the Christian spirit is at risk at this moment.... Since the fall of the Roman Empire, Catholics have not had a greater mission than the salvation of the world, not by clericalism which the Church disapproves and which we do not want at any price, but the salvation of the world by the Cross of Jesus Christ.[37]

In 1941, the same prelate had expressed his ideas in another way, but in a clear Gallican and anti-ultramontane manner: "For us, totalitarianism and clericalism signify the same error, the same confusion. Render unto God what is God's and unto Caesar what is Caesar's. The two powers, temporal and spiritual, are distinct. Each has its rights and its duties. To confuse them would be a suffocation, an oppression, a regression of 2,000 years."[38] As an indication of the new wave of broad-mindedness in the province of Quebec, *Aujourd'hui*, a monthly Jesuit review reproduced this speech. In addition, Father Gaudreault, the Provincial of the Dominican Order, wrote a critical article on the Popular Social School (*l'École Sociale Populaire*), generally an anti-liberal religious group. In this pamphlet—which had been approved by the Archbishop of Montreal, Monsignor Charbonneau—Gaudreault defended Father G. H. Lévesque, dean of the Social Science Faculty of Laval University. Levesque had been the object of criticism by the *École Sociale Populaire* in the past for supporting non-confessionality in the co-operative movement. Gaudreault severely condemned the language and exaggeration in the writings of those who wanted to exclude non-Catholics from social, commercial, and economic fields. Finally, in a pub-

---

36 Ibid., p. 188.

37 Ibid., p. 188.

38 Ibid., p. 188.

lic conference at the Democratic Institute, Lucien Parizeau gave a talk entitled "The Tyranny of Myths," in which he attacked Groulx's promotion of the legend spread about Dollard Désormeaux being a hero of French Canada. While praising Désormeaux's courage when he defended himself and his band against forces superior to his, Parizeau established the reality. At the head of sixteen youths of Ville Marie (Montreal) and a handful of Hurons, Désormeaux had ambushed some Iroquois returning from a hunt, in order to rob them of their furs. However, the Iroquois, numbering two hundred, defended themselves and massacred the French. Thus, he condemned the creation of myths not based on the true history.[39]

The Democratic Institute was very active in 1945–46. Lectures were given in the auditorium of the High School of Montreal, and in the Windsor Hotel. The talks were on various subjects. J.-C. Harvey spoke on May 9, 1945. His address was entitled, *La peur* ("Fear"), published in *Feuilles Démocratiques*.[40] Fifteen years before the publication of Brother Anonymous's famous letters in *Le Devoir*, and then his book *Les insolences du Frère Untel*, Harvey exposed the dominant element of fear among the French-Canadian people—a fear that resulted in the suffocation of "so many of our liberties." J. P. Desbiens (Brother Anonymous) would write about the lamentable state of education in the province of Quebec, the universal usage of "joual"—the garbled pronunciation and grammar of the French language in the province—and the harmful effect of the patron saint of

---

39   Lucien Parizeau. *La tyrannie des mythes. Feuilles Démocratiques* I. 9. 1946, p.2.

40   The Democratic Institute continued its activities with conferences on teaching by Prof. André Morize from Harvard University, who asserted among other things that all those who know only one language are like semi-blind people advancing in life with a single eye. He presented a humanistic speech, pushing for reforms in the teaching of literature that tended to develop a critical spirit in youth. The *Feuilles Démocratiques*, the organ of the Institute Démocratique, continued in publication for two years (1945–47) with articles, often by Senator Bouchard and by Charles-E Holmes, on the question of a national flag; "The Great Pity of Rural Education" by Gilbert Larue; "Religion, Must it Divide Us" by the Reverend Claude de Mestral; "The Separatism of Mr. Anatole Vanier" by André Fallières; an open letter from T.-D. Bouchard to "My Friend Mr. Chaloult" in which he explained the difference between anti-clerical belief and the belief in the Catholic religion, and between patriotism and ultra-nationalism; "Bilingualism: A World Problem" by Prof. John Huges; "Democracy and Canadian Opinion" by Abbé Arthur Maheux; "Antisemitism in Canada" by Peter I. Browne; "The Science of Man to the Atomic Age" by Dr. J.S. Anseleme Bois; and "The Tyranny of Myths" by Lucien Parizeau already quoted.

Quebec, "Notre Dame de la Trouille" (Our Lady of Being Scared to Death). Harvey asserted:

> What do we fear? Well, we fear the supreme power, the power about which you are thinking at this time and that no one of you dares to name. The lone power that, in this part of Canada, causes everyone to tremble. It is clerical power.... Weigh well my words: *it is not precisely religion, not even the Church, before which it is necessary to bend. No, I speak of clerical power....* To live in fear is to live without liberty.... When a government adopts bad laws, sometimes absurd, in the sole goal of pleasing clerical power, it is not free, it is fearful.... When a physician, an attorney, a notary, a manufacturer, a merchant, or any other whose means of livelihood depend on the French Catholic population, never publicly reveal their thoughts, never show their liberal spirit in the light of day, they are not free, they have fear.... This has nothing to do with religion itself, nor with morals ... it is for this reason ... that so many of our liberties are smothered. When peoples believe they are threatened by the loss of a situation, a job, or a clientele; or under the threat of a systematic boycott or a campaign of general defamation each time that their views are not accepted in high places ... it is not difficult to understand the instinct of self-preservation.[41] (Emphasis added.)

Harvey underscored that from birth until their mid-twenties, with rare exceptions, French Canadians undergo a clerical "bewitchment." "The generous illusions and the disinterestedness of youth have been channelled," he declared, "so that they serve as ghosts, and contribute to maintain the people in a state of old age: in the myths of superstition and the cult of racist prejudices." As for the teaching of history, he stated:

> The masters of teaching and false historians such as Groulx have made an incredible effort to inspire this youth with depressing and harmful fanaticism, to parade it ceaselessly in the cemetery of history and dead ideas, to maintain it in a dominating oppression as

---

41   J.-C. Harvey; *La peur,* Conference given May 9, 1945 in the Auditorium of the High School of Montreal, under the auspices of the Democratic Institute of Canada, reproduced in *Feuilles Démocratiques,* Vol. 1945, I, no.1, p. 2.

totalitarian from the point of view of the mind as does any Nazi or
Fascist power.[42]

Harvey ended his speech by quoting from Roosevelt, who had placed
the Freedom from Fear in fourth position among the fundamental liberties
listed in the Atlantic Charter. He repeated the American president's famous
Depression-era phrase, "We have nothing to fear but fear itself!" He counseled
his compatriots to take risks. Joy in living, he said, does not consist in obeying
our worst instincts. There is infinitely more happiness in doing good than in
doing evil. Evidently, though, Harvey, his friend Senator Bouchard and Abbé
Maheux suffered much for speaking so forthrightly.

Archbishop Charbonneau of Montreal also learned, to his chagrin, that it
was not wise to support causes displeasing to the occult powers. He actively
supported the strikers of the Asbestos Company in 1949. Charbonneau was
not among Duplessis's favourites because of his independence and his support
of poor people and the unemployed. Indeed, he is reputed to have thrown
Duplessis out of the Episcopal Palace on one occasion.[43] He accepted invitations from Irish ecclesiastical authorities, putting himself at odds with some
of the ultramontane bishops. He expressed the wish to be the representative
not only of French-speaking Catholics, but of all Montrealers. To the horror of
the other bishops, he advocated the admission of non-Catholics to unions and
co-operatives, as had Abbé Maheux. Charbonneau formulated a new charter
for the University of Montreal that would give more importance in the administration to lay members—unacceptable to Duplessis and several ultramontane
bishops. He reorganized several departments, and introduced a Department of
Psychology, which included the study of psychoanalysis.

Charbonneau advocated better education for French Canadians, and supported the law introduced by Godbout requiring compulsory education
then ignored by Duplessis upon his return to power in 1944. Through two
complicated trusts, the Archbishop bought *Le Devoir*, enlisting the vigorous
anti-Duplessists Gérard Filion, André Laurendeau and Antonio and Jacques
Perrault to serve on the editorial board—a frankly hostile gesture. For all these

---

42   Ibid., p. 8.

43   Renaude Lapointe; *L'Histoire Bouleversante de Msgr. Charbonneau* (Montréal: Éditions du
     Jour. 1962). See also Hector Laferté, *Derrière le trône, Mémoires d'un parlementaire québécois
     1936–1958*, (Sillery: Les Éditions Septentrions, 1998, p. 332–325).

reasons, Maurice Duplessis became a bitter enemy of Charbonneau. Moreover, the Archbishop of Rimouski, the ultramontane Msgr. Georges Courchesne, collected a list of charges against Charbonneau, a list that he presented in person in Rome. It is apparently true that Charbonneau was a poor administrator, often leaving letters unanswered. He also seemed to have aroused the hostility of the papal delegate of Rome in Ottawa, Monsignor Antoniutti, who found his frankness unpleasant. Duplessis threatened to stop the granting of funds to the diocese of Montreal if Charbonneau was not dismissed. He sent two ministers to Rome to have him fired. Charbonneau did not suspect the power of his enemies. The result was indeed his dismissal. The Pope ordered Charbonneau to resign or to accept an apostolic administration, which would have had him play merely a decorative role. In spite of his protests, it was too late. He did not see this coming and neglected to find friends in Rome. Charbonneau was banished to Victoria, BC. He clandestinely boarded an airplane at dawn with two suitcases and seventy dollars in his pocket. Because of his popularity, the authorities announced his resignation and departure only a week later. In his book *O' Canada*, Edmund Wilson, an eminent American literary critic, suggests that the conflict between Charbonneau and the Chief (Duplessis) was so dramatic that it should provide the theme for a theatrical play.[44] And indeed, *Charbonneau et le chef* was staged some years later.[45]

The list of those labeled and punished as enemies of the Church is long. As Guibord was banished from the Catholic cemetery in the late nineteenth century for belonging to the Institut Canadien, so too was Louis-Antoine Dessaulles, an anti-clerical and Liberal seigneur, banished to Belgium and Paris. Bouchard suffered for his frankness and was kept from advancement by Gouin and Taschereau, then fired by Godbout after his speech in the Senate. Jean-Charles Harvey had suffered because of his 1936 book *Les demi-civilisées*. Abbé Maheux and Father G. H. Lévesque were persecuted at Laval University; and then there was Archbishop Charbonneau. Even in 1960 the forces of narrow-mindedness

---

44   Edmund Wilson, *O' Canada*, p. 197.

45   *Charbonneau et le chef,* a historical drama in two acts by John Thomas McDonough adapted by Paul Hebert and Pierre Morency, premiered at the Theatre du Trident, March 1971, directed by Hébert. It was revived at the Trident in May 1972, and was performed with Duceppe and Lemieux at Compagnie Jean Duceppe, November 1973. It subsequently toured, including to the National Arts Centre, and premiered in English at the Siadye Bronfman Centre in April of 1975.

were still powerful enough to chastise Brother Anonymous, Jean-Paul Desbiens. He was banished to Rome to engage in theological studies. His superior Jacques Tremblay, who had encouraged him to publish his *Insolences,* was banished to Europe. The Marist Order subjected the two Brothers to intense pressure to resign. Senator Jacques Hébert, in a preface to Desbien's book, recounts the efforts of the Marist Order's superior to suppress its publication after it had already gone to press. In short, even while celebrating the new liberalism, it is necessary to take note of the obvious power still retained by the ultramontanes right up to the 1960s.[46]

The days of the Democratic Institute were numbered. Founded during the war in 1943 with the support of the leftists, the alliance between them and the Liberals began to unravel in the atmosphere of the Cold War. Several Liberal leaders left the Institute. The party itself decided to put an end to its collaboration, as demonstrated by the resignation of Jean-Louis Gagnon, honorary secretary of the Institute, who had become the chief organizer of the Liberal Party. D'Hont reported to Bouchard that Gagnon had tried to induce him to resign as well, and thereby precipitate the end of the Institute.[47] In spite of these resignations, with the help of the loyal d'Hont a meeting was held to fill the vacant positions.

In June of 1946, *Le Jour* of Jean-Charles Harvey closed down. In an effort to replace it Bouchard founded *Le Clairon-Montréal.* He had the help of the respected intellectuals Charles Hamel as political editor, and his friend the writer Claude-Henri Grignon, mayor of Ste.-Adèle, as literary editor. In 1950, the newspaper's name became the *Le Haut-Parleur* (*The Loudspeaker*). On the philanthropic level, Senator Bouchard was active in promoting the establishment of the Foyer Dieppe, a lodging-house for epileptic patients, named in memory of the son of its financial backer, Georges Savoy of Saint-Jean d'Iberville, a philanthropist and vice-president of the Democratic Institute. Paul Savoy had died in the raid on Dieppe in 1942. The Foyer had no denominational character

---

46 *Fonds* T.-D.B., ANQ, P-10/2. To demonstrate that provincialism and narrow-mindedness were still omnipresent, there is an anonymous letter in the ANQ *Fonds* Bouchard, reporting in the 1950s that the St. Joseph Hospital of Trois-Rivières refused the donation of an iron lung, an orthopedic table and an anaesthetic machine because they were donated by the local Kiwanis and Rotary clubs (Protestants). This occurred during the polio epidemics of that period.

47 *Fonds* Bouchard, ANQ 10/2, February 2, 1946.

and accepted handicapped people of all races and religions. Among its officers were Dr. Baruch Silverman of the Department of Psychiatry of McGill
University and Dr. C. M. Hincks of the National Committee of Mental Health
in Toronto. Despite the opposition of the clericals who accused Savoy of being a
poor Catholic, the lodging-house was opened on November 11, 1946. Abbé E.
Galtier addressed a letter to his friend Savoy:

> As for the accusation … that you are not a good Catholic—it makes
> me laugh. There are people who truly believe that one is a good
> Catholic only if one can produce proof of confession and devotion.
> Poor people who judge others by their own narrow petty measure …
> Christ does not judge those who claim to represent him and speak in
> his name…. The first quality of a good Christian is charity.[48]

Always generous, Senator Bouchard contributed even to the needs of
his enemies. During a collection to save *Le Devoir* he donated $100. In
December of 1946 he sent a check to a friend, a priest in Saskatchewan, and
another to a priest in Saint-Hyacinthe, to reserve a place at the Midnight
Mass in the Cathedral at New Year for himself.[49]

In 1946, he defended his causes with the help of Conrad Langlois, one
of the lecturers at the Institute. To demonstrate the narrow-mindedness of
the nationalists, on August 3, 1946, Langlois sent a memo to Bouchard
quoting extracts from *Relations*, the Jesuit monthly review, which accused
the French, of France of upsetting Quebec's school system by establishing
Stanislas and Marie-de-France Colleges, both based on France's curriculum.
"We discover," the article proclaimed, "French officials in the act of infiltrating…. The precautions taken by our authorities in allowing Stanislas to
establish itself here are justified and the distrust warranted."[50] In June of
1947, Cardinal Gerlier, the French Primate, presided over the distribution
of prizes at Stanislas College. He expressed a wish for increasingly closer
ties between the France of yonder and the France of here. But, he asked,
what "incited spirits misled by chauvinism to protest on all rooftops that

---

48   T.-D.B., *Mémoires*, III, p. 185.

49   ANQ *Fonds* Bouchard, P-10/42.

50   Honoré Bettez, " Les révélations du rapport Abadie," *Relations*, Montréal, aôut, 1946, pp.
      231–232.

the French high school was a den of dissolution and hell? Can one find a stupider, more dishonest and more disconcerting statement?"[51]

In order to please the clericals, the Duplessis government proposed a law to co-ordinate teaching in the province under the direction of the Church. The law extended the jurisdiction of the Council of Public Education to all teaching in technical schools, arts and trades schools, agricultural schools, furniture schools, the graphic art school, *l'École de Beaux Arts*, as well as the *École des haut etude commerciales*. The law was later modified, leaving the *École de beaux Arts* of Montreal and Quebec under the jurisdiction of the Provincial Secretary. In the Legislative Council, Sir Thomas Chapais then successfully proposed an amendment also leaving the *École des haut etude commerciales* under the Provincial Secretary's jurisdiction.

Senator Bouchard was not at all demoralized, and remained very active on the public scene. He gave a pan-Canadian speech under the auspices of the Canadian Broadcasting Corporation, in both official languages, stimulating a good deal of correspondence. He also continued his attachment to the Canadian Unity Alliance. Federal Conservative leader Arthur Meighen joined the Alliance and gave him a list of names of other possible supporters.[52] Bouchard was the popular Honorary Colonel of the Saint-Hyacinthe Regiment. One day he had to choose between a press conference and a speech to the Young Liberals of Canada.[53] He spoke in English for the women of the Outremont Club during the winter, and corresponded with Cécile's friend, the world-renowned Sino-American author Lin Yutang. Bouchard sent Lin Yutang a copy of the first chapter of his memoirs in English, entitled, "Early Struggles." On a trip to France and England, Cécile met Lord Beaverbrook during an evening at the High Commissioner of Canada's residence in London. He said to her: "He is quite a man, your father."[54]

In October of 1947, at the age of sixty-five, Télesphore-Damien Bouchard suddenly had his first stroke. This resulted in a slowing of his activities, but did not put a stop to them. He won a suit brought against

---

51   T.-D.B., *Mémoires,* III, p. 205.

52   *Fonds* Bouchard ANQ, P-10/2, January 9, 1947.

53   Ibid., January 24, 1947.

54   Cécile-Ena B., personal communication to Chisholm, p. 203.

him by a citizen of Saint-Hyacinthe whom he had named as a member in the Order of Jacques Cartier. The judge found that no damage had resulted to the plaintiff's reputation or to his commercial activity as a coal merchant. Bouchard telegraphed Premier Duplessis, who had accused him once again in Chambers, this time of having profited from the purchase of a Cadillac from the Department of Roads when he was minister. "I invite you to repeat these accusations outside Chambers," was his challenge.[55]

Gérard Filion, publisher of *Le Devoir* and later named by Harvey as a member of the OJC, (which he denied), wrote an article appearing on November 8, 1947, defending the independence of his newspaper. He stated that he was neither for nor against Duplessis, and quoted a variation of a classic expression: "I call a cat a cat and Bouchard a rogue." Against the advice of his attorney, Bouchard sued Filion for $10,000. Knowing T.-D. Bouchard, he continued, "If you decide to take action, let me know when."[56] Filion's lawyer argued that no one could prove that he was the Bouchard named by Filion. Some years later, Bouchard was awarded $200. The judge found that there was no malice, and that the article had been written without the intention of causing injury. Interviewed later by Elspeth Chisholm, Filion—by then president of Marine Industries Ltd.—asserted that to defend himself he had said that since there were so many Bouchards in the province, nobody could say that he was referring to the senator. Nevertheless:

> Bouchard brought three of his employees to court to assert that when they read the phrase in the newspaper that Bouchard was a thief, they immediately thought of their boss. It was a good joke. I had to pay the fine, but I have to tell you that some months later when *Le Devoir* was broke ... I received a check of $100 from T.-D. Bouchard. He was this type of person; he fought with everyone; but he was decent. He did things in private, which he would not do in public.[57]

Bouchard made this gesture despite growing concerns about money. It was, after all, before Medicare. The cost of his illness—hospital stays,

---

55   *The Montreal Star,* March 19, 1948.

56   *Fonds* Bouchard ANQ, P-10/1, November 8 and 11, 1947.

57   Gerard Filion, personal communication to Chisholm, p. 205.

nurses, and his domestic servants—began to mount. In Saint-Hyacinthe he maintained a small team of servants, including a chauffeur. When in Ottawa, Cécile-Ena helped to push him to Senate in a wheelchair so that he would be present at the number of sessions required to receive his salary. He sought without success employment with the *Ottawa Citizen* as author of a regular column. The publisher, H. H. Southam, wrote that he regretted his negative decision, but since half his readers were Catholic it would be imprudent to have contentious articles written weekly by "Teddy" Bouchard. Moreover, Southam refused to consider the publication of his memoirs.[58]

With his usual energy, in 1948 he organized a committee of prominent citizens, starting with members of the Institute and the Alliance, to erect a monument dedicated to the memory of the province's most illustrious son, Sir Wilfrid Laurier, who had been Bouchard's own political idol throughout his whole career. Thirty years after Laurier's death there was no monument in Quebec, although there was a statue outside the East Block of Parliament in Ottawa. This was the last campaign of subscriptions that Bouchard organized. Before his final physical deterioration, with the assistance of Maurice d'Hont, this robust man worked intensively to collect money for this patriotic project. At the end of four weeks, they had collected the required sum. They asked the Montreal sculptor Émile Brunet, who was then residing in Paris, to create two copies of a large statue of the first French-Canadian Prime Minister of Canada—one for Dominion Square in Montreal, and the other for Quebec City. Émile Brunet had sculpted the existing statue of Laurier in Ottawa. He was also the creator of a bust Bouchard's father Damien Bouchard, and of the tombstone of Blanche-Corona Cusson Bouchard. The bust of Damien had been commissioned to commemorate his activity in the union and was titled "Pioneer of the Emergent Working Class, 1854–1912." Damien's statue stood on its pedestal across from Bouchard's house on Girouard Boulevard, but when the house was sold it was moved to the cemetery. It later disappeared without a trace. Brunet's tombstone dedicated to Blanche-Corona is still present in the cemetery of Saint-Hyacinthe, over the graves of Senator and Mrs. T.-D. Bouchard, Father J. A. Brousseau and Cécile-Ena Bouchard. It is still a beautiful sculpture.

---

58   *Fonds* Bouchard ANQ, P-10/1, February 5, 1948.

**The statue of Damien Bouchard,
"Pioneer of the emergent working class," which has disappeared.**

During the summer of 1948 Bouchard was again the victim of a stroke, which left him blind for some weeks. He asked Cécile-Ena to summon a priest, "in case something happens to me; I am born Catholic and I die Catholic."[59] In the end he recovered, although he would lose a lot of weight in the following years. He regained his strength by attacking Canon Groulx, who had just delivered a lecture full of demagoguery, deprecating the Canadian Confederation. Until then, the Tricolor of France and the Union Jack of Great Britain were flown at public occasions, representing the two countries of Canada's origin. Everywhere in Quebec during first half of the century, the Tricolor had fluttered during celebrations as a sign of the attachment of French Canadians to France. King appointed a committee to study a proposal for a national flag. Quebec nationalists rejected the suggestion of the committee because the proposed flag included both the Union Jack and the Tricolor. Canon Groulx favoured an exclusively Quebec flag—a blue flag with a white cross and the lily of France at the corners (as we have noted, a

59   C.-E.B., personal communication.

design of the Order of Jacques Cartier), the exact reproduction of the standard of pre-Revolutionary France. Bouchard remarked, "It had been found in the royal storage shelves of Louis XIV."[60]

Bouchard believed that a truly Canadian flag would facilitate a better understanding between the founding races, reminding citizens that they were all citizens of the same country despite their different origins. He inveighed against the Duplessis government, which adopted a slightly modified version of the white lily flag. He noted, "[The flag is] a real challenge to English-speaking Canadians who live on the banks of the Saint Lawrence. This flag is and will remain a bone of contention because it symbolizes the domination of the Catholic majority over the minority."[61] Bouchard found it ironic that the OJC and Groulx promoted the adoption of this flag—"the ideal of a middle-age mentality"—even though the canon had neglected to inform the people that this flag was, in fact, the standard that the Huguenots had brought to New France. (See citation from *L'Emerillon*, Chapter 10.)

Bouchard was present during the inaugurations of the statues of Sir Wilfrid Laurier in both Montreal and Quebec City. Before the ceremony in Quebec, he met Duplessis on Osborne Street. Duplessis greeted him, taking him fondly by the shoulders. "My dear old Tée-Dée" he exclaimed, "my old friend, my old enemy. How are you, old fighter?"[62] And on April 20, 1959, Bouchard sent a formal letter of congratulation to Duplessis on his sixty-ninth birthday, using the formal (*vous)* form of address and ending with the formal *Je me souscris, monsieur le Premier ministre, votre tout respectueux.* On April 23, Duplessis replied, paying tribute to an old enemy (and in the familiar *tu* form of address):

> Frankly, I do not understand the impersonal and ceremonious tone of your letter. We have been colleagues for a long time in the Assembly and even though I am completely convinced that I am in the right and you are in error, these differences of opinion have never prevented me from appreciating the sincerity of your errone-

60   T.-D.B., *Mémoires,* III, p. 207.

61   Ibid., p. 208.

62   C. Black; *Duplessis,* II p. 564.

ous passion, your incontestable talents, although poorly applied,
and your love of work, as you surely know. "[63]

Maurice Duplessis admired T.-D. Bouchard for his frankness, his belli-
cosity and his independent character more than some members of his own
party, whom he often treated with disdain. He admired Bouchard more than
did some Liberals, who were often embarrassed by these very same character
traits. Black writes: "But Duplessis saw in him a formidable and courageous
adversary, neither an aristocrat like Taschereau, nor a good-natured man
such as Godbout, nor a gentleman such as Marler, nor an opportunist such
as Lapalme. Bouchard and Duplessis recognized in each other their tough-
ness, their staying power, their follow-through and bold deeds, their political
instinct, determined to win."[64]

During the 1950s, Bouchard continued to attend sessions in Ottawa, and
directed his newspaper as well as the Yamaska Press. Jean-Charles Harvey
wrote a new novel, again with sexual scenes. As he found it difficult to find
a publisher, T.-D. offered the services of Yamaska Press. However, as a prud-
ish man of the nineteenth century, he asked Harvey to clean up the erotic,
"dirty" sections. Before this could be done sickness hit Bouchard again.[65]
Since Cécile-Ena had never had a sense for business and could not manage
the enterprise, he was forced to sell his newspaper *Le Haut-Parleur* in 1957,
and *Le Clairon* and the Yamaska Press in 1959. In 1957 he sold his home in
Saint-Hyacinthe for $50,000 and took up residence on Côte Ste. Catherine
Road in Montreal. He had accumulated debts amounting to $90,000, but
according to Cécile he managed to pay them off. The last years of his life
were very expensive, as he incurred huge costs for nurses who worked on
three eight-hour shifts.[66] For these reasons and because of old age, he became
suspicious and irascible even towards those who had served him well—such
as Maurice d'Hont, who eventually left him. When the former Abbé—now
Monsignor—Maheux visited him a few years before his death, he found him

---

63   Ibid., p. 565.

64   Ibid., p. 564.

65   It was published a few years later, *Les Paradis de Sable*. J.-C. Harvey.

66   Garde Gaudrault, personal communication.

sitting at his desk in the process of studying Russian and Esperanto. He confessed that he found the study of Russian difficult.[67]

Another adoptive son took d'Hont's place. This was Father Milot, who had been astounded one day to find T.-D. Bouchard among the people attending a Dominican retreat in Saint-Hyacinthe. As he wrote in the preface to the second volume of Bouchard's memoirs, Father Milot had met Father Brousseau on a train, where he learned of the esteem that the latter held for Bouchard. Father Milot and Doctor Segall were with T.-D. on the evening of his death, while Cécile-Ena was out. At 10:30 on the evening of November 13, 1962, the nurse called Doctor Segall to confirm Bouchard's death. He would have been eighty-one years of age on December 20. He had wanted so much to vote for the Liberals of Jean Lesage in the elections held the next day.

The population of the City of Saint-Hyacinthe and the province of Quebec, and the political elite of the entire country, expressed their tribute to Télesphore-Damien Bouchard. His body lay on view in his home on Côte des Neiges Road in Montreal, and then in the city hall of Saint-Hyacinthe for two days, where thousands of people passed before their mayor of twenty-five years. Accompanied by an impressive procession to the Church of Our Lady of the Rosary, where the funeral service was conducted, and then to the cemetery. Honorary pallbearers were Dr. Harold N. Segall, his physician and friend for over thirty years; Raoul Jobin, opera singer and friend; Georges Marler, representing the provincial government; Senator Cyrille Vaillancourt, president of the Caisse Populaire Federation of Quebec; Mtre. Philippe Pothier, representative of the city council of Saint-Hyacinthe; Senator J. E. Lefrançois; Mtre. Léon Mercier-Gouin; and Judge Victor Chabot. Bouchard's death was mourned throughout the province and across Canada.

It was an impressive funeral, attended by thousands and covered by all Quebec newspapers, which featured eloquent tributes. *La Presse* printed a front-page picture and a long obituary. It read in part: "A great figure of Canadian and Quebec politics, Senator T.-D. Bouchard, who was one of the most controversial people of his time, died yesterday at the age of 80."[68] The newspaper then reviewed his career and ended with the following tribute: "In Télesphore-Damien Bouchard, the province loses an extraordinary politician, to whom one can pay homage, as he never hid his fundamental positions in

---

67   Abbé Maheux, personal communication to Chisholm, p. 210.

68   *La Presse, 14 novembre* 1962.

order to avoid creating enemies." His death was also reported in the other major newspapers: *The Gazette, Le Soleil* and *The Montreal Star. The Gazette* noted: "He was one of the first advocates of publicly owned hydro-electric power during his 28 years in the Quebec Legislature, one of the main issues in today's Quebec provincial election. He also served as first president of the Quebec Hydro-Electric Commission. Senator Bouchard also supported changes in Quebec's educational system."[69] *The Montreal Star* noted that he had "served a long and distinguished career."[70] *La Voix de l'Est* splashed a photo of the funeral cortege on the front page: "The City of Saint-Hyacinthe paid an energetic and last homage to one of the most brilliant sons in its history."[71] It concluded by quoting the final tribute from *La Presse.* Of course, his death was also front-page news for *Le Clairon.*[72] "[He was] one of the most eminent Canadians and a precursor of the economic, social, and political liberation of the province of Quebec." Even *Le Devoir* reported his death on November 15 with a tribute to his campaign to nationalize hydroelectricity and his support for reforms in the educational system of Quebec.[73] *Le Devoir* praised his *activité débordante*—his exuberant enthusiasm for work: "In the morning, he was first to arrive in his office, and the last to leave." The city council of Chomedy, Quebec, passed a resolution at the end of 1962 approving the expenditure of $5,000 to erect a monument in his honour.[74]

He was buried in the family plot in the Saint-Hyacinthe cemetery beside his beloved Blanche-Corona and Abbé Brousseau, over which rose the beautiful sculpture by Émile Brunet.[75]

---

69   *The Gazette,* November 13, 1962.

70   *The Montreal Star,* November 14, 1962.

71   *La Voix de l'Est,* 20 *novembre* 1962.

72   *Le Clairon,* 24 *novembre* 1962.

73   *Le Devoir,* 15 *novembre* 1962. The article mistakenly claims that Bouchard became MLA at the age of twenty-three and that he took over the newly nationalized Montreal Light, Heat and Power Company as president in 1943.

74   *Le Clairon,* 24 *novembre* 1962. I have been unable to discover if the monument was ever built.

75   In 1987, Cécile-Ena was buried at this site. The author (FMG) and Dr. H.N. Segall attended her funeral.

St-Hyacinthe rend un dernier hommage au sénateur Télesphore-Damien Bouchard

The funeral procession of the Honourable Senator T.-D.
Bouchard. The honorary pallbearers were: Senator Léon-Mercier
Gouin, the Honourable George Marler, Richard Hyde,
Senator Eugène Lefrançois, Senator Cyrille Vaillancourt,
Raoul Jobin and Dr. Harold N. Segall.

Playing the piano and studying Russian in his retirement.

At Bouchard's eightieth birthday party and the launching of his
autobiography, *Mémoires*, 1961. Seated are Émile Bouchard,
T.-D. Bouchard and Msgr. Maheux.
Standing from right to left are Mr. Marina Doye,
Father Paul Trempe, Cécile-Ena Bouchard and Father Albert Milot.

At the same celebration. Standing: Father Milot;
Louis St. Laurent, former Prime Minister of Canada;
and Jean Lesage, premier of Quebec.

With friends Raoul Jobin—the celebrated Quebec
opera singer—and his wife.

CONCLUSION

For twenty years I fought to against the forces that threaten our existence more and more, without ever receiving the necessary support from the intelligentsia.... The Jewish minority ... expresses its opinion openly and underhandedly."[1]

The complaint of Dr. Philippe Hamel cited above expresses his deep disappointment that his ultramontane views had not prevailed in Quebec. In spite of the contradiction between "openly" and "underhandedly," the statement underscores the frustration of the xenophobic ultra-nationalist movement in attempting to control the destiny of Quebec. T.-D. Bouchard's life story describes his struggles, from early on in his career, with this "enemy." The fact that the majority of the French-Canadian people did not subscribe to the appeals of the ultra-nationalists at that time is stressed in Hamel's lament.

Télesphore-Damien Bouchard was a leading light trying to pull his fellow French Canadians towards the values of the radical *rouges* of the nineteenth century. He should be classed in the category of *rouges* that Fernande Roy noted: "that the flame of their views may have grown dimmer but it was never extinguished." Roy asks: "Was liberalism triumphant or dominant at the turn of the century? That remains to be seen, but in any case, liberalism was definitely an active force not confined to the fringe of ideological debate."[2] In the view of Conrad Langlois, a journalist who worked for Bouchard for five years, he was

---

1   Letter from Philippe Hamel to Dr. Pierre Jobidon, 22 *novembre* 1948, Rumilly, *HPQ* XXXIII, p. 124.

2   Fernande Roy, *Progrès, Harmonie, Liberté. Le libéralisme des milieux d'affaires francophones au tournant du siècle.* (Montréal: Boréal, 1988), p. 283. See also Fernande Roy, *Histoire des idéologies au Québec aux XIXe et XXe siècles,* (Montréal: Boréal Express, 1993) p. 45. "Did the defeat of the reds really mean the end of liberalism in Quebec? Of course not," and p. 115, "Liberal ideas had been present in Quebec society since the end of the eighteenth century. They became entrenched with time, into the next century, and became dominant in the twentieth century."

inwardly a timid and insecure person.[3] Cécile-Ena confirmed this view, attributing these traits to his working-class origin.[4] For this reason, he girded himself to attack vigorously and never to give quarter. He thus sometimes overreacted, harming his own political career. All those who evaluated his contribution agree that he was ahead of his time. In the words of Yves Michaud—who had been a teenaged apprentice, later editor, and then publisher of *Le Clairon*—Bouchard was an infuriating and provocative fighter, and an idealist. He was one of the most-discussed politicians of his day, and a great partisan of democratic reforms in French Canada.[5] Bouchard was certainly among the outstanding leaders of Quebec in the first half of the twentieth century—along with Gouin, Taschereau, Godbout and Duplessis. He had progressive ideas that he defended vigorously. He was in favour of abolishing the seigneurial annuity. He campaigned for compulsory and free education, bilingual education, freedom of expression, the municipalization and then the nationalization of electric power, and the municipal taxation of manufacturers and clerical institutions in his city. He was an early proponent of the vote for women. At the same time, he was against socialism. Privately, he would rant against union leaders and against paid holidays for his workers. He defended the rights of owners to reward ability and to fire the incompetent. He was the author of the improved Quebec Worker Accident Compensation Act of 1935. He was also a staunch proponent of closed bids for government public works, and a fierce opponent of patronage.

Of course, as Ralph Heintzman has pointed out, patronage was a way for French Canadians, frustrated by the lack of advancement in large English-controlled industrial and financial institutions, to obtain employment.[6] "Economic needs encouraged *Québécois* to exploit the political process for advancement."[7] Unemployment had been evident throughout the nineteenth and twentieth centuries. Louis-Hippolyte LaFontaine had established a pattern of patronage appointments for the next century.[8] "The sudden opening of the entire range of government jobs

3   Conrad Langlois; *Le T.-D. Bouchard que J'ai connu*; La Patrie, 22–28 *novembre* 1962.

4   Interview of C.-E. Bouchard with Céline Legaré, *La Patrie*, 22–28 *novembre* 1962.

5   Yves Michaud, *La Patrie, 22 novembre, 1962.*

6   Ralph Heintzman, " The Political Culture of Quebec, 1840–1960," Canadian Journal of Political Science/Revue canadienne de science politique, XVI, 1983, 1–59.

7   Ibid., p. 3.

8   Jacques Monet, pp. 116–117, 257–258, 277–284.

and appointments offered partial relief ... for the continuing problem of unemployment."[9] "For the great silent mass," Heintzman remarks, "the most dramatic
form of evidence [of unemployment] is the unceasing flow of emigration to the
United States." Emigration was the single most important social fact in nineteenth
century Quebec, which is not yet sufficiently recognized. It exercised a profound
influence on ideology, politics, economic policy, and even literature."[10] The role of
patronage in Quebec politics was also emphasized in Harold Angell's work.[11]

How should we judge Bouchard now? There is no doubt that he was a har-
binger of the Quiet Revolution. In regards to all his progressive goals, he was
a leader who was sixty years ahead of his time. His anti-clericalism—fighting against the stranglehold that the Church exercised on Quebec society and
politics—was certainly a portent of the radical and sudden change in church-
society relations in the 1960s. He was also a resolute foe of the ultra-nationalist
elements of French-Canadian society. T.-D. Bouchard was known as "the devil
from Saint-Hyacinthe"—a description not without substance.[12] Conrad Black
has called him one of the most remarkable mayors of twentieth-century Quebec,
the man who made Saint-Hyacinthe a beautiful city and the greatest anti-clerical
political leader since Papineau.[13] The *Ottawa Citizen* compared him to Edouard
Herriot of France, predicting that Bouchard's name would become as historically
important as that of Laurier.[14] A major Quebec history text mentions Bouchard
briefly as having belonged to the radical wing of the Liberal Party, of having
served as president of the Farmers Association, and as having been a leader in
the battle for educational reform.[15] As noted, there is no published biography of
Bouchard except for the laudatory account of his life between 1935 and 1944, by

---

9   Heintzman, p. 15.

10   Ibid., p.11.

11   Harold M. Angell, "Quebec Provincial Politics in the 1920s," M.A. thesis, Department of
     Economics and Political Science, McGill University, 1960.

12   Jean-Noël Dion. *Le Courrier de Saint-Hyacinthe,* 21 aôut 1987.

13   Black, pp. 318–319.

14   Editorial, *The Ottawa Citizen,* July 17, 1944.

15   L.D.R., p. 487, 531, 557.

Robert Saint-Germain and Yves Bibeau, in the form of their Master's thesis at the University of Sherbrooke.[16]

Bouchard's outstanding characteristic was his courage. He always remained steadfast in the face of the "enemy," no matter what the outcome. Perhaps he had been trying to overcome his feelings of inferiority, but in any event, he stood up for his principles. His greatest hours were as acting Leader of the Opposition, facing Duplessis in his first *Union Nationale* mandate from 1936 to 1939. He did not allow Duplessis to get away with any accusations, or with the absence of government programs. In fact, Duplessis greatly admired him, as did Duplessis's two biographers—each coming from different viewpoints—Conrad Black and Robert Rumilly.[17] His astonishing and aggressive opposition to Duplessis during those years no doubt worked to the advantage of the Liberal Party and contributed to the victory of 1939.

A convinced federalist with a love of Canada as a whole, Bouchard fought Henri Bourassa for the latter's erratic behaviour in betraying Bouchard's hero Sir Wilfrid Laurier, even though fundamentally Bourassa had been a federalist. Bouchard hated the ultramontane view of church-state relations. Although constantly accused of Freemasonry, atheism, and even Protestantism, he was a believing Catholic, often attending mass secretly so that it would not appear that he was doing so out of political self-interest.[18]

Bouchard's stands on educational reforms in 1912 and 1919 no doubt contributed to keeping him out of the Gouin and Taschereau cabinets. Another factor

---

16   Robert Saint-Germain and Jacques Bibeau, M.A. Thesis (History) *Télesphore-Damien Bouchard; Un chef du Parti Libéral, (1935–1944)* Université de Sherbrooke, *novembre* 1973.

17   In the English edition of Black's biography, *Duplessis*, there are only three photographs of people other than Duplessis: King and Taschereau together, Cardinal Leger and T.-D. Bouchard and daughter.

18   An exchange of letters between Monsignor Decelles, Bishop of Saint-Hyacinthe and T.-D. Bouchard, the mayor, in 1927, confirms that Bouchard was a practicing Catholic. Monsignor Decelles requests that T.-D.B.attend mass and confession at Easter (March 19, 1927). In a very friendly reply, T.-D.B. confirms that he will do so gladly, but not in the local church, so as not to give his enemies the opportunity to call him hypocritical. (March 22, 1927) ANQ, P-10/1. He kept this secret practice even from his close friends. However, Judge Marcel Nichols is of the opinion that T.-D.B. kept the faith rather loosely. In his last will dated January 26, 1961 Bouchard states that he leaves his daughter to determine the details of his funeral and for the masses sung or celebrated for the repose of his soul after his death. Will no. 607, Montreal, 26 janvier 1961.

may have been Gouin's antipathy for someone of plebeian origins. Bouchard's insistence on open bidding and surveillance of the terms of tenders led to conflict within his party—with activists and organizers, as well as with ministers. His innovative approach to the economic crisis of the 1930s aroused the disapproval of many interested parties. Nevertheless, he held to his views. He said that the duty of the elected was to give a proper accounting to the public, not by passing popular laws out of a self-interested concern with re-election. If the elected could not convince the electorate through education that theirs was the proper course, then they deserved to lose. This philosophy consoled him when he was defeated as MLA in 1919 and as mayor in 1930, as well as after his dismissal as president of Quebec-Hydro in 1944. All who knew him drew attention to his lack of bitterness and to the spirit of forgiveness he extended to his enemies.

On the municipal level, T.-D. Bouchard guided the destiny of Saint-Hyacinthe for over twenty-five years. His achievements included the outdoor municipal swimming pool; the City Hall; and many parks, bridges, underpasses and fairgrounds. He introduced a plan to redress the plight of the poor during the Depression; and at the same time ensured strict control of the city's finances, allowing Saint-Hyacinthe to be singled out for praise by all Canadian newspapers. His home town has remembered him by naming a bridge, a park and a street after him.

T.-D. Bouchard certainly had faults. He was stubborn and vain. He often pursued his goals with a self-destructive single-mindedness. According to T.-D., reclusiveness had been widespread in his family, manifested on the male side by the preference for the tranquil rural life, and on the female side by membership in religious orders. As an example, he describes the closed life of an aunt, Sister Bouchard of the Hotel-Dieu of Saint-Hyacinthe. Although the rules of the congregation had stipulated sixteen as the age of admission, she was admitted to the order at thirteen by special permission. She never left the convent until, in her old age, permission was granted for birthdays or holidays. T.-D. recalled visiting with her on her birthday. Dr Harold Segall confirmed this solitary aspect of Bouchard's character, remarking on the long periods of silence at the Bouchard dinner table, where he was frequently the guest. The Honourable Judge Marcel Nichols disagrees with this assessment of T.-D. He found Bouchard to be an outgoing person. Over twenty years in the 1940s and 1950s, Bouchard frequented almost daily the Nichols household across the street from his own home, gossiping about political life, recounting his memories, playing cards and occasionally playing the piano.

The family's relationship was so close that, as mentioned earlier, Marcel and his brother Jacques called T.-D. *pépère* (grandpa).

Bouchard's relationship with Godbout was strained by the former's feeling that a clerical background had tainted his leader. As well, there was the natural strain between a leader out of legislature and a very effective acting House Leader. When the cabinet was formed in 1939, there was no doubt who was the most powerful minister. There was much material in the situation for cartoonists and comics. Although said to be arrogant when in power, Bouchard always worked for the common good. This allegation of arrogance was no doubt a comment on his rigid integrity, which enraged his colleagues and party activists who resented the lack of a level of patronage that had been the norm for Quebec.

Credit for the progressive reforms of the Liberal administration of 1939–1944 certainly go to both Premier Godbout and Bouchard. The vote for women would certainly not have survived Cardinal Villeneuve's initial attack with a weaker person than Godbout leading the cause. He stood up to the cardinal and delivered on a campaign promise. The law regarding compulsory and free education must also be attributed to both of these men who were imbued with a common desire to see French Canada progress. The creation of Hydro-Quebec perhaps owes more to Bouchard than to Godbout, but this is certainly debatable. There is no doubt that Bouchard's performance before the Lapointe Commission in 1935 helped turn the tide towards nationalization of the province's electrical resources. As we have shown, he really was the star of these hearings, appearing in over eighteen hours of testimony, well-prepared with documents and calculations. Godbout showed that he considered Bouchard the only man who could properly administer the merged institution when, offering Bouchard the presidency of Hydro-Quebec, he declared that if Bouchard did not take the job he would annul the law of nationalization of the major power companies of Montreal. Certainly, Bouchard's stewardship during his two months at Hydro-Quebec demonstrated that he was in command. He almost immediately reduced the price of electricity. Godbout's dismissal of Bouchard after his famous speech in the Senate may be termed either political realism or ignoble weakness. In any case, it did not help his campaign, although perhaps nothing would have saved the Liberal Party from Duplessis's effective use of the autonomy issue, regarding which Godbout stood on shaky ground.

In spite of his political and financial success, Télesphore-Damien Bouchard remained true to his working-class roots. He laboured constantly to improve the condition of the poor. Growing up in poverty, he never neglected to increase his personal fortune so as to spare his family that curse; but he was always careful to separate public and private functions. Even as a young man he refused to accept mediocrity. He demanded excellence of himself and from his entourage. He celebrated his own rise in society—"to the upper town"—and held that progress through education was an achievement within the reach of all people. He held that the backwardness of French-Canadian society was attributable to poor education and widespread illiteracy. His major preoccupation was the progress of the French-Canadian nation within a united Canada. This led to his conclusions about the lack of education in the province, and to his conflict with the narrow-minded clergy and an inert, inward-looking society.

St. Germain and Bibeau emphasize that, although the public memory of T.-D. Bouchard may be that of a belligerent, small-town opponent of the clergy, in private life he had the soul of a poet. They remark on his honesty; how candid he was about the one-sided nature of his relationship with his wife, Blanche-Corona. He loved her completely, and she did not reciprocate. He told this story publicly in his published memoirs. I regard him as a tragic hero because of this personal sadness and because of his political banishment after his Senate speech—a speech which like tragic heros of the past he felt impelled to deliver, in spite of his awareness that it would lead to his political isolation. Bibeau and St. Germain celebrate him as having contributed greatly to the development of Saint-Hyacinthe, and as having been one of the principal precursors of the Quiet Revolution of the 1960s:

> In attacking the inertia and conservatism of an inward-looking society, in attacking the dominant clericalism, Bouchard chose a difficult course at the beginning of the century, and over a long career he had to suffer the consequences … a perpetual battle.… Very early, he acquired a reputation as an implacable fighter. He never backed away from a fight. He always held that the triumph of his ideas was more important than personal honours and success.… He left the impression of a difficult, violent man, without sensitivity.… However, far from the public scene … in his *Mémoires* he recounts with great tenderness his first love as an adolescent and then his first meetings with she who became his wife.… A certain number of Maskoutains and Quebecers may only remember the MLA from Saint-Hyacinthe as a small, quarrelsome man who waged a cruel fight against the priests … few remember that Bouchard contributed to the great development of the City of Saint-Hyacinthe, that he was one of the principal

authors of the "Quiet Revolution" in Quebec, and one of the most fervent defenders of the French-Canadian nation.[19]

Thus, Télesphore-Damien Bouchard stands out as a representative of his people, in a long line of nineteenth-century *rouges*—Liberals on the radical side of the party—such as Papineau, Doutre, Dessaulles, Langlois and Langelier. Although he modified the *rougisme* of those nineteenth-century *rouges* to correspond with Laurier's views on the Liberal Party, Bouchard remains among the few politician/journalists of the first half of the twentieth century to have distinguished himself as outstanding in this tradition. He maintained the radical *rouge* anti-clerical position, and their burning hopes to eliminate the Church from control of education and social agencies. Yet again, Bouchard could be regarded as typical of many French Canadians who, contrary to the wishes of the Philippe Hamels of the period, did not espouse the extreme ethnocentric views of the nationalists. He could be considered typical of the many French Canadians who historically were broad-minded, accepting the indigenous native culture early on, and then other cultures after the British conquest.

The awakening and expression of this open-mindedness certainly had its highs and lows. Yet, for the first part of this century, in spite of the alleged clerical control, the *rouges* ("from Hell") were elected consistently from 1897 to 1936. In his controversial book, Ronald Rudin has reviewed the diverse views of Quebec historians towards such questions as whether the Church controlled everything and everyone in Quebec; whether the peasants were backward or typical of the stage of North American development; whether the conquest was a tragic turning point in Quebec history; the rate of modernization; whether Quebec's development was normal in the North American context; and whether the divisions in Quebec were based on class rather than race.[20] Rudin analyzes the classical Groulx approach (anti-English—that the Conquest was the cause of all the suffering in French Canada, and that the ideal was a rural, anti-modernist society). He contrasts Groulx's views with those of François-Xavier Garneau on the Conquest (that it was not the Conquest, which may in some way have been providential). Certainly, historiography today is a long way from the classical 1950s and '60s debates between the "Montreal school" (the modification

---

19   S.-G. & B., pp. 266–269.

20   Ronald Rudin: *Making History in Twentieth-Century Quebec* (Toronto: University of Toronto Press, 1997).

of Groulx's views by Maurice Seguin, Michel Brunet and Guy Fregault of the Université de Montréal—however, all viewed the conquest as a disaster)[21] and that of the "Quebec school" (Garneau, Thomas Chapais, to some extent Marcel Trudel, and especially Fernand Ouellet, who felt that the Conquest was providential).[22] Rudin then criticizes the revisionists, whose thesis is that Quebec's development was normal as compared to Ontario and North America, and who downplayed some factors, notably the power of the Church and the rate of urbanization.[23] There is an extensive literature of commentary on Rudin's thesis.[24] The textbooks by Linteau, Durocher and Robert, and by Young and

---

21   Jean Lamarre, *Le devenir de la nation québécoise, selon Maurice Seguin, Guy Frégault et Michel Brunet* (Sillery: Les éditions du Septentrion, 1993).

22   Rudin, Chapter 3, "The Maître and his successors: The Montreal Approach," pp. 93–128 and Chapter 4, "Maybe It Was Our Fault: The Laval Approach," pp. 129–170.

23   Rudin, Chapter V, pp. 171–218.

24   There is extensive historiographical commentary on Rudin's views, both for and against. See
Brain Young. "New Wine or Just New Bottles," *Journal of Canadian Studies*, no. 30 (1995–96): 194–98.
Brian Young. *Y a-t-il une nouvelle histoire du québec? Bulletind'histoire politique* 4, no. 2 (1995–96): 7–11.
Brian Young and John Dickinson, Toronto, 1988. *A Short History of Quebec: A Social and Economic Perspective* (Toronto: Copp Clark Pitman, 1993). Bruno Deshaies. "De Groulx 'a l'École de Montréal: Une Impasse." *Bulletin d'histoire politique* 7, no. 1 (1998–1999): 119–26. Eric Bedard, *Bulletin d'histoire politique* 7, no. 1 (1998–1999): 127–32. Fernand Ouellet, "La Modernisation de l'Historiogarphie et l'Emergence de l'Histoire Sociale," *Recherches sociographiques* 26 (1985): 11–83.
      Fernand Ouellet, "La Révolution Tranquille, Tournant Révolutionnaire?" In *Les Années Trudeau; La Recherche d'une Société Juste.*, edited by Thomas Axworthy & Pierre Elliot Trudeau, 333–62 (Montreal: Le Jour, 1990). Gilles Bourque, *Du Révisionnisme en Histoire Du Québec, Bulletin d'histoire politique* 4 (1996): 45–51. Jacques Beauchemin and Gilles Bourque, "Making History in Twentieth Century Quebec," *Bulletin d'histoire politique* 7, no. 1 (1998–1999): 152–56. Jacques Rouillard, *"La Révolution Tranquille: Rupture Ou Tournant?" Journal of Canadian Studies* 32 (1998): 23–51. Jean-Marie Fecteau, *"La Quête d'une Histoire Normale: Réflexion sur les Limites Épistomologiques Du 'Révisionisme' Au Québec," Bulletin d'histoire politique* 4, no. 2 (1995–1996): 31–38.
      Jean-Marie Fecteau, "Between Scientific Enquiry and the Search for a Nation: Quebec History as Seen by Ronald Rudin," *Canadian Historical Review* 80 (1999): 641–66. Jean-Paul Bernard, *"Histoire Nouvelle et Révisionnisme," Bulletin d'histoire politique* 4, no. 2 (1996): 53–55. Jocelyn Letourneau, *La Production Historienne Courante Portant sur le Québec et Ses Rapports avec la Construction Des Figures Identitaires d'une Communauté Communicationnelle,*

Dickinson are expressions of this revisionist interpretation of Quebec history, in Rudin's view. A study of the life of Télesphore-Damien Bouchard truly confirms the complexity and richness of Quebec's history.

The Liberal reign of Godbout from 1939 to 1944 advanced Quebec into the twentieth century with much-needed legislation. From 1944 to 1959, the Duplessis regime returned to many of the autocratic practices of the nineteenth century. The narrow-minded elite held sway. Then came the Quiet Revolution and a reawakening of the French-Canadian people, which had come to acknowledge its own potential. Télesphore-Damien Bouchard had always stressed this potential, which he foresaw would obtain through open interchange with fellow Canadians and other citizens of the world, and through advances in education. His nephew Charlemagne Bouchard quotes him as follows: "I came from the

Recherches sociographiques 36 (1995): 9–45. John A Dickinson, *Commentaires sur la Critique de Ronald Rudin, Bulletin d'histoire politique* 4, no. 2 (1995–96). Marlene Shore, "Ronald Rudin, Making History In Twentieth Century Quebec," *Revue d'histoire de l'Amérique française* 53 (2000): 625–28.

Michel Sarra-Bournet, *Pour une Histoire Postrévisioniste, Bulletin d'histoire politique* 4, no. 2 (1995–1996): 25–29. P.M. Senese, P.-A. Linteau, R. Durocher, and J.C. Robert, *Histoire Du Québec Contemporain: De la Confédération À la Crise* (1867–1929), *Histoire sociale— Social History* 15 (1982): 278–80 (Montréal: Boréal, 1979, 1989). Patrice Regimbald, "Ronald Rudin, Making History in Twentieth Century Quebec," *Bulletin d'histoire politique* 6, no. 3 (1997–1998): 147–55. Paul-André Linteau, *De l'Équilibre et de la Nuance dans l'interprétation de l'Histoire Du Québec, Bulletin d'histoire politique* 4, no. 2 (1995–1996): 13–19. Paul-André Linteau, René Durocher, and Jean-Claude Robert: François Ricard. *Quebec Since 1930* (Toronto: James Lorimer & Company, 1991). Pierre Trépanier, *Débats: Faire de l'Histoire À la Manière de Ronald Rudin, Bulletin d'histoire politique* 7, no. 1 (1998– 99): 106. Ramsay Cook, "Ronald Rudin: Making History in Twentieth Century Quebec," *Histoire sociale/Social History* 32 (2000): 120–23. Richard Jones, 1997, *American Historical Review* 104 (1999): 557–58.

Ronald Rudin, Book review, "Paul-André Linteau—Histoire de Montréal Depuis la Confédération," (Montréal: Les Éditons Du Boréal, 1992), p. 613, *Histoire sociale—Social History* 25 (1992): 423–25. Ronald Rudin, "Revisionism and the Search for a Normal Society: A Critique of Recent Quebec Writing," *Canadian Historical Review* 73 (1992): 30– 61. Ronald Rudin, *Au-delà du révisionisme, Bulletin d'histoire politique* 4, no. 2 (1995–1996): 57–73. Ronald Rudin, *Making History in Twentieth Century Quebec*, Toronto: University of Toronto Press, 1997. Ronald Rudin, "On Difference and National Identity in Quebec Historical Writing: A Response to Jean-Marie Fecteau," *Canadian Historical Review* 80 (1999): 666–76. Serge Gagnon, *À Propos de Ronald Rudin, Bulletin d'hsitoire politique* 7, no. 1 (1998–1999): 133–51. Yves Gingras, *Une Sociologie Spontanée de la Connaissance Historique, Bulletin d'histoire politique* 4, no. 2 (1995–1996): 39–43.

common people, and I had a surplus of their qualities: love of justice; love of liberty; and a devotion to open-minded ideas."[25] His outstanding characteristic was his courage. He had the courage to stand up for what he believed in, at a time when "fear" of doing so pervaded the province. He had the courage to fight the occult, chauvinistic forces, which had captivated the elite. He had the courage to defend "others." He had the courage to urge progress for his fellow French Canadians. He certainly was a man two generations ahead of his time, and a major contributor to the birth of a new Quebec.

**Photograph by Karsh. The president of Quebec-Hydro.
The only picture of Bouchard smiling.**

---

25   Charlemagne Bouchard, *La Patrie* 15–21 *novembre* 1962

Abbreviations

ANO National Archives, Ottawa
ANQ Archives nationales du Québec (Quebec City)
AMSH Archives de la municipalité de Saint-Hyacinthe
ASSH Archives Séminaire Saint-Hyacinthe
CHR Canadian Historical Review
HPB Histoire de la province du Québec
H. P.-B. Hélène Pelletier-Baillergon
L.-D.-R. Linteau, Durocher and Robert
RHAF Revue d'histoire de l'Amérique française
R. R. Robert Rumilly
S.-G. & B. Robert Saint-Germain and Jacques Bibeau
T.-D. B. Télesphore-Damien Bouchard

Appendix
Note on the Order of Jacques Cartier

As noted, the first public report on the OJC came from Jean-Charles Harvey, who published a brief note in *Le Jour* in 1939. However, it was in November of 1941 that Harvey published a sensational series over seven weeks—an open exposé with banner headlines such as: *The Ku Klux Klan of French Canada; Sectarian nationalists, anti-British, anti-Semitic, prohibitionists, Vichyards, colonists form a secret society, The Order Of Jacques Cartier, Members of parliament, members of the clergy, bureaucrats, journalists belong. A Conspiracy to take over all the levers of power.* Harvey named about fifteen well-known personalities belonging to the OJC, among whom were Edouard Lacroix, Maxime Raymond, Ligori Lacombe, René Chaloult and Louis Depire. Harvey denounced the methods of *la patente.*

"By underhanded methods they arrange to introduce everywhere their choice of individuals, to eliminate men with open minds from several important positions, all those who hold dear democratic institutions dear and to good relations between Canadians of diverse origins and for the unity of our country. The OJC is a conspiracy against intelligence, tolerance, freedom, and progress, in favour of the most destructive elements of French Canada." *Le Jour,* 15 *novembre* 1941.

Harvey published extracts from *L'Émerillon,* the Order's secret newspaper, demonstrating direct links between the OJC and the Saint Jean-Baptiste Society, the Buy At Home League *(L'achat chez nous),* the *Action canadienne de jeunesse catholique* and the *Caisses populaires.* He accused several newspapers of serving the interests of the OJC, notably: *Le Devoir, L'Action catholique, Le Droit, L'Évangeline, La Boussole* (the official newspaper of the OJC), *L'Oeil and L'Action nationale.* He revealed the existence of a list of 262 names of merchants, tradesmen, professionals and businessmen "judged worthy of patronage by the OJC." He suggested that the failed Gouin-Duplessis movement had been inspired in part by this group. At least two, maybe three members of Duplessis's first cabinet had been "commanders" of the OJC, as were several Members of the Legislative Assembly. It is important to remember that this society included a small portion of the total population. Its influence has been questioned, but its existence acknowledged. Even in 1959, Daniel Johnson complained to the editor-in-chief of *MacLean's Magazine,* after his election as leader of the *Union Nationale,* that he had faced a coalition formed by the OJC to oppose him and to support Jean-Jacques Bertrand instead.

In his biography of Jean-Charles Harvey, Marcel-Aimé Gagnon maintains that he had obtained his information about the OJC from T.-D. Bouchard. Certainly Bouchard followed the activities of the OJC closely. Harvey's letter to Bouchard in December of 1941, asking him if he had seen Harvey's series on the OJC and asking him to watch for the follow-up articles, does not mention any debt to Bouchard.

Charles-Henri Dubé, in his well-documented article in *Le Magazine Maclean* in May of 1963, states that Harvey's information had come from Edmond Turcotte, previously the editor of *Le Canada,* not Bouchard. Yves Lavertu establishes the link in his recent biography of Harvey. At the time, Turcotte worked in Bouchard's ministry. No doubt Bouchard's thick file on the OJC had found its way to Harvey through Turcotte's hands. (Marcel-Aimé Gagnon, J.-C. *Harvey, précurseur de la révolution tranquille* (Montreal: Beauchemin, 1970). Lavertu, p. 272–279.)

In 1963 Dubé, previously a high-ranking official of the OJC, revealed the structure of the Order. He did so, he said, after years of reflection and hesitation, and with "The firm moral conviction that true democracy was unthinkable in Quebec as long as the Order, which consisted of a state within a state, continued to infiltrate and direct municipal councils, school commissions, social organizations, administrations, etc., bringing everywhere an inherent fault of every secret society, directing its power to control other societies with suspicion, division, favouritism, a spirit of caste, and the many problems which follow." Charles-Henri Dubé, *Le Magazine Maclean, mai* 1963, p. 24.

Dubé described his recruitment in Saint-Jean in 1953, where Monsignor Coderre had appointed him secretary-general of the new social services of the diocese. He had been invited to join an "honest, patriotic, Catholic, etc., association." He underwent a rigorous initiation, called VAPDA *(voyage au pays des ancêtres);* "blindfolded … a bad quarter of an hour" one Sunday afternoon. Dubé compared the Order's initiation to that of the Freemasons, including secret passwords and secret signs. The candidates had to request admission through an intermediary who struck several knocks on the door. The candidates had to drink from the cup of bitterness, pass through several obstacles, pass a test of fire, and to swear solemnly to keep the Order's secrets. The Grand Commander who presided explained the symbolic meaning of each test. It ended with a shout on the part of the whole assemblage *standing with their arms extended at 45 degrees!* "Discretion! Discretion! Discretion!" (Shades of *"Heil?"*) They were forbidden to tell anyone, including their wives, anything about the Order. In Dubé's own case, when the lights came on, he was surprised to see on the stage so many people whom he recognized, including Monsignor Coderre.

Dubé quoted Harvey's exposé and confirmed the close association of the Order with the Church. Each cell, each *commanderie,* had a chaplain—usually the local priest. There was also a regional chaplain appointed with the approval of the local bishop, and a General Chaplain at the Supreme Council level, named by the Assembly of French-Language Bishops of Canada. The secretariat published *L'Émerillon,* as well as several bulletins; took care of finances; and organized a triennial congress. Dubé rose quickly to become local secretary, then regional secretary. Five years later, when he began to question the practice of favouritism and the honesty of some Montreal bureaucrats in the city administration and in the school commission, his local cell was dissolved. He was offered the status of "isolated member"; a special category reserved for difficult members or high-ranking civil or religious authorities who wished to hide their membership. In describing the history of the Order, Dubé mentioned Bouchard's 1944 Senate speech: "Another sensational denunciation, which resulted in no end of insults and difficulties for its author, including the loss of the presidency of Hydro-Quebec, it shook the province ... If I have dwelled on these two denunciations [Harvey's and Bouchard's], it is because they describe the history of the OJC generally. Ignoring the excess of language in style at that time, and some far-fetched or in any case premature conclusions—such as that of T.-D. Bouchard saying that the OJC was separatist, which went against its pan-Canadian nature—I can confirm that the facts brought out by Bouchard and Harvey are generally true." Dubé, p. 65.

Dubé linked the fortunes of the *Union Nationale* and those of Jean Drapeau's Civic Action League, to the influence of the OJC, "or [the two groups were] at least controlled by members of the Order." He also linked *Le Devoir* to the Order, at least during the 1930s and 1940s: "it was practically impossible to obtain an important position ... [at *Le Devoir*] without being a member." The names of several highly placed Order members associated with *Le Devoir* were mentioned, such as Pierre Vigeant (some said he was the Grand Chancellor), Gérard Filion, Pierre Laporte, and René Paré. They represented the authority of the Order in the region of Montreal." Claude Ryan, invited to Saint-Jean to give a talk, is reported to have expressed the wish that no-one in the audience belonged to the OJC: "I hope that none of you belong to the Order of Jacques Cartier. If by chance you have belonged, I recommend that you do not waste your time." Ryan stressed that the threat to democracy and the effectiveness of the Order was due to the apathy of the majority of the population and the passion for power of the initiated.

"The members of the Order take a malignant pleasure in holding leading positions ... their adversaries do not benefit as they do from a fraternal secret society to concentrate their action and especially to prepare elections ... what is important is membership in the Order, not the competence of those who will be chosen for a leader's job ... One understands how easy it is for the OJC to pass slogans into civic societies and to mobilize public opinion, truly into a tidal wave ... they generally use tested techniques of getting members to send letters, messages, and telegrams to the public authorities or enterprises being targeted." Dubé, p. 67.

In its bulletin of October 15, 1956, the OJC complained about the lack of strict hierarchical obedience: "We are astonished every time to discover that chapters do not follow orders from the CX [Suprême Commanderie]." Dubé confirmed Harvey's and Bouchard's contention that the most-infiltrated organizations were the Saint-Jean-Baptiste Society, the *Caisses populaires*, the Canadian Association of French-Language Educators, the Association of French-Canadian Youth (which had taken the place of the ACJC), the Federation and the Associations of Education, and school commissions across Canada,—parent-teacher associations, etc. He describes several examples of infiltration and undue influence by the Order in the campaigns for the *fleur-de-lis* flag, and against the Fulton Bill to repatriate the British North America Act in 1963.

Dubé also describes its laudable, successful campaigns for bilingual stamps; bilingual currency; federal publications in French; French in the social services, on notices, and commercial labels; and the provincial nationalization of electricity. Even though, up to the 1960s, the Order was a pan-Canadian movement, it had also infiltrated the independence groups. One week before the congress of the R.I.N. *(Rassemblement pour l'indépendance nationale),* Dubé reported that he was able to predict to his friends that Marcel Chaput, expelled from the Order in Ottawa for his separatist ideas, would not be re-elected president, thanks to a team of brothers of the OJC. He concluded his article by quoting the words of Pope Benedict XV, who had commented on the animosity aroused by Regulation 17—the Ontario law limiting the use of French in schools (June 1918). "We wish to severely warn anyone amongst the clergy or the congregants, who, contrary to evangelical doctrine and our proscription, dare in the future to nourish or excite animosity which has divided Canadians until now." Dubé, p. 74

Certainly there has not been an organization more active in promoting discord between the two ethnic groups of Canada than the OJC, states Dubé, pointing out the OJC's failure to obey the papal injunction. This was particularly true of discord between the French Catholics and the Irish Catholics: according to *L'Émerillon*: "… the worst enemies of Canadians of French origin and of Catholic faith are the Irish Catholics." *L'Émerillon, Mars 1958.*

Abbé Maheux, Bouchard's great friend, wrote to him concerning the referendum on conscription in 1942: "In the campaign taking place at this moment, one can see the influence of the ultra-nationalists … the work of the Order of Jacques Cartier. This Order advised its members in *L'Émerillon* that its three organs are *Le Devoir, L'Action Catholique* and *La Bousole.* These are the same three newspapers—and the only ones—that are carrying out a campaign against my book *Your History is an Epic,* and against my opinions … It seems that the harm comes from the nationalist group and the Montreal section of the Order. *Le Devoir* boycotted my book; Mr. Georges Pelletier forbade the personnel of his bookstore to sell my book. When I spoke to him reproachfully, he did not deny it. What fanaticism!" ANQ *Fonds* Bouchard, P-10/14. Letter A. Maheux to T.-D. Bouchard.

Dubé's article once again focussed provincial attention on the secret OJC. It produced a sensation. At meetings of the OJC it was the sole subject of discussion. Jean David wrote an article for the English-language edition of *Maclean's Magazine* based on Dubé's piece of June 15, 1963. One year later it was Roger Cyr's turn to expose the organization in a series of articles published in March and April of 1964, just prior to the OJC's May congress. The provincial council of the society, presided over by Rosaire Morin, published a manifesto calling for less power for Ottawa, and for the establishment of an Estates General. The Order that had defended the rights of French-speaking people throughout Canada for forty years could not confine its program to one province, and refused the manifesto. The most active Quebec members resigned *en masse.* Rosaire Morin lured the majority of former OJC brothers to the newly formed Order of Jean Talon, a Quebec-oriented OJC. Then Morin resigned the presidency to devote himself to the Estates General of French Canada. One year after Morin's departure, the executive resigned. From forty thousand members in 1960, the OJC numbered only twelve thousand several years later. (Claude Marcil, *L'Ordre de Jaques Cartier, Perspectives, La Tribune,* 23 *octobre* 1976.) Bouchard's claim that his speech was so effective that the OJC's membership—estimated to have been eighteen thousand in 1944—had been drastically reduced, does not seem to hold up.

Laliberté concludes the book based on his doctoral thesis with the proposition that the *Parti Québécois* is the legitimate heir of the OJC because of its plans for "unitary nationalism, its desire for national hegemony, its platform of financial control, its preoccupation with control of the diffusion of ideological information, and its recourse to referendums rather than traditional general elections." This judgment must be countered by the very democratic structure of the *Parti Québécois* as compared to that of the OJC. Nevertheless, the xenophobic opinions of some PQ adherents do resemble those of the OJC. When their supporters shout *le Québec au québécois* or speak of *Québécois "pure laine"* they remind one of the OJC. When Jacques Parizeau blames the "ethnics" for the failure of a referendum and Pierre Bourgault (recently given almost a state funeral) speaks of eliminating the vote for the non-*pure-laine Quebecois*, they are following in the footsteps of the OJC. It should be noted that this xenophobic element has been severely chastised by the leaders of the PQ—premiers Lucien Bouchard and Bernard Landry.

Bibliography

PRIMARY SOURCES

Archives de la Société d'histoire de Saint-Hyacinthe: Fonds T.-D. Bouchard: two boxes of documents.

Archives Municipale de Saint-Hyacinthe

Archives Nationale de Québec: Fonds T.-D. Bouchard: 85 boxes containing documents, letters, newspaper clippings, and copies of all the speeches of T.-D. Bouchard

Archives de L'Archévechie de Trois-Rivières

Chisholm, Elspeth. Unpublished. *Life of T.-D. Bouchard.* Ottawa: National Archives.

Saint-Germain, Robert; Jacques Bibeau. *Télesphore-Damien Bouchard; Un Chef du Parti Libéral; (1935–1944).* Masters thesis, Université de Sherbrooke, November 1973.

Susan Mann (Trofimenkoff) Robertson *The* Intstitut Canadien, *an Essay in Cultural History.* Masters thesis, University of Western Ontario, 1965.

Mandements du Québec, NS II,

Extract of Acts; Cathedral of Saint-Hyacinthe

Street Directories, Saint-Hyacinthe, ASSH.

Jugement de la Cour Supérieure. No. 135, 4 Avril, 1910.

Newspapers:

L'Union, Le Devoir, Le Clairon, The Gazette, Le Soleil, The Montreal Star, Le Nouveau Monde, Le Canadien, Le Journal de Trois-Rivières, La Croix de Paris, La Libre Parole, La Patrie, Le Travailleur, La Presse, Le Nationaliste, l'Avenir du Nord, Sherbrooke Daily Record, Le Courrier de Saint-Hyacinthe, L'Évenement, L'Action Catholique, Maclean's Magazine, Saturday Night, The Ottawa Citizen, La Voix de l'Est.

Bouchard, Cécile-Ena, cache of private letters and memorabilia provided by Mme. Claire Simard-Odermatt

SECONDARY SOURCES

Anctil, Pierre. *Le rendez-vous manqué; Les Juifs de Montréal face au Québec de l'entre-deux-guerres.* Montréal: Institut Québécois de Recherches sur la Culture, 1988.

———. *Le Devoir, les Juifs et l'Immigration.* Montréal: Institut québécois de recherche sur la culture, 1988.

Asselin, Olivar, La grève de l'internat, *L'Ordre*, 1934. Reprinted in O.

Asselin, *Pensée Française.* Éditions de l'Actions canadienne-française, 1937.

Barette, Antonio. *Mémoires.* Montreal: La Librairie Beauchemin, 1966.

Beauchemin, Jacques; Bourque, Gilles. 1998–1999. Making history in twentieth century Quebec. *Bulletin d'Histoire Politique* 7(1): 152–156.

Bedard, Eric, 1998–1999. *Bulletin d'histoire politique* 7(1): 127–132.

Behiels, Michael D., *Prelude to Quebec's Quiet Revolution, 1945–1960.* Montreal & Kingston: McGill-Queen's University Press, 1985.

Bellavance, Claude. *Shawinigan Water and Power, 1898–1963, Formation et Déclin d'un Groupe Industriel Au Québec.* Montréal: Boréal, 1994.

Bernard, Jean-Paul. *Les Rouges, Libéralisme, Nationalisme et Anti-Cléricalisme au milieu du XIX siècle,* Montréal: Les presses de l'Université du Québec, 1971.

———. 1996. Histoire nouvelle et révisionnisme. *Bulletin d'Histoire Politique* 4(2): 53–55.

Bernard, Phillipe and Dubreif, Henri. *The Decline of the Third Republic, 1914–1938*. Cambridge: Cambridge University Press, 1985.

Bettez, Honoré, 1946. Les révélations du rapport Abadie. *Relations*. Montréal, Aug. p. 231–232.

Black, Conrad, *Duplessis*, Vol. I: *L'ascension*; Vol. II: *Le pouvoir*. Montréal: Les éditions de l'Homme, 1977.

Bliss, Michael. *Plague: A Story of Smallpox in Montreal*, Toronto: Harper-Collins Publishers, 1991.

Boismenu, Gérard. *Le Duplessisme, Politique, Economique et Rapports de Force, 1944–1960*. Montréal: Les Presses de l'Université de Montréal, 1981.

Bouchard, Télesphore-Damien. *Mémoires de T.-D. Bouchard*, Vol I, *Ma vie privée* Vol II, *Gravisant la colline*, Vol III, *Quarante ans dans la tourmente politico-religieuse*. Montreal: Les Presses Beauchemin, 1960.

Bourassa, Henri, "Mr. Bourassa's Reply to Capt. Talbot Papineau's Letter." In *Readings in Canadian History*, edited by R. Douglas Francis and Donald B. Smith, pp. 353–60. Toronto: Holt, Rinehart and Wilson of Canada, 1982.

Bourque, Gilles. 1996. Du Révisionnisme en histoire du Québec. *Bulletin d'histoire Politique* 4:45–51.

Bray, R. Matthew. "'Fighting as an Ally': The English-Canadian Response to the Great War." In *Readings in Canadian History*, edited by R. Douglas Francis and Donald B. smith, pp. 322–44. Toronto: Holt Rinehart and Winston of Canada, 1982.

Bredin, Jean-Denis. *The Affair; The Case of Alfred Dreyfus*. New York: George Brazillier Inc. 1986.

Brown, Michael Gary. *Jew or Juif? Jews, French Canadians and Anglo-Canadians 1759–1914*. Philadelphia: Jewish Publication Society, 1987.

Carter, Sarah. *Aboriginal People and Colonizers of Western Canada to 1900*. Toronto: University of Toronto Press, 1999.

Chaloult, Réné. *Mémoires Politiques*. Montréal, Éditions du Jour, 1969.

Chastenet, Jacques. *Déclin de la Troisième. 1931–1938*. Paris: Hachette, 1962.

Chisholm, Elspeth. *T.-D. Bouchard, a Biography.* Unpublished. National Archives. Ottawa.

Choquette, Msgr. C.P. *Histoire de la Ville de Saint-Hyacinthe*. Sainte Hyacinthe: Richer et Fils, 1930.

Comeau, Paul-André. *Le Bloc populaire 1942–1948*. Montréal: Québec/ Amérique, 1982

Cook, Ramsey, *French-Canadian Nationalism*. Toronto: Macmillan, 1969.

———2000, Ronald Rudin: Making History in Twentieth Century Quebec. *Histoire sociale/Social History* 32:120–123.

Crunican, Paul. *Priests and Politicians: Manitoba Schools and the Election of 1896.* Toronto: Univ. Toronto Press, 1974.

———1991, Book review of Perrin's *Rome in Canada,* in the *Catholic Historical Review*, 177, and 344.

Dandurand, Raoul. *Les Mémoires du Sénateur.* Québec: Marcel Hamelin, Les Presses de l'Université Laval, 1967.

De la Grave, Jean-Paul. *Histoire de l'information au Québec.* Montréal: Éditions de la Presse, 1980.

DeCelles, Alfred Duclos. *Scènes de moeurs électorales.* Montréal: Librairie Beauchemin, 1919.

Delisle, Esther. *Le Traître et le Juif, Lionel Groulx, Le Devoir et le délire du nationalisme d'extrême droite dans la province du Québec 1929–39.* Montréal: L'Étincelle Éditeur, 1992.

Desbiens, J.P. *Les insolences du frère untel,* Montréal: Les Éditions de l'Homme, 1960.

Deshaies, Bruno, 1998–1999. De Groulx à l'école de Montréal: une impasse. *Bulletin d'Histoire Politique* 7(1): 119–26.

Dickinson, John and Young Brian. *A Short History of Quebec,* Mississauga: Copp Clark Pitman, 1993.

———1995–1996, Commentaires sur la Critique de Ronald Rudin. *Bulletin d'histoire politique* 4, no. 2.

Dion, Jean-Noel, 1988, "Aux Origines du Quétaine"; *Le Courrier de Saint-Hyacinthe.* March 9, 16, 23.

Dirks, Patricia. *The Failure of l'Action Libérale Nationale,* Montreal and Kingston: McGill-Queens University Press, 1991.

Dubé, Charles-Henri. *Le Magazine Maclean,* May, p. 24, 1963.

Dufour, Pierre and Jean Hamelin. *Honoré Mercier*, DCB, XII, Toronto: University of Toronto Press, pp. 719–728, 1990.

Dumont, Fernand, 1969, "Idéologies Au Canada Français (1850–1900): Quelques Réflexions d'Ensemble." *Recherches sociographiques* 10,145–69.

Dupont, Antonin. 1972, "Louis-Alexandre Taschereau et la législation sociale au Québec, 1920–1936," *Revue d'histoire de l'Amérique française,* 26(3): 397–426.

Dutil, Patrice, *Devil's Advocate; Godfroy Langlois and the politics of Liberal Progressivism in Laurier's Quebec,* Outremont: Robert Davies, 1994.

Drumont, Edouard, *Le testiment d'un antisémite,* Paris: E. Dentu, 1891.

———. *La France Juive,* Paris: Librairie Marion et Flammarion, 1886.

Eid, Nadia F., *Le Clergé et le Pouvoir Politique Au Québec,* Montréal: Éditions Hurtubise, 1978.

Fay, Terrence J., *A History of Canadian Catholics: Gallicanism, Romanism, and Canadianism,* Montreal and Kingston: McGill-Queen's University Press, 2002.

Fecteau, Jean-Marie. 1995–1996, "La Quête d'une Histoire Normale: Réflexion sur les Limites Épistomologiques du Révisionisme Au Québec." *Bulletin d'histoire politique* 4, no. 2, 31–38.

————, 1999, "Between Scientific Enquiry and the Search for a Nation: Quebec History as Seen by Ronald Rudin." *Canadian Historical Review* 80, 641–666.

Flanagan, Thomas, *Louis 'David' Riel; 'Prophet of the New World'* Rev. ed. Toronto: University of Toronto Press, 1996.

————. *Riel and the Rebellion: 1885 Reconsidered* (Toronto: University of Toronto Press, 2000)

Fraser, Blair, *Maclean's Magazine*, August 15, 1944

Gagnon, Jean-Louis. *Les Apostasies*; Vol. I *Les Coqs du Village*; et Vol. II *Les dangers de la vertu*, Ottawa: La Presse, 1985.

Gagnon, Marcel-Aimé. *J-C Harvey; précurseur de la révolution tranquille*, Montréal: Beauchemin, 1970.

Gagnon, Serge. *Quebec and its Historians; The Twentieth Century*, Montreal: Harvest House, 1985.

————.1998–1999, "À Propos de Ronald Rudin." *Bulletin d'hsitoire politique* 7, no. 1, 133–151.

Gallichan, Gilles. *Honoré Mercier, La politique et la culture,* Sillery: Septentrion, 1994.

Genest, Jean-Guy. *Godbout*, Québec: Éditions Septentrion, 1996.

Gingras, Yves. 1995–1996, *Une Sociologie Spontanée de la Connaissance Historique. Bulletin d'histoire politique* 4, no. 2, 39–43.

Gossage, Peter. *Families in Transition, Industry and Population in Nineteenth Century Saint-Hyacinthe*, Montreal & Kingston: McGill-Queen's University Press, 1999.

Guttman, Frank M. "The Bouchards of Saint-Hyacinthe and Dr. H. N. Segall"; *Essays in Honour of the 90th Birthday of Dr. H.N. Segall,* The Osler Library. Montreal: McGill University Press, 1989.

Hamelin, Jean and Marcel. *Les mœurs électorales dans le Québec*, Montreal: Éditions du jour, 1962.

Hart, Arthur Daniel. *The Jew in Canada: A Complete Record of Canadian Jewry from the Days of the French Régime to the Present Time*, Toronto-Montreal: Jewish Publications, 1926.

Harvey, Fernand. "Children of the Industrial Revolution in Quebec" In *The Professions: Their Growth or Decline?* edited by J. Dufresne/Reprinted in translation by Robert Russel in R. Douglas Francis and Donald B. Smith. Readings in Canadian History, pp. 195–204, Montreal-Toronto: Société de Publication Critère Holt, Rinehart and Winston of Canada, 1979.

Hathorn, Ramon and Patrick Holland. *Images of Louis Riel in Canadian Culture* Lewiston: Edwin Mellen Press, 1992.

Hogue, Clarence, Bolduc, Andre, and Larouche, Daniel. *Québec, un Siècle d'Élecricité*, Montréal: Libre Expression, 1979.

Horton, Donald J., *André Laurendeau, French-Canadian Natioanlist, 1912–1968*, Toronto: Oxford University Press, 1992.

Hudon, Théophile. *L'institut canadien de Montréal et l'affaire Guibord: une page d'histoire*, Montréal: Librairie Beauchemin, 1938.

Jobin, Carol. *Les Enjeux Économique de la Nationalisation de l'Électricité*, Laval: Éditions Coopératives Albert Saint-Martin, 1978.

Jones, Richard. 1999. Book review. Ronald Rudin—Making History in Twentieth-century Quebec. *American Historical Review* 104:557–558.

Kermoal, Nathalie. 1997. *Les femmes lors de la résistance de 1870 et de la Rebellion de 1885, Prairie forum*, 19, 153.

Lacouture, Jean, *Léon Blum*. Paris: Éditions du Seuil, 1977.

Laferté, Hector, *Derrière le trône, Mémoires d'un parlementaire québécois 1936–1958*, Sillery: Septentrion, 1998.

Laliberté, G.-Raymond, *Une Société secrète: L'Ordre de Jacques Cartier* Montréal: Hurtubise, 1983.

Langlais, Jacques, and Rome, David, *Juifs et Québécois français, 200 ans d'histoire commune*, Montréal: Fides, 1986.

Lamonde, Yvan, *Louis-Antoine Dessaulles, Un seigneur libéral et anticlérical,* Montréal: Fides, 1994.

———and Claude Corbo, *Le rouge et le bleu, une anthologie de la pensée politique au Québec de la conquête è la révolution tranquille,* Montréal: Les presses de l'Université de Montréal, 1999.

———. *Histoire sociales des idées au* Québec, 1760–1896, Montréal: Éditions Fides, 2000.

Lapierre, Laurier, *Les Relations Entre l'Église et l'État Au Canada Français.* In *L'Église et le Québec,* edited by Marcel Rioux, 31–45. Montréal: Éditions du jour, 1961.

Lapointe, Renaude, *L'Histoire Boulversante de Mgr. Charbonneau,* Montréal : Éditions du Jour, 1962.

Laurier, Wilfrid, *Le Libéralisme Politique;* Conference given at the Club Canadien de Québec, June 26 1877.

Lavertu, Yves, *L'affaire Bernonville, Le Québec face è Pétain et à la Collaboration (1948–1951),* Montréal: VLB, 1994.

———. *Jean-Charles Harvey, Le Combattant* Montréal: Les Édtions Boréal, 2000.

Letourneau, Jocelyn. 1995. La Production Historienne Courante Portant sur le Québec et Ses Rapports avec la Construction Des Figures Identitaires d'une Communauté Communicationnelle. *Recherches sociographiques* 36, 9–45.

Levitt, Joseph, *Henri Bourassa and the Golden Calf,* Ottawa: Les Éditions de l'Université d'Ottawa, 1972.

Linteau, Paul-André, Durocher, Réné, and Robert Jean-Claude, *Histoire du Québec contemporain,* Vol I. *De la confédération à la crise, Vol II,* also with François Ricard *Le Québec depuis 1930,* Montréal: Boréal, 1979–1989.

———, 1995–1996, De l'Équilibre et de la Nuance dans l'Interprétation de l'Histoire Du Québec. *Bulletin d'histoire politique* 4, no. 2, 13–19.

Mann Trofimenkoff, Susan. *Visions Nationales;* St. Laurent, Quebec: Éditions Trécarré, 1986.

Marcil, Claude. L'Ordre de Jacques Cartier; Perspectives. *La Tribune*, October 23, 1976

Marion, Séraphin. 1962. *Libéralisme Canadien-Français d'Autrefois et d'Aujoud'hui. Cahiers des Dix*, 27, 9–45.

McLean, Donald George. *1885, Métis rebellion or government conspiracy?* Winnipeg: Pemmican Publications, 1985.

Miller, J. R., 1988, "From Riel to the Métis," *Can. Hist. Rev.*, 69, 11.

————. *Skyscrapers, Hide the Heavens, A History of Indian-White Relations in Canada,* 3rd Edition, Toronto: University of Toronto Press, 2000.

Miner, Horace. *Study of St. Denis,* thesis, University of Chicago, Chicago: Phoenix Books-University of Chicago Press, 1939.

Monet, Jacques. *The Last Canon Shot*, Toronto: University of Toronto Press, 1969.

Monière, Denis. *Le Développement des idéologies au Québec, des origines à nos jours*, Montréal: Québec/Amérique, 1977.

Morin, Maurice. *Bio-Bibliography Analytique de Discours et Conférences de L'Honorable Télesphore-Damien Bouchard,* Thèse pour la Faculté de Lettres, section bibliothéconomie, Université Laval, 1964

Morton, Desmond, *Ministers and Generals; Politics and the Canadian Militia, 1868–1904*, Toronto: University of Toronto Press, 1970.

————. "An Introduction," in *The Queen v Louis Riel. The social History of Canada.* General Ed. Michael Bliss, Toronto: University of Toronto Press, 1974.

————. *The last war drum; the North West campaign of 1885*, Toronto: Hakkert, 1971.

Neatby, H. Blair, *Laurier and a Liberal Quebec; a Study in Political Management,* Toronto: McClelland & Stewart, 1973.

Nemni, Max and Monique, *Young Trudeau: 1919–1944 Son of Quebec, Father of Canada*, Translated by William Johnson, Toronto: Douglas Gibson Books, 2006.

Oliver, Michael, *The Passionate Debate; The Social and Political Ideas of Quebec Nationalism*, Montreal: Véhicule Press, 1991.

Ouellet, Fernand. 1985. *La Modernisation de l'Historiogarphie et l'Emergence de l'Histoire Sociale. Recherches sociographiques* 26: 11–83.

———. *"La Révolution Tranquille, Tournant Révolutionnaire?"* In *Les Années Trudeau; La Recherche d'une Société Juste.*, edited by Thomas Axworthy & Pierre Elliot Trudeau, 333–62, Montreal: Le Jour, 1990.

Parizeau, Lucien. 1946, La tyrannie des mythes. *Feuilles Démocratiques* I. 9.

Parkman, Francis, *France and England in North America*, New York: The Library of America, 1983.

Payment, Diane P., *"La vie en Rose?* Métis Women at Batoche, 1870–1920."
From, *Rethinking Canada; The Promise of Women's History*, ed. Veronica Strong-Boag and Anita Clair Fellman, Toronto: Oxford University Press, 1997.

Pelletier-Baillargeon, Helen, *Olivar Asselin et son temps,* Montréal: Fides, 1996.

Perrin, Roberto, *Rome in Canada: The Vatican and Canadian Affairs in the Late Victorian Age,* Toronto: University of Toronto Press, 1990, p.8.

Pouliot, Léon, *Mgr Bourget,* Montréal : Beauchemin, 1955.

Price, Roger, *A Concise History of France,* Cambridge: Cambridge University Press, 1993.

Pomeryols, Catherine, *Les intellectuels québécois: formation et engagements 1919–1939,* Paris: L'Hartmattan, 1996.

Quinn, Herbert F., "The Formation and Rise to Power of the Union Nationale." In *Readings in Canadian History*, edited by R. Douglas Francis and Donald B. Smith, 433–46, Toronto: Holt, Rinehart and Wilson of Canada, 1982.

Raynault, Adhémar; *Témoin d'une époque,* Montréal: Éditions du jour, 1970.

Regimbald, Patrice 1997–1998, Ronald Rudin, Making History in Twentieth Century Quebec. *Bulletin d'histoire politique* 6, no. 3): 147–55.

Regehr, T. D., *The Beauharnois Scandal : A Story of Canadian Enterpreneurship and Politics,* Toronto: University of Toronto Press, 1990.

Rouillard, Jacques. 1998. *La Révolution Tranquille: Rupture Ou Tournant? Journal of Canadian Studies* 32): 23–51.

Roy, Fernande, *Progrès, Harmonie, Liberté. Le libéralisme des milieux d'affaires francophones au tournant du siècle,* Montréal: Boréal, 1988.

———. *Histoire des idéologies au Québec aux XIXe et Xxe siècles,* Montréal: Boréal Express, 1993.

Rudin, Ronald, *Making History in Twentieth-Century Quebec,* Toronto: University of Toronto Press, 1997.

———, 1992, Book review. *"Paul-André Linteau—Histoire de Montréal Depuis la Confédération" Histoire sociale-Social History,* 25): 423–25.

———. 1992. Revisionism and the Search for a Normal Society: A Critique of Recent Quebec Writing. *Canadian Historical Review* 73: 30–61.

———, 1995–1996, "Au-Delà Du Révisionisme" *Bulletin d'histoire politique* 4, no. 2 57–73.

———, 1999, "On Difference and National Identity in Quebec Historical Writing: A Response to Jean-Marie Fecteau" *Canadian Historical Review* 80, 666–76.

Rumilly, Robert, *Histoire de la Province du Québec Vol I–XXXIV* Montréal: Fides, 1940-1977.

———, *Maurice Duplessis et son Temps, 1: 1890–1944, II: 1944–1959,* Montreal: Presses de l'Université de Quebec, 1971.

Sack, Benjamin G., *Canadian Jews—Early in This Century,* Montreal: National Archives, Canadian Jewish Congress, 1975.

Sarra-Bournet, Michel. 1995–1996, *Pour une Histoire Postrévisioniste Bulletin d'histoire politique* 4, no. 2, 25–29.

Sauve, Todd, 1998, "[Louis Riel] may have been crazy, Prof. [Tom] Flanagan, but he did the West a lot of good," *Alberta Report*, 25.

Schull, Joseph, *Laurier,* Toronto: MacMillan, 1965.

Senese, Phyllis A., 1986, *La Croix de Montréal: 1893–95* CCHA. Historical Studies, 53, 81.

———. (Sherrin) *The World, the Flesh and the Devil: The Crusade of Lionel Groulx, 1878–1967,* PhD Thesis; York University, 1975.

———,1982 Book Review, P-A Linteau, R. Durocher, and J. C. Robert, Histoire Du Québec Contemporain: De la Confédératon À la Crise (1867–1929)." *Histoire sociale-Social History,* 15, 278–80.

Shore, Marlene. 2000, Book Review, "Ronald Rudin, Making History InTwentieth Century Quebec" *Revue d'histoire de l'amérique française,* 53, 625–28.

Silver, A. I. *The French-Canadian Idea of Confederation 1864–1900,* Toronto: University of Toronto Press, 1982.

Skelton, D. *Life and Letters of Sir Wilfred Laurier,* Volume 1,: Toronto : McClelland and Stewart, 1965.

Sociètè d'histoire régionale de Saint-Hyacinthe, *Saint-Hyacinthe: 1748–1998* Sillery: des Éditions Septentrion,1998.

Sprague, D. N., *Canada and the Métis, 1869–1885,* Waterloo, Ontario: Wilfrid Laurier Press, 1988.

———, 1985, "Deliberation and Accident in the Events of 1885," *Prairie Fire: A Manitoba Literary Review,* 6.,

Stanley, G. F. G, in *1885 and After; Native Society in Transition,* ed. F. Laurie Barron and James B. Waldram, Regina: University of Regina Press, 1986.

Tacel, Max, *La France et le monde au XXe siècle,* Paris: Masson, 1989.

Talbot Papineau, Captain, "An Open Letter from Capt. Talbot Papineau to Mr. Henri Bourassa." In *Readings in Canadian History*, edited by R. Douglas

Francis and Donald B. Smith, 345–53, Toronto: Holt, Rinehart and Winston of Canada, 1982.

Teboul, Victor, *Mythe et images du Juif au Québec Essai d'analyse critique,* Montréal : Éditions de la Grave, 1977.

———. "Juifs et Canadiens," deuxième cahier du cercle juif de langue française, edit. Naïm Kattan, Montréal: Éditions du Jour, 1967.

Thomas, Hugh, *The Spanish Civil War,* 3rd edition, New York: Harper and Row, 1977.

Trépanier, Pierre. 1998–1999, *"Débats: Faire de l'Histoire À la Manière de Ronald Rudin." Bulletin d'histoire politique* 7, no. 1, 106.

Trudel, Marcel, *L'Influence de Voltaire Au Canada, Volume II, de 1850–1900.* Montréal: Les Publications de l'université Laval, Fides, 1945.

Vigod, Bernard L., *The Political Career of Louis-Alexandre Taschereau,* Kingston and Montreal: McGill-Queens Press, 1986.

Wade, Mason, *The French Canadians, 1760–1945,* Toronto: MacMillan, 1955.

Ward, N., *A Party Politician: The Memoirs of Chubby Power,* Toronto: Macmillan, 1966.

Wilson, Edmund, *O Canada,* Toronto: Ambassador Books, 1964.

Young, Brian *Georges-Etienne Cartier,* Montreal–Kingston: Mcgill-Queens University Press, 1981.

———, 1995–1996, "New Wine—or Just New Bottles?" *Journal of Canadian Studies,* no. 30, 194–98.

———1995–1996, "Y a-t-Il une Nouvelle Histoire Du Québec?" *Bulletin d'histoire politique* 4, no. 2, 7–11.

Index

978-0-595-40302-8
0-595-40302-6